# Economics of Change in Less Developed Countries

DAVID COLMAN and FREDERICK NIXSON

*University of Manchester*

Philip Allan

First published 1978 by

PHILIP ALLAN PUBLISHERS LIMITED
MARKET PLACE
DEDDINGTON
OXFORD OX5 4SE



0 86003 011 3 (hardback)
0 86003 112 8 (paperback)

Reprinted 1980, 1982

Typeset by MHL Typesetting Ltd, Coventry
Printed in Great Britain by The Camelot Press Limited, Southampton

# Contents

# List of tables

# Introduction

Recent years have seen a flood of books, journals and articles concerned with the problems of the poor two-thirds of the world's population. Although much attention has been devoted to the analysis of the characteristics and structures of the economies and societies within which the poor live, too often a stereotype of both the people and their societies is presented. While this stereotype has now progressed beyond describing the people as 'primitive' or their societies as 'backward', the 'popular' image remains of a basically stagnant, or only slowly changing less-developed world, essentially homogeneous, confronting a small group of rich, developed economies.

In order to simplify analysis of the problems of development it is conventional to classify those countries typified by widespread poverty under one of a number of alternative labels, such as less-developed countries (LDCs), underdeveloped countries (UDCs), developing countries, the Third World, satellite, periphery or dependent economies or simply as poor countries. The dividing line between them and the developed or rich countries is a purely arbitrary one, since as is discussed in Chapter 1 there is no wholly objective criterion of development. But although problems of classification exist, they are not insurmountable and there is general agreement as to which countries should be included in the 'less developed' category. Nevertheless, there is in reality a high degree of diversity of economic, social and political conditions between the countries classed as less-developed or as in the Third World. Argentina and Afghanistan, Brazil and Botswana, Uganda and Uruguay, have achieved different levels of economic and social development and face very different problems.[1] But they can all be categorised as 'underdeveloped' or 'less developed' given that the vast majority of their populations exist at a very low level of material welfare, and that their economic structures can be described as 'distorted' or 'disintegrated', and that their growth processes are subject to a variety of economic, technical, political and social constraints. By 'distortion' or 'disintegration' we mean that the less developed economies and societies are dualistic structures in the broadest sense of that term – subsistence production and production for the market co-exist, old and new technologies are used side-by-side, new social classes have arisen alongside the traditional strata. These countries have also been unbalanced by the fact that, historically, the direction of their economic development was controlled and influenced for a long period, directly or indirectly, by foreign colonial powers.

As already noted there are several collective terms in use for the poor and poorer countries which are the subject of development economics. These terms are however not exact synonyms for one another, and each has its own subjective overtones. Thus, the term 'developing countries' implies that all poor countries are making progress and developing; this not only suggests an optimistic gloss to the problems of development, but it may actually be incorrect for specific countries over particular intervals in time. Likewise, the term 'underdeveloped countries' has a special meaning in theories which define it as an unfavourable condition caused by the actions of international capitalism and imperialism; moreover, it somewhat ambiguously implies that underdeveloped countries have failed to fulfil some (unstated) potential for development. By contrast the term 'less-developed countries' suggests simply that such countries are less-well developed than others. None of the terms is ideal but for the sake of convenience we use the term 'less developed countries' (LDCs). There are however occasions when other terms have been used. For example, when discussing statements or statistical presentations by other authors which employ the terms developing or underdeveloped countries it has often seemed appropriate to use the same terminology. In like fashion we tend to employ the term developed countries (DCs) for the better-off countries, but for reasons of emphasis they are on occasion referred to as either rich or industrial countries.

Since the attainment of political independence, the majority of LDCs have consciously attempted to change the structure of their economies. Many of them have achieved impressive rates of growth of national income and this has been accompanied by, and has led to, often quite significant structural changes. Change has thus been rapid and substantial, although not necessarily in a direction that everyone would consider desirable from a normative standpoint.

One of the primary objectives of this book is to analyse the changes that are taking place in LDCs at the present time, to examine the problems that the processes of change are generating, and to look at the agents of change themselves. Our own thinking on these issues, as reflected in the structure and contents of the book, has been influenced by the observation (Szentes 1971, part 2, chapter 1) that there are two aspects or sides of underdevelopment; the external, international aspect, which from the historical point of view is of primary importance; and the internal aspect, which from the point of view of future development, is of increasing importance. While not in any way wishing to minimise the need for changes in the structure of international economic and political relations (and the relationships between rich and poor countries are discussed in Chapters 4 and 5) we have concentrated discussion on the internal aspect of the development process. Thus we pay particular attention to the question of economic inequality within LDCs and the impact that different income distributions are likely to have on the development process. We analyse the process of agricultural and industrial development within LDCs, and although we place particular emphasis on one of the major external agents of change, the TNCs (transnational corporations), we are most interested in the impact of their activities on the nature and characteristics of the development process within LDCs themselves.

This emphasis on internal socio-political and economic changes is because it is apparent that it is the structure of the LDC that determines the effectiveness with which it can bargain (for example) with TNCs and thus influence the impact the latter have on the course of development. It is the LDC government that is responsible for the economic policies pursued; and although external agencies (the World Bank, bilateral aid agencies, TNCs etc.) offer advice, and pursuade or coerce LDC governments into accepting certain general strategies of development, nevertheless they more often work within the internal framework created or maintained by the LDC government. For example, TNCs or aid agencies cannot be fairly blamed for the creation of inequalities within LDCs. TNCs in particular respond to, and hence exacerbate, inequalities within the LDCs, but the basic responsibility for their presence lies with the LDC government.[2] In a similar manner, the implementation of the proposed measures which make up the package generally referred to as the New International Economic Order (NIEO) would be unlikely to benefit the vast majority of the population of LDCs unless there are radical changes within the latter. In any case, it could be argued that LDCs cannot afford to wait for changes in international economic relationships. They must get on with the job of economic development, irrespective of the external situation, although it is necessary at the same time to fight for changes in the international sphere.

Although it is the intention of this book to concentrate attention on the internal aspects of the development process, this should not be taken to mean that we are primarily concerned with policy issues. Obviously we have not entirely been able to escape saying what we think LDCs should be doing. But we feel that in the development literature too much emphasis has been placed on policy recommendations without any attempt being made to assess the chances of such policies being adopted. There have, for example, been many impressive reports by international bodies advocating specific development policies for LDCs, but they have often had a greater effect on academic economists than on the countries at which they were aimed. All too often policy recommendations have been made without due consideration of their political acceptability to the authorities in the LDCs, or their feasibility given international pressures. In development economies in particular, neglect of the political environment is fatal when it comes to making policy recommendations (unless, as often appears to be the case, the latter are intended more as academic exercises than proposals aimed at the real world).

One other point needs to be made. We do not regard this book as a textbook on the principles of economic development, as we believe that there is no generally agreed body of theory or doctrine that is unambiguously 'development economics'. Rather we have focussed our attention upon the processes of change affecting LDCs and upon those issues which we feel that readers of the contemporary literature should have some familiarity. Nevertheless, our efforts to work within a strict word limit have required considerable selectivity in the topics covered. Consequently, despite exceeding the intended length by fifty per cent, some important issues have received only limited coverage. There is for example no detailed discussion of the relationship between rapid population growth and development in the LDCs. Also we would have liked to expand the treatment of the socio-economics of poverty and of the human implications of underdevelopment. However, to emphasise that these are the central causes of concern in development economics, Chapter 7 on the World Food Problem is included. Another area which in an ideal world we would have liked to expand on is rural development – this differs from agricultural development in that the emphasis is on rural communities rather than on farmers and farm workers. For reasons that become apparent in the book (see Chapter 6) there is an increasing policy emphasis on rural development, but as it is a rather amorphous subject it would not fit comfortably into the structure of the book. Its limited coverage, as with other topics, is regrettable, but unavoidable.

## Notes

1 The exception that must be made to this generalisation is the Peoples Republic of China. Although poor, it is not included in our category of less-developed countries. Throughout the book we have attempted to compare and contrast Chinese policies with those of the conventionally defined LDCs.

Likewise, countries such as Cuba, North Korea, and Vietnam are excluded from our strictures.

2 This is not to deny that LDC governments are not responsive to foreign pressures or that they are in league with foreign interests. If the LDC government significantly threatens foreign interests, the latter are often able to remove it and replace it with a more malleable administration. But this fact does not alter the substance of the argument.

## Reference

Szentes T. (1971), *The Political Economy of Underdevelopment*, Budapest, Akademiai Kiado.

## ACKNOWLEDGEMENTS

The preparation of this book has made demands on both our families and colleagues and so we are happy to acknowledge their encouragement, assistance and advice. Phillip Leeson in particular was most generous in the time and effort he devoted to reading and commenting on successive drafts. His advice led to improvements in both form and content. Professor Wat Thomas, John McInerney, Colin Kirkpatrick and Stephen Tidman read and offered valuable comments on individual chapters. F. Tore Rose of the UN Centre on Transnational Corporations made a number of valuable comments on Chapters 9 and 10. We have not accepted all the suggestions made to us and none of those mentioned above is in any way responsible for the opinions expressed in the book. Likewise, all errors and omissions remain our responsibility.

We would also like to thank the typists who grappled successfully with various drafts. Rajinder Jasdhoar and Edith Gillett carried most of the burden, with support from Jennifer Vaughan.

We acknowledge with thanks the permission of the following publishers to reprint various tables reproduced in the book: Basil Blackwell (table 5.2); The Institute of Economic Affairs (table 1.1); Methuen (table 6.2) and Oxford University Press (table 3.1 and table 9.1).

The book is dedicated to Lucy, Sophie, Matthew, Jonathan and Andrew.

DAVID COLMAN
FREDERICK NIXSON
Manchester, April 1978

# List of abbreviations

| | |
|---|---|
| CIMMYT | International Maize and Wheat Improvement Centre |
| DAC | Development Assistance Committee of OECD |
| DC | Developed Country |
| ECAFE | Economic Commission for Asia and the Far East |
| ECLA | Economic Commission for Latin America |
| EEC | European Economic Community |
| EFTA | European Free Trade Area |
| FAO | Food and Agriculture Organisation of the U N |
| GATT | General Agreement on Trade and Tariffs |
| GDP | Gross Domestic Product |
| GNI | Gross National Income |
| GNP | Gross National Product |
| GSP | Generalised System of Preferences |
| IBRD | International Bank for Reconstruction and Development |
| ICA | International Coffee Agreement |
| ICOR | Incremental Capital-Output Ratio |
| ICRISAT | International Crops Research Institute for the Semi-Arid Tropics |
| ILO | International Labour Organisation |
| IMF | International Monetary Fund |
| IRRI | International Rice Research Institute |
| ISA | International Sugar Agreement |
| ISI | Import Substituting Industrialisation |
| IWA | International Wheat Agreement |
| LDC | Less Developed Country |
| MGC | Marginal Growth Contribution |
| NI | National Income |
| NIEO | New International Economic Order |
| OECD | Organisation for Economic Co-operation and Development |
| OPEC | Organisation of Petroleum Exporting Countries |
| RWG | Redistribution With Growth |
| SMP | Social Marginal Product |
| TNC | Transnational Corporation |
| UDC | Underdeveloped Country |
| UN | United Nations |
| UNCTAD | United Nations Conference on Trade and Development |
| UNRISD | United Nations Research Institute for Social Development |
| WFP | World Food Problem |
| WHO | World Health Organisation |

# 1

# The concept and measurement of development

At the outset it is necessary to clarify the meaning of 'development'. While this is by no means a simple matter, there is, as discussed in section 1.1, a broad measure of agreement about it. Having defined development, the question then is how to measure it? As will become clear in section 1.2, however, this is rather more problematic. In fact the direct measurement of development turns out to be unmanageable, and instead various rather crude indicators have to be used – indicators are measurable variables which are assumed to be directly correlated with development. As will be seen, there are doubts as to whether any available indicators are particularly highly correlated with development, but there is a (rather grudging) acceptance that national income per person is as useful as any; certainly it is the most widely used. This measure of agreement is important because it provides the essential requirement for the classification of countries according to their state (or rate) of development, and for the subsequent testing of hypotheses about the causes of development.

In classifying countries by their state of development a strict numerical ranking could be adopted, but more usually they are arbitrarily classified into groups. A commonly used device is to classify countries, other than the centrally planned, into two groups: those countries with the highest per capita incomes (almost exclusively the industrialised capitalist ones) are classified as developed countries; the larger number of countries which rank lower on this scale are classified as developing, less-developed, or underdeveloped (according to the preferred terminology). While at many points in the book we shall accept this crude division of countries into two groups, it is recognised that the groups are by no means homogeneous. In particular, there are important differences between the less-developed countries, and where it is considered appropriate further arbitrary sub-divisions can be made within the group of developing countries. This further sub-division may also be made according to the per capita income criterion, as for example when employing the UN categories of low, middle, upper-middle, and high income developing countries. Alternatively, sub-division may be made according to some other characteristic such as when distinguishing the oil exporting developing countries from those without oil, or in separating developing countries with a high proportion of industrial exports from those almost wholly dependent upon primary commodity exports. While we recognise the arbitrariness of the distinction between developed and less-developed countries, and also between different categories of less-developed countries, we accept the conventions about the usefulness of such distinctions throughout this book.

## 1.1 What is Development?

Development can be considered either as a process of improvement with respect to a set of values or, when comparing the relative levels of development of different countries, as a comparative state of being with respect to such values. The values in question relate to desired conditions in society. Self-evidently, there is no universal agreement about what these desired conditions should be; individuals certainly have different preferences regarding their life-style and relationships with the rest of society; and through their political manifestos nations express different collective (majority or minority) views about the desired state of society – views which change through time. Inevitably, therefore, the rate or the relative level of a country's development are normative concepts whose definition and measurement depend upon the value judgements of the analysts involved.

The assertion that development is a normative concept which will be measured differently by different people constitutes a serious charge, but is one which affects all areas of the social sciences and it is not unique to development studies. For as Myrdal observes (1970, p.42) the fact is 'that value premises are needed even in the theoretical stage of establishing facts and factual relations. Answers can only be given when questions have been asked. A view is impossible except from a viewpoint.' Not only are value judgements an inevitable part of deciding what concepts and relationships should be employed to answer questions such as 'what causes development?' or 'has development occurred in any specific instance?', but value judgements are also necessary in deciding how to represent concepts empirically. For example, in defining gross domestic product, should unpaid, housewives' services be included, and if so how should they be valued? Similarly, what procedures should be used to measure the volume and value of food produced for own consumption and not exchanged in the market? These questions can only be resolved judgementally, there being no obvious objective procedures.

It has thus to be recognised that value judgements are inescapable elements of factual study in the social sciences. They are, however, especially prominent elements in development economics precisely because a central aspect of the subject is to formulate criteria for development, and also because many of the commonly chosen criteria are difficult to define and measure. Consequently, there would appear to be plenty of scope for judgemental disagreements about what development is, what are its most important goals, and what are the relationships between aims. Certainly there has recently been extensive debate about these issues in the literature, but this, while demonstrating the existence of disagreements about how development is caused and what weights should be assigned to specific goals, nevertheless demonstrates a broad measure of agreement about the main categories to be achieved in development.

Possibly this measure of agreement is not surprising if, as Seers has said (in Baster 1972), 'Surely the values we need are staring us in the face, as soon as we ask ourselves: what are the necessary conditions for a universally accepted aim, the realisation of the potential of human personality?' Based on this value premise, that the ultimate aim and yardstick of development is that implied by the question, Seers identifies a number of objectives for development in the poorest countries. These are: (1) that family incomes should be adequate to provide a subsistence package of food, shelter, clothing and footwear; (2) that jobs should be available to all family heads, not only because this will ensure a distribution of income such that subsistence consumption levels will be generally achieved, but because a job is something without which personality cannot develop; (3) that access to education should be increased and literacy ratios raised; (4) that the populace should be given an opportunity to participate in government; and (5) that national independence should be achieved in 'the sense that the views of other governments do not largely predetermine one's own government's decisions.' As progress is made towards the economic goals, that is as 'undernourishment, unemployment and inequality dwindle', Seers argues that the 'educational and political aims become increasingly important objectives of development.'

Seers' list of development criteria or objectives is similar in basic respects to those suggested by others. Myrdal, for example, adopts as 'instrumental value premises' (i.e. criteria for assessing development) certain 'modernisation ideals' which are (1) rationality, (2) development and development planning, (3) rise of productivity, (4) rise of levels of living, (5) social and economic equalisation, (6) improved institutions and attitudes, (7) national consolidation, (8) national independence, (9) democracy at the grass roots, and (10) social discipline.

Similarly, to Streeten, who participated in the preparation of Myrdal's magnum opus *Asian Drama* (1968), 'development means modernisation, and modernisation means transformation of human beings. Development as an objective and development as a process both embrace a change in fundamental attitudes to life and work, and in social, cultural and political institutions' (Streeten 1972, p.30). More specifically, Streeten (p. 15) sees the process of development in terms of progress in a number of interrelated dimensions: (1) output and incomes, (2) conditions of production, (3) levels of living (including nutrition, housing, health and education), (4) attitudes to work, (5) institutions and (6) policies.[1]

Little purpose would be served by presenting yet other proposed lists of development criteria. They would inevitably include many of the components common to the lists above, and would tend to lend some support to Seers' assertion that the criteria of development are largely self-evident. Whether this is true or not, the lists of values presented do indicate the extent to which there is agreement about certain key criteria, and that development is a multidimensional process or set of objectives, in which the dimensions are economic, social, political and cultural in the widest sense of these terms. But the lists also indicate clearly that strong personal values intrude into conceptions of development. This is well borne out in Myrdal's approach; even his initial general characterisation of development in terms of 'modernisation ideals' amounts to a strong value judgement, namely that modern methods and attitudes (presumably as revealed in some of the wealthier nations) are preferable to more traditional approaches (as found in the poorer countries?). While a majority of people may agree with this value premise, there are undeniably others who would dispute it. The personal nature of the value judgements is even more evident in some of the individual criteria. 'Social discipline', which for Myrdal largely involves stamping out corruption in what he calls the 'soft state', is liable to widely differing interpretations. Similarly, 'national consolidation' and 'democracy at the grass roots' have different meanings to different people and political systems.

It should also be reiterated that there is no agreement as to what weights to assign to each of the individual objectives for the operational purposes of policy formulation and measurement of development. This is partly due to the inevitable differences in personal values, but it is also due to the need for the weights to be changed with changes in the level of development. Whatever its causes, this problem of not being able readily to represent development as a single variable creates serious problems in the study of development. This emerges most clearly when we examine theories of development which, as is discussed in Chapter 2, tend to circumvent the problem by analysing only selected subsets of development objectives. The problem also poses appreciable problems for measuring development – an issue taken up in the next section of this chapter.

One important conclusion which emerges from the attempt to define development is that as a process it is not synonymous with economic growth. It is conceivable that, in a particular country, average GNP per capita might have risen, while at the same time income inequality increased, the poor became poorer, and negative progress was made to other development goals. Such a situation might be classed as economic growth with negative development in that, although average incomes may have risen, the economic lot of the mass of the population would have deteriorated and negative or no progress would have been made in transforming personal attitudes and institutions in the manner required by the modernisation ideals. Conversely, it is possible to envisage development with negative growth. This might occur where (as perhaps recently in Mozambique) a major restructuring occurs in attitudes, political institutions and production relations (by such means as land reform and villagisation) which creates the conditions for future development, but at a short-run cost of reduced GNP due to disruption of the previous production and distribution system. Thus we must agree with Streeten (1972, p. 31) when he says 'Just as there can be economic growth without development there can be development without economic growth.'[2]

## 1.2 Measuring Development

Interest in measuring development is intense. Everyone who reads this book is likely to have accepted some statistical notion about the level of development of his/her own country in comparison to certain others, and will either feel satisfaction or concern about its relative position. At a national level such pride or concern has a central role in the political process and in engaging electoral support for the policies of political parties or governments. And in development studies, the focal point of concern is often the statistical evidence of a widening gap between the standards of living in the richer (so-called developed) countries and the poorer (less-developed) ones (LDCs).

The fact is, however, that it is extremely difficult to measure comparative levels of development. The statistical methods available may be thought fairly reliable for obtaining acceptable measures of rates of growth of living standards and of ordinal rankings as to whether one country is more developed than another, but there are appreciable doubts as to whether it is possible to obtain cardinal measures of by how much or how many times one country is more developed than any other.

The fundamental cause of the measurement difficulty lies with the definition of development. As identified in the previous section, the criteria or objectives by which development is to be judged or measured are qualitative ones. Such criteria as the standard of living, health levels, the educational level, and the extent of grass-roots participation in government are all qualitative ones which cannot be measured directly. They have to be measured indirectly using indicators which are directly measurable quantities. Thus among the many possible indicators of a 'nation's state of physical health' might be included the number of people per trained doctor, the rate of child mortality, or the average life expectancy; and for the standard of living one might use such indicators as average national income per person, the proportion of families with piped water to their living quarters, the proportion of households supplied with electricity, and so on.

This multiplicity of possible indicators for any given general dimension of development simply compounds the problems arising from the existence of several general dimensions.[3] Firstly, no quantitative indicator is capable of exactly measuring a qualitative criterion. Secondly, no one indicator can conceivably approximate the qualitative levels attained with respect to all the major dimensions of development, especially when it is remembered that these are economic, social, political and cultural. Thirdly, there are appreciable difficulties in deriving a method (weighting scheme) whereby various indicators for different qualities can be added together into a single index measure of a country's level of development.

Since the concept of development only acquires substance through a process of measurement it is important (in the light of the foregoing statement of the problems of measurement) to examine briefly some of the major alternative proposals for development indicators, and some of the criticisms levelled at them. Most effort to date has been devoted to the development of economic indicators, and it reflects this fact that most of the rest of this section is devoted to economic indicators, and little to political indicators, social indicators or combinations of these.

*Economic Indicators of Development*

It is natural that analysts should want to employ a single indicator of development rather than a set of separate ones. It is attractive not only because it simplifies (at least in a mechanical sense) the task of producing theoretical models of development, but also because it facilitates communication and thought to consider a single series of numbers rather than several simultaneously.

In practice, one indicator has dominated all others, and that is national income or gross national product (GNP) per capita.[4] This is the name given to a series which can be calculated for any country, using a specific basic set of measurement rules which have been devised in the Western industrial countries to measure their overall level of income or production. It is important to note that the measurement rules used for adding together the values of different economic activities were not derived with any concept of development in mind, but to produce indicators of annual levels of production and income. Consequently, a love–hate relationship has developed about the use of GNP as a development indicator. In its favour are that (1) it is an indicator of key activity, the provision of goods and services, an increase in which is almost[5] a necessary condition for development, (2) the measurement rules, which are complex, have evolved over time and are well known and understood, and (3) most member countries of the United Nations (UN) produce estimates of GNP for inclusion in UN official statistics. Against GNP as a development indicator are that (1) it is an indicator only of some economic aspects of development – it makes no allowance for changing income distribution – and it has no direct implications for the other non-economic criteria, (2) it is a heavily value-loaded indicator, and the subjective element is larger in countries with poor statistics and large subsistence sectors than in countries where a much smaller proportion of transactions bypass the market, and (3) irrespective of any deficiencies GNP may have as a measure of national economic activity, there are additional problems in using it for making international comparisons. Most of these points are perfectly obvious ones – but in view of the frequency with which GNP is encountered in international 'league tables' of development they deserve a certain amount of amplification.

Regarding the first point, there is no way in which a simple total of the value of goods and services produced can reflect details of income distribution. It is, therefore, quite possible for any increase in average GNP per capita to be due to the increased incomes and consumption of only a relatively few richer members of society and to be accompanied by a worsening income distribution (as Chapter 3 on economic inequality reports, this relationship may even be characteristic of certain stages of development). In this case, depending upon the weight assigned to income inequality as a criterion for development, it is possible for an increase in GNP per capita to apparently signal an increase in social welfare when it has in fact diminished.

The question of the value-loaded nature of GNP as a development indicator is a somewhat broader one, but basically it revolves around the appropriateness of using market prices to value social welfare. Thus, returning to the question of income distribution it is observed that the prices and quantities of goods and services consumed depend upon the prevailing income distribution. To the extent that the distribution may be highly unequal, increases in measured GNP may give a poor indication of the extent to which social need is increasingly satisfied; certainly, given any level of GNP the pattern of consumption might be markedly changed by changing the distribution of income. This consideration is amplified by major doubts arising in relation to the possibility that, because of market imperfections, the market prices used for valuing components of GNP are appreciably different from the appropriate social valuations. Not only may prices be distorted by the existence of monopolistic forces, by policy intervention, and by the possibility that the pricing of public goods may be to some extent arbitrary; but also 'many aspects of the quality of life and the environment fall outside the market calculus' (Baster 1972, p.3) and therefore have a zero price, which clearly does not reflect their social worth. Thus there are a number of well-recognised sources of potential bias in GNP as a measure of the social value of national income.

In making international comparisons of development levels the general procedure is to take each country's own estimate of GNP calculated in local currency units and then to convert these into some common currency unit, usually the US dollar, for comparative purposes. It has to be recognised that there are several sources of bias in this procedure. One of these is that the subjective elements in the measurement procedure may be resolved differently in different countries, resulting in a lack of standardisation between countries' estimates. In richer countries a high proportion of domestic services are purchased in the form of washing machines, vacuum cleaners and refrigerators; housing construction and repair costs are mainly in the form of purchased inputs; and food is largely purchased rather than home produced. Thus a high proportion of the consumption of these services is provided in the form of traded labour and consumer products which will be recorded by the normal national accounting procedures. But this is not so in poor countries where only a small proportion of such services will be purchased. This is particularly significant (because it constitutes a high proportion of total product) in the case of food, a high proportion of which is consumed directly by the producer and his family. But it is also true of house construction, household and other services much of which are provided by family labour in LDCs. Hence in poor countries a high proportion of these important services is supplied without involving trade of a conventionally accountable type. If, as is often the case, due to lack of statistical evidence, national income accounts omit or inadequately allow for the consumption of such non-traded goods and services, the resultant GNP estimates will be biased in favour of the rich and against the poor countries precisely because a higher proportion of total economic activity takes a non-traded form in the latter. This is a serious problem and as Seers describes it (in Baster 1972, p.23):

> But what are all the voluminous tables of national income accounts really worth? So far as the Third World is concerned, much of what they ought to cover is virtually outside the scope of official statistics. This applies above all to output of domestic foodstuffs, even the staples, let alone subsidiary crops which come under the general heading of 'market gardening' (American 'truck farming'), not to speak of fish, forest products, etc. Extremely rough methods of estimation are often used, much of the output being assumed to rise in proportion to the increase in rural population, an increase which is in turn assumed to be some constant arbitrary rate in the absence of registration of births and deaths, or data on migration. Secondly, we know very little about construction in the countryside by the farming community itself; this apparently amounts to a good deal if one takes account not only of building houses, but also clearing land, digging wells and ditches, constructing fences and hedges, etc. Thirdly, there are practically no basic data on domestic service and other personal services, even those which are remunerated.

Another bias arising from the use of national income accounting statistics as welfare measures is that some items which are in fact necessary and unavoidable costs of living are treated implicitly as benefits. This is true of the costs of travelling to work. To the extent that such costs may be a significant item in the accounts of rich countries and negligible in poor countries, comparison of GNP levels will exaggerate the extent of the gap between rich and poor.

There is also a major complex of biases for comparative use of national accounts statistics which arises from the choice of an exchange rate to convert from local currency units to (say) US dollars. In the first place, where a country operates a multiple exchange rate system it may be difficult to decide which rate to use. For example (Open University 1975, Table 2) Colombia apparently operates four separate and highly variable exchange rates for different classes of transaction, so that it may be necessary to impute an exchange rate for the sort of purpose being considered here.

More importantly, the choice of any exchange rate carries with it certain implications for the relative prices of non-traded goods and services which may be quite inappropriate and misleading. Consider, for example, an exchange rate between the pound sterling and US dollar of £1 = $1.80. A simplified interpretation of this is that (before allowing for transport costs) £1 will buy for a Briton a basket of traded American goods which would cost an American $1.80, and conversely $1.80 will buy a basket of British traded goods which would cost a Briton £1. Applying this exchange rate to an estimate of UK GNP to convert it to its dollar equivalent involves implicitly assuming that £1's worth of those British goods and services which are not traded would cost $1.80 in the USA. This is unlikely to be true. A pound's worth of car servicing in the UK may cost substantially more than $1.80 if carried out in the USA, and the same with house construction costs, electrical repairs and so forth. In that case comparing USA national income per capita with the dollar equivalent (at £1 = $1.80) of UK national income per capita will overstate the margin by which the average American is better off than his British counterpart.

The magnitude of this class of bias is likely to be far larger when comparing income levels in the USA to those of the poorest countries. Indeed, the absurd results which could occur from a welfare interpretation of such comparisons are well demonstrated by Usher (1966). He reproduces UN data which indicate that for 1963 the USA had a GNP of $2,790 per capita and Ethiopia, toward the bottom of the league, only $40 per capita. As Usher asks, what conceivable meaning can be accorded to the notion that the average Ethiopian lived on 11 cents a day? A person would have starved in the USA unless he had far more than that, and yet most Ethiopians survived. The only possible conclusion is that Ethiopian prices for basic commodities were much lower relative to those in the USA than implied by the exchange rate, that the dollar cost of subsistence was much lower in Ethiopia than the USA, and that the implied ratio of American to Ethiopian living standards of 70 to 1 was a sizeable exaggeration. It is obvious that if Ethiopia's output of goods and services were valued at American prices in the first place, instead of being valued at local prices and then converted at the dollar exchange rate, then its national income would appear substantially larger than one-seventieth of the USA's. By the same token, valuing the USA's output of goods and services at Ethiopian prices would appreciably reduce the estimate of their value relative to Ethiopian output.

These observations are at the basis of the so-called 'binary comparison' method (Usher 1966, p.28). This method assumes that the 'true' ratio of two countries' living standards lies in between the values of the two ratios obtained by first valuing both countries GNP at the prices of one country and then at those of the other, and that it is approximated by the geometric average of these two ratios. The application of these principles is illustrated in table 1.1 (taken from Usher 1966) which indicates what happens to the ratio of the national income (NI) in the USA to that of five other countries when

**Table 1.1** *Real national incomes per head expressed as percentages of the real income per head of the United States*[a]

| | (1) Conventional[b] comparison | (2) All values at US prices | (3) All values at local prices | (4) Geometric average of (2) and (3) |
|---|---|---|---|---|
| UK (1955) | 42 | 64 | 51 | 57 |
| France (1955) | 47 | 56 | 43 | 49 |
| Italy (1955) | 19 | 35 | 24 | 29 |
| USSR (1955) | – | 45 | 22 | 31 |
| China (1952) | 2.5 | 6.1 | 1.8 | 3.3 |

*Source:* Usher 1966, p.35

[a] There are special difficulties associated with calculating national income for the USSR and China, and less weight should be given to the comparisons for these two countries.

[b] National income calculated at local prices, then converted into dollars by an exchange rate.

the pricing assumptions are changed. Column 1 shows the conventional comparison in which the NIs of the five countries are first valued at their local prices and then converted at an official dollar exchange rate. In column 2 the ratios are recalculated after the NIs of the five countries have been calculated directly at USA prices – in all relevant cases this is seen to reduce the apparent gap between USA and other living standards. When, in column 3, USA NI is valued at the prices of the five other countries the gap between USA and other living standards is seen to be greater than under the assumptions of column 2, but in the cases of the UK and Italy is still less than under the conventional comparison of column 1. Naturally, in column 4 the geometric mean of the two binary comparisons generates estimates of relative living standards which lie between the two binary estimates; but the important feature of this result is that the estimated living standards of the relevant four countries are estimated to be closer to those of the USA than is implied by the conventional comparison. This highlights one of the most important inadequacies about the conventional national income comparison, namely that it exaggerates the gap between rich and poor countries. Having said this, however, it should be emphasised that there is no way of equating a halving of the ratio between NI per capita in two countries (from, say, 20:1 to 10:1) with a halving of our degree of concern for the poorer country. There is no definable correspondence between 'units of concern' and ratios or gaps between NI per capita, although presumably most people would accept that there is some direct correlation between them. Thus it is not a matter of indifference whether the ratio is 20:1 or 10:1. One of these values will be a better indicator of relative welfare than the other, but how much better is not assessable.

What the preceding illustration and calculations show is that it is possible, by repricing methods, to adjust the conventional national income estimates so that their performance as relative welfare indicators is improved. However, these methods cannot overcome all the problems, and in any case the binary pricing approach is laborious and involves the statistician in a whole new set of subjective judgements. Naturally therefore, consideration has been given to alternative economic indicators of development, most of which appear to represent a short-cut to the common pricing approach. Usher (1966) mentions two of these: (1) the social adequacy method and (2) the not unrelated direct attempts to measure levels of living. In the social adequacy method, for 'each country, income per head in local currency is divided by an estimate of the bare cost of subsistence; ratios arrived at in this way are then treated as measures of real income. The one attempt to compare incomes by this method, a comparison of Japan and the United States, raised the ratio of Japanese to American income almost 600 per cent over what it appears to be when national incomes are compared through the foreign exchange rate' (Usher 1966, p.37). The main obvious difficulty with this procedure is in defining the cost of subsistence in each country. The concept of subsistence may be defined (not without difficulty) as a purely physiological level, but is often defined to include a psychological component for consumption thought to be socially necessary, e.g. the minimum quality of housing demanded by the average European is far higher than that expected in poor African countries. But this sort of judgemental hurdle is found with all measurement procedures, including Usher's second class of method. In this, following Clark and Haswell (1964, Ch. 4) an attempt might be made to 'measure' living standards in terms of a key welfare indicator such as 'grain equivalent'. In this the value of all goods and services would be divided by the local price of a standard measure of grain so that national income for countries could be expressed and compared in terms of so many grain equivalents. Interesting though this is, none of the proposed alternatives have yet supplanted national income as the main economic indicator of development.

### *Mixed and Non-Economic Indicators of Development*

Various experiments have been conducted to derive development indicators which either combine non-economic dimensions with economic ones or produce indicators of only non-economic aspects

**Table 1.2** *UNRISD list of core indicators of socio-economic development*

Expectation of life at birth
Percent population in localities of 20,000 and over
Consumption of animal protein, per capita, per day
Combined primary and secondary school enrolment
Vocational enrolment ratio
Average number of persons per room
Newspaper circulation per 1,000 population
Percent economically active population in electricity, gas, water, etc.
Agricultural production per male agricultural worker
Percent adult male labour in agriculture
Electricity consumption, kWh per capita
Steel consumption, kg per capita
Energy consumption, kg of coal equivalent per capita
Percent GDP derived from manufacturing
Foreign trade per capita, in 1960 US dollars
Percent salaried and wage earners to total economically active population

*Sources*: UNRISD, *Contents and Measurement of Socio-Economic Development*, Geneva 1970, p.63.

of development such as, for example, in Adelman and Morris' attempt (in Baster 1972) to produce an indicator of political development as measured by the degree of political participation. Nearly all of these experiments have involved creating a single index number of development for each country and, therefore, encounter all the basic problems of index number construction. The main ones are: (1) that all component series should be reduced to a common unit of measurement in order, for example, to be able to add together the contributions to the state of development of life expectancy, percentage adult male labour in agriculture and energy consumption per capita, which are three of the 16 core indicators selected by UNRISD for socio-economic development (reproduced here as table 1.2); and (2) to find a weighting scheme to ensure an appropriate relative valuation of each of the separate indicators.[6] This is not the place to consider in detail the ingenious procedures which have been devised to normalise and weight various lists of separate indicators and to combine them into a single measure. These are quite helpfully and briefly sketched out in Open University (1975). As this same publication points out (p. 37), however, none of these alternative proposed procedures has made much progress in supplanting GNP (or GDP) per capita which 'remains the most comprehensive and widely used indicator of development levels. While recognising its inherent weaknesses it is still the most convenient measure of the level of development. Many studies show that economic and social indicators are highly correlated with the level of GDP per capita, and therefore a ranking based on their combination is relatively close to a ranking based on per capita GDP alone.'

## Notes

1 For those who are interested, Streeten provides a detailed breakdown of the criteria which should be considered within each of these six groups.

2 It is clear that this depends upon the time-scale of one's observations, and not everyone would agree with Streeten. For example Szentes (1971, p.14) argues that 'any distinction between the theories of "development" and "growth" can at best only be accepted for practical reasons . . . (but) by no means as a scientific distinction. The terminological distinction on a semantic basis is unacceptable, because development always and everywhere involves and presupposes the dialectic of quantitative and qualitative changes, of evolution and revolution. And even if a purely quantitative "growth" can be observed in a given place and at a given time within the framework of the existing structure or system, it is not only the consequence of a previous qualitative change but it also inevitably paves the way for a new one.'

3 For a full discussion of proposed development indicators and of the problems associated with them see the various contributions to Baster (ed.) (1972).

4 It should be observed that the national income measure most commonly used is in effect gross national income (GNI). This has to be distinguished from net national income (NNI), which equals GNI minus the allowance for capital depreciation. Thus, while GNI measures the income equivalent to the total value of production in society, NNI indicates the value of the product available for consumption and net new investment, and is therefore probably a better welfare indicator. These two income measures have their exact value equivalents in gross national product (GNP) and net national product (NNP). All of the four measures referred to so far include within them any net property income from abroad, the value of which does not reflect local productive activity – in the LDCs this flow is typically negative as a reflection of repatriated profits by companies and capital export by wealthy individuals. By subtracting net property income from GNP a measure is obtained of gross domestic product (GDP). If the difference between GNP and GDP is large, in so far as the latter is a measure of the total goods and services produced within the economy (before allowing for capital depreciation) it is the better indicator of the productive capacity of the economy and its employment potential.

5 As has already been said, if as GNP increases negative progress is made towards other development goals such as equality or political participation, negative development might be judged to occur.

6 NB. In deriving an index for national income, all the various goods and services are measured in common units of money and the weighting scheme is provided by their prices.

## Bibliography

Baster N. (ed.) (1972), *Measuring Development,* Cass.

Clark C. and Haswell M.R. (1964), *The Economics of Subsistence Agriculture,* Macmillan.

Myrdal G. (1968), *Asian Drama: An Inquiry into the Poverty of Nations,* Allen Lane (London), Pantheon (New York).

Myrdal G. (1970), *The Challenge of World Poverty,* Penguin.

Open University (1975), *International Comparisons of Levels of Development,* Statistical Sources Unit 15, Open University Press.

Streeten P. (1972), *The Frontiers of Development Studies,* Macmillan (especially Ch. 3).

Szentes T. (1971), *The Political Economy of Underdevelopment,* Akademiai Kiado, Budapest.

UNRISD (1970), *Contents and Measurement of Socio-economic Development,* Geneva.

Usher D. (1966), *Rich and Poor Countries,* Eaton Paper 9, Institute of Economic Affairs.

# 2
# Economic theorising about development

## (A) A METHODOLOGICAL NOTE

Where a theory purports to relate to some aspect of the real world it is inevitably a simplified representation of the true situation. For, in the social sciences at least, if it were not a simplification it would be the real world itself, and that is not amenable to treatment in a classroom or textbook. It follows that some theories may entail a greater degree of simplification than others; that is they may be either more partial, or more general (in the sense of abstracting from a number of different situations) and less 'realistic'. However, to describe a theory as partial or general is not necessarily to denigrate it. The tests of a good (useful) theory are that the derived relationships (a) are not immediately obvious, i.e. they require the theory to generate them, (b) are verifiable, and (more strongly) are verified by observations in the real world, and (c) are non-trivial and useful to planners and policy makers. If a very simple set of hypotheses and assumptions can generate important conclusions which satisfy all of these three tests then it is a useful theory. Furthermore, simplicity is a virtue, in the sense that there is no advantage in devising an elaborate theory when a very simple one generates the same conclusions. It is this which explains Friedman's statement that 'Truly important and significant hypotheses will be found to have assumptions that are wildly inaccurate representations of reality, and, in general, the more significant the theory the more unrealistic the assumptions (in this sense). A hypothesis is important if it "explains" much by little, that is if it extracts the common and crucial elements from the mass of complex and detailed circumstances surrounding the phenomena to be explained and permits valid prediction on the basis of them alone. To be important, therefore, a hypothesis must be descriptively false in its assumptions; it takes account . . . of none of the attendent circumstances, since its very success shows them to be irrelevant . . . ' (Friedman 1966, pp. 14 and 15).

The reason for this methodological preamble is that much of the theorising about development by economists in the post-1945 era, that is in the period when a separate literature of development economics has emerged, is now under attack. It is under attack for being both excessively simple and unreal – charges levelled at much economic theorising – and because of an alleged lack of rigour in comparison to other branches of economic theory (for a fuller critique of the theory see section 2.4). While this is a patently unsatisfactory state for the theory to be in, its existence can be explained at least in part by the methodological propositions stated above. For it was natural in the infancy of the subject for economists to seek simple theories and simple policy prescriptions for hastening material progress in the poorest countries. Moreover, it must have seemed plausible at that time that simple development models would provide powerful prescriptive tools, given the apparent success of the industrialised countries at economic management using Keynesian macroeconomic theory, and given also the earlier usefulness of Adam Smith's liberal trade principles of economic management. Because, also, most of the early development theorising was conducted by North American and European academics it is quite understandable that attempts should be made to follow the Keynesian example and build a development theory using nationally defined aggregate variables such as saving and investment. However, the theories propounded in the 1950s and early 1960s have been subjected to a rigorous test of usefulness in the last two decades by the newly independent LCDs seeking to develop national policies for economic and social betterment, and by common consent the theories have been found wanting. Not only have the predictions of the theories not been verified in a number of instances, but it has been found that variables of crucial importance to the LCDs are excluded from consideration by many of the theories, and that preoccupation with national aggregates and averages leads to the ignoring of spatial, interpersonal and intersectoral distribution problems of vital interest to LCDs.

As interest in development has grown so it has become apparent that the dimensions of this process are numerous and that producing generalised theories to explain it requires highly complex models. This is true even if the main focus is on the economic dimensions of development and the social and political aspects are largely ignored, which is the typical characteristic of economic theorising on the subject. However, one general consequence of theoretical complexity, which can be measured in terms of the number of variables and relationships between them, is that no simple propositions may emerge to aid planners and policy makers. It tends to be true that only restricted (closed) theoretical systems produce simple general conclusions. For example, for economies which are assumed to have no international sector (trade and aid), theory suggests clear relationships between domestic saving and economic growth. Where, however, an international sector is assumed to exist no such simple relationships exist between national economic aggregates (as is discussed more fully in Chapter 5). When theories are made more complex, deduced relationships for policy purposes emerge more readily when the theory is expressed numerically rather than in general algebraic form. Since, however, the numerical information required (about such things as marginal propensities to consume and import, and the rates of population and export demand growth) differs from economy to economy, it is apparent that complex theory is more suitable as an aid to planning and policy in individual countries, and that typically few useful conclusions will emerge which are generalisable to all underdeveloped countries.

Increasingly, economists have come to recognise what Seers (1963) called 'The limitations of the special case'. In particular, Seers has attacked attempts to apply to economic management in underdeveloped countries theories which were devised solely with the developed countries in mind. Seers' logic demands also that it be accepted that there is a diversity of types of underdeveloped economy, and that few simple generalisations will be applicable to all of these simultaneously. Thus, even if it is restricted to the economic domain, the prospects for the emergence of an acceptable general theory of development look poor. When the social and political dimensions of the problem are added, since these cannot truly be isolated from the economic, the prospect of a general development theory (comparable to the Keynesian macroeconomic theory for industrial countries) recedes still further.[1] Recognising this, many would probably now argue that to try and explain 'the development process' by any simple generalisable economic theory is undesirable. Instead it might be agreed that it is possible to identify some problems common to many poor countries and to develop partial theories to analyse these, or alternatively to identify groups of countries with essentially identical problems and to build theories for each of these groups.

In view of the preceding critical observations it may well be asked 'what purpose is served by presenting a brief survey of development theory?' There are in fact several objectives which can be identified in response to this question. In the first place it has to be recognised that, whatever their currently perceived imperfections, the various theories to be discussed have commanded support and influenced development policy at different times and in different places. Therefore, in studying the way in which development policy has evolved in different countries and at the international level, it is necessary to have an understanding of the influence of theoretical views about development. Moveover, these theoretical views have themselves changed in response to experience and deeper understanding of development processes, and it is instructive to gain some appreciation of the progress which development theory has made. Perhaps the most important justification for reviewing theories of development and criticisms of them is the insight this provides into the nature and dimensions of the development process. For, when particular theories were expressed or adopted it was because it was felt that they addressed themselves to some crucial variables and relationships in the development process, in a way which helped either to comprehend the process or to formulate policy to accelerate and, if necessary, initiate it. If subsequently these theories have been found wanting and have been modified, it is mainly because their simplifying assumptions have been too strong and the domain to which they relate has proved too limited. In other words, these theories have tended to ignore factors which have subsequently been found to be of considerable importance to developing countries. By examining both the content and some of the alleged shortcomings of the theories we can gain some idea of what domain development theory should ideally cover. To a large extent it is in these shortcomings that we identify many of the main topic areas for discussion later in the book, since it is now felt that no proper understanding or theory of the development process can ignore the special features of underdeveloped economies which have not been accounted for in most of the formal theory. Amongst these topics are such things as foreign ownership of firms, dependence upon foreign technology, barriers to international trade, problems of income distribution and nutrition, and requirements for institutional reform.

## (B) THEORIES OF DEVELOPMENT

### 2.1 Theories of Capital Accumulation

*Harrod–Domar Growth Model*

An important early stimulus to economic theorising about development was the Harrod–Domar growth model, so called because essentially the same theory was independently produced by the two named authors (Harrod 1939; Domar 1946). In neither case were the authors concerned with developing countries. Their prime intention was to explore the conditions for stable economic growth in developed countries. The basic assumptions made were (1) that aggregate supply and demand would be balanced when investment ($I_t$) in any period equalled the change in national income ($Y_t - Y_{t-1}$) times the capital–output ratio ($k$), where $k$ indicates the value of capital required to produce one unit of output by value in a single period, and (2) that at equilibrium in a closed economy intended investment would equal intended savings ($S_t$). (Note that the first assumption, of an accelerator process, involves a third which is that new capital comes into full production instantaneously.) These assumptions thus produce the equilibrium condition that

$$I_t = S_t = k(Y_t - Y_{t-1}) \qquad (2.1)$$

By dividing $S_t$ and $(Y_t - Y_{t-1})$ both by $Y_t$ to produce $s$, the savings rate, and $g$ [equal to $(Y_t - Y_{t-1})/Y_t$], the growth rate, we obtain the Harrod–Domar growth equation

$$s = kg \quad \text{or} \quad g = \frac{s}{k} \qquad (2.2)$$

Thus the Harrod–Domar model defines the equilibrium conditions for steady economic growth. Despite the fact that the theory was not conceived with the underdeveloped countries in mind, and that its behavioural assumptions and implications are open to question (see, for example, the critique by Ackley 1961, Ch. 18) it has nevertheless exercised considerable influence on development economics. The immediate attraction of the model was that it relates one of the primary objectives of development, the rate of economic growth, to what is often considered its major limiting factor, investment. There is some doubt as to whether it is the level of savings which restricts investment in underdeveloped countries, as application of the Harrod–Domar formula would seem to imply, or whether, as Cairncross (1962, Ch. 3) has argued, it is limited opportunities for profit that restrain the level of investment with saving levels adjusting to the scale of investment opportunities that exists. Despite this doubt attempts have been made to employ the model, with appropriate allowances for capital depreciation, to answer such questions as: (1) what rate of savings (and hence investment) is necessary to achieve a target growth rate, given the assumed capital–output ratio of a specified economy? or (2) what saving and investment patterns will maximise consumption over time (e.g. Goodwin 1961)?

Little purpose would be served by considering in detail here all the refinements and extensions which have been proposed to make the Harrod–Domar theory more relevant for planning or expository uses. There are some obvious changes which will not be discussed further such as introducing capital depreciation into the model so that not all saving contributes to a net addition to capital stock, or the introduction of gestation lags so that net new investment only makes its full contribution to output after a few years. There are, however, other refinements which introduce either significant concepts or issues which feature in later chapters, and these are worthy of mention.

One simple but important extension of the model is to introduce foreign trade. This is typically done (Bruton 1955; UNECAFE 1960, p. 82) by rephrasing the model such that

$$g = \frac{s}{k} + \frac{b}{k} \qquad \text{where } b = \frac{\text{imports} - \text{exports}}{Y} \tag{2.3}$$

The significance of this is that imports can only exceed exports (and $b$ be positive) if a country is in receipt of either aid, credit or foreign investment. Such a capital transfer enables additional investment to occur. The income-generating effects of this additional investment may, as in equation 2.3, be assumed to be the same as would occur from investment financed by domestic saving. Thus, this 'opening up' of the model indicates a strategic growth-generating role for aid and credit to poor countries. Unfortunately, however, this particular treatment of the international sector fails to portray the full importance of that sector. For equation 2.3 implies that, if trade is in balance on current account, $b$ will equal zero and higher volumes of trade will have no beneficial effect upon economic growth. According to Bruton's own theorising this is not adequate. For he himself argues that, despite import-substituting industrialisation (see Chapter 8), poor nations need to import raw materials plus many capital and intermediate products which they cannot manufacture themselves, and that their ratio of imports to national income may well not decline as income increases. Thus it is argued that domestic savings and transfers of foreign capital are not perfect substitutes for one another and that economic growth may be constrained by a *foreign exchange gap*. By this is meant that the import purchasing power conferred by the value of exports plus capital transfers may be inadequate to support the level of growth permitted by the level of domestic saving. Conversely, a *savings gap* may be said to exist where domestic savings are inadequate to support the level of growth which could be permitted given the import purchasing power of an economy and the level of other resources. This *two-gap* theory, that investment and development are restricted by levels of either domestic saving or import purchase capacity, is clearly not adequately explained by the extended Harrod–Domar model in equation 2.3, and requires a more elaborate formulation such as that by Chenery and Bruno (1962) for the case of Israel.

If import purchasing capacity is deemed to be the limiting constraint upon economic growth, then the two-gap theory indicates a strategic role for aid and other forms of foreign capital flow, namely to finance a deficit in the current account of the balance of payments to cover a high rate of capital goods imports. This important argument has been used to justify persistent current account deficits for a large number of LDCs. However, the increasing problem of external indebtedness in many of these LDCs has led to questioning of this justification, and constitutes an issue of sufficient magnitude to warrant separate examination in Chapter 5 on foreign exchange flows and indebtedness.

*Mahalanobis' Model*

By considering simply aggregate investment, the basic Harrod–Domar model in effect assumes that all forms of investment are equally productive and also that capital is infinitely flexible as to what it can produce. Neither assumption is realistic, as is recognised by those extensions to the model which allow for different sectoral capital–output ratios, and for the level of investment in any particular sector to affect capacity in other sectors. Among the most celebrated of these extensions is the two-sector model developed by Mahalanobis (1955) which provided part of the basic rationale for the Indian Planning Commission's draft second five-year plan of India for 1951 to 1956. This model was employed in establishing national level, sectoral targets for the plan, and in so far as the proposals for achieving these were implemented by government the model may be said to have influenced economic policy, particularly with respect to the recommended emphasis on the development of heavy industry.

The Mahalanobis model shares the assumptions of the Harrod–Domar model that output is a function of capital only, that at equilibrium in the economy the output of any one sector (the $i$th) will equal its stock of capital times its output–capital ratio ($b_i = 1/k_i$), and that there is no international sector. The two sectors are defined to be producing consumption and investment goods respectively. In the investment goods sector two types of machine are assumed to be made, those required to produce consumption goods and those required to make more machines. Since all savings are invested in machines it follows that:

(1) The rate of growth of consumption goods output depends in the short-run upon that sector's share of the new machines produced in any period (i.e. its share of new investment).

(2) The rate of growth of consumption goods output ultimately depends upon the share of new investment in the investment goods sector – the larger this sector becomes, the greater the

economy's capacity to produce machines for consumption goods manufacture.

(3) If the marginal rate of savings ($s'$) is raised above the average rate ($s$), the share of new investment to the heavy goods sector can be increased at the expense of the consumption goods sector since the marginal growth rate in consumer demand will be correspondingly reduced. Thus if a country can raise its savings rate (which implies $s' > s$) it is in a position to increase its rate of investment in productive capacity to permit future consumption levels to exceed what they otherwise would be.

(4) When the average and marginal rates of saving are equal ($s = s'$), an equilibrium, in which machine capacity is fully employed, is achieved when the rates of growth of national income, investment and consumption are equal to the investment goods sector's share of investment times its output–capital ratio.[2]

A particular merit of this model is that it pushes questions of inter-sectoral development choice to the forefront. In particular, it draws attention to the capital goods sector, and argues that its capacity needs to be expanded if higher growth rates are to be attempted.[3] However, it is far too partial a model to permit a full exploration of the issues of sectoral emphasis in development planning. This is partly because it does not contain any explicit mechanism relating demand for the products of the consumer goods sector to the growth and distribution of national income and also because, as always, the sectoral interdependencies, which are forced by assuming an economy without trade, are relaxed as soon as trade is admitted. Even if demand for exports is stagnant a range of alternative sectoral development policies becomes possible, as Raj and Sen (1961) showed in their re-examination of the Mahalanobis model. (Obviously the foreign trade possibilities of a country are of considerable significance for its sectoral development strategy, an issue which is pursued at length in the chapters on trade, Chapter 4, and industrialisation, Chapter 8.) These limitations are, however, susceptible to treatment in full-scale planning models in which there may be a high level of sectoral disaggregation, plus systems to represent domestic and export demands as well as assumptions about the prices at which imports and foreign capital will be available. When all these features are incorporated into planning models, they yield results about sectoral interdependency which depend entirely upon the precise numerical assumptions made about demand and import supply, and are specific to a particular economy. One of the few generalisable results of such models will be that higher rates of domestic saving will lead over time to higher levels of national income and consumption.

This question of raising the saving rate of underdeveloped countries, which was brought into sharp focus by the models just discussed, became a key article of faith in the economic development literature. Thus Lewis (1954, p. 155) argued that 'The central problem in the theory of economic development is to understand the process whereby a community which was previously saving and investing 4 or 5% of its national income or less, converts itself into an economy where voluntary saving is running at about 12 to 15% of national income or more'. And Rostow (1956, p. 25) argued that a necessary condition for a country to launch itself into sustained economic growth is 'a rise in the rate of productive investment from (say) 5% or less to over 10% of national income (or net national product)'. Of course, the Harrod–Domar–Mahalanobis models do nothing to answer Lewis' question about the process through which this change in the savings–investment rate occurs, although they do incorporate the rationale for the target rates employed by Lewis and Rostow. If one accepts an average capital–output ratio of 4:1 (Mahalanobis, 1955, p. 24, accepted that for India it would lie between 3:1 and 5:1) and a population growth rate of 2.5% per annum, then investment equal to 10% of national income would be necessary to maintain average per capita output at a constant level. A higher rate of investment will be required to permit per capita output to increase – according to the theory, investment rates of 14% and 18% would lead to per capita output growth of 1% and 2% respectively. Thus the theory implies that there is a 'critical minimum effort (which) would enable the economy to escape the gravitational pull of population increase' (Myint 1964, p. 103).

*Theoretical Relatives of the Harrod–Domar–Mahalanobis Models; Big Push and Balanced Growth*

In an early statement of the notion that poor countries need to raise their savings–investment rate sharply, Rosenstein-Rodan (1943) writing about Eastern Europe suggested that what these poor countries needed was a 'big push' of industrial investment. The reasons for this recommendation were, however, deeper than that of simply needing to increase investment. The argument was that investment in any single industry in a poor country was unlikely to be financially attractive or successful because of the very small size of the market for its product. Expanding output in any one industry would create income for the workers in that industry, but since these workers would not spend all of this income on their own product insufficient demand would be created to absorb the extra output. The necessary level of demand, it was argued, would only be created if several industries expanded simultaneously (i.e. by a big investment push) so that the demand for the output of one industry would be created by increasing the incomes of workers in other industries. Once the initial big push had occurred, a sufficiently broadly based market would have been created to provide the incentive for further investment. The same reasoning was used by Nurkse to put the case for balanced growth (Nurkse 1952, Ch. 1). As Nurkse put it (p. 12): 'An increase in production over a wide range of consumables, so proportioned as to correspond with the pattern of consumers' preferences does create its own demand.' Thus the arguments for the 'big push' and for 'balanced growth' are essentially the same.[4] Note that both arguments appear to advocate a strategy of developing industry rather than agriculture, a course followed by the USSR and also by India in its second five-year plan. In both these cases, however, the relative neglect of agriculture led to food supply and balance of payment problems which necessitated policy changes to increase investment in agriculture, and it seems clear that the big-push and balanced-growth theories have tended to be interpreted in ways which underestimate the economic role of the agricultural sector. Another criticism which has been levelled at these theories is that they over-emphasise the large-scale aspect of industrial investment. As, for example, Furtado (1954) pointed out, large-scale output is associated with the capital-intensive production techniques employed in the industrial countries. There are other more labour-intensive technologies which are viable in small-scale production and are not constrained by the smallness of the market. The big-push and balanced-growth arguments rather took for granted the appropriateness of capital-intensive production techniques. In so doing they underplayed the problem of inelastic supplies of capital and other factors of production facing many of the LDCs. For if a particular factor is in short supply, expanding one industry, far from creating external economies to the benefit of other industries, may by bidding up the cost of the factor create external diseconomies, so disadvantaging other industries (Fleming 1955).

Another weakness of the balanced-growth argument, as naively presented, was the absence of specific recognition that not all industries produce final goods but that some are clients for the products of the others. Recognition of this fact of backward and forward linkages between industries, plus the recognition of limited decision-making capacity and resource availability led Hirschman (1958) to propose, in diammetric opposition to the balanced-growth view, that sectoral investment strategies of *unbalanced growth* should be pursued. In these the State would initiate or support large-scale investment in a leading sector. Although the chosen industry might initially have excess capacity and operate at a private financial loss, the proposition is that it would create the necessary external economies to induce the development of supplying and client industries. More specifically, it was argued that expansion of the leading sector would create both new opportunities and bottlenecks elsewhere in the economy which would stimulate a secondary wave of investment and entrepreneurship. This is an argument which at first glance would appear to have particular relevance to those economic functions now generally managed by the public sector, such as railways, ports and roads, which involve large lumps of indivisible investment. However, this reveals something of the tautological character of the unbalanced-growth proposal, which is that there is always a gestation lag associated with investment; particularly so with public infrastructure investment, and never does one expect railways or roads to begin operating instantaneously at full capacity. The fact is that neither the unbalanced or balanced growth models provide adequate descriptions of the industrial development process, or operational policy prescriptions to achieve it. It hardly needs saying that the underdeveloped countries are a highly heterogeneous collection, so that the appropriate pattern of structural transformation differs for each country and depends upon its assumed national objectives, resource endowments and its prospects for trade, population growth, etc. Given suitable assumptions about these functions and parameters, programming techniques provide methods for calculating possible development plans. Exercises of this type are now numerous (see for example, Adelman and Thorbecke 1966) and incorporate within them the basic logic of the Mahalanobis model.

Note also that the justification of the big-push and balanced-growth theories requires the assumption of no foreign trade, or of poor export prospects. For, if there were strong foreign demand for the product of an industry, small domestic market size would not be synonymous with lack of investment incentive. Certainly, Nurkse (1952) in suggesting the need for a development policy of balanced growth specifically assumed that export demand for the industrial products of poor countries would be low, and that industrialisation in these countries would therefore be controlled by the size of the home market.

*Analysis Relating to Capital–Output Ratios (k)*

The apparent prospect of using simple accelerator models of the Harrod–Domar and Mahalanobis types as crude planning aids led to extensive empirical and theoretical examination of sectoral and aggregate capital–output ratios. For planning purposes it was the incremental capital–output ratios (ICORs) relating marginal increases in capital to increases in output which were considered relevant. While naturally these were found to exhibit greater variation than the average capital–output ratios, they exhibited stability in certain ways, such as between countries with a similar level of prosperity, and in certain comparable economic sectors of different countries. Nevertheless, they varied in other dimensions and, not surprisingly, $k_i$ was found to differ with the sector, $i$, of the economy (Lewis 1955, Ch. 5); thus in underdeveloped countries agriculture exhibits a lower capital requirement per unit of output than does manufacturing industry and the public sector. Also, as expected where capital becomes more abundant relative to labour as a result of economic growth, it has been observed that aggregate capital–output ratios change over time as a result of both (1) structural change within countries towards the more capital-intensive sectors and (2) increased capital intensity within sectors. Because these two aspects of change are relatively slow they do not of themselves preclude the possibility of identifying and employing $k_i$ for planning purposes. However, there is an obvious weakness for planning of treating capital–output ratios as predetermined when in fact they are adjustable through planning. Clearly, when capital is scarce it is desirable to pursue policies which minimise the size of the aggregate ratio for any given combination of outputs, which brings us back again to the problem of choice of production technique (which is the subject matter of Chapter 10). But it also raises the question of work organisation; for as Reddaway (1962, App. C) identified, $k$ may be reduced by, amongst other things, non-capital-using sources of productivity increase, changes due to the introduction of multiple shift working, and changes in capacity utilisation as a result of changes in demand. It is obvious that the second of these factors is amenable to deliberate adjustment, as is the first to the extent that work study and 'learning by doing' may lead to a more efficient use of resources.

More importantly these three points made by Reddaway indicate the limitations of attempting to explain output changes in terms of capital only. Leaving labour out of the theory might be justified where it is assumed to be in unlimited supply, and where the labour input per unit of capital remains constant, i.e. where labour and capital are complementary. However, even with ample labour, if it is feasible to adjust the number of shifts worked or their length, labour and capital become substitutes, and variations in both labour and capital have to be studied to explain output changes. In cases where the labour supply is limited, capital growth will be constrained to the rate of labour supply growth unless, as is usually the case, capital can be substituted for labour. Where this is so output changes again have to be explained by changes in both capital and labour. To a large extent it was because labour supply was thought not to be a limiting factor in the LDCs that in the early theorising it may have seemed adequate to omit it from consideration. This, however, ignored the facts (1) that not all the LDCs were overpopulated relative to their resources – there has been a tendency for thinking about development to be dominated by the special case of the highly populated Asian countries – and (2) that labour is not homogeneous in quality, and that there may be shortages of skilled manpower in countries with an abundance of unskilled labour.

Reddaway's first point also highlights the possibility of output changes without any readily measurable changes in capital or labour use, through technological change. In fact it is arguable that technological change is not generally dissociated directly (disembodied) from capital and labour, but is 'embodied' in the sense that it is associated with the introduction of improved machines or with the training of, and investment in, labour (c.f. Solow 1962). The intense empiricism sparked off by the attempt to test hypotheses related to disembodied and embodied technical change is not of interest here. What is important is to recognise, as more recent analytical and planning models do, the contribution of technical change to economic development. The need for policies to actively steer and promote technological change is extensively pursued in the later chapters on agriculture, industry and the transnational corporation, although some important policy aspects, such as health and education to improve the productive capital embodied in human beings, are not specifically examined in this book.

## 2.2 Theories of Economic Dualism

Theories of economic dualism – to be distinguished from the sociopolitical dualism of Boeke (1953) – have been ostensibly more concerned with describing certain aspects of the structural transformation which occurs within a developing economy than with generating tools to assist in planning development. The influence and attractiveness of this line of theorising is due to a considerable extent to the fact that it fills an important theoretical vacuum. As Fei and Ranis (1966) explain this, neither theories of growth of a post-Keynesian type for mature industrial economies nor classical theories of growth in agrarian economies are adequate to analyse the development of contemporary underdeveloped economies. For these latter countries are not agrarian in the sense that virtually their whole economy is based upon traditional agricultural and handicraft production; nor are they mature economies in which capitalist (or state-capitalist) modes of production are employed in all sectors. Rather, they are dualistic economies in which a modern dynamic capitalist sector exists alongside a (usually larger) traditional sector which is dominated by subsistence agriculture. The theories about economic dualism specifically relate to this type of economy and seek to provide an explanation of how a primarily agrarian economy is transformed via a dualistic state into a mature economy.

From a different standpoint Szentes (1971) also considers the theories of dualism to be a step forward. As he puts it (p. 83) 'That the phenomena and problems of dualism have received such a prominent treatment in the theory of development is doubtless a significant step forward towards a better understanding of the real nature and mechanism of underdevelopment. Instead of the superficial, quantitative characteristics, the idea of dualism calls attention to structural diseases, to certain peculiarities of the operation of the system, that is to say, it emphasises the need for a much more complex analysis.' At the same time Szentes feels, although this will not be pursued here, that 'Owing to the separation of the economic and social sides of dualism, sociological dualism becomes unexplainable, while economic dualism is simplified to the problem of technical coefficients and the asymmetry of production functions.'

The dual economy theory was first formally stated in a seminal article by Lewis (1954), and has been the subject of numerous extentions and modifications, most notably by Ranis and Fei (1961, 1966), Jorgenson (1961, 1967), and by Lewis himself (1968). No attempt will be made here to consider specific points of difference between these authors, but their combined work will be drawn upon in a generalised presentation of the main characteristics and propositions of the theory.

The dual economy is assumed to be divisible into two sectors which we will designate 'industry' and 'agriculture'. Alternative labels may be applied such as 'modern' and 'subsistence', or 'capitalist' and 'non-capitalist'. But irrespective of the nomenclature used, the essential distinction is between (1) that small and rapidly growing sector which uses relatively large amounts of capital, with labour hired for a contractual wage or salary, and (2) the much larger sector dominated by subsistence agriculture, where little capital is used, labour productivity is low, and where payment is more in kind than in cash.

Despite the claim of Ranis and Fei that the theory explains how an agrarian economy with no modern industrial sector is transformed into a mature industrial economy, it should be pointed out that all the models of dualism require an embryo capitalist industrial sector as an initial condition. What the models in fact describe is how, and under what conditions, industry may grow from small beginnings to overtake agriculture in size; but in none of the models is there an explanation of how the industrial seed appears. Perhaps this latter is not truly necessary since all LDCs have at least some indigenous entrepreneurs and modern industrial plant. It is, however, interesting to note in passing that in many countries the initial injection of industrial capital often came largely from abroad, and that many indigenous industrial managers and entrepreneurs started their professional careers in foreign-owned companies (often preceded by training in foreign educational institutions); these circumstances clash somewhat with the assumptions (stated below) of a closed economy and no foreign ownership. Nevertheless, it is clear that massive structural economic change (development) does not take place without facilitating institutions – markets and legal controls – and it is likely that there is a link between the institutions favourable to the emergence of the first modern industry in a country and those needed for its further expansion. It is true that Fei and Ranis (1966) discussed the significance of the emergence of a class of capitalist entrepreneurs among agricultural landlords, and Lewis (1954) likewise discussed the role of the entrepreneur, but no attempt is made to incorporate the conditions for the growth of entrepreneurship into the formal models.

The main assumptions of the dual economy theory are:

1. The economy is a closed one in which there is no international trade in goods and no foreign ownership of capital.[5] The principal significance of this assumption is that imports cannot be used to supplement locally produced food and agricultural raw material supplies, and sufficient resources have to be employed in agriculture to ensure an adequate marketed agricultural surplus to feed industrial workers and their families.

2. It is assumed that land for agricultural production is in fixed supply (which is effectively true for the majority of LCDs) and that no reproducible capital is required in agriculture. Thus labour is the one factor of production free to be adjusted in agriculture during the process of structural transformation.

3. It is assumed that there is exogenously given technological change in both agriculture and industry which increases the productivity of all factors of production. Note that without this assumption for the agricultural sector, the maximum potential food and agricultural raw material supply would be fixed by assumption 2.

4. In industry, output is taken to be a function of capital and labour, and these two factors are assumed to be substitutes for one another.

5. It is further assumed that the whole of capital's share of industrial output is saved and reinvested in additional industrial capacity; that is only owners of capital are assumed to save.
6. Two alternative sets of assumptions may be made relating to the productivity of agricultural labour. The usual assumption is that there is disguised unemployment in the agricultural sector such that the marginal product of a labourer is zero. Such a situation can occur where the system of land tenure grants some land use rights to every family (either directly or through a feudal system) and where each family subsists by sharing out amongst its members the product of the family holding. Under this system, agriculture forms a sink in which everybody not supported by employment in industry can find a livelihood, and it enables non-productive family members to consume at the level of the average product per person. While all family members may do some work and hence be productive at the margin, particularly in the peak agricultural labour requirement period at harvest, it is nevertheless probably true, in view of the short length of the average working day and the long periods of slack labour time, that many labourers could be withdrawn without any reduction of agricultural output because the remainder would work harder. In these conditions it may be assumed that there is initially an infinitely elastic supply of labour from agriculture to industry at a subsistence wage ($\bar{w}$) which has real purchasing power equivalent to a constant basket of food.

   There has been an extended debate as to whether or not LDCs have disguised unemployment in agriculture in the above sense. Although in the review of the literature on this subject Kao, Anschel and Eicher (1964) concluded that early empirical studies pointed to its existence on a small scale, the widespread open unemployment now evident in the urban areas of Africa, Asia and S. America suggest that it is a common phenomenon — for note that, since the urban unemployed are not supported directly through employment in the modern industrial sector, they must by the definitions of the two-sector model be part of what is labelled as agriculture.[6]

   Despite the fact that the evidence for many countries thus seems consistent with the existence of zero marginal product for 'agricultural labour', the assumption that this is so is not crucial for the dual-economy theory. And Jorgenson (1967) accepted instead, as an initial condition of the agrarian economy, that agricultural labour has a positive marginal product, but one which is less than the institutional subsistence wage ($\bar{w}$). In this circumstance it can still be assumed that initially there will be an elastic supply of labour to industry at the subsistence wage ($\bar{w}$), but it has to be accepted that any transfer of labour to industry has an opportunity cost in terms of agricultural output.

7. It is assumed that there is some maximum level of population growth ($\bar{p}$) but that actual growth may be restricted below $\bar{p}$ by a Malthusian mechanism. For, with everyone assumed to be receiving a minimum subsistence food ration, a population growth rate higher than that of food supplies would not be possible over any length of time. Thus the population growth rate may be restricted to the rate of growth of food production if the latter is less than $\bar{p}$. Note that, because of the assumed technological change in agriculture, even an economy with disguised agricultural unemployment could support a rate of population growth equal to that of this technological change.

8. It will be readily appreciated from the preceding paragraph that a critical determinant of the dynamics of population growth within the model is the assumption that the subsistence food ration is both a minimum and a maximum. Although this is usually explicitly assumed within the theory, the question naturally arises as to why, when a worker with a zero marginal product leaves agriculture, his former share of food consumption should be released to sustain him in industrial employment rather than being consumed by the remaining agricultural population to raise their living standard above the subsistence level. If the food is not released with the migrating worker the supportable growth of the industrial labour force and of the whole population would be reduced.

Given the above assumptions, including that initially the marginal productivity of agricultural labour is zero, the theory yields a number of deductive propositions: Because there is disguised unemployment, the industrial sector is in a position to develop rapidly subject only to its rate of capital accumulation. For provided that those remaining in agriculture do not start to eat what was formerly allocated to the disguised unemployed who shift to industry, complementary quantities of food and labour can be transferred from agriculture to industry and there is no reduction in total agriculture supply. With reasonable assumptions about capital's share of industrial output and about capital depreciation rates, it can be shown that the rate of growth of industrial output and employment would be high (and accelerating because of technological change). It can also be shown that this rate will be higher than any plausible rate of population growth. Thus it follows that industry will eventually absorb all the disguised unemployed and the economy will reach a turning point, usually referred to as the shortage point, and pass into a second phase in which further labour transfer into industry reduces agricultural output.

Unless technological change (productivity growth) in agriculture exceeds the maximum rate of population growth, $\bar{p}$, in this second phase, (a) the supportable rate of population growth will be reduced below that of the first phase, because agriculture supply growth due to technological change will be partially offset by a reduction in the productive labour force in agriculture, and (b) there will be a tendency for a shortage of marketed agricultural product to appear causing higher agricultural prices and a worsening of industry's terms of trade. This last effect will be due to the higher wage cost (in terms of industrial product) of maintaining the wage's purchasing power for agricultural products, and will tend to cause some substitution of capital for labour in industry. This higher wage cost will also reduce industry's profits and tend to retard its growth rate.

As more labour is sucked into industry in the second phase of the theoretically described process another turning point, the commercialisation point, will be reached at which the marginal productivity of the remaining agricultural labour force rises to a level at which the marginal supply price of labour to industry exceeds the institutional wage ($\bar{w}$). From this point on, in the third phase of development, continued expansion of the industrial workforce will be accompanied by a higher real wage rate. When this is combined with any worsening of industry's terms of trade as a result of growing agricultural supply shortage, industrial expansion will be further retarded. In this third phase, agriculture will be forced through competition for labour into a state of commercialisation which involves adopting modes of capitalist economic behaviour similar to those operating in the industrial sector. Thus the economy will have achieved the transition from an agrarian economy (at the begining of phase one) to a mature economy describable by neo-classical analysis.

Despite their various shortcomings the dual-economy models have made a notable contribution to theorising about development. In contrast to the Harrod–Domar–Mahalanobis models they focus attention upon certain aspects of agriculture, which in most LDCs is the largest economic sector in terms of employment and contribution to GNP. In particular, they emphasise the strategic importance of a marketed surplus of agricultural output and the crucial importance of technical change in generating such a surplus in the face of an expanding population. Although in the exposition above, this surplus has been treated simply as a food and raw material transfer to industry, it is in reality more than this. It is also a monetary flow from industry to agriculture arising out of payments for food, which (a) generates demand for the products of industry and creates the incentive for further industrial expansion, and (b) is a source of saving, both voluntary and through taxation, which may be used to finance investment in either agriculture or industry.[7]

Another distinguishing feature of the dual-economy theorising is that it places prime emphasis upon the employment of people plus the distribution of income between them. In doing this it introduces the troubling problem of population growth as a central dynamic force of structural transformation, alongside the dynamos of technological change and capital accumulation.

While there are many criticisms which can be levelled at the dual-economy models, as at any theory which makes strong simplifying assumptions, there are just one or two which should be indicated here. The models have, and this is a point which recurs throughout this book, helped to suggest a falsely optimistic picture of the ease with which poor, untrained rural dwellers can be assimilated into the industrial labour force. In fact a large number of LDCs have not yet reached the stage where the scale of growth of the industrial labour force is sufficient to require a decline in the agricultural labour force. As is indicated in Chapter 6 (table 6.2) the number of workers in the agricultural sector has been growing rapidly in the LDCs, and may be expected to continue to grow for a fair number of years. For not only do the activities which fall under the umbrella label of industry not generate as much demand for labour (in terms of numbers of people rather than value of labour) as the numerical assumptions accompanying the theorising imply, they also tend to require skilled (high valued) rather than unskilled labour. Thus a large differential emerges between the wages of unskilled urban-industrial workers and agricultural labour. This differential attracts agricultural workers to the towns on the offchance of obtaining skilled jobs and a high wage. In reality most of the migrants are not qualified for the employment they seek and they end up unemployed or in the 'informal sector' in the urban areas. The models also tend to overstate the capacity for reinvestment of the profits in industry, and to underestimate the savings potential in agriculture. Conspicuous consumption by industrial entrepreneurs and foreign ownership of industry (a topic extensively dealt with in Chapters 8 and 9) will both reduce the rate of industrial capital formation below the 100 per cent reinvestment level of the theory.

## 2.3 Rostow – The Stages of Economic Growth

Rostow's stage theory of economic growth was intended as a direct counter to the Marxist stage theory of capitalist development, and his 1960 publication was entitled *The Stages of Growth: A Non-Communist Manifesto.* Rostow's basic proposition was that all countries are located in one of a hierarchy of developmental stages. These were identified as (1) the traditional society, (2) the transitional stage: the preconditions for take-off, (3) the take-off, (4) the drive to maturity, and (5) the stage of high mass consumption. The currently wealthy industrial countries are identified as those which have passed through the take-off stage and are ensconced in stages 4 or 5. Since most of these countries are capitalist, the argument that in stages 4 and 5 they achieve a stable condition for self-sustaining growth and wealth presents a direct challenge to the Marxist argument of a violent end to the capitalist system.

The poor countries are required in Rostow's scheme to build a launching platform for development in the preconditions stage. In this, radical facilitating changes are required to occur in agriculture, transport and international trade, and entrepreneurial spirit and capacity has to emerge. The required changes in agriculture are towards a market-orientated economy in which food and agricultural raw materials become increasingly available to other sectors of the economy; the development of the transport sector and other social infrastructure has an obvious and vital role in economic growth; while export expansion is seen as a necessary accompaniment of increased capital imports and industrial specialisation. The critical stage is seen as the take-off, when in the space of one or two decades the rate of investment increases sharply from about 5 per cent of GNP to over 10 per cent. During this stage, leading economic sectors are assumed to emerge which create investment opportunities elsewhere in the economy and provide the basis for further investment and self-sustaining growth in stages 4 and 5.

Because of the widespread appeal of Rostow's theory it also attracted a good deal of critical attention (see for example the contribution of Kuznets to Rostow 1963; Szentes 1971, Ch. 5; and Baran and Hobsbawm 1961). The main burdens of this criticism are as follows. In the absence of any clear distinction between the end of one phase and the beginning of the next the theory becomes tautological; the rich countries have definitionally achieved the transition from an earlier condition, which may be described as traditional, to one of maturity or high mass consumption, whereas the poor countries have equally self-evidently failed to accomplish the transition or achieve take-off. Furthermore, even for the rich countries, it is by no means certain that they have achieved a self-sustained growth and thus escaped the fate predicted by the Marxists, for as Kuznets observes (in Rostow 1963, p. 41) 'no growth is purely self-sustaining or self-limiting'.

Yet another important line of criticism is that Rostow's theory in effect assumes that the still underdeveloped countries are in a traditional (or, more probably, preconditions) stage, essentially the same as that from which the now-rich countries started their development. This is an implication which is widely disputed, as will be made more fully clear in section C below. For instance, it may be argued that in the traditional stage countries are not totally stagnant but change, albeit slowly, in response to historic forces which differ from one country to another. But more importantly, it is argued that the condition of the now-poor countries has been shaped by markedly different forces from those which had prevailed in rich countries before their industrial revolution (take-off). The history of colonialism, and the transmission of various influences from the rich countries, make the condition of the now underdeveloped countries markedly different from that of the rich countries when they were at a comparable stage of GNP per capita, and raise obvious doubts about whether they can follow the same development path.

## 2.4 Critique

The volume of criticism which has been directed against the theorising discussed in this section (section B), is such that serious doubts must be entertained as to whether economic development theory passes the test of 'goodness and usefulness' stated in the first paragraph of the chapter. While it is not possible to review the full range of criticism here, it is felt to be worth drawing the attention of readers to some of the more general points.[8]

The main set of charges against the theorising stems from the fact that (at least up until the last few years) most of the influential theorists have not been nationals of the LDCs. They have mainly originated in the industrial market economies, but also include some economists from centrally planned countries, and their work in development economics has been greatly influenced by the environment and methods for examining problems in their own countries. While this is quite understandable, it is now widely accepted that this influence has introduced a variety of methodological and ideological biases into the study of development economics.

These biases manifest themselves in a number of interrelated ways. There is for example Seers' (1963) charge that there has been a marked propensity for theorists to argue for the generality of what are in fact special cases. An extreme form of this tendency has been the assumption, most evident in Rostow's stage theory of growth, that the underdeveloped countries are in the early stages of a development process, similar to that undergone by the currently industrialised nations, which will eventually change them into industrial nations. This assumption of the similarity of the path of progression is certainly rejected by Marxist theorists – who themselves are not immune from the charge of having introduced ideological biases in their approach to development (e.g. see Seers 1963). Also, as is referred to elsewhere in this book (Chapters 4 and 6), the international environment within which the LDCs are now operating is appreciably different from that surrounding the DCs at a comparable stage in their development, so that there is ample reason to suppose that their patterns of development may be different. The tendency to generalise from the special case also takes other forms. One of these is to assume, at least implicitly, that LDCs are basically similar to one another and that the same theoretical model is applicable to all of them. It is, however, fairly obvious that the problems of a highly populated country like India, differ from those of an oil-rich country such as Iran, which in turn differ from those of a sparsely populated country such as Papua–New Guinea. The diversity among the LDCs makes it unlikely that a single theoretical model can simultaneously provide an adequate basis for development policy in all countries. If this is now recognised, that in itself represents progress.

Attention has been vigorously drawn to a related form of bias by Streeten (1972, especially in Ch. 5), Myrdal (1970, Ch.1), and Szentes (1971, Part 1). This is that economists of all persuasions have in their development theories tended to misapply concepts and categories carried over from, for example, Keynesian macroeconomics or Marxist doctrine. As one illustration of this, Streeten points out that in Western orthodox models the conventional distinctions between what are variables and what are parameters (constants) are based upon (among other things such as ideological factors, vested interests, and convenience of measurement) the assumption that certain institutions and attitudes are given and adapted. In LDCs such institutions and attitudinal behaviour may not exist – indeed Chapter 1 mentions the possibility that underdevelopment may be identified by the very absence of certain institutions and attitudes – and they may need to be classified as variables to be acted upon rather than as parameters. Thus, for example, in considering the role of capital formation on economic growth, it may be feasible in Western economies to assume that adequate supplies of skilled manpower are or will be available, and that ready markets exist for the product. In LDCs, however, it is probable that the capacity to absorb (utilise) capital is limited by shortages of trained manpower, lack of complementary facilities, and limited market size. In such situations the level of capital formation has to be planned in conjunction with many complementary factors such as, for example, the provision of skilled manpower. This latter point is generally recognised in the development literature which places considerable emphasis on the role of education, but so far no satisfactory development models have been presented which integrate educational and more conventional economic variables together.

The theoretical problems arising out of the definition of concepts extend to Streeten's point that definitions and rules of measurement need to be changed when moving from the context of DCs to that of LDCs. Streeten's point is in fact that items themselves may need to be aggregated differently in the two separate situations. For example, food, which is always aggregated into consumption in developed countries, should possibly be classed with investment in countries where malnutrition inhibits the working capacity of labour.

A far more fundamental problem for the formulation of an acceptable theory of development is the failure to agree upon a readily measurable definition of what development is. Analytically, problems and disagreements about the value of development theories seem inevitable if it is agreed, as suggested in Chapter 1, that development can only be perceived in terms of improvement in several key indicators. The problems arise from the lack of any consensus as to precisely which indicators should be selected as the key ones, and from the nomination of indicators which are not readily measurable, e.g. those for institutional and attitudinal changes. It is hard to see how formal theories can be constructed to satisfy the critics if the critics themselves do not suggest operational ways of dealing with the qualitative variables they wish to see incorporated into the theory. It is not surprising that theorists have concentrated their attention upon measurable variables such as gross domestic product and capital formation. They could hardly have done otherwise, and the inclusion of qualitative variables might in any event expose the analysis to even more serious sources of subjective bias. While attempts to improve the relevance of existing models are necessary, it seems unlikely that all of the criticisms of development theory can possibly be met.

## (C) AN ALTERNATIVE VIEW OF DEVELOPMENT: UNDERDEVELOPMENT AND DEPENDENCE

### 2.5 Introduction

In this section, we present a brief survey of what may be called alternative views of the problems of development and underdevelopment. These views have developed largely within the structuralist/

Marxist framework of analysis and have given rise to the theory of dependency. It has now become a commonplace in the literature on economic development to describe or characterise LDCs as dependent economies. The condition of dependency, it is argued, encompasses all or most of the following features:

1. From their common historical background (colonialism), LDCs have inherited particular structures of production and trade, in particular, the production of primary commodities (raw materials and foodstuffs) for export to the developed capitalist economies.
2. They were initially dependent on imports for their manufactured goods requirements; with the gradual establishment of import-substituting consumer goods industries, they have become dependent on imports of intermediate and capital goods.
3. Partly as a result of industrial development, they are heavily dependent on imports of foreign technology, although this form of dependency covers many other spheres of activity – agriculture, communications, education, medicine, and so on.
4. The LDCs are in general deeply penetrated by foreign capital, largely in the guise of the transnational corporation (TNC), with its associated patterns of production, consumption, marketing, expertise, etc.
5. At a very general level, there exists a condition of cultural, psychological, social and political dependence; nominal political independence has been gained by all but a few LDCs, but this has not been matched by economic independence, a phenomenon which was first generally recognised in the early 1960s (at least in independent Africa) and which gave rise to the concept of 'neo-colonialism' (see, for example, Nkrumah 1965).[9]

Dependency theory itself has largely originated in Latin America and the Caribbean (for an example of the latter, see Girvan 1973). O'Brien (1975) shows that dependency theory contains two basic strands of thought:

1. The 'structuralist' tradition of the UN Economic Commission for Latin America (ECLA). This emphasised the failure of exports to stimulate growth because of the alleged long-run secular decline in the terms of trade between primary products and manufactured goods and the consequent need for industrialisation behind protective barriers (the move from an outward-orientated to an inward-orientated development path). The subsequent 'failure' of this import-substituting industrialisation strategy – industrialisation has not brought with it the expected developmental and modernisation benefits – has led to the realisation that the forms of

dependency may have changed but that the essential condition has not been eliminated. The structuralist analysis of these problems is discussed in the chapters on trade, income distribution, industrialisation and the TNC and will not be further pursued in this section.[10]

2. A Marxist perspective deriving from the work of Baran (1957), Frank (1967, 1969, 1972), Dos Santos (1973) and others. It is to a discussion of this latter influence that we devote the rest of this section. It should be pointed out that there is considerable overlap in the views of structuralist and Marxist writers and particular writers are not always easy to categorise. Indeed, the question of who is, or is not, a 'Marxist' has generated much controversy, but these problems will not be pursued in this section.

## 2.6 The Concept of Underdevelopment

The basic starting point of the analysis of underdevelopment and dependence is the recognition that underdevelopment is not a condition that all countries experience, or a stage that all countries pass through, before development. Rather, development and underdevelopment are regarded as opposite sides of the same coin (Frank 1967, p.9). It is held that the development of some countries actively led to the underdevelopment (or distorted development) of others, and that underdevelopment is thus a 'normal' part of the development of the world capitalist system. Szentes (1971, p. 132) argues that:

> the socio-economic state of the developing countries is not merely 'economic underdevelopment', not just a sign of not having participated in development, of their having fallen behind in progress, but it is the product of a specific development, which is most closely connected with, moreover derived from, the development of capitalist world economy.

The development gap between developed and less-developed countries (that is, the difference in the levels of productive forces) widened as a result of colonialism and the interaction of the two groups of countries. In the LDCs themselves, the establishment of 'alien' forms of economic and social/political organisation and the external orientation of these countries led to a pattern of development very different from that which would have occurred if their development had been based mainly on internal socio-economic forces.

A complete understanding of the present position of LDCs must thus begin with an analysis of colonialism, seen as the consequence of the emergence and development on a world scale of a specific social system, the objective product of capitalism at a certain stage of its development (Szentes 1971, Part 2, Ch. 1).[11] From a Marxist viewpoint, colonialism is seen as essentially an economic phenomenon, the earliest period of which was associated with piracy, the plunder of treasure from foreign lands, and the slave trade (the period of so-called primitive capital accumulation). As industrial capitalism developed in western Europe, the nature of its impact on the rest of the world changed. An international division of labour was established in which colonial possessions were formally incorporated into the spheres of interest of the metropolitan powers and functioned as suppliers of minerals and agricultural raw materials to the metropolitan powers, as markets for industrial products, as areas of expanded investment opportunities (and thus as a regular source of income to the metropolitan powers), as well as fulfilling strategic and political functions.

Large areas of the world were thus incorporated into the expanding world economy through the vigorous outward thrust of the rapidly growing societies of western Europe. New patterns of production and trade were introduced along with more advanced technical, scientific and infrastructural facilities. New cultural and religious values were also introduced. But in this process, old societies, institutions, cultures and values were partially, if not completely, destroyed and the processes of change (albeit slow) that were taking place in these societies were retarded and distorted.[12]

*Marx on India*

Marx wrote several articles analysing the impact of British rule on India (Marx 1853, 1973; see also Kiernan 1974). Marx regarded Asian society as stagnant, based on a village system described as 'undignified, stagnatory and vegetative'.[13] He argued that Britain's conquest of India had a two-fold mission:

(a) destructive – the plunder and annihilation of the old Asiatic society (including the destruction of native communities and the elimination of Indian industries), and

(b) constructive – the laying of the material foundations of Western society in Asia. This regeneration consisted of, *inter alia,* (i) the political unification of the country, (ii) the establishment of private property in land, (iii) the creation of a class of Indians 'endowed with the requirements for government and imbued with European science', (iv) the establishment of a communication network, especially the development of a railway system, leading to the creation of 'fresh productive powers'.

The latter was considered to be most important. Industrial interests in the UK (the so-called millocracy) recognised the need to pursue policies expanding the Indian market for UK manufactured goods (especially textiles) and to ensure guaranteed and regular supplies of raw cotton to the UK mills. Railways were needed to develop the production and export of cotton and other raw materials but, Marx argued:

> You cannot maintain a net of railways over an immense country without introducing all those industrial processes necessary to meet the immediate and current want of railway locomotion, and out of which there must grow the application of machinery to those branches of industry not immediately connected with railways. The railway system will therefore become, in India, truly the forerunner of modern industry'
>
> (Marx 1973 edition, p. 323).

In turn, industrialisation would dissolve the caste system and other impediments to social change.

But as Kiernan (1974, pp. 189–191) notes, emancipation from the past proceeded more slowly than Marx expected. Indian religion and social habits retarded social change; since there was no Indian State there was no tariff policy to protect Indian industry; capital flowed into land rather than into industry and the countryside was able to absorb surplus labour power.

Baran (1957, Ch. 5) has stressed the point that capitalist penetration developed some of the prerequisites of capitalist development but blocked others, mainly through (i) the removal of the previously accumulated and currently generated economic surplus which retarded capital accumulation, and (ii) the destruction of indigenous industries. Capitalist development was 'distorted' to suit the purposes of Western imperialism (Baran 1957, p. 144).[14] Of major importance for Baran was the nature of the wealthy class, either surviving from pre-colonial times or created under colonial rule. This was a class that either could not or would not develop into an autonomous bourgeoisie, and was thus incapable of establishing the capitalist mode of production in its own country. Rather it was a 'comprador bourgeoisie' whose position was dependent on, and allied to, foreign interests.

Baran has been classified by some as a 'neo-Marxist' and controversy has arisen over the relationship between 'neo-Marxism' and 'classical' Marxism. Foster-Carter (1974, p. 69) argues that

> the rise of a neo-Marxist school centered on the problem of underdevelopment (albeit conceived very differently from its original bourgeois meaning) . . . must be seen against a backcloth of the perceived inadequacy, not only of bourgeois descriptions and prescriptions, but also of traditional Marxist ideas about 'backward' countries.[15]

But Leys (1975, Ch. 1) has maintained that there is no necessary conflict between Marx's views on India and the 'neo-Marxist's' views of the non-development of contemporary LDCs. From Marx's writings on Ireland Leys argues that, had he lived long enough, Marx would have produced a theory of underdevelopment along the lines of today's 'neo-Marxists' and that thus there is no real inconsistency between Marx and Baran regarding the latter's insistence on the part played in the process of underdevelopment by surplus transfer:

> Underdevelopment theory is thus partly a correction and partly an expansion of Marx's interpretation of history, an extension of his method and central ideas which, in a world scale, was still in embryo at his death.
> (Leys 1975, p. 7).

Underdevelopment theory should thus be the history of LDCs viewed in their own right, rather than merely seen as sources of primitive capital accumulation for the western economies.[16]

Dos Santos (1973) makes a similar point when he argues that theories of imperialism are essentially eurocentric, that is, imperialism is analysed from the standpoint of the problems of the advanced capitalist country. Until recently, little attention has been devoted to its impact on LDCs, but Dos Santos believes that the study of the development of LDCs must give rise to a theory of dependence. It is within this context that we must briefly discuss the work of Andre Gunder Frank.

### *Andre Gunder Frank*

In his work on Latin America, Frank coined the now famous expression 'the development of underdevelopment' (used by many others – for example, Rodney 1972) to refer to the continuous process by which capitalist contradictions and capitalist development generate underdevelopment in the peripheral satellite countries whose economic surplus is expropriated, whilst generating development in the metropolitan centres that appropriate the surplus. The 'contradictions' that Frank refers to are:

(i) *The expropriation/appropriation of the surplus.* Using Baran's (1957) concept of 'potential' or potentially investible economic surplus (an economic surplus that is not available to society because its monopoly structure prevents its production or, if it is produced, it is appropriated and wasted through luxury consumption), Frank argued that the non-realisation and unavailability for investment of 'potential' economic surplus was due essentially to the monopoly structure of capitalism (Frank 1969, pp. 6–7). Chile (the country Frank was analysing) was always subject to a high degree of monopoly, both external and internal, and the external monopoly resulted in the expropriation of a considerable part of the economic surplus produced in Chile and its appropriation by another part of the world capitalist system. Furthermore:

> The monopoly capitalist structure and the surplus expropriation/appropriation contradiction run through the entire Chilean economy, past and present. Indeed, it is this exploitative relation which in chain-like fashion extends the

> capitalist link between the capitalist world and national metropolises to the regional centers (part of whose surplus they appropriate), and from these to local centers and so on to large landowners or merchants who expropriate surplus from small peasants or tenants and sometimes even from these latter to landless laborers exploited by them in turn . . . at each point the international, national and local capitalist system generates economic development for the few and underdevelopment for the many.
>
> (Frank 1969 ed. pp. 7–8)

(ii) *Metropolis – satellite polarisation.* The metropolis expropriates the economic surplus from its satellites and appropriates it for its own economic development, leading to polarisation in which there is development at the centre and underdevelopment at the periphery. One important corollary of this thesis is that, if it is in fact the case that satellite status generates underdevelopment, then it follows that the weaker are metropolis–satellite relationships (for example, at times of war and economic depression), the greater are the possibilities for the local development of the satellite. We briefly return to this point in Chapter 8.

(iii) *The contradiction of continuity in change.* The structural essentials of economic development and underdevelopment are continuous and ubiquitous throughout the expansion and development of the capitalist system, even though important historical changes have taken place in specific parts of the system, in this instance Chile.

Two major implications of Frank's analysis require brief mention. At the political level, the conclusion is drawn that the Latin American bourgeoisie is incapable of undertaking its historic task, that is it cannot adopt independent, nationalist policies leading to a democratic political system and independent national development. This is because of its origins and economic connections. What exists, Frank argued in a later work (Frank 1972), is a lumpenbourgeoisie, a class which is a passive or active tool of foreign industry and commerce, and whose interests are thus identical.

The second major point is that, according to Frank, most of Latin America was incorporated into the world capitalist system during the very first phase of its colonial history, and thus it does not make sense to speak of feudal, semi-feudal or archaic elements in Latin American society. This also undermines the concept of the dual economy which has dominated much orthodox and Marxist thinking about LDCs.

Frank's work has been extensively criticised from many different quarters (the extensive bibliography given in Frank 1977 illustrates the reaction his work has provoked; Booth 1975 provides a good survey of the work of both Frank and his critics). In his later work (1972, 1977), Frank has answered some attacks from the left by stressing that underdevelopment must be understood and defined in terms of social classes and that dependence 'should not and cannot be considered a purely "external" relationship imposed on Latin America from abroad and against their wishes. Dependence is also, and in equal measure, an "internal", integral element of Latin American society' (Frank 1972, p.3). We return to this point below.

A significant criticism has been made by Laclau (1971) who argues that Frank confuses the two concepts of the capitalist mode of production and participation in a world capitalist economic system. The precapitalist character of the dominant relations of production in Latin America

> was not only *not* incompatible with production for the world market, but was actually intensified by the expansion of the latter. The feudal regime of the haciendas tended to increase the servile exactions on the peasantry as the growing demands of the world market stimulated maximisation of their surplus.
>
> (Laclau 1971 p. 30)

Furthermore, Laclau maintains that to affirm the feudal character of relations of production does not necessarily involve maintaining a dualistic thesis (in which dualism is taken to imply that no connections exist between the 'modern' and 'traditional' sectors of the economy). As the above quote shows, the connections between the two sectors ('feudal' and 'modern') were strong and it is necessary to examine the system as a whole and show the 'indissoluble unity that exists between the maintenance of feudal backwardness at one extreme and the apparent progress of a bourgeois dynamism at the other' (p. 31). Booth (1975) argues that a major gap in Frank's analysis is a discussion of the interconnections between different modes of production combined in a single, national or international, economic system.

From another viewpoint Cardoso (1972) has argued that dependency, monopoly capitalism and development are not contradictory terms and that there is occurring a kind of dependent capitalist development in some LDCs. Taking into account the characteristics of contemporary industrial development and the operations of TNCs in LDCs (issues discussed in Chapters 8–10) in countries such as Argentina, Brazil, Mexico and India, there is an 'internal structural fragmentation', linking the most advanced parts of these economies to the international capitalist system. Separate from, although subordinate to, these advanced sectors, the backward economic and social sectors became 'internal colonies' and a new kind of dualism is created (Cardoso 1974, p. 90).[17]

A final point deserves mention. Frank has used the expression 'ultra-underdevelopment' to describe regions such as the Brazilian

North-East where once active primary export economies eventually declined, creating conditions of poverty and stagnation. But Frank also argues that underdevelopment is a structural condition, created simultaneously with the metropolitan centres and the incorporation of the satellite into the world capitalist economy. From this it follows that 'ultra-underdevelopment' must be the consequence of 'ultra-incorporation' of the satellite into the metropolitan sphere. It could thus be argued that the most 'ultra-underdeveloped' part of Latin America is (or will be) oil-rich Venezuela 'where contemporary rather than past colonialism assumes its most extreme forms' (Frank 1972, p. 22). Frank therefore agrees to distinguish between the 'active' development of underdevelopment (Venezuela) and the 'passive' state of ultra-underdevelopment in the exporting regions of earlier periods in the development of world capitalism. Booth (1975, pp. 76–77) argues that this 'leaves us in a mess' and that 'the terminology upon which Frank has chosen to rely fails to serve as an unambiguous and internally consistent scheme for classifying the varied historical processes and states of affairs identified by him'.

Frank's analysis may be relevant to agro–mineral societies but his pursuit of a general explanation of underdevelopment obscures the diversity of economic structure and experience. Both open, export-orientated economies and 'inward-looking' semi-industrialised economies are in some sense dependent, but the nature of the 'dependency' differs markedly in the two cases. In view of these problems, it would perhaps be better to abandon the idea of underdevelopment as an active process in the contemporary world and concentrate instead on the varied processes of change that are actually taking place.[18]

## 2.7 The Concept of Dependency

What clearly emerges from the above discussion is that dependency cannot be viewed as a purely external phenomenon and this is a point that is stressed by a leading dependency theorist, Dos Santos (1973). Dos Santos defines dependence as a 'conditioning situation, in which the economies of one group of countries are conditioned by the development and expansion of others' (p. 76). That is, dependence is based on an international division of labour which allows industrial development to take place in some countries while restricting it in others, 'whose growth is conditioned by and subjected to the power centres of the world' (p. 77). The concept of dependence must take into account the articulation of dominant interests in both the metropolitan centres and the dependent societies – domination is only possible when it is supported by local groups which profit from it ('External domination, in a pure sense, is in principle impracticable') (p. 78).[19]

From this analysis follows a most important conclusion:

> . . . if dependence defines the internal situation and is structurally linked to it, a country cannot break out of it simply by isolating herself from external influences; such action would simply provoke chaos in a society which is of its essence dependent. The only solution therefore would be to change its internal structure – a course which necessarily leads to confrontation with the existing international structure.
>
> (Dos Santos 1973, p. 79)

## 2.8 Dependency Theory – A Reappraisal

We noted at the beginning of this section that the concept of dependence has been incorporated into orthodox development economics, but the concept has been both misinterpreted and misused by supporters and critics alike. Too often the concept is reduced to a mere listing of the characteristics of LDCs (structure of production, patterns of trade, importance of foreign capital, etc.) or a description of different types of dependency (financial, technical, cultural, etc.).[20]

A critic of the concept of dependency (Lall 1975) for example, after discussing so-called static and dynamic characteristics of dependence, concludes that the concept as applied to LDCs is impossible to define and cannot be shown to be related causally to the continuation of underdevelopment. He argues that it makes more sense to think in terms of a pyramidal structure of socio-political dominance in the capitalist world, 'with the top (hegemonic) position held by the most powerful capitalist country and the bottom by the smallest and poorest ones, and a more or less continuous range occupied by various developed and less developed countries, with relative positions changing between the two' (Lall 1975, p.803).

But the concept of dependence is empty of meaning if it fails to analyse the class structure of the LDC and the relationships that exist between the domestic ruling class and foreign interests, in the way suggested by Dos Santos. Given that the concept of dependency is not encompassed by a list of the characteristics of LDCs, or the processes of change taking place within them, it also follows that the theory of dependency does not fall within the positivist–deductive methodology discussed in Section A of this Chapter. We cannot appeal to empirical evidence to prove or disprove the existence of dependency. In O'Brien's words (1975, pp. 11–12), the concept of dependence is a 'higher level or general hypothesis', the objective of which is

> to define the problem or area of interest and to try and show how lower level, more specific *ad hoc* hypotheses fit within this framework . . . The theory of dependency therefore represents a framework of reference within which various heterogeneous phenomena are analysed to see how they link and interact with each other to form a total system.

Even accepting that the concept of dependency can only be used in a meaningful sense within a basically Marxist analytical framework, the concept has come under increasing attack by those writing from an explicitly Marxist viewpoint. Kay (1975, pp. 103–4) argues that the concept of dependence 'fails to grasp the real nature of the process of underdevelopment . . (it) . . is an eclectic combination of orthodox economic theory and revolutionary phraseology'. Leys (1977) condemns underdevelopment and dependency theory for its theoretical repetition and stagnation, the existence of fundamental problems of analysis which it cannot solve (for example, the meaning of development, the concept of 'exploitation') and its co-option by 'developmentalists allied to international capital' (Leys 1977, p.92), a point also emphasised by Frank (1977).[21]

It is undoubtedly the case that dependency theory has provided many important insights into the characteristics of LDCs and the interaction between them and developed capitalist economies. But its Marxist critics argue that it is necessary to move forward to a different kind of theory and a more clearly defined relation between theory and practice. In Leys' words, what is needed is a genuine historical theory which 'will allow us to analyse the process of combined and uneven development of capitalism on a world scale, as it has been experienced . . . in particular countries, and hence as it presents itself to any one of them now' and which will permit the drawing of conclusions relevant to contemporary struggles within these countries (Leys 1977, pp. 100–101).

## Notes

1 It is significant to note that industrial countries are choosing to place increasing reliance upon regional and sectoral policies to supplement generalised economic policies of a Keynesian type, which may be interpreted as indicating that macroeconomic models are proving over-simple in practice even in these countries.

2 In the Mahalanobis planning exercise the output–capital ratios are adjusted for capital depreciation. This adjustment involves adding replacement requirements to the capital side of the ratios. For example, if a machine which does not depreciate produces annual output equivalent to one third of its cost, the output–capital ratio is 1:3, but if the machine depreciates and has to be replaced every third year the adjusted ratio will be 1:4.

3 It is easier to accept this emphasis in the Indian context in which Mahalanobis wrote. Despite low average per capita incomes in India, its huge population creates a sizeable market for heavy industrial products and steel which, given the availability of coal and iron ore, justified the development of heavy industry. In LDCs with much smaller populations, and without the required raw materials, heavy industry is difficult to justify and does not receive the same emphasis, although, as Frances Stewart (1976) has argued, the capital goods industry is an important force for technical progress. (Issues relating to heavy industry are more fully discussed in Ch. 10).

4 Although as Myint (1964) states the big push theory results from logic relating the investment rate through the output–capital ratio to the rate of population growth, whereas the balanced growth theory evolved from wider concerns about the vicious circle between poverty, small markets and lack of investment incentives.

5 It is true that Lewis (1954) did discuss an open dualistic economy model. However, as previously noted, most of the generalisations which emerge about relationships in a closed economy disappear when trade is permitted.

6 That those in the urban 'informal sector' should be classified as in the agricultural sector emphasises the arbitrariness of dividing an economy into only two sectors. It is appropriate in this case, however, to the extent that the majority of such people may have moved to the urban areas because they perceive the opportunities to be better than in the rural areas from which they have moved. Nevertheless, that the marginal product should be zero for 'agricultural labour' defined in this way cannot be taken to imply that the same is true for those remaining in rural areas and actually working the land.

7 Note that without such savings from agriculture out of this surplus the average consumption levels in agriculture would exceed the subsistence level by the amount of industrial product consumed; and unless, as is most certainly the case, the industrial wage were actually higher than the subsistence level, agricultural workers would have higher consumption levels than those in industry.

8 Those wishing to pursue these matters further are recommended to read Streeten 1972, part 1; Szentes 1971, part 1; Myrdal 1970, Chs. 1 and 2; and Seers 1963.

9 Neo-colonialism was defined, in a resolution at the All-African People's Conference, Cairo, 1961, as 'the survival of the colonial system in spite of the formal recognition of political independence in emerging countries which become the victims of an indirect and subtle form of domination by political, economic, social, military or technical means'. Quoted in Leys (1975, p. 26).

10 Leys (1977) re-emphasises the point that dependency theory has largely emerged from a continually revised interpretation of the process and characteristics of the development experience (largely of Latin America), mainly from an orthodox (i.e. non-Marxist) viewpoint. He concludes: 'The main stream of UDT (underdevelopment and dependency theory) can thus be seen as eventuating in *radical structuralism* – i.e. as a structuralist analysis of the obstacles to capitalist development in the

third world in which progressively more and more of what were originally seen as means to structural change – international manufacturing companies, third world governments and the interests they mostly represent, etc. – come to be seen as yet further structures which themselves need to be changed' (p. 97).

11 Barratt Brown (1974, Ch. 1) uses the concept of imperialism to 'encompass the outward drive of certain peoples (generally, since 1600, nation states) to build empires – both formal colonies and privileged positions in markets, protected sources of materials and extended opportunities for profitable employment of labour' (p. 22). The term 'imperialism' is more commonly used (by Marxists) to describe the outward expansion of monopoly capitalism over the past 100 years (Lenin, *Imperialism – The Highest Stage of Capitalism).*

12 It is wrong to regard all pre-colonial societies as stagnant, backward, primitive, etc. Hodgkin (1972) notes that 'technological advance and social change, in a centralising, modernising direction were . . . taking place in a number of African societies in the late eighteenth and nineteenth centuries, as a result both of internal forces and external stimuli.' (p. 106).

13 Fernbach in his Introduction to Marx (1973 edition, pp. 26–27) notes that Marx was later to revise his views on the stagnant character of Indian society and to deny that the west European path of historical development was a necessary model for all societies.

14 India is usually quoted as the classic example of this process. It has been estimated that in the early decades of the twentieth century, Britain annually appropriated over 10% of India's GNP and this figure would have been higher in the eighteenth and nineteenth centuries. For a different view, see Mukerjee (1972).

15 For a criticism of Foster-Carter see Taylor (1974).

16 Leys presents a broad outline of what he considers to be the main elements of underdevelopment theory: plunder and extortion – the slave trade – the period of primitive capital accumulation; the extraction of the investible surplus; the development of new social strata; the replacement of primitive by capitalist accumulation; replacement of direct rule by independent governments; external orientation of LDC economies; monopoly elements – force, trading companies, commodity markets, technology; import-substituting industrialisation and the TNC.

17 In another article, Cardoso (1973) characterises the process as 'associated dependent development'. This process is dynamic in so far as the interests of TNCs, in the era of production for the domestic market, become compatible with the internal prosperity of dependent economies; that is, the production and sale of goods to upper/middle income groups requires the growth of some sectors of the dependent economy. But this path of development has its costs: it 'is based on a regressive profile of income distribution, emphasises luxury consumer durables as opposed to basic necessities, generates increasing foreign indebtedness and contributes to social marginality and the under-utilisation and exploitation of manpower resources' (p. 149).

18 A further point deserves brief mention, Frank (1977, p. 362) states

that he has never had the temerity to claim to be a Marxist nor the desire to deny it, and thus we must avoid the mistake 'which Laclau makes – of reading Frank as a theoretically naive Marxist' (Leaver 1977, p. 114). Leaver also suggests that 'the almost universally accepted conflation of Baran and Frank' must be challenged, but he does not develop this argument.

19 The situation is not static; there is interaction between the conditioned situation and the conditioning situation and changes in either can affect the other; the situation of dependence itself alters with changes in the centre and changes in the dependent structures, redirecting the dependency relationship. (Dos Santos 1973, p. 78).

20 Szentes (1971, Part II, Ch. 2) enumerates the various forms of dependence (both external and internal) but does so within an explicitly Marxist framework.

21 Warren's (1973) critique of dependency is discussed in Chapter 8.

## Bibliography

Ackley G. (1961), *Macroeconomic Theory,* Macmillan.

Adelman I. and Thorbecke E. (eds) (1966), *The Theory and Design of Economic Development,* The Johns Hopkins Press.

Agarwala A.N. and Singh S.P. (eds) (1958), *The Economics of Under-Development,* Oxford University Press.

Amin S. (1974), *Accumulation on a World Scale: a Critique of the Theory of Underdevelopment* (2 vols), Monthly Review Press, New York.

Baran P. (1957), *The Political Economy of Growth,* Monthly Review Press, New York.

Baran P.A. and Hobsbawm E.J. (1966) 'The stages of economic growth: a review', *Kyklos,* Vol. 14, Reprinted in Wilber (1973).

Barber W.J. (1967), *A History of Economic Thought,* Penguin Books.

Barratt Brown M. (1974), *The Economics of Imperialism,* Penguin.

Beckford G. (1972), *Persistent Poverty: Underdevelopment in Plantation Economies of the Third World,* Oxford University Press, New York.

Boeke J.H. (1953), *Economics and Economic Policy of Dual Societies.*

Booth D. (1975), 'Andre Gunder Frank: an introduction and appreciation' in Oxaal I., Barnett T. and Booth D. (eds), *Beyond the Sociology of Development,* Routledge and Kegan Paul.

Brookfield H. (1975), *Interdependent Development,* Methuen.

Bruton J. (1955) 'Growth models and underdeveloped economies', *Journal of Political Economy,* Vol. 63, reprinted in Agarwala and Singh (1958).

Cairncross A.K. (1962), *Factors in Economic Development,* George Allen and Unwin.

Cardoso F.H. (1972), 'Dependent capitalist development in Latin America', *New Left Review,* No. 74, July–August.

Cardoso F.H. (1973), 'Associated-dependent development: theoretical and practical implications', in Stepan A. (ed) (1973), *Authoritarian Brazil,* Yale University Press.

Chenery H.B. and Bruno M. (1962), 'Development alternatives in an open economy: the case of Israel', *Economic Journal,* Vol. 72.

Domar D. (1946), 'Capital expansion, rate of growth and employment', *Econometrica,* Vol. 14.

Dos Santos T. (1973), 'The crisis of development theory and the problem of dependence in Latin America', in Berstein H. (ed) (1973), *Underdevelopment and Development*, Penguin.

Fei J.C. and Ranis G. (1966), 'Agrarianism, dualism and economic development', Ch. 1 of Adelman and Thorbecke (eds) (1966).

Fleming J.M. (1955), 'External economies and the doctrine of balanced growth', *Economic Journal,* Vol. 65, Reprinted in Agarwala and Singh (eds) (1958).

Foster-Carter A. (1974), 'Neo-Marxist approaches to development and underdevelopment', in de Kadt E. and Williams G. (eds.) (1974), *Sociology and Development*, Tavistock.

Frank A.G. (1967), *Capitalism and Underdevelopment in Latin America,* Monthly Review Press, New York; Modern Reader Paperback Edition 1969.

Frank A.G. (1969), *Latin America: Underdevelopment or Revolution,* Monthly Review Press, New York.

Frank A.G. (1972), *Lumpenbourgeoisie: Lumpendevelopment: Dependence, Class and Politics in Latin America,* Monthly Review Press, New York.

Frank A.G. (1977), 'Dependence is dead, long live dependence and the class struggle: an answer to critics', *World Development,* Vol. 5, No. 4.

Friedman M. (1966), *Essays in Positive Economics,* University of Chicago Press.

Furtado C. (1954), 'Capital formation and economic development', in Agarwala and Singh (eds) (1958).

Girvan N. (1973), 'The development of dependency economics in the Carribbean and Latin America: review and comparison', *Social and Economic Studies,* Vol. 22, No. 1, March.

Harrod R.F. (1939), 'An essay in dynamic theory', *Economic Journal*, Vol. 49, No. 1.

Hirschman A.O. (1958), *The Strategy of Economic Development,* Yale University Press.

Hodgkin T. (1972), 'Some African and Third World theories of imperialism', in Owen R. and Sutcliffe R.B. (eds) (1972), *Studies in the Theory of Imperialism,* Longman.

Jorgenson D. (1961), 'The development of a dual economy', *Economic Journal* Vol. 71.

Jorgenson D. (1967), 'Surplus agricultural labour and the development of a dual economy', *Oxford Economic Papers,* Vol. 19.

Kao C.H.C., Anschel K.R. and Eicher C.K. (1964), 'Disguised unemployment in agriculture: a survey', Ch. 7 in Eicher C.K. and Witt L.W. (eds) (1964), *Agriculture in Economic Development,* McGraw-Hill.

Kay G. (1975), *Development and Underdevelopment: A Marxist Analysis,* Macmillan.

Kiernan V.G. (1974), 'Marx and India', in *Marxism and Imperialism,* Edward Arnold.

Laclau E. (1971), 'Feudalism and capitalism in Latin America', *New Left Review,* No. 67, May–June.

Lall S. (1975), 'Is "dependence" a useful concept in analysing underdevelopment?', *World Development,* Vol. 3, Nos. 11 and 12.

Leaver R. (1977), 'The debate on underdevelopment: "On situating Gunder Frank"', *Journal of Contemporary Asia,* Vol. 7, No. 1.

Lewis W.A. (1954), 'Economic development with unlimited supplies of labour', *Manchester School*, Vol 22, Reprinted in Agarwala and Singh (eds) (1958).

Lewis W.A. (1955), *The Theory of Economic Growth*, Allen and Unwin.

Lewis W.A. (1968), 'Reflections on unlimited labour', Princeton Special Paper.

Leys C. (1975), *Underdevelopment in Kenya: The Political Economy of Neo-Colonialism*, Heinemann.

Leys C. (1977), 'Underdevelopment and dependency: critical notes', *Journal of Contemporary Asia*, Vol. 7, No. 1.

Mahalanobis P.C. (1955), 'The approach of operational research to planning in India', *Sankhya: The Indian Journal of Statistics*, Vol. 16, Parts 1 and 2.

Marx K. (1853), 'The East India Company – Its history and results' and 'The future results of the British rule in India', Reprinted in Fernbach D. (ed..) (1973), Karl Marx, *Surveys from Exile*, Political Writings, Vol. 2, Penguin.

Marx K. (1853), 'The East India Company – Its history and results' and 'The future results of the British rule in India', Reprinted in Fernbach D. (ed) (1973), Karl Marx, *Surveys from Exile*, Political Writings, Vol. 2, Penguin.

Marx K. and Engels F. (1971 edition), *Ireland and the Irish Question*, Progress Publishers, Moscow.

Meier G.M. (ed.) (1970),*Leading Issues in Economic Development* (2nd edn), Oxford University Press.

Mukerjee T. (1972), 'Theory of economic drain: impact of British rule on the Indian economy 1840–1900', in Boulding D.E. and Mukerjee T. (eds) (1972), *Economic Imperialism*, University of Michigan Press.

Myint H. (1964), *The Economics of the Developing Countries*, Hutchinson University Library.

Nkrumah K. (1965), *Neo-Colonialism: The Last Stage of Imperialism*, Heinemann.

Nurkse R. (1952), *Problems of Capital Formation in Underdeveloped Countries*, Blackwell.

O'Brien P.J. (1975), 'A critique of Latin American theories of dependency', in Oxaal I., Barnett T. and Booth D. (eds) (1975), *Beyond the Sociology of Development*, Routledge and Kegan Paul.

Raj K.N. and Sen A.K. (1961), 'Alternative patterns of growth under conditions of stagnant export earnings', *Oxford Economic Papers*, Vol. 13.

Ranis G. and Fei J.C. (1961), 'A theory of economic development', *American Economic Review*, Vol. 51, Reprinted in Eicher and Wit (eds) (1964).

Reddaway W.B. (1962), *The Development of the Indian Economy*, Allen and Unwin.

Rodney W. (1972), *How Europe Underdeveloped Africa*, Bogle–L'Ouverture Publications London, and Tanzania Publishing House, Dar es Salaam.

Rosenstein-Rodan P.N. (1943), 'Problems of industrialisation of Eastern and South-Eastern Europe', *Economic Journal*, Vol. 53, Reprinted in Meier 1970.

Rostow W.W. (1956), 'The take-off into self-sustained growth', *Economic Journal*, Vol. 66, Reprinted in Agarwala and Singh (1958).

Rostow W.W. (1960), *The Stages of Growth: a Non-Communist Manifesto*, Cambridge University Press.

Rostow W.W. (ed) (1963), *The Economics of Take-Off into Sustained Growth*, Macmillan.

Seers D. (1963), 'The limitations of the special case', *Bulletin of Oxford Institute of Economics and Statistics*, Vol. 25, No. 2.

Stewart F. (1976), 'Capital goods in developing countries', in Caircross A. and Puri M. (eds) (1976), *Employment, Income Distribution and Growth*, Macmillan.

Streeten P. (1972), *The Frontiers of Development Studies*, Macmillan.
Solow R.M. (1962), 'Technical progress, capital formation and economic growth', *American Economic Review*, Vol. 25.
Sunkel O. (1969), 'National development policy and external dependence in Latin America', *Journal of Development Studies*, Vol. 6. No. 1.
Sunkel O. (1973), 'The pattern of Latin American dependence' in Urquidi V. and Thorp R. (eds), *Latin America in the International Economy* ,Macmillan.
Szentes T. (1971), *The Political Economy of Underdevelopment*, Akademiai Kiado, Budapest.
Taylor J. (1974), 'Neo-Marxism and underdevelopment – a sociological phantasy', *Journal of Contemporary Asia*, Vol. 4, No. 1.
UN Economic Commission for Asia and the Far East (ECAFE) (1960), *Programming Techniques for Economic Development.*
Wilber C.K. (1973), *The Political Economy of Development and Underdevelopment*, Random House.

# 3
# Economic equality and economic development

## 3.1 Introduction

We noted in Chapter 1 the distinction that is now commonly made between the concepts of economic growth and economic development. The concept of economic development raises a number of normative issues, one of the most important of which concerns the degree of economic equality thought to be necessary or desirable, both as a means of stimulating economic growth and as a development objective.

Although many LDCs have experienced rapid rates of growth of GDP over the past two decades, it has become increasingly obvious that this process has brought little, if any, benefit to a substantial minority, or perhaps even a majority, of the population of these countries. Economists, planners and international agencies are expressing growing concern over the fact that perhaps one third (the World Bank's estimate) of the population of LDCs has received no net benefit from growth. In some countries, the proportion of the population excluded from receiving the benefits of growth will be even higher and, in certain cases, large sections of the population may have sunk into even greater poverty as the result of the specific processes of change taking place within these societies.

Economic and social inequalities exist in many overlapping forms in LDCs. Inequalities in the distribution of income and wealth (especially land) are perhaps the most obvious, but inequalities between rural and urban areas, different regions and different tribes and ethnic groups are all important and raise difficult policy issues. In the case of regional inequalities, tensions can arise which may ultimately lead to armed conflict if not solved. Differential access to modern sector facilities (education, health, housing, employment) is both a cause and a consequence of economic and social inequalities in general. Many see unemployment as the prime cause of inequality and thus stress the need to create widespread employment opportunities within the LDC as a step towards the elimination of poverty and inequality. The International Labour Office in Geneva is a strong supporter of this argument, although it also focuses attention on the problem of the 'working poor', that is, those whose income falls below some specified minimum, even though they have a full-time job (see ILO 1972, Ch. 3). Unemployment is also, of course, a symptom of inequality.

In this chapter, we are concerned with the distribution of income and specifically with (1) the impact of economic growth on the pattern of income distribution over time and (2) the influence of the distribution of income on economic growth. We will argue that greater equality is a necessary condition if economic growth and development are to occur which will beneficially affect the lives of the mass of the population.

The concept of economic equality encompasses, in Tawney's (1964, pp. 48-9) words, equality of 'circumstances, institutions, and manner of life' and as such refers to more than merely the distribution of income. But we shall assume that a society that aims at broad equality in its income distribution will also be concerned with the elimination of those other economic and social inequalities referred to above.[1]

## 3.2 The Distribution of Income in LDCs

Measurement of the degree of income inequality in LDCs is by no means straightforward, and there is no ideal way of empirically comparing differences in income distributions between countries. In the first place the necessary data are frequently unobtainable for LDCs, and when available are not highly reliable. Secondly, conceptual problems exist as to the basic unit for which the data should be analysed (whether it should be the individual, the nuclear family, or the household), the period over which income should be measured, and the definition of income that should be used (a problem of particular importance in LDCs). Thirdly, there are various alternative measures of inequality, and countries are liable to rank differently according to the measure chosen.

Basically there are two types of measure of inequality: there are measures which express the whole frequency distribution of the population by income level, and there are single-valued measures which summarise such distributions. Since, in ranking countries according to their degree of income inequality, it is simpler to use a single-valued index, this type of measure is often used. However, different summary indices lead to conflicting rankings and measures of the extent of inequality and as Knight (1976, p. 169) has argued 'There is no "right" index. Different indices have different properties and different value judgements implicit in them'.

Of the single-valued measures of inequality the Gini coefficient is perhaps the most frequently used. This measure is calculated as the ratio of the areas under two different Lorenz curves. A Lorenz curve shows in this case, the proportion of total income received by the bottom *x* per cent of income receivers (for all values of *x* up to and including 100%). The Gini Coefficient is in fact the ratio of the area under the Lorenz curve for the actual income distribution to that under the curve for an exactly equal distribution of income. (The Coefficient always has a value of less than or equal to one.)

But for simple expository purposes it is probably more revealing to examine simplified frequency distributions of income rather than single-valued summary measures. Accordingly, table 3.1. presents data which the World Bank has compiled for 66 countries, both developed and less-developed. This table cross-classifies countries according to (1) their level of overall inequality, and (2) their level of per capita income. It should be stressed that the classifications used are arbitrary and the 'moderate' and 'low' inequality categories should not be interpreted as meaning that the distribution of income is in some sense acceptable or poses no particular problems.

Keeping in mind the various qualifications, the data in table 3.1 clearly show a higher degree of inequality in less-developed than in developed countries. Approximately half of the LDCs fall in the high-inequality category and a further one third display moderate inequality. These same proportions apply also to the middle-income category of countries, and contrast markedly with those for the high-income countries which, with the exception of Finland, France and Venezuela, are equally distributed between the moderate- and low-inequality categories. More specifically, the relatively high income inequality of the poorer countries is revealed by the large number of them in which the richest 20% of the population receive over 60% of the GNP, and in which the poorest 40% of the population receive less than 10% (or slightly more) of GNP. By contrast in the developed countries, in only two cases (France and the Federal Republic of Germany) do the richest 20% of the population receive more than 50% of GNP, although the percentage of GNP received by the poorest 40% is below 15% in a number of cases. Thus, without allowing for the countries omitted from table 3.1, there is strong evidence that income is distributed more unequally in poor than in rich countries.

Various theories have been advanced in an attempt to explain the determinants of income distribution (summarised in Cline 1975).

**Table 3.1** *The distribution of income: cross-classification of countries by income level and equality*

| | *High inequality* (Share of lowest 40% less than 12%) | | | | | *Moderate inequality* (Share of lowest 40% between 12% and 17%) | | | | | *Low inequality* (Share of lowest 40%, 17% and above) | | | | |
|---|---|---|---|---|---|---|---|---|---|---|---|---|---|---|---|
| | *Country/ Year* | *Per capita GNP (US $)* | *Lowest 40%* | *Middle 40%* | *Top 20%* | *Country/ Year* | *Per capita GNP (US $)* | *Lowest 40%* | *Middle 40%* | *Top 20%* | *Country/ Year* | *Per capita GNP (US $)* | *Lowest 40%* | *Middle 40%* | *Top 20%* |
| *Income up to US $300* | Kenya (1969) | 136 | 10.0 | 22.0 | 68.0 | Burma (1958) | 82 | 16.5 | 38.7 | 44.8 | Chad (1958) | 78 | 18.0 | 39.0 | 43.0 |
| | Sierra Leone (1968) | 159 | 9.6 | 22.4 | 68.0 | Dahomey (1959) | 87 | 15.5 | 34.5 | 50.0 | Sri Lanka (1969) | 95 | 17.0 | 37.0 | 46.0 |
| | Philippines (1971) | 239 | 11.6 | 34.6 | 53.8 | Tanzania (1967) | 89 | 13.0 | 26.0 | 61.0 | Niger (1960) | 97 | 18.0 | 40.0 | 42.0 |
| | Iraq (1956) | 200 | 6.8 | 25.2 | 68.0 | India (1964) | 99 | 16.0 | 32.0 | 52.0 | Pakistan (1964) | 100 | 17.5 | 37.5 | 30.0 |
| | Senegal (1960) | 245 | 10.0 | 26.0 | 64.0 | Madagascar (1960) | 120 | 13.5 | 25.5 | 61.0 | Uganda (1970) | 126 | 17.1 | 35.8 | 47.1 |
| | Ivory Coast (1970) | 247 | 10.8 | 32.1 | 57.1 | Zambia (1959) | 230 | 14.5 | 28.5 | 57.0 | Thailand (1970) | 180 | 17.0 | 37.5 | 45.5 |
| | Rhodesia (1968) | 252 | 8.2 | 22.8 | 69.0 | | | | | | Korea (1970) | 235 | 18.0 | 37.0 | 45.0 |
| | Tunisia (1970) | 255 | 11.4 | 53.6 | 55.0 | | | | | | Taiwan (1964) | 241 | 20.4 | 39.5 | 40.1 |
| | Honduras (1968) | 265 | 6.5 | 28.5 | 65.0 | | | | | | | | | | |
| | Ecuador (1970) | 277 | 6.5 | 20.0 | 73.5 | | | | | | | | | | |
| | El Salvador (1969) | 295 | 11.2 | 36.4 | 52.4 | | | | | | | | | | |
| | Turkey (1968) | 282 | 9.3 | 29.9 | 60.8 | | | | | | | | | | |
| | Malaysia (1970) | 330 | 11.6 | 32.4 | 56.0 | Dominican Republic | 323 | 12.2 | 30.3 | 57.5 | Surinam (1962) | 394 | 21.7 | 35.7 | 42.6 |

| | | | | | | | | | | | | | | | |
|---|---|---|---|---|---|---|---|---|---|---|---|---|---|---|---|
| *Income US $300–750* | Colombia (1970) | [illegible] | [illegible] | [illegible] | [illegible] | Iran (1968) | 332 | 12.5 | 33.0 | 54.5 | Greece (1957) | 500 | 21.0 | 29.5 | 49.5 |
| | Brazil (1970) | 390 | 10.0 | 28.4 | 61.5 | Guyana (1956) | 550 | 14.0 | 40.3 | 45.7 | Yugoslavia ((1968) | 529 | 18.5 | 40.0 | 41.5 |
| | Peru (1971) | 480 | 6.5 | 33.5 | 60.0 | Lebanon (1960) | 508 | 13.0 | 26.0 | 61.0 | Bulgaria (1962) | 530 | 26.8 | 40.0 | 33.2 |
| | Gabon (1968) | 497 | 8.8 | 23.7 | 67.5 | Uruguay (1968) | 618 | 16.5 | 35.5 | 48.0 | Spain (1965) | 750 | 17.6 | 36.7 | 45.7 |
| | Jamaica (1958) | 510 | 8.2 | 30.3 | 61.5 | Chile (1968) | 744 | 13.0 | 30.2 | 56.8 | | | | | |
| | Costa Rica (1971) | 521 | 11.5 | 30.0 | 58.5 | | | | | | | | | | |
| | Mexico (1969) | 645 | 10.5 | 25.5 | 64.0 | | | | | | | | | | |
| | South Africa (1965) | 669 | 6.2 | 35.8 | 58.0 | | | | | | | | | | |
| | Panama(1969) | 692 | 9.4 | 31.2 | 59.4 | | | | | | | | | | |
| *Income above US $750* | Venezuela (1970) | 1004 | 7.9 | 27.1 | 65.0 | Argentina (1970) | 1079 | 16.5 | 36.1 | 47.4 | Poland (1964) | 850 | 23.4 | 40.6 | 36.0 |
| | Finland(1962) | 1599 | 11.1 | 39.6 | 49.3 | Puerto Rico (1968) | 1100 | 13.7 | 35.7 | 50.6 | Japan (1963) | 950 | 20.7 | 39.3 | 40.0 |
| | France (1962) | 1913 | 9.5 | 36.8 | 53.7 | Netherlands (1967) | 1990 | 13.6 | 37.9 | 48.5 | United Kingdom (1968) | 2015 | 18.8 | 42.2 | 39.0 |
| | | | | | | Norway (1968) | 2010 | 16.6 | 42.9 | 40.5 | Hungary (1969) | 1140 | 24.0 | 42.5 | 33.5 |
| | | | | | | Germany, Fed Rep. (1964) | 2144 | 15.4 | 31.7 | 52.9 | Czechoslovakia (1964) | 1150 | 27.6 | 41.4 | 31.0 |
| | | | | | | Denmark (1968) | 2563 | 13.6 | 38.8 | 47.6 | Australia (1968) | 2509 | 20.0 | 41.2 | 38.8 |
| | | | | | | New Zealand (1969) | 2859 | 15.5 | 42.5 | 42.0 | Canada (1965) | 2920 | 20.0 | 39.8 | 40.2 |
| | | | | | | Sweden (1963) | 2929 | 14.0 | 42.0 | 44.0 | United States (1970) | 4850 | 19.7 | 41.5 | 38.8 |

*Note:* The income shares of each percentile group were read off a freehand Lorenz curve fitted to observed points in the cumulative distribution. The distributions are for pretax income. Per capita GNP figures are taken from the World Bank data files and refer to GNP at factor cost for the year indicated in constant 1971 US dollars.

*Source:* Chenery *et al.* (1974), Chapter 1, pp. 8–9.

These theories have in general emphasised explanations of functional income shares. It has usually been assumed that individuals possess various quantities of the factors of production (land, labour, capital and enterprise) which determine their income shares and hence the size distribution of personal incomes (Adelman and Morris 1973, p. 142). Knight (1976) points to the need for an explanation of the distribution of the ownership of factors among households, and argues that the distribution of assets is determined primarily by historical, institutional and political forces, although economic forces and government policies are important. The distribution of political power in most LDCs is very uneven and is probably correlated with the distribution of income and wealth, with causation running both ways (from wealth to political power and vice versa). Knight concludes that:

> Economists should be prepared to enter more explicitly into the realm of political economy. There is need for a more realistic theory of government than is normally assumed, and for a study of the relationships between the distribution of political power and the distribution of income. By examining the economic interests of the different groups in society, and the extent to which government policies are consistent with these interests, it may be possible to throw light on the role, the sources and the effects of political power.
>
> (Knight 1976, p. 174)

Given the present state of our knowledge, any attempt at explaining the distribution of income has to be eclectic. For the purposes of this chapter, it is sufficient to state that the economic structure, the system of property ownership and social relations, market forces constrained by the economic and socio-political environment within which they operate, government fiscal and social policies, and political, legal and social institutions are all factors which, acting together, determine the distribution of income and wealth in any country.

In an attempt to investigate empirically the interactions between economic growth, political participation and the distribution of income in LDCs, Adelman and Morris (1973) constructed 35 indicators, taken from the 48 indicators listed in table 3.2, of economic, social and political influences which could be expected, on theoretical grounds, to affect the distribution of income. Analysing data for 43 countries (for the 1950s and early 1960s) Adelman and Morris (1973, Ch. 4) found that, on average, the poorest 60% of the population received 26% of total income. Their share was inversely related to the extent of socio-economic dualism and positively related to the level of social and economic modernisation and the expansion of secondary and higher education. The income share of the poorest 60% was smallest where 'a sharply dualistic development process had

**Table 3.2** *Adelman and Morris: 48 qualitative measures of social, economic and political characteristics of LDCs*

*Socio-cultural indicators*

Size of the traditional agricultural sector
Extent of dualism
Extent of urbanisation
Importance of the indigenous middle class
Extent of social mobility
Extent of literacy
Extent of mass communication
Degree of cultural and ethnic homogeneity
Degree of social tension
Crude fertility rate
Degree of modernisation of outlook
Predominant type of religion
Level of socio-economic development

*Political indicators*

Degree of national integration and sense of national unity
Degree of centralisation of political power
Extent of political participation
Degree of freedom of political opposition and the press
Degree of competitiveness of political parties
Predominant basis of the political party system
Strength of the labour movement
Political strength of the traditional elite
Political strength of the military
Political and social influence of religious organisation
Degree of administrative efficiency
Extent of leadership commitment to economic development
Extent of direct government economic activity
Length of colonial experience
Type of colonial experience
Recency of self-government
Extent of political stability

*Economic indicators*

Per capita GNP in 1961
Growth rate of real per capita GNP, 1950/51–1963/64
Abundance of natural resources
Gross investment rate
Modernisation of industry
Industrialisation, 1950–63
Character of agricultural organisation
Modernisation of techniques in agriculture
Improvement in agricultural productivity, 1950–63
Adequacy of physical overhead capital
Effectiveness of the tax system
Improvement in the tax system, 1950–63
Effectiveness of financial institutions
Improvement in financial instutions, 1950–63
Improvement in human resources
Structure of foreign trade
Rate of population growth
Country size and orientation of development strategy.

*Source:* Adelman and Morris, 1973, pp. 15–16

been initiated by well-entrenched expatriate or military elites ideologically oriented to receive most of the benefits of economic development' (p. 160) and the authors found no support for the hypothesis that economic growth raised the share of income of the poorest groups of the population.[2]

The average share of income received by the top 5% of the population was 30%. Their share was higher in resource-rich countries, but in all countries the extent of the direct economic role of the government has an important moderating influence. The average share of the top 5% was significantly smaller in countries with large public sectors and important government net investments than in predominantly private enterprise economies.

The average share of the middle 20% of the population (the two deciles clustered around the median income) was 12%. This was the only share that appeared to vary systematically with the level of development although the relationship was non-linear. The major influence differentiating between countries with respect to the share of this income group was the extent of socio-economic dualism.

Adelman and Morris concluded thus:

> ... our analysis supports the Marxian view that economic structure, not level of income or rate of economic growth, is the basic determinant of patterns of income distribution.
>
> (Adelman and Morris 1973, p.186)

The methodology used by Adelman and Morris, their manipulation of data and their interpretation of the results have all been criticised (see, for example, Lal 1976; Cline 1975). Knight (1976) has pointed out that their results may indicate symptoms or non-causal associations, or that the direction of causation may be the opposite to that suggested. Equally important are the criticisms that can be made of the authors' attempts to quantify essentially non-quantifiable factors (especially political and socio-cultural variables) and their classification of countries on this basis. The dependence on cross-section data is also open to criticism although, in inferring dynamic relationships from cross-section data, the authors (pp. 187–88) make explicit their assumption that average country traits associated with successive development levels represent the path of change of a typical LDC undergoing economic growth.

## 3.3 Economic Growth and Income Distribution Over Time

A number of empirical studies published recently (Adelman and Morris 1973; Paukert 1973; Chenery *et al.* 1974; Chenery and Syrquin

1975, Ch. 3; Ahluwalia 1976) have broadly supported the hypothesis first advanced by Kuznets of a 'long swing in the inequality characterising the secular income structure: widening in the early phases of economic growth when the transition from the pre-industrial to the industrial civilisation was most rapid; becoming stabilised for a while; and then narrowing in the later phases.' (Kuznets 1955, p. 18)

Kuznets' analysis was largely based on the historical experience of developed western economies (the USA, the UK and Germany) and he was at pains to point out that it was dangerous to draw conclusions from historical experience and apply them to contemporary LDCs. But this warning was rarely heeded and orthodox analysis advanced the idea of a conflict between equity and economic growth.[3] One of the most influential models of development, the 'Lewis model' (Lewis 1954) (discussed in Chapter 2, section 2.1), postulated that the level of saving in a society depended on the functional distribution of income, rather than on the level of income. His model suggested that income must be redistributed in favour of the class that saves and invests (the capitalist class) in order to ensure capital accumulation and growth. Following this line of argument in Pakistan, for example, the concept of 'functional inequality' was promoted. That is, inequality was regarded as a positive virtue, and whenever there was a conflict between growth and equity, the latter was usually sacrificed without hesitation (Maddison 1971, p. 85).

Lewis (1976, p. 26) has recently re-emphasised the link between growth and inequality, stating that 'Development must be inegalitarian because it does not start in every part of an economy at the same time'. He argues that growth takes place in enclaves within the LDC and that this process can generate inequalities both between the enclave and the 'traditional sector' and within the enclave itself. Distribution will depend on the pattern of growth, the main ingredients of which are the original distribution of property, the economic structure and dependence on foreign resources.

The orthodox view that inequality was essential for growth was vigorously challenged by Myrdal (1968, Ch. 12; 1971), who argued that quite the opposite was the case and that greater equality was in fact a necessary pre-condition for more rapid economic development:

> ... inequality and the trend towards rising inequality stand as a complex of inhibitions and obstacles to development and that, consequently, there is an urgent need for reversing the trend and creating greater equality as a condition for speeding up development.
>
> (Myrdal 1971, pp. 63–64)

He argued that the consequences of an unequal distribution of income were malnutrition, poor housing, poor education, etc. for the vast majority of the population, which in turn led to low levels of productivity. A redistribution of income to these groups would lead to an increase in production through increasing the consumption, and hence the health and productivity, of the poor. On the other hand, the 'middle classes' indulged in conspicuous consumption and wasteful expenditures (including the export of capital), instead of living frugally and saving and investing a substantial part of their income. Myrdal argued that social inequalities resulted from economic inequalities and in turn reinforced them, and both were a cause, and a consequence, of poverty.

Myrdal (1971) noted the apparently paradoxical situation that, although the policy declarations of most LDC governments favoured greater equality (in many cases, some form of 'socialism' was the development objective) inequality was increasing in most LDCs. The paradox was resolved by reference to the distribution of political power in LDCs. The classes that held power were unlikely to implement measures that would produce a distribution of income less favourable to them and their supporters. But as the masses were thought to be 'passive, apathetic and inarticulate', political changes could not be expected to occur as a result of pressure from below and would thus ultimately have to come about as a result of changes within the ruling classes themselves. We return to this point below.

*Empirical Evidence*

Paukert's (1973) data (*circa* 1965) show an increase in inequality as countries move from the below \$100 per capita income level to the \$101–\$200 level and beyond. The peak of inequality is reached in countries with a per capita income of between \$200 and \$500. Countries in the \$501–\$1,000 range, with the exception of the Republic of South Africa, have a significantly lower degree of inequality.

Ahluwalia's (1976) analysis confirms this basic pattern and further shows that the 'turning point' (that is, the point at which the share of income of different groups begins to change) occurs at different levels of per capita income for different income groups. For example, the share of the top 20% begins to decline at a per capita income of \$364 (in 1965–71 prices) but the income share of the bottom 60% only begins to improve at a per capita income level of \$412 and the figure for the bottom 20% is \$593 (Ahluwalia 1976, Table 1, p. 311). Ahluwalia remarks that if there is a 'trickle down' process at work, it takes a long time to reach the lower income groups.

Care must be taken when using cross-section data and, ideally, dynamic relationships should be inferred from time-series data. In his study of Puerto Rico, Argentina and Mexico, Weiskoff (1970) examines the relationship between economic growth and income distribution over time, although the data used are limited and thus they do not permit a systematic study of secular trends. In all three countries different measures of inequality give different results.

During the period 1953–1963, Puerto Rico experienced a rapid growth of real incomes accompanied by an increase in inequality in the distribution of income (as measured by the Gini ratio). The bottom 60% and the top 5% of the population lost, relatively, and the middle strata gained. In Mexico during the period 1950 to 1963, economic growth was again rapid but, according to the Gini coefficient, inequality increased from 1957 to 1963, following a period of greater equality between 1950 and 1957. The income shares of the bottom 30% of families declined throughout the entire period, and again it was the middle-income groups that gained at the expense of other groups. In Argentina, the period 1953 to 1961 was marked by political revolution, recession and a slight real growth of incomes. All the measures show an increase in inequality between 1953 and 1959 (a year of severe recession) with a movement to equality in the 1959–1961 period (although income distribution was still more unequal in 1961 than it had been in 1953). During the entire period only the top 5% of families increased their income share.

The time-series data thus give limited support to the notion that growth and equality are inversely related at least at low levels of economic development. Returning to the cross-section studies, the relationship between inequality and per capita income takes the form of an inverted U-shaped curve as first postulated by Kuznets (1955). Inequality is low in an unchanging, 'traditional' society but increases as the shift from agricultural to industrial activities and the move of population from rural to urban locations occurs. Kuznets (1955, pp. 7–8) suggested that inequality within the urban sector was greater and thus overall inequality increased as this sector grew more than proportionately to the rest of the economy. In addition, the concentration of savings in the upper income groups led to the concentration of an increasing proportion of income-yielding assets in the hands of this group, which in turn led to larger income shares in the future. At more mature levels of development, inequality begins to decrease. Thus we find that both extreme economic underdevelopment and high levels of economic development are associated with greater income equality (Adelman and Morris 1973, p. 188).

Although cross-section data appear to indicate an inverted U-shaped relationship between inequality and per capita income, there is no necessary fixed relationship between equity and growth. It is not necessarily the case that high growth rates require an unequal distribution of income, nor that high growth rates are responsible for an unequal distribution of income. China's economic growth record has been more impressive than that of India and yet it is generally agreed that it is a more egalitarian society (Weisskopf 1975). Other things being equal, we would expect to find a less unequal distribution of income in a country effectively pursuing explicity socialist objectives than in a country following a free enterprise development path. Thus a great deal depends on the economic and social-political structure of the economy in question and its broad developmental objectives.

The argument that there is an inevitable conflict between equity and growth is not valid either on theoretical or empirical grounds. Cline (1975, p.374) stresses the point that there is 'no inexorable theoretical basis justifying a worsening of the distribution (of income) in the course of development' and Ahluwalia concludes that 'there is little firm empirical basis for the view that higher rates of growth inevitably generate greater inequality' (in Chenery *et al.* 1974, Ch. 1, p. 13), even though his data seem to support the inverted U-shaped relationship. A conflict may exist in particular cases, but the explanation must be sought in the specific circumstances of each individual case and not in terms of a generalised relationship.

## 3.4 The Distribution of Income and Economic Growth

### *Income Distribution and Savings*

We have already noted above the widely held view that an unequal distribution of income (distributed in favour of profits) is necessary to ensure a high rate of savings and hence growth, as profit receivers are assumed to save a higher fraction of their incomes than wage earners.

This view is dependent upon both a particular view of the growth process (conceived of in terms of the Harrod–Domar model – see Chapter 2, section 2.1) and a particular interpretation of the development experience of the capitalist economies of the West. It is argued that the lessons of that experience are of significance to LDCs. Economic development was partly due to, and accompanied by, the rise to power of an indigenous capitalist class which allegedly saved and invested, in a productive manner, a substantial proportion of its income. The capitalist class abstained from lavish consumption, worked hard and in general lived a life according to a rigorous religious code, the 'Protestant Ethic'.

The argument that this experience (or more accurately, this particular interpretation of history, one which not everyone would accept) is of relevance to today's LDCs must presuppose the existence of a capitalist class in LDCs similar to that which existed in 19th century Europe and North America. Whether or not such a class exists is a key question in the political economy of development, and is referred to in several places in this book (see particularly Part C of Chapter 2). Kuznets (1955, p.22) noted the absence of a substantial 'middle class' in LDCs, that is, there was a sharp contrast between the vast majority of the population whose average income was well below the generally low countrywide average and a small top group with a very large relative income excess. Weiskoff's (1970) data discussed above, on the other hand, suggest that this class might have been growing in certain countries in recent years.

Other writers, for example Fanon (1967) and Baran (1957) have argued that an independent capitalist class, devoted to the national development of the LDC economy, does not, and cannot, exist. Baran in particular argued that a comprador class would develop (see Part C of Chapter 2).[4] A distribution of income in favour of this class would not therefore lead to a high rate of savings and hence economic growth.

The middle- and upper-income groups in LDCs are in any case subject to economic and social pressures very different from those faced by their nineteenth century counterparts in western Europe and North America: savings are likely to flow into 'safe' investments – either abroad (capital flight) or domestically into real estate and other non-productive forms; expenditure on foreign travel and conspicuous consumption is likely to be greater; the hoarding of gold, jewellery, etc. may be a prevalent social trait. The government too may be unable or unwilling to promote rapid capital accumulation – much public expenditure may be wasteful and contribute nothing to the development effort.

The empirical work that has been carried out on the determinants of saving in LDCs (reviewed in Snyder 1974) suggests that, *inter alia*, current income, wealth holdings and the distribution of income are of importance. But the work is still at an early stage and firm conclusions cannot yet be drawn.

It is possible, however, to provide a qualified answer to an alternative question: what would be the effect of income redistribution on savings and growth? Cline (1972), who attempts to quantify this effect, argues that the impact of income redistribution on savings depends on the nature of the consumption function. Only a non-linear Keynesian consumption function unambiguously leads to a decline in aggregate savings when income is redistributed from high-income to low-income recipients. Cline (1972, Ch. 4) applies such a consumption function (estimated from family budget studies) to the new or simulated levels of income for the new income distributions and aggregates the implied savings to determine new aggregate personal savings for comparison with the original personal savings. Assuming an income redistribution to the degree of equity in the UK and using a log–linear form of the consumption function, he finds that there would be little decline in personal saving in Argentina, a decline of 5.5% in Brazil, 7.6% in Mexico and no change in Venezuela (where a linear consumption function is used). The impact on savings of a radical income redistribution would thus vary but would not be as drastic as is usually assumed, given that other major sources of savings (government savings, the retained earnings of incorporated enterprises and foreign savings) would not be adversely affected.

Cline next calculates the impact on growth of the hypothesised income redistribution, using a Harrod–Domar type relationship. Depending on the assumptions made, the redistribution would entail a sacrifice of annual growth of approximately 1% in Brazil and Mexico, 0.65% in Argentina and zero in Venezuela (with the linear function) or a maximum of 1.0% with an alternative specification of the consumption function. Cline stresses that these calculations are overestimates (because of the consumption function assumed) and they assume an income redistribution unlikely to be realised in practice. Nonetheless, the vast majority of the populations of Argentina, Brazil and Mexico would benefit if the strategy of redistribution with slower growth was selected.

*Income Distribution and Consumption*

Different income groups consume different bundles of goods and thus the distribution of income is an important determinant of the pattern or composition of aggregate consumption. A highly unequal income distribution is likely to increase the demand for sophisticated durable consumer goods, luxuries, etc., and depress the demand for basic, essential mass-consumption items, for example textiles.[5] The composition of imports is also affected in so far as upper- and middle-income groups are more likely to consume imported goods or import-intensive domestically produced goods (although, as we note in Chapter 10, the poor may also consume such goods). This in turn has important consequences for those countries attempting to industrialise on the basis of import-substituting industrialisation (ISI). Industries established will often be producing non-essentials consumed by the wealthier classes and the needs of the poor may be neglected (these issues are discussed in greater detail in Chapter 8).

In principle, income redistribution in favour of the poor would increase the demand for essential goods (in the production of which there are greater possibilities for the utilisation of labour-intensive methods of production, thus stimulating employment – see Chapter

10) and reduce the demand for non-essentials, thus easing the balance of payments constraint. Taking an optimistic view of the course of events, greater equality could stimulate the demand for foodstuffs, thus increasing agricultural output, incomes and employment, and act as a check on rural–urban migration and rapid urbanisation.

On the other hand, a very different scenario can be imagined. The additional demand for foodstuffs might have to be met by increased imports, worsening the balance of payments constraint, and other sectors also may not be sufficiently flexible to respond to increased demands, thus generating inflationary pressures. What has been referred to as the problem of 'structural-lock' emerges. The structure of industry which developed with a particular (or only slowly changing) distribution of income may be unable to respond rapidly to the new pattern of demand in the post-redistribution situation. In other words, there is an imbalance between the country's production and demand structures. Excess capacity in some sectors and shortages in others, inflationary pressures, a worsening balance of payments position and perhaps social tension and political unrest are the more likely outcomes of attempts at effective income redistribution in many LDCs (especially the more 'developed' Latin American economies).

Recent years have seen the publication of the results of a number of simulation exercises which have attempted to test the hypotheses discussed above (summarised in Cline 1975). Tokman (1976) in his work on Venezuela made projections for 1985 for aggregate consumption, assuming that consumption expanded more rapidly for lower- than for upper-income groups. He concluded that the structure of consumption did not change significantly in the event of changes in income distribution benefiting lower-income groups, the main variations being a fall in expenditure on services and an increase for processed and non-processed foods. The effect of income redistribution on employment was also insignificant if no account was taken of the possibilities of using alternative technologies.

Foxley's work on Chile (Foxley 1976b) defines as a redistributive target an absolute level of basic consumption required by a typical family. He concludes that even radical consumption redistribution will not affect the rate of growth of the economy significantly and thus redistribution and growth are not necessarily correlated in a positive manner (p. 190). But the effect on employment is positive and reinforced if government expenditure on social services (health, education, housing) is also used as a redistributive instrument.

Finally, we refer once more to Cline (1972). He calculates the change in final demand resulting for each product sector from an income redistribution and uses input–output analysis to determine the change in imports. He finds that the final import effect is very small and that income redistribution has little effect on growth through its import repercussions. The basic reason for this is that the higher import coefficients applied to smaller absolute production changes of the declining group (transport equipment, rubber, metallurgy and electrical machinery) yield a fall in imports approximately equal to the rise in imports from the smaller import coefficients applied to much larger absolute production increases in agriculture and processed foodstuffs.

The results of these simulation exercises do not provide strong support for the hypothesised effects of income redistribution. Cline (1972, p. 179) concludes that while the effects are in the theoretically correct direction, they are of minor importance and thus there is little empirical evidence to support the view that income redistribution would be a powerful stimulus to economic growth (although conversly, even radical redistribution would not do irreparable damage to growth prospects). In addition, in the absence of more direct measures, income redistribution may not have a dramatic effect on either the balance of payments or employment. We refer again to the latter problem in Chapter 10. For the present, however, we must emphasise the point that it is highly unlikely that a radical income redistribution will occur whilst 'all other things remain equal'. Social, political and institutional changes are likely to accompany, and be complementary to, income redistribution policies. Indeed, the simulation exercises discussed above can be used to support the argument that income redistribution is likely to be ineffective in the absence of radical reforms in other areas. We must therefore now turn to a discussion of policy issues.

## 3.5 The Policy Implications

There are in principle a variety of policy instruments available to governments pursuing the objective of a more equal distribution of income, although they are not all equally effective. Incomes policies can be used to control (or prevent) income increases for middle- and upper-income groups whilst permitting the incomes of poorer groups to rise relatively to all other groups. Discriminatory pricing policies can be used to reduce the price of certain goods and services which account for a large proportion of the total expenditure of the poor or, alternatively, such goods can be distributed directly to the recipients. Goods and services can be provided on a collective basis (collective consumption), for example, education and health facilities, fiscal policies (taxes and subsidies) and transfer payments to the poor can be used, either on their own or in conjunction with these policies.

Many of these policies have as their prime objective greater equality of consumption. A less orthodox approach to the problem of achieving greater income equality is to emphasise the need to create large-scale employment opportunities via the encouragement of labour-intensive sectors (construction, for example) and technologies. The spread of educational facilities is also seen as a means of promoting equality objectives.

But the most radical (and, in principle, the most effective) policies relate to the ownership of the means of production. Gross inequalities in the ownership of property give rise to similar inequalities in the distribution of income and thus many would argue that a more equal structure of property ownership (or state ownership of productive assets) is an essential precondition for a more equal income distribution. In the majority of LDCs, the ownership of land is highly unequal and emphasis is therefore placed on the need for effective land reform in order to promote agricultural growth, rural development, greater employment and greater equality (these issues are discussed in Chapter 6).

Although an abundance of policy instruments exists and both LDC governments and international organisations emphasise the necessity and/or desirability of greater equality, few LDCs apart from those that have experienced revolutionary changes and have deliberately pursued egalitarian (socialist) policies, are moving towards greater equality. Economists are at present devoting much effort and ingenuity to the problem of evolving redistributive strategies but are paying little attention to political questions and the likelihood of such policies being actively implemented. As in other areas of development economics, too much attention is paid to policy prescription while the analysis of socio-economic structures (if considered at all) is relegated to second place.[6]

There are no overwhelming reasons why the ruling groups in LDCs should pursue egalitarian policies, especially if such policies are harmful to their own economic and political interests. As Myrdal notes:

> It has never occurred in recorded history that a privileged group, on its own initiative and simply in order to give reality to its ideals, has climbed down from its privileges and opened its monopolies to the unprivileged. The unprivileged have to become conscious of their demands for greater equality and fight for their realisation ... But when that pressure from below is almost totally absent, as in most underdeveloped countries, we should not be surprised that the inegalitarian social and economic stratification from colonial times is preserved and that development moves in the direction of greater inequality.
>
> (Myrdal 1971, pp. 88–89)

It is possible that enlightened self-interest plus popular pressure may lead the ruling groups to attempt to bring about a less unequal distribution of the benefits of growth, if only to strengthen their own position. But in the contemporary world, the repression of such popular movements is a more likely outcome. As Leys (1975, p. 6) argues:

> . . . in Africa, Latin America and South-East Asia most governments closely control political activity and harass or suppress 'radical' parties, where political organisation is not banned altogether.

These problems are of particular relevance to strategies of redistribution with (or from) growth (RWG) which are being promoted by a number of influential organisations at the present time (for example, the International Labour Office – ILO 1972; the World Bank – Chenery *et al.* 1974).

The ILO (1972) in its report on Kenya advocated the maintenance of rapid growth, the stabilisation of the incomes of the top 10% of the population for a number of years, and the channelling of the income and resources which growth would have brought to this group into various forms of investment which would benefit the poorest 40% of the population (Jolly 1976). The policy proposals involved a wide range of government initiatives aimed at expanding the resources available to the poor. The strategy was not to be based on direct income transfers from rich to poor but on investment which would provide the unemployed and the working poor with the basis for earning a reasonable minimum level of income.

In a further development of this approach by Chenery *et al.* (1974), the target growth rate is so defined as to give a higher weight to the growth of incomes of the poorer groups, and 'target' poverty groups (in both rural and urban areas) are identified and public investment redirected to raise the productive capacity and incomes of these groups.[7] The conclusion is reached that:

> . . . there is considerable potential for raising income in low-income groups through a policy of 'investment transfers'. Such a strategy, although operating at the margin, can achieve substantial improvements in patterns of asset concentration over time. If income in the poorer groups is constrained by lack of physical and human capital and access to infrastucture, the reallocation of public resources can provide a powerful mechanism for removing these constraints. The extent of resource transfer involved – 2 per cent of GNP per year for twenty-five years – is not small, but it should be feasible in many countries. (Chenery and Ahluwalia in Chenery *et al.* 1974, Ch, XI, pp. 234–35.)

The RWG strategy is explicitly reformist and evolutionary and it is argued that such a policy is less likely to face opposition from vested interests. Although presented as a politically neutral and technical document ('a framework for analysing the interconnections between economic growth and redistribution' – Jolly 1976, p. 48), one of its major critics, Colin Leys (1975) has argued that the Chenery *et al.* publication is, in fact, a 'highly political document' (p. 4) and must be viewed as such. Leys maintains that the authors of the Report assume the LDCs will continue to be predominantly capitalist economies in which income distribution is determined mainly by the distribution of ownership of productive capital, and that political power in these societies will continue to be based primarily on the private ownership of capital. Social revolution ought to be avoided and the status quo maintained. In other words, capitalist development in LDCs must be given a more 'human' and 'acceptable' face, leaving intact the social, political and economic structures within which poverty and inequality have their roots.

Stewart and Streeten (1976) argue that economic growth is by definition vital if effective redistribution is to occur with a RWG strategy, but redistribution may adversely affect the growth rate in so far as it involves a switch from the consumption and production of high technology goods to the consumption and production of goods for the poorer groups. Technological advance has neglected the latter and

> . . . a policy which switched a substantial amount of resources to them would thus almost certainly reduce the rate of growth measured in conventional terms, at least for a time . . . To the extent that the switch in resources was successful, the source of redistribution – the extra incomes generated by advanced technology among the elite – would dry up. (p. 396)

But the basic problem remains one of political feasibility. There are no obvious reasons why ruling groups should adopt even mildly reformist RWG strategies. Advocates of RWG argue that in the absence in the foreseeable future of radical political changes in LDCs, a reformist strategy is, in effect, better than nothing and the only chance that exists to alleviate the lot of the poor. As Leys (1975, p.8) shows, this position allows RWG to be presented as 'a realistic and humane response to the improbability that radical changes will bring about radical improvements in the lot of the poor'. But given the uncertainty surrounding future developments in LDCs and at the same time, the role of foreign interests and international organisations in influencing the extent and direction of change, Leys feels that the Report's judgement that radical social changes are 'unlikely' takes the form of a programme rather than a prognosis. This approach enables the advocates of RWG to promote it as an alternative 'technical' approach to development, to be prefered to the advocacy or pursuit of revolutionary change.

## 3.6 Conclusions

The gap between rhetoric and reality is perhaps greatest in the field of development and equality. Governments proclaim political and economic objectives of an egalitarian, even socialist, nature but pursue policies that have the opposite effect. Other governments deliberately create greater economic and social inequalities, creating demand profiles favourable to TNCs (as in Brazil – see Chapter 8), and channelling resources to already engorged ruling groups.

Greater economic and social equality should be regarded both as a goal of development and as a means by which growth and development can be accelerated. The objective of redistribution is not merely to take from the rich to give to the poor, nor merely to redistribute poverty, but to create the conditions within which the development effort can be maximised. Income redistribution must thus be viewed in a dynamic context and cannot be separated from complementary social, political and institutional changes. Redistribution cannot take place in a political vacuum and the most radical redistributions in LDCs have occurred during, and as part of, social and political upheavals of a fundamental kind. The objective of greater equality can only be achieved by the elimination of the political, social and economic structures within which inequality is located, and we do not hold out much hope for RWG-type solutions.

We would argue that radical changes, that is changes in the distribution of the ownership of productive assets, are a necessary but not a sufficient condition for economic development. Land reform, for example, must be accompanied by measures aimed at the promotion of agrarian reform. It may in fact be the case that income redistribution has little overall effect on employment if steps are not taken at the same time to design and produce goods which are 'appropriate' in terms of the needs they meet and the production technologies that they utilise. The characteristics of the goods produced in the post-redistribution environment are thus of importance in this context (this issue is further discussed in Chapter 10).

The short-run costs (in terms of economic growth forgone) of radical changes may be high and in any case are likely to be increased by both domestic and foreign opposition (sabotage, 'destabilisation', etc.) to such measures. The difficulties involved in the specification of 'basic needs' and development objectives, the redirection of resources towards the creation of 'desirable' products and technologies, the re-orientation of the productive structure to meet the needs of the mass of the population, the mobilisation of the population to work on community-based development projects, the replacement of material by moral incentives, the re-evaluation of the role of the market and the creation of effective and efficient development planning structures are all problems that remain to be solved. But the existence of such problems cannot be used as an argument against radical changes as they are problems that ultimately must be faced and tackled by all LDCs.

## Notes

1 Tawney argues that '. . . in spite of their varying characters and capacities, men possess in their common humanity a quality which is worth cultivating, and that a community is most likely to make the most of that quality if it takes it into account in planning its economic organisation and social institutions – if it stresses lightly differences of wealth and birth and social position, and establishes on firm foundations institutions which meet common needs and are a source of common enlightenment and common enjoyment. The individual differences of which so much is made . . . will always survive, and they are to be welcomed, not regretted. But their existence is no reason for not seeking to establish the largest possible measure of equality of environment, and circumstance, and opportunity. On the contrary, it is a reason for redoubling our efforts to establish it, in order to ensure that these diversities of gifts may come to fruition'. (Tawney 1964, pp. 55–56.)

2 Indeed, Adelman and Morris (1973) advance the hypothesis that the poorest 60% of the population may experience an absolute as well as a relative decline in their average income, and they conclude that 'The frightening implication of the present work is that hundreds of millions of desperately poor people throughout the world have been hurt rather than helped by economic development' (p. 192). Lal (1976) vigorously challenges this viewpoint, arguing that Adelman and Morris's evidence does not support their conclusions. Lal also attempts to challenge the ethical underpinnings of egalitarian policies and objectives.

3 Johnson (1958) stated the orthodox view thus: '. . . the cost of economic equality may be great to any economy at a low level of economic development that wishes to grow rapidly, particularly as it is evident that historically the great bursts of economic growth have been associated with the prospect and the result of big windfall gains; it would therefore seem unwise for a country anxious to enjoy rapid growth to insist too strongly on policies aimed at ensuring economic equality and a just income distribution' (p. 159). Implicit in this and similar arguments is the view that more rapid growth in the present means greater equality in the future through the higher income 'trickling down' to the poor. The creation of more and better-paid jobs and government redistributive policies (progressive taxation, free education, etc.) made possible by the higher level and rate of growth of income are essential elements in this process. Even accepting the existence of these redistributive mechanisms in contemporary LDCs, it can still be argued that expectations

are such that the length of time required for such 'trickling down' to be effective is politically unacceptable.

4 Fanon (1967, p. 141) directed his invective against the bourgeoisie in LDCs: 'A bourgeoisie similar to that which developed in Europe is able to elaborate an ideology and at the same time strengthen its own power. Such a bourgeoisie, dynamic, educated and secular, has fully succeeded in its undertaking of the accumulation of capital and has given to the nation a minimum of prosperity. In underdeveloped countries, we have seen that no true bourgeoisie exists; there is only a sort of little greedy caste, avid and voracious, with the mind of a huckster, only too glad to accept the dividends that the former colonial power hands out to it. This get-rich-quick middle class shows itself incapable of great ideas or inventiveness. It remembers what it has read in European textbooks and imperceptibly it becomes not even the replica of Europe, but its caricature'. Such views have been challenged by, among others, Warren (1973). See the discussion in Chapter 8.

5 The classification of goods and services into 'essentials' and 'luxuries' is in practice difficult and the terms 'essential consumption' and 'luxury consumption' are imprecise in content. Nevertheless the attempt must be made by any country that wishes to pursue an effective redistributive policy. An essential item in one country may be considered a luxury in another and thus 'Factors to be considered in the definition of consumption categories include the historical and political framework, the level of per capita income, and national habits and traditions'. (Ffrench-Davies 1976, p. 114.)

6 '. . . it seems difficult to avoid the conclusion that much wasted ingenuity has been put into devising *forms* of redistribution, when it is not lack of ingenious schemes but a basic political contradiction between the schemes and the real as opposed to nominal objectives of decision makers, that is critical'. (Stewart and Streeten 1976, p. 396.)

7 It is argued that RWG also involves (i) accelerating GNP growth by raising savings and allocating resources more efficiently with benefits to all groups in society, (ii) redistribution of existing assets and (iii) transfer of income to support the consumption of the poorest groups. But the redirection of public investment is the dominant element. (Ahluwalia and Chenery in Chenery *et al.* 1974, Ch. 2; Jolly 1976, pp. 46–47.)

## Bibliography

Adelman I. and Morris C.T. (1973), *Economic Growth and Social Equity in Developing Countries*, Stanford University Press.

Ahluwalia M.S. (1976), 'Inequality, poverty and development', *Journal of Development Economics*, Vol. 3, December.

Baran P. (1957), *The Political Economy of Growth*, Monthly Review Press, New York.

Cairncross A. and Puri M. (eds) (1976), *Employment, Income Distribution and Development Strategy*, Macmillan.

Chenery H.B., Ahluwalia M.S., Bell C.L.G., Duloy J.H. and Jolly R. (1974), *Redistribution With Growth*, Oxford University Press.

Chenery H.B. and Syrquin M. (1975), *Patterns of Development 1950–1970*, Oxford University Press.

Cline W.R. (1972), *Potential Effects of Income Redistribution on Economic Growth: Latin American Cases,* Praeger, New York.

Cline W.R. (1975), 'Distribution and development: a survey of literature', *Journal of Development Economics,* Vol. 1.

Elliott C. (1975), *Patterns of Poverty in the Third World,* Praeger, New York.

Fanon F. (1967), *The Wretched of the Earth,* Penguin.

Ffrench-Davies R. (1976), 'Policy tools and objectives of redistribution' in Foxley (ed.) (1976b).

Figueroa A. (1975), 'Income distribution, demand structure and employment: the case of Peru', *Journal of Development Studies,* Vol. 11, No. 2, January; Reprinted in Stewart F. (ed.) (1975), *Employment, Income Distribution and Development,* Frank Cass.

Foxley A. (1976a), 'Redistribution of consumption: effects on production and employment' in Foxley (ed.) (1976b).

Foxley A. (ed.) (1976b), *Income Distribution in Latin America,* Cambridge University Press.

International Labour Office (1972), *Employment, Income and Equality: A Strategy for Increasing Productive Employment in Kenya,* Geneva.

Johnson H.G. (1958), 'Planning and the market in economic development', *Pakistan Development Review,* Vol. VIII, No. 2, June, Reprinted in *Money, Trade and Economic Growth,* Allen and Unwin, 1962.

Jolly R. (1976), 'Redistribution with growth', in Cairncross and Puri (eds) (1976).

Knight J.B. (1976), 'Explaining income distribution in less developed countries: a framework and an agenda', *Oxford Bulletin of Economics and Statistics,* Vol. 38, No. 3, August.

Kuznets S. (1955), 'Economic growth and income inequality', *American Economic Review,* Vol. 45, No. 1, March.

Lal D. (1976), 'Distribution and development: a review article', *World Development,* Vol. 4, No. 9.

Lewis W.A. (1954), 'Economic development with unlimited supplies of labour', *Manchester School,* May.

Lewis W.A. (1976), 'Development and distribution', in Cairncross and Puri (eds) (1976).

Leys C. (1975), 'The politics of redistribution with growth', *Institute of Development Studies Bulletin,* Vol. 7, No. 2, August.

Maddison A. (1971), *Class Structure and Economic Growth: India and Pakistan Since the Moghuls,* Allen and Unwin.

Myrdal G. (1968), *Asian Drama,* Penguin.

Myrdal G. (1971), *The Challenge of World Poverty,* Penguin.

Paukert F. (1973), 'Income distribution at different levels of development: a survey of evidence', *International Labour Review,* September.

Snyder D.W. (1974), 'Econometric studies of household saving behaviour in developing countries: a survey', *Journal of Development Studies,* Vol. 10, No. 2, January.

Stewart F. (ed.) (1975), *Employment, Income Distribution and Development,* Frank Cass.

Stewart F. and Streeten P. (1976), 'New strategies for development: poverty income distribution and growth', *Oxford Economic Papers,* Vol. 28, No. 3, November.

Strassman W.P. (1956), 'Economic growth and income distribution', *Quarterly Journal of Economics,* August.

Sturmthal A. (1955), 'Economic development, income distribution and capital formation in Mexico', *Journal of Political Economy*, June.

Tawney R.H. (1964), *Equality*, Allen and Unwin (first published 1931).

Tokman V. (1976), 'Income distribution, technology and employment in the Venezuelan industrial sector', in Foxley (ed.) (1976b).

Warren B. (1973), 'Imperialism and capitalist industrialisation', *New Left Review*, No. 81, September–October.

Weiskoff R. (1970), 'Income distribution and economic growth in Puerto Rico, Argentina and Mexico', *Review of Income and Wealth*, December. Reprinted in Foxley (ed.) (1976b).

Weisskopf T.E. (1975), 'China and India: contrasting experiences in economic development', *American Economic Review Papers and Proceedings*, Vol. LXV, No. 2, May.

# 4

# The international setting: trade

It is hardly surprising that problems of trade between the underdeveloped and developed countries should dominate the agendas of international agencies concerned with economic affairs. For economic relationships between countries are largely definable in terms of the patterns of trade and exchange existing between them. Certainly the pattern of trade between the developed and underdeveloped countries yields a fairly clear picture of their economic relationships, the predominant feature of which is that the poorer countries exchange primary commodities (agricultural produce and minerals) with the richer ones in exchange for manufactured capital and consumer goods. Using GATT definitions of trading areas, the industrial areas dominate the trade of the developing areas; from 1970 to 1973 the former accepted 73% of all the latter's exports and contributed 69% of their imports (GATT 1974). Of these exports from the developing to the industrial areas no less than 77% was accounted for by primary commodities (of which somewhat over half was fuels), while 80% of the reciprocal trade was in manufactures. Approximately half of these developing-area imports has consisted of engineering products and motor vehicles, which include essential capital items for development, and of the remainder many, like various chemicals, constitute essential goods which cannot be produced locally.

This picture of the poorer nations exchanging primary commodities for manufactured capital and consumer goods is the focus of many issues in economic development. It is a pattern of trade which has persisted from a past in which, under colonial domination, the trade of LDCs was subservient to the needs of the metropolitan countries. Through it, the colonies provided a captive market for the manufactured products of the colonising country while in return supplying it with raw materials and tropical foodstuffs. Questions which arise in the post-colonial era revolve around whether the basic relationships of the colonial period have changed. Does the pattern of trade contribute to the growth and development of poorer nations, or does it largely serve to reinforce the hierarchy of rich and poor nations? Is this pattern preserved by protective policy actions of the richer countries designed to maintain their economic advantage over poorer countries? Do the institutions controlling international trade hinder economic development by passing on most of the gains from trade to the richer nations? In other words, is the system of international trade inherently unfair to the poorer nations? These are essentially long-term questions about the capacity of international trade to promote economic development. But there are also short-run issues concerning the possible economic disadvantages of reliance upon primary products for the bulk of export earnings. For example, do prices and revenues of primary commodities exhibit greater short-run instability than those for manufactured goods and, if so, does such instability hamper development?

## 4.1 Can Trade Lead to Development?

As far as orthodox international trade theory is concerned the answer to this question is undoubtedly affirmative. The theory of comparative advantage argues that, by specialising in the production and trade of those commodities for which they have the relative lowest production costs, all countries including the developing ones can increase their consumption (and value of production) levels above those achievable by autarkic production with no trade. The further elaboration of this theory attributed to Hecksher and Ohlin, in which countries should specialise in the production and trade of those commodities requiring intensive application of their most abundant resource, leads to an additional conclusion. This is that free trade and specialisation in production will tend to bring about factor-price equalisation, that is to eliminate international differences in incomes paid to labour and other factors of production. Thus the elementary theory of trade argues strongly that trade will not only promote development in the poorer countries (in the form of higher consumption and production) but that it will also reduce the income gap between them and the richer countries.

These arguments have had a pervasive influence since the theory of comparative advantage was first published by Ricardo in 1817, and have led policy makers to emphasise trade expansion as a means of promoting development. However, the persistence of large international differences in per capita incomes has led to doubts about the relevance of the assumptions of neo-classical trade theory and about the capacity of the existing system of trade to improve the relative incomes of underdeveloped countries. Some critics argue that the failure of the trade system to generate the expected improvement of incomes in the LDCs is due to the existence of barriers to trade (such as tariffs, quotas and domestic support schemes) erected by the developed countries, so that the theoretical conditions of free competitive trade are not met in practice. Certainly, there is some truth in these criticisms. For instance, in 1973 D. Gale Johnson estimated that eliminating all barriers to agricultural trade would have increased the export revenues of developing countries by US $2,000 million (Johnson 1973). Also, meetings of UNCTAD repeatedly stress the importance to the underdeveloped countries of trade liberalisation.

Other critics, however, argue more fundamentally that some of the explicit assumptions of trade theory, which lead to the proposition that free trade will help provide a solution to underdevelopment, are defective, and that in practice the current international trade system (or a freer version of it) can only serve to reinforce the differential economic status of developed and underdeveloped countries. Kitamura emphasises the weakness of the static assumptions of the theory regarding the fixity of production technology and of the stocks of productive resources (Kitamura 1968). He argues theoretically 'that in a changing world of capital accumulation and technical progress, free trade does not tend to maximise the welfare of the less-developed countries nor to ensure their balance of trade...' and that 'international trade if not assisted by the consciously guided transfer of factors of production, has no inherent tendency to equalise income and productivity levels. Indeed, the trade mechanism works the other way round – in favour of the progressive countries and against stagnant ones'.

The principal justification for this extremely important viewpoint is the argument that, although some developed countries may well have high wage rates relative to those in underdeveloped countries, because of traditionally high rates of productivity growth and technological change the ratio of productivity to wage rates may still be higher in the richer countries. In this situation, as accepted by some Marxist economists (Barrat Brown 1974, Ch. 10), capital will be attracted to these rather than the poorer nations thus extending the technology gap and increasing the international difference in wage levels. It follows that, if free trade is unlikely to increase the relative capital endowment of the underdeveloped countries, international income disparities are only likely to be reduced if conscious decisions are taken to direct capital to the LDCs in the form of aid, technical assistance and preferential trade arrangements.

Kitamura is not alone in recognising the weakness of applying static theory to a changing world. Indeed, it can be argued that this has a long history of recognition. For it has long been accepted that it is difficult to introduce an industry to a new country in the face of international competition without financial loss in the short and medium runs. It is therefore generally agreed that such 'infant industries' should be protected from competition in the early stages by the imposition of import tariffs and other measures.

Another fundamental set of criticisms of free trade as a mechanism for promoting development is directed at the theory's implicit assumptions that there are no basic institutional differences between nations in the way their production and trade are managed. One very influential criticism is that in many developing countries the main exporting industries have, until recently at least, been dominated by foreign interests. Often the firms responsible for production have been, and are, foreign owned, and in many instances they established their position in the colonial era of the 18th and 19th centuries. When first established in such activities as mining and plantation agriculture the main function of these firms was to serve the markets and secondary industries of the metropolitan countries. This, it can be argued, strengthened the competitive position of manufacturing industry in the wealthy countries so that it is now very difficult for those poorer countries with small domestic markets to establish viable industries since so many of them exhibit marked economies of size. In addition, it is observed that in many cases foreign firms operating in developing countries have found that the safest and most remunerative investments for their profits have been in the already industrialised countries, with the result that there has been a massive repatriation of profits from the poorer to the richer countries.

This clearly reinforces Kitamura's argument above about trade reinforcing the dominance of the richer countries, and in part this may be attributed to a lack of commitment by foreign firms to the developing countries in which they operate. Also, although it is not only foreign firms which are responsible for exporting capital, it clearly lends substance to the charge that foreign capital operates in an exploitative role within the developing countries. Further evidence of this is found in the enclave nature of much foreign owned primary industry. This is clearly noticeable in both plantation agriculture and mining (Beckford 1972), which tend (a) to export virtually all of their output, (b) to be capital intensive relative to much of the rest of the economy and to import most of their capital equipment, (c) to be demanding of the provision of roads, railways, ports and other forms of social capital and (d) to promote few backward linkages into input-supplying industries or forward linkages into secondary industry. These features do much to account for the main charge made against foreign ownership of industry, which is that it has not tended to reinvest its profits in the expansion of the local developing economies but has used them 'exploitatively' for the benefit of the richer nations. They may also cause there to be a weak relationship between export and GNP growth in the developing countries. Bairoch (1975, p. 108) goes as far as to assert that there was almost no relationship between those two measures. This, however, conflicts with the earlier, more optimistic, conclusion of Kravis (1970, p. 867) that there was a statistically significant positive relationship between increases in exports and real GNP for 37 non-oil exporting LDCs in the period 1950–1965.

A somewhat different argument, associated with the names of Prebisch and Singer, also leads to the conclusion that institutional differences cause the industrialised nations (the Centre) to 'exploit' the underdeveloped primary producing ones (the Periphery) through international trade (Prebisch 1967; Baer 1961). Prebisch's main challenge is directed at the validity of the trade theory assumption of classically competitive factor and product markets in both the Centre and the Periphery. Neo-classical economic theory suggests that, where competition exists, technological changes which result in increased general productivity will lead to reduced product prices. Prebisch argues that this process operates at the Periphery, competing down export prices to the benefit of consumers at the Centre. However, at the Centre more monopolistic forces are believed to operate, particularly in the labour market where union power is seen as extracting the gains from increased productivity in the form of higher wages, and in the product market where firms are seen as having sufficient market power to pass on higher wage costs in the form of higher prices to consumers at the Periphery and at the Centre. Thus it is argued that, as a result of differences in competitive structure, the prices of primary exports from the Periphery are depressed relative to those of imported manufactured items and trade will act as an 'exploitative' force on behalf of the Centre. Certainly there is a widespread belief that the terms of trade of primary for manufactured goods has shown a steady swing in favour of manufactures. If true, and this will be examined in more detail in section 4.2, this evidence would tend to lend support to the Prebisch hypothesis.

A more extreme view of the adverse effects of trade on development is held by those economists who have used Marxian value analysis to derive the proposition that trade is a form of unequal exchange. This concept is particularly associated with the name of Emmanuel (1972) and is that advanced countries exploit poor countries by obtaining more labour for less through trade. There are a number of ambiguities in this argument, exemplified by Emmanuel's own changes of position, among which are different views of precisely how the institutions governing trade might bring about unequal exchange (Barrat Brown 1974, Ch. 10). There is in addition the problem of the non-homogeneity of labour in different countries; this is that because the inherent productivity (due to a higher investment in training, nutrition, etc.) of, say, the average German worker is higher than that of the average Indian worker, it is difficult to evaluate clearly the meaning of unequal exchange. Despite these question marks, the concept of unequal exchange appears to have had a significant impact upon thinking about trade and development.

Trade theory also directs comparatively little attention to the influence of transport, handling and insurance charges upon the patterns of and rewards from trade. The fact is, however, that the major share of the transport charges in international trade accrue to richer nations such as Japan, Norway, the USA and the UK which own substantial merchant fleets. Since on bulky cargoes such as ores, oil and grains, ocean transport charges may account for a significant percentage of the landed price of the commodity, it is clear that the maritime nations derive substantial freight revenues from trade and that little accrues to the underdeveloped countries, as in general these do not own major shipping lines.

Supported by some of the arguments just sketched out, there is no doubt that many believe that the present system of international trade does not contribute greatly to the elimination of underdevelopment and that it contributes the lion's share of the spoils to the industrial and oil-rich nations. Spreading acceptance of this view has led to increasing demand for reform of world trade and to the institution of special measures of trade credit and preference to create a New International Economic Order more favourable to the poorer nations.[1]

## 4.2 Trade Policy for Development

It follows from the diversity of views considered in the last section about the effects of trade upon economic development that divergent strategies have been proposed for the trade policy of developing countries and have been espoused by such countries. Despite the obvious importance of identifying and examining these approaches to trade policy, only a brief description will be presented here to avoid duplication of material elsewhere in the book. For as Haq asserts 'Trade should not be regarded as a pace-setter in any relevant development . . but as a derivative. The LDCs should first define a strategy for attacking their problems of unemployment and mass poverty. Trade possibilities should be geared to meeting the objectives of such a strategy'. (Streeten 1973, p. 101). Thus formulation of trade policy strategy constitutes a part of a development planning process which simultaneously establishes policies for industrial and agricultural expansion. It is this simultaneity which inevitably leads to policy strategy aspects bearing on trade also being discussed in the chapters on industrial development (Chapter 8), agricultural development (Chapter 6) and models of development (Chapter 3).

One trade strategy, pursued particularly by China and in less rigorous form by Tanzania, is to severely restrict and control trade with the industrialised countries. The basis of this policy is a different philosophy of development, in that these countries would reject many of the economic changes arising from comparatively free trade as constituting development. They would argue that under 'free trade', in which private traders and transnational corporations import where it is profitable for them to do so, there will be a tendency to supply the comparatively rich urban elite with foreign luxury goods and to engage in promotional activity to sell 'socially unnecessary' goods and a 'Western' set of aspirations unsuited to the state of the country's development. Such tendencies would not only be socially divisive but they would divert scarce foreign exchange from 'socially desirable' investment to luxury consumption. Instead China, and like-minded countries, pursue a basic policy of economic self-sufficiency and export only in order to be able to import 'socially desirable products' (basically capital items and, if necessary, food) when there is a marked advantage in the exchange.

The majority of countries, however, do not formulate their trade strategies from the standpoint that free trade leads to contamination by polluting western consumerism. Nevertheless, as a reflection of the theoretical attitudes expressed above, plus some pragmatic ones about the export prospects of individual countries, countries other than China and Tanzania have adopted basically 'inward-looking policies'. Where notions of unequal exchange, the exploitative nature of trade, or just sheer export pessimism hold sway, development policy has concentrated on minimising dependence upon imports. This has entailed emphasis on building up domestic industries to substitute home-produced for imported products — 'import-substituting industrialisation' (ISI) as this is usually referred to, is extensively discussed in Chapter 8. In many cases pursuit of this strategy has required the imposition of extreme measures of trade protection (tariffs, import quotas, embargoes) to overcome the limitations inherent in producing for what is often a small market. Such policies, as we shall consider elsewhere (Chapter 6), have in many cases led to under-emphasis on the agricultural sector, the neglect of which has led to serious development bottlenecks in several countries. They have also tended to reduce incentives to exporting industries, since these have to pay higher prices for some domestically produced imports than their overseas competitors, and they also suffer from over-valued exchange rates with respect to 'free trade' levels. Nevertheless, inward-looking trade and development strategies have held an important place in the developing countries during the 1960s and 1970s. And as Haq opines, 'import substitution strategy carries fewer risks for the harassed policy makers because high-cost goods produced under protective walls can still be shoved down the throats of the local populations by closing down any decent alternative. ... as far as the LDC policy makers are concerned (the) high element of risk is fairly decisive in their attitude towards outward looking strategies.'

Whether or not the strength of support for inward-looking trade/development policies has increased or not is a matter of opinion. Nevertheless there are many who reject the pessimistic view of the relationship between trade and development and who are critical of the results of ISI. These economists feel that the outward-looking alternative is more appropriate, with its emphasis on export expansion, gains from specialisation in trade and relatively low and selective levels of protection for domestic industry. Myint, for example, in his review of the prospects for the South East Asian economy envisages a rapidly expanding and healthy demand for the area's exports, and advocates a dismantling or reduction of many of the measures of protection for domestic industries (Myint 1971, pp. 31, 32). Similarly, Kravis in his interesting analysis of the relationship between trade expansion and growth takes an optimistic view of the trade prospects of the LDCs (Kravis 1970). On the basis of analysis of historical data, Kravis argues that the rate of increase of demand for the primary exports of the LDCs is currently at least as great as it was for the now-developed countries during their period of rapid industrialisation in the late 19th century, while the rate of increase in demand for their manufactured products is substantially greater. If correct, this rather undermines any arguments that currently underdeveloped countries are disadvantaged by markedly worse export demand prospects than those facing the industrialised countries at a comparable stage in their development. Of course, not all LDCs have promising export prospects but, as Kravis argues, this may be due to deficiencies in supply conditions within countries rather than to any deficiency in export demand. Certainly as is indicated in Chapter 8, a number of LDCs have experienced considerable success in pursuing outward looking policies. Countries such as Singapore, Korea, Hong Kong and Taiwan have demonstrated simultaneously high rates of growth in manufactured exports and GNP. It is this experience which has led many experts (e.g. some contributors to Streeten 1973) to support the efficacy of an outward-looking policy of export expansion in the products of secondary industry as a sound basis for development.

**Table 4.1:** *Developing countries' shares in the import markets of four developed regions by commodity groups, 1964 and 1972* (Percentage share of total imports)

| *Commodity group* | *EEC(a)* | | *EFTA(a)* | | *United States* | | *Japan* | |
|---|---|---|---|---|---|---|---|---|
| | *1964* | *1972* | *1964* | *1972* | *1964* | *1972* | *1964* | *1972* |
| Agricultural products | 51.2 | 47.1 | 31.9 | 30.0 | 63.8 | 52.9 | 36.9 | 36.2 |
| Raw materials including fuel | 55.0 | 62.8 | 45.8 | 46.3 | 55.6 | 46.9 | 53.7 | 56.0 |
| Raw-material-intensive manufacturing | 24.9 | 24.0 | 14.2 | 9.6 | 17.2 | 14.6 | 35.8 | 41.9 |
| Labour-intensive manufacturing | 17.2 | 14.8 | 17.4 | 17.0 | 23.4 | 26.3 | 9.4 | 26.8 |
| Skill-intensive manufacturing | 2.1 | 4.3 | 2.7 | 3.0 | 3.8 | 5.8 | 5.0 | 4.5 |
| Total | 37.7 | 37.5 | 24.5 | 19.0 | 36.0 | 23.7 | 40.3 | 41.9 |

(*a*) Share in trade with non-member countries.
*Source:* Fels and Glisman (1975, Table 1)

## 4.3 Barriers to Manufacturing Export Growth

Despite the fact that a number of comparatively small developing countries – which are not among the poorest of that group – have succeeded in creating the necessary industrial supply conditions to rapidly expand their manufactured exports, the evidence is that the developing countries as a whole are experiencing difficulty in penetrating industrial export markets. As table 4.1 shows, the trade shares developing countries hold in the manufactured goods markets of the rich countries are substantially smaller than in those for raw materials and for agricultural products, although shares in the latter declined between 1964 and 1972 to all four developed regions. Furthermore, the developing countries have had difficulty in retaining such shares as they do have in manufactured export markets, except in the category with the smallest share, skill-intensive products, in which they achieved rapid rates of export growth to all areas other than Japan.

The data in table 4.1 are hardly conclusive, but the declining shares of developing countries in EEC and EFTA imports of raw-material-intensive manufactures and labour-intensive goods, and in USA imports of the former, lend support to the view that the trade policies of the rich countries are biased against manufactured imports from developing countries. For it is precisely in these two categories of manufacturing that the developing countries might be expected to have a comparative advantage since they supply a substantial proportion of the developed countries' raw materials and have large quantities of cheap unskilled labour.

The failure of the developing nations to achieve greater shares of the manufactured imports of industrialised countries has been assessed by many to be a demand problem arising from policies by the latter countries to restrict the growth of certain classes of imports. Such policies have been pursued for a variety of reasons, including the prevention of rapid rundown of domestic industries such as textiles and to provide short-run support for the balance of payments.

The policy measures employed to control imports can be broadly classified into tariff and non-tariff barriers, and it is argued that the industrial countries have used these in such a way that they discriminate most heavily against the exports of developing countries. For example, it is observed that many developed countries employ a 'cascading' or 'escalating' system of import tariffs in which the rate of tariff increases with the degree of processing an item has undergone. Thus Helleiner (1972, p. 70) noted that the USA had tariffs of zero on raw hides and skins, 10% on finished leather and 13% on leather footwear. There are many other examples, but it can be seen readily that such tariff systems restrict the opportunities for the developing countries to build up raw material processing industries for export, and encourage them instead to continue exporting raw materials so that the processing jobs are maintained in the rich countries. Not only that, but the tariff systems of industrial countries appear to discriminate more against the manufactured products of developing countries than against those of other highly industrialised competitors – the formation of tariff-free trading areas, such as the European Economic Community, is one factor contributing to this discrimination. Thus Little, Scitovsky and Scott (1970, p. 273) showed that in the 1960s the average effective tariff imposed by industrial countries on manufactured imports from developing countries was 22.6%, as opposed to 11.1% for all their manufactured imports. Admittedly these levels of tariff were lower than they had been before the Kennedy Round of the General Agreement on Trade and Tariffs (GATT) and have been reduced still further as a result of subsequent meetings of GATT.

During the 1960s, recognition that there was tariff discrimination by developed countries against processed and manufactured imports from LDCs led to pressure (orchestrated within UNCTAD) for the granting of certain tariff exemptions for such imports. As a consequence, the major industrial countries have, during the 1970s, introduced Generalised Systems of Preference (GSPs) to grant preferential access, through abolition or reduction of tariffs, to certain classes of imports from designated LDCs. For example, GSP schemes were introduced by the EEC and Japan in 1971, and by the USA in 1976. Although it is possibly too early to assess fully the impact of such schemes on LDC exports, the view is already emerging (Murray 1973a and 1973b; Baldwin and Murray 1977; and Morton and Tulloch 1977, pp. 169-175) that, due to restrictions written into the various GSP schemes, the DCs have effectively managed to severely restrict the value of the concessions made.

To appreciate the limited impact of the GSP schemes upon LDC exports it has first to be noted that most primary commodities are not subject to tariffs and that, since these constitute such a large proportion of LDC exports, approximately 60% of their total exports to the DCs are not dutiable. Of the remaining 40% (approximately) of dutiable exports, a large proportion is either totally excluded from the GSP schemes or is given only limited preference. Most dutiable processed agricultural goods (which constitute a large proportion of total exports) are excluded, and those which are included are only eligible for reduced, as opposed to zero, tariffs. Thus it is mainly to manufactured goods that the GSP schemes relate. But not even all of these are covered; and for those which are eligible preferential access may only be available up to specified ceilings on the total exports of LDCs and the exports from particular countries. As a result of all these restrictions, possibly no more than 10% of all LDC exports stand to benefit from the various GSP schemes. Furthermore, unless (and there is evidence of reluctance by the DCs to permit this) the ceilings are raised sufficiently to allow for the growth rate of LDC exports this proportion will fall.

Not only is the total impact of the GSP schemes limited, but it is spread unevenly between the LDCs. Because the schemes are directed towards industrial products the immediate benefits tend to accrue mainly to that small group of better-off LDCs which dominate the LDCs exports of manufactured products; Baldwin and Murray (1977) identify Taiwan, Mexico, Yugoslavia, South Korea, Hong Kong, Brazil, Singapore, India, Peru, Chile, Argentina and Iran as the countries which gain most. It is, however, precisely because of the strong competitive position of some of these countries in certain markets that some products are excluded from the schemes and ceilings are placed upon the eligibility of others. In particular, the country ceilings on preferential access are designed to limit the extent to which these economically stronger LDCs can benefit from the trade-creating effects of the GSP schemes. In so far as such country quotas are not effective for the poorest countries with a low proportion of manufactured exports, the poorest LDCs should tend to benefit in time from the trade diversion effect. This is that trade will tend to be switched to cheaper sources, from suppliers without preferential access on their marginal exports (because they have exceeded their quota) to those which are eligible for preferential treatment. However, the difficulty here is that the most weakly industrialised LDCs may be unable to capitalise on any tariff advantages they possess because of lower capacity to cope with non-tariff barriers to trade. Non-tariff barriers are of various types and include packaging and marking regulations, health regulations for foodstuffs, safety regulations, import quotas, variable levies, production subsidies in importing countries, and policies whereby government departments purchase primarily domestically produced goods. Walter (1971) has presented empirical evidence that these barriers discriminate against the manufactured exports of the least industrialised LDCs. He proposes, as arguments to explain the evidence that the LDCs are less able to cope with the frequent changes and many details of the legislative barriers, that these barriers principally operate against the class of products exported by LDCs, and that these countries are hampered by shortages of credit in financing the long delivery delays incurred for border inspections.

It thus appears that trade restrictions by rich countries do limit the opportunities of LDCs to profit by outward-looking trade strategies. At the same time, however, it seems (and is logical) that the main beneficiaries of any general dismantling of tariff barriers to trade will be the better-off, more industrialised LDCs, and that it might do little to assist many of the poorest countries to increase their exports of manufactured products. This may explain why so many poor countries have rejected outward-looking policies in favour of an inward-looking policy of import substituting industrialisation.

## 4.4 Issues Relating to Export Dependency on Primary Commodities

### *Terms of Trade*

By terms of trade is meant the value (price) of one commodity bundle in terms of another. A decline in the terms of trade for a specified bundle of goods means that a given quantity of it can only buy a smaller quantity of some other bundle than was formerly the case. To calculate a terms of trade series therefore requires the construction of two indices of value. Unfortunately, however, there is no uniquely correct way of constructing indices, and in the case of the terms of trade there are a number of alternative concepts of the comparison to be made. Thus among typical alternatives we may have the valuation of one commodity in terms of all others (the commodity terms of trade), the valuation of a standard bundle of exports in terms of imports (the net barter terms of trade), or we might use the net barter terms of trade adjusted for a volume index of exports (the income terms of trade); there are also other theoretical possibilities (Clement *et al.* 1967, p. 129). This lack of specificity about how to measure the terms of trade creates appreciable latitude for disagreement between analysts when examining the critical question of whether or not the terms of trade for developing countries as a whole have been declining in terms of their imports from richer nations. For this is the hypothesis put forward by Prebisch and others who reason that international trade mainly benefits the richer nations.

However, there are reasons other than those proffered by Prebisch as to why the terms of trade for primary commodities and hence developing countries may tend to decline. In particular it is noted that income elasticities of demand for agricultural commodities fall as income rises so that demand for them increases more slowly than for manufactured goods. It follows that any tendency for the ratio of productivity to demand growth to rise more rapidly in agriculture than in industry will cause a relative decline in agricultural product prices. Any global tendency for decline in agriculture's terms of trade has been magnified for the underdeveloped countries by the industrial countries' pursuance of policies of paying their farmers more than world prices. The output expansion effects of these policies have increased the industrial countries' exportable surpluses of some agricultural commodities and reduced their import demand for others. It is also noted that, as a result of technological advances, synthetic substitutes are being continuously developed to compete with those agricultural commodities which are industrial raw materials, e.g. nylon and polyester for natural fibres, and plastics for rubber. Continuous reductions in real production costs for these synthetic substitutes coupled with the ability to control their quantity and quality has placed a powerful constraint upon the prices of natural raw materials. In addition there is a tendency for technological advance to reduce the weight of metal and other minerals required to produce a unit of manufactured goods; hence the rate of growth of demand for the minerals tends to be slower than that of the end product. Then there is also the tendency for structural change away from such industries as textiles, shipbuilding and iron casting towards those like electronics and aircraft manufacture, which are much less dependent upon raw materials. Thus there are several hypotheses to explain a decline in the terms of trade for primary commodities and consequently for those of developing countries. It is therefore clear that any general evidence of this effect cannot be interpreted as confirming the validity of any one hypothesis, but will be consistent with all of them.

**Table 4.2** *Changes in the terms of trade*

| | *Commodity terms of trade for primary[(a)] products (1963=100)* | | | | *Net barter terms of trade for developing countries* | | |
|---|---|---|---|---|---|---|---|
| | *All primary ÷ manufactured* | *Food ÷ manufactured* | *Ag. non-food ÷ manufactured* | *Minerals ÷ manufactured* | *All[(a)] developing (1963 = 100)* | *Major[(b)] oil exporters (1969= 100)* | *Non-oil[(b)] exporters (1969= 100)* |
| 1950 | 133 | — | — | 113 | 112 | — | — |
| 1952 | 122 | — | — | 109 | 106 | — | — |
| 1954 | 120 | 127 | 119 | 109 | 112 | — | — |
| 1956 | 114 | 109 | 118 | 112 | 107 | — | — |
| 1958 | 106 | 106 | 101 | 110 | 104 | — | — |
| 1960 | 101 | 96 | 107 | 99 | 104 | 110 | 90 |
| 1961 | 98 | 93 | 103 | 102 | 102 | — | — |
| 1962 | 107 | 104 | 108 | 93 | 98 | — | — |
| 1963 | 100 | 100 | 100 | 100 | 100 | — | — |
| 1964 | 102 | 104 | 101 | 101 | 101 | — | — |
| 1965 | 100 | 100 | 100 | 101 | 99 | — | — |
| 1966 | 98 | 99 | 98 | 98 | 101 | — | — |
| 1967 | 94 | 97 | 90 | 110 | 100 | — | — |
| 1968 | 94 | 95 | 91 | 109 | 101 | — | — |
| 1969 | 94 | 95 | 92 | 95 | 101 | 100 | 100 |
| 1970 | 92 | 95 | 86 | 95 | 100 | 98 | 99 |
| 1971 | 97 | 96 | 85 | 107 | 101 | 114 | 93 |
| 1972 | 104 | 102 | 93 | 110 | 101 | 117 | 94 |
| 1973 | 126 | 124 | 127 | 123 | 111 | 137 | 100 |
| 1974 | 175 | 134 | 119 | 276 | 156 | 331 | 96 |
| 1975 | 154 | 114 | 93 | 257 | 147 | 321 | 86 |

(a) Calculated using data in the UN Monthly Bulletin of Statistics, September issues.

(b) *Source:* OECD, 1974 Review, *Development Cooperation*, Table II–3, Paris, November 1974, and IMF *Annual Reports.*

Turning to the empirical evidence, the relationship between primary and manufactured goods prices appears to be characterised by short periods in which the terms of trade move sharply in favour of the former; the evidence in table 4.2 indicates that such short periods occurred from 1950 to 1954 and 1973 to 1974, and less markedly in 1962 to 1964. Typically these short periods seem to be interspersed by longer ones in which prices for manufactures rise relative to those of primary commodities. It is on the basis of the evidence of these longer periods that most economists tend to argue that the primary commodity terms of trade show a secular tendency to decline, and certainly examination of the data from 1950 up until

1972 lends strong support for this view. The post-1972 situation is somewhat less clear, but it does appear that following the temporary boom in commodity prices in 1973–1974 their real level has subsequently fallen back, in many cases to around the levels of the 1960s. Certainly UN projections up to 1985 envisage real commodity prices remaining below their levels in the 1950s and stabilising about their level in the 1960s (UN 1975). This being so, it is understandable that there is common support for the hypothesis of secularly declining terms of trade for primary commodities. Such a conclusion should perhaps be viewed with some slight caution in view of the interesting analysis recently published by Bairoch (1975). A careful examination of data for the period 1870 to 1938 leads Bairoch (pp. 112, 113) to conclude that during this period 'in fact a real secular improvement occurred in the terms of trade of primary products vis-à-vis manufactures'.[2] Analysis of the subsequent period up to 1970 led him to conclude that only in the post-1938 period did the behaviour of primary commodity and manufactured goods prices conform to the Prebisch hypothesis. It is possible but, as previously stated, unlikely that this latter conclusion will be reversed by the price experience in the post-1970 period.

Accepting then that the terms of trade for primary products has in the recent past shown an underlying tendency to decline, the question naturally arises as to whether this in itself is evidence that trade benefits the importers of such commodities more than the exporters? All that can be stated unequivocally is that, with the same volume and composition of exports, the developing countries and other predominantly primary commodity exporters would have been better off as a group if the relative prices of their exports had been higher. For a variety of reasons the terms of trade cannot be interpreted as an index of welfare. In the first place, if productivity in the agricultural and extractive industries of the developing countries had risen faster than demand at constant real prices then there could probably have been an increase in the purchasing power of exports and in the economic rents accruing to them, in spite of a decline in the commodity terms of trade. In fact the developing countries have increased their volume of exports in such a way that their income terms of trade (buying power) has increased. The crucial point, however, is that this growth of import purchasing power has lagged behind that of the industrialised nations, because not only has the growth of world trade in agricultural and mining products lagged behind that in manufactures, but the developing countries' share of total trade in primary commodities has steadily fallen – from 40.5% in 1955 to 34.7% in 1972 (Stern and Tims 1975, p. 227). Understandably, faced with the more rapid growth in demand for manufactured goods the underdeveloped countries have been attempting to diversify their exports to include more manufactures and to reduce their dependency on primary commodities. It is the measure of their (limited) success at this diversification which largely explains why the net barter terms of trade of the developing countries (table 4.2) did not decline between 1960 and 1970 in line with the primary commodity terms of trade.[3]

Another reason for rejecting a simplistic welfare interpretation of terms of trade indices relates to the quality factor. A ton of wheat or bauxite remains of much the same quality over time in terms of productive services. The same is not true of manufactured items such as vehicles, textile machines or refrigerators. These have changed markedly over time in the sense of providing improved services. If therefore the terms of trade between, say, wheat and motor cars remained constant over time then wheat producers would become progressively better off in terms of motor car services. In this situation even declining wheat-to-car prices would not necessarily rule out a welfare gain to wheat exporters.

Of course, the concept of the terms of trade for developing countries is a statistical *tour de force* which covers up wide variations in changes in the terms of trade for individual commodities and countries. A striking illustration relates to the experience of oil and the oil-producing countries; as indicated in table 4.2 the terms of trade for this commodity and group of countries has improved substantially since 1972 relative to other commodities and countries, and it is unlikely that export dependence upon oil is viewed as a medium-term liability. There are, however, other commodities whose prices have over fairly long periods fared relatively well in international trade. Among these are cocoa, sugar, coffee, and bauxite which account for a high proportion of the exports of a number of developing countries. Indeed, as several authors (Little *et al.* 1970; Maizels 1968) have pointed out, there are a number of commodities likely to exhibit rapidly growing export markets which the underdeveloped countries can expect to exploit successfully. In fact all the commodities named above as having shown favourable relative price movements feature in Maizels' classification of commodities likely to display rapid growth in world trade (Maizels 1968, p. 153), along with others such as hardwood, fishmeal, citrus fruit and meat. Of course, in export markets for some of these commodities the developing countries are competing against the developed countries, and it is only with tropical agricultural commodities (plus oil) that the developing countries have a dominant share of world trade. It is also the case that for tropical agricultural products world trade represents a high proportion of world production, with the consequences that general efforts to expand such exports are very likely to depress export prices in the face of relatively inelastic demand, and that increased market shares are won at the expense of other developing countries. In markets for minerals, and agricultural commodities produced in both temperate and tropical areas, world trade typically does not constitute a high proportion of world production. In these markets, expansion of exports by developing countries is less likely to depress prices and, in the absence of barriers to trade, is as likely to be at the expense of the developed as of the developing countries.

Despite these favourable export opportunities for some primary commodities and hence countries, the net barter terms of trade for many underdeveloped countries are likely to continue to decline. This is because their exports are composed primarily of commodities with poor price prospects, while at the same time they are heavily dependent upon raw material imports such as oil which are expected to maintain their real price. Indeed, as table 4.2 shows, the group of non-oil-exporting developing countries, which includes most LDCs, failed to benefit in their net barter terms of trade from the relative increase in primary commodity prices. For some of the most populous of these non-oil-exporting countries (including India, Indonesia, Egypt and Ethiopia) it seems unlikely on the basis of past trends (GATT 1974, p. 110) that export volume growth will be sufficiently high to offset the decline in net barter terms of trade and to produce substantial growth in import purchasing power. It is countries such as these which fail to obtain the expected long-run benefits from trade and which cannot rely upon export stimulated economic development.

### *Short-Term Instability of Export Earnings*

A widely accepted hypothesis which has exercised an important influence on international trade policy is that, because of their reliance upon primary commodities, the export earnings of underdeveloped countries exhibit a high degree of short-run instability. As an ancillary proposition it is argued that such instability is damaging to the growth and development prospects of these countries. This follows because it is assumed that fluctuating exports will cause fluctuations in the capacity to import the capital goods on which growth and development depend.

With regard to variations in the value of commodity trade at the world market level it is popularly argued that, because of price inelastic demand, short-term shifts in aggregate demand or supply of primary products lead to price changes of greater proportionate magnitude than those in the volume of trade. It should, however, be observed that a given proportionate reduction of demand will tend to have a greater adverse effect upon total export earnings for a commodity than an equivalent proportionate supply increase. From the standpoint of international trade policy this is an important distinction, since demand shifts are beyond the control of the exporters but are mainly dependent upon fluctuations in the level of economic activity in the industrial countries. It is evident that such fluctuations have been large – witness the world economic boom of 1972–1974 and the subsequent recession of 1975–1977 – and precisely because they have not originated in the economic conditions of the underdeveloped countries there is a basis for arguing that the rich countries should compensate poorer ones for any damage caused to their economies by such fluctuations.

Of course, the export earnings of an individual country for a particular commodity need not move in line with total world export earnings from that commodity. Exports from a particular country may increase at a time of world supply shortage and high prices (and vice versa), so that they may fluctuate more than world export earnings of that commodity. Few countries, however, are dependent solely upon one export product, and export concentration ratios have declined indicating a steady process of export diversification by the majority of developing countries. It is therefore probable that there are offsetting movements in the earnings from different products which will damp down fluctuations in total export earnings, except at times of extreme world economic recession or boom when all commodity prices will tend to move together.

Empirical evidence about export earning instability has not substantiated the view that it represents a grave problem for the underdeveloped countries. MacBean (1966), in his analysis for the period 1946–1958, even went so far as to conclude that although the export revenues of developing countries were more unstable than those of developed countries, the difference was not marked. MacBean's analysis also failed to discover much empirical support for the hypotheses that export instability tends to increase if (a) primary commodities constitute a higher proportion of total exports, (b) a smaller number of commodities dominate the primary export fraction, or (c) if exports are mainly destined for one geographic market, e.g. the former colonising nation. Various writers have, however, been critical of MacBean's work. Ady (1969), for example, argues that his methods of analysis have systematic biases which play down the extent of instability in the underdeveloped countries. And, in contradiction of MacBean, Erb and Schiavo-Campo (1969) found evidence that export earning instability in the underdeveloped countries during 1954–1966 was significantly higher than in developed countries. These authors did, however, also allow that the general problem of instability between 1954 and 1966 was less than in the period 1946–1958 studied by MacBean. Thus the evidence available does not suggest that the developing countries as a group suffer extreme export instability as a consequence of their reliance on primary products. However, this does not rule out the possibility of exceptional variability for some commodities and countries. Certainly some commodities such as rubber, cocoa and cotton have experienced much higher earnings instability than others, e.g. bananas, sugar and petroleum (MacBean 1966, p. 51). However, it does not appear that the more volatile commodities were responsible for the higher levels of instability in those countries where this was greatest. Rather, exceptional export earning instability was mainly due to special internal factors, often political, which influenced the volume of exports.

The concern with short-term export instability is due to the hypothesis that it hampers development. Since instability is defined in such a way that on average downswings equal upswings, 'the hypothesis is equivalent to stating that the damaging effects of downward export fluctuations are greater than the beneficial effects of upward deviations' (Schiavo-Campo and Singer 1970, p. 167). Support for this form of the hypothesis is along the lines that unanticipated increases in foreign exchange earnings cannot be exploited readily for investment because of shortages of complementary local factors of production (particularly skilled human capacity) and thus tend to be dissipated on consumer goods, whereas unexpected shortfalls in earnings lead to cutbacks in capital equipment imports and delays in investment projects.

Again, the empirical analysis which has been conducted, largely by MacBean, fails to support the hypothesis that export earnings instability reduces economic growth in the poorer countries. There may be various sound explanations for this, such as, for example, that commodity tax policies tend to reduce the impact of earnings fluctuations upon the private sector and enable governments to pursue stabilising policies. MacBean (1966, pp. 86, 87) also suggests that the expatriate firms, which dominate the export sector, expect a fluctuating pattern of receipts and tend to take and repatriate their profits only in years of high earnings, thus stabilising export revenue flows into the exporting economy.

The negative quality of the empirical analysis need not be, and clearly has not been, accepted as indicating that export earning instability is not a problem for developing countries. The analysis does not preclude the possibilities that (a) certain countries are severely handicapped by export fluctuations, (b) in periods other than that for which the analysis has been conducted a widespread problem has existed, and (c) that, although differences in economic growth rates between countries cannot be adequately explained by differences in export instability, such rates might have been higher in all countries given greater stability. In view of these possibilities it is perhaps not surprising that in international trade negotiations many participants adhere to their *a priori* views about the harmful effects of export variability upon development, and of the need for stabilisation policies to be implemented. This pressure has led to the introduction of a variety of policies to create export stability for some underdeveloped countries. The exact measures are discussed below, but it is worth noting that, because stabilisation can be interpreted as simply the smoothing out of payments over time without any need for continuous long-term transfers from one group of countries to another, it is much easier to reach international agreement on stabilisation policies than for policies to counteract any secular tendencies for decline in the terms of trade of particular nations, since these latter require a net secular transfer of funds to disadvantaged nations.

## 4.5 Policies to Increase the LDCs Share of the Benefits from Trade

The preceding discussion has highlighted a number of issues relating to international trade which cause concern to developing countries. Most significantly there is the feeling that the LDCs are not receiving a fair share of the expansion of world trade and that they are not being paid adequately for the share that they do have. This amounts to concern that the export earnings of the LDCs are not rising fast enough. Added to this is concern that too high a proportion of the export revenues which 'do accrue' to the developing countries are subsequently exported as profits by foreign-owned or transnational companies. In addition there is wide acceptance of the view that heavy reliance upon primary commodities leads to fluctuations in export earnings which disrupt the development plans of poorer countries.

Increasing awareness of these problems coupled with more sophisticated political representation by the LDCs in international bodies has led to mounting pressure for changes in the conduct of international trade. Manifestations of this pressure have been the creation and convening in 1974 and 1975 of the World Food Council under the aegis of the UN Food and Agricultural Organisation. Also, in 1974 the sixth special session of the UN General Assembly adopted as a resolution the Programme of Action on the Establishment of a New International Economic Order. This resolution has been the basis for a series of negotiating meetings of the UN including those of the Fourth UN Conference on Trade and Development (UNCTAD IV) in Nairobi in 1976, and it 'embodies a six-point plan covering buffer stock arrangements, a common financing facility for the management of commodity markets, a network of supply and purchase agreements (multilateral commodity schemes), transfer of primary processing activities from rich to poor countries, index linking of prices of primary commodity exports from poor countries to the prices of their imports, and ... as a residual measure, a system of compensatory financing to stabilise and guarantee poor countries' export earnings from commodity exports' (Wall 1976, pp. 17, 18). At UNCTAD IV the proposals were shaped into an 'Integrated Programme for Commodities, the central core of which was proposals for the setting up of a 'common fund' to finance the holding of international buffer stocks of primary commodities (UNCTAD 1974). It was suggested that as much as $6,000 million would eventually be required to finance buffer stocks of up to ten commodities (cocoa, coffee, copper, cotton, jute, rubber, sisal, sugar, tea and tin), and that up to seven other commodities (bananas, bauxite, iron ore, meat, rice, wheat and wool) should be included in the integrated programme. To date no agreement has been reached upon these and other proposals for a New International Economic Order, and considerable technical and political obstacles to agreement have been encountered, some brief insights into which are provided in the remainder of this chapter.[4]

### *International Commodity Agreements*

At the international level the record of achievement of producing a new trade deal for the developing countries has been poor even in the most successful sphere of action, that of stabilising prices through the operation of multilateral trade agreements or buffer stock schemes. There is a history of trade agreements for primary commodities stretching back to the 1930s. The history is a patchy one, however, in that agreements have been negotiated for comparatively few commodities, and that the agreements which have been concluded have tended either to break down or to be less than wholly successful in terms of their stated objectives.

The objectives have differed from one International Commodity Agreement to another. The International Wheat Agreements (IWAs), for example, were in the nature of multilateral contracts between major exporting and importing nations. The aims of successive IWAs were to introduce an element of price stability into international trade, to guarantee markets to exporting countries in times of high production, and to assure supplies to importing nations in periods of shortage. These objectives were to be achieved by undertakings from importing countries to guarantee to purchase annually from the group of signatory exporting countries a fixed quota of wheat at no less than an agreed floor price, while the exporting countries undertook to supply the importers with a quota of wheat at no more than the negotiated ceiling price. The agreements were thus designed to stabilise prices in the range between the floor and ceiling prices,[5] to help exporting countries in years of surplus supply and importing countries in years of shortage. To what extent the IWAs were successful in achieving these ends is debatable, and it is accepted that their apparent success between 1949 and 1971 was mainly due to the domestic policies of the two major wheat exporters, the USA and Canada. Further, it is difficult to see how the IWAs could have succeeded of themselves without linking agreements (which did not exist) for the other major traded grains such as rice, maize and barley which substitute for wheat over a range of uses.

The various frictions that arose with the International Wheat Agreements are instructive in terms of the difficulties likely to be encountered in obtaining multilateral trade agreements for a wider range of commodities. The conflict of interest between wheat importing and exporting countries has made it impossible to agree upon floor and ceiling prices since 1971 and the agreement is effectively in abeyance. It is inevitable that importers should be tempted to renege on their commitments when supplies are ample and wheat prices are below the agreed floor, and for exporters to do likewise when world prices exceed the ceiling. Thus, for example, the UK as a major wheat importer was not a signatory to the agreements in 1956 and 1959.

There has also been the problem that some important trading nations, such as Russia (except in 1962), have not signed the IWAs and have thus been in a potential position to benefit by the restraint of the signatory countries when wheat prices lay outside the negotiated range. Similarly, the USA and EEC were not members of the 1969–1973 International Sugar Agreement (ISA), but chose instead to enter into independent agreements for the supply of their sugar imports. Also the UK's imports of sugar under the Commonwealth Sugar Agreement were conducted outside the framework of the ISA.

A completely different system for achieving price stability and guaranteeing markets and supplies is embodied in the buffer stock element of the International Tin Agreement which has been operating uninterruptedly since 1956. Again, this is an agreement between the major exporting countries and most of the major importing countries (with the notable exception of the USA). The countries provide the necessary financial backing to operate a buffer stock of up to 20,000 tons of tin. The buffer stock manager is empowered to buy up tin when prices fall below an agreed floor and to sell tin when prices reach a predetermined ceiling. In this way the stock should be self-financing after the initial funding, and it operates as a source of supplementary demand in periods of low prices and of supplementary supply when prices are high. What is significant for the prospects for buffer stock schemes for other commodities is that the tin stock has proved difficult to manage in practice. Even when the range between ceiling and floor prices has been relatively large '... it has been necessary at times to impose export quotas to reinforce the action of the buffer stock in preventing the price from falling below the agreed floor. At the other end of the range unless a buffer stock is very large, it will become exhausted in the effort to check the upswing of prices, and beyond a certain point the buffer stock manager is unable to prevent further upswing of price' (Commonwealth Secretariat 1975). In addition, there may be a reduction in commercial stocks and a transfer of costs from the private sector to the buffer stock, in which case the latter no longer constitutes a net addition to total stocks.

It has to be recognised that stabilisation of prices does not entail simply smoothing out 'natural' fluctuations in market prices. Instability to producers can be reduced by imposing a variable commodity tax by specially created monopsonist purchasing agencies such as the export crop marketing boards found in some developing countries. More importantly at the international level of trade, wholesale price stability can be increased as a by-product of policies to restrict supply and push up prices. Note that such restriction requires the imposition of production or export quotas and generates a situation where particular producers or countries could profitably produce more than their quota allotment. Collective supply restriction policies will benefit producers (exporters) when, as is typical of most primary products, total demand is price inelastic, since in these cases any reduced volume of sales will be more than offset by increased prices thus causing increased total revenue. International action of this type has been taken for several commodities. In the case of coffee the action has been taken with the agreement of importing countries within the framework of the International Coffee Agreement (ICA); for oil there has been the dramatic unilateral action taken in 1973 by the OPEC cartel of major oil-exporting countries; and equally effectively, since 1974 Morocco and the USA have pushed up phosphate fertiliser prices by cutting back the extraction rate of phosphate rock.

However, there do appear to be distinct limitations on the scope for extending this type of action to other commodities. Favourable conditions for successful agreement to restrict supply exist when:

1. There are no close substitutes for the commodity so that the price

elasticity of demand is low even in the medium and long-run – following the oil price rise there is a marked upsurge of investment in nuclear power and coal production.

2. There are few producing countries so that potential conflicts of interest in reaching agreement are reduced; or there is a small number of countries dominating export sales which can undermine the position of the other exporters if they fail to comply with any agreement, e.g. Brazil has sufficient market power to manipulate the international coffee market independently.

3. The production and distribution systems within countries are oligopolistic (as in metals) rather then atomistic (as in agriculture). Where atomistic structures exist it is very difficult to control non-quota sales.

4. The commodity is storable so that sale of surplus product can be deferred.

5. It is also helpful if storage is cheap, as with oil and phosphate rock which can be stored in the ground at zero financial cost.

There are very few commodities which satisfy even most of these favourable conditions for the implementation of output restriction and buffer stock types of ICA, and it is doubtful if many more of such schemes will emerge to assist the level of stability of the commodity export earnings of developing countries.

*International Compensatory Finance Schemes*
It is questionable whether a commodity-by-commodity approach is appropriate to the trade problems of the developing countries. A more fundamental approach would be to try and increase the level and stability of earnings from total commodity and product exports. One proposal which recognises this calls for the index linking of commodity export prices to the import prices paid by developing countries. It is, however, unlikely that much progress will be made in this direction in view of the formidable technical problems of producing the indices and of the potential for conflicts of interest even among developing countries. For example, the interests of the oil- and non-oil-exporting countries conflict sharply, and the non-oil-exporting developing countries have suffered more than any other from the changes in relative commodity and product prices since 1972.

There has, however, been progress on another proposal, that of providing compensatory finance to offset unanticipated falls in the export earnings of developing countries. One scheme with a compensatory financing element is the Lomé Convention signed in 1975 between the European Economic Community and 46 developing countries. This export earnings stabilisation element (STABEX) is, however, of a limited nature and applies only to exports to the EEC of a number of selected commodities and simple processed items.[6]

STABEX makes available 75 million units of account per annum (1 u.a. = US $1.15 in February 1976) for the five years from 1975, which can be drawn from by any signatory country in the rather stringent event that its earnings from exports to the EEC of one or more of the covered products, taken separately, has fallen by at least 7.5% below the average level of earnings of the preceding four years. Although 22 of the signatory developing countries may be required to repay without interest any stabilising finance received from STABEX, no repayments are required from the other 24. Thus to some extent this scheme is not simply stabilising, but includes an element of earnings support. As Wall (1976) points out, however, the funds made available by STABEX are relatively small and in so far as they may be a substitute for other forms of aid paid by EEC member countries they may not represent additional aid.

A second more general compensatory finance scheme for developing countries is operated by the IMF to compensate for uncontrollable reductions in countries' overall export earnings below their estimated medium-term trend. General borrowing limits under this scheme are restricted in any 12 months to an additional 25% of a country's quota with the Fund, with total compensatory borrowings limited to 50% of the quota. Countries taking advantage of this facility are expected to repay loans within three to five years so that this scheme does not contain any income support element but is of a purely stabilising character.

As a stabilising device the generality of the IMF scheme makes it far more attractive than the individual commodity schemes which have been discussed. For in contrast to them there is no need to negotiate trade quotas, to agree upon price ranges for specific qualities of produce or to consider a wide range of other technical details.[7] From the poorer developing countries' point of view, however, repayment of the loans may be difficult even in periods of high export earnings, and the scheme is not a substitute for the net transfer of resources to these countries as envisaged in the resolution proposing a New International Economic Order.

*Other Policies*

The experience with International Commodity Agreements and the new compensatory finance schemes for export earnings gives rise to appreciable scepticism as to whether international negotiation is likely to generate a New International Economic Order, and to greatly transform the pattern of trade arising from the competitive economic forces now operating. It is true that there are other negotiated policies which affect trade patterns. There are, for example, narrowly based trade arrangements between countries, such as the old Commonwealth preference system which granted tariff exemptions on trade between countries of the British Commonwealth; the old Commonwealth Sugar Agreement now superseded by EEC arrangements; and there are the trade agreements between the United States and various Caribbean and Latin American countries which have entailed an element of price support for exports of sugar and coffee to the USA. In addition, initiatives have been taken by the developing countries themselves to form regional customs unions such as the East African Community (which broke up in 1977) and the Central American Common Market. It was hoped that the setting up of such communities would, through the creation of larger regional market units, enable local industries to take advantage of economies of size in production, lead to increased industrial activity within each Community, and generate a rapidly increasing volume of intraregional trade. The outcome of these experiments has fallen somewhat short of expectations, and there is no evidence that this type of policy provides for a radical improvement in individual countries' benefits from trade.

Countries also have some capacity to act individually to expand their economies through trade. The whole of commercial and industrial policy has implications for trade in that changes in industrial structure and activity influence import demand and export content. Some authors (Little *et al.* 1970, Ch. 4) have argued that in many cases developing countries appear to have pursued policies of industrialisation which have reduced the potential benefits from trade and international specialisation, and to the extent that this is true they have some scope to improve their own position. This issue is dealt with more fully in Chapter 8, but it is evident from the discussion there that the majority of developing countries experience great difficulty in devising policies which greatly increase their rates of development and export growth.

## Conclusion

The share of the developing countries in world trade is declining as the value of world trade expands. Some commentators (Kravis 1970) have, however, suggested that the failure of the LDCs to reap greater benefits from expanding world trade is substantially due to deficiencies in the economic policies and internal structures of these countries, and cannot be attributed simply to deficiency of demand for their products. It can also be argued that the LDCs declining share of trade is not as serious as it first appears. For a large and rapidly increasing component of the exports by developed countries is accounted for by reciprocal trade in similar manufactured products, e.g. motor cars exchanged for motor cars. Nevertheless there is widespread acceptance of the view that international trade has not worked to the advantage of the poorer nations in the manner anticipated by neo-classical economic theory. This feeling has been compounded by the increasing volume of literature which asserts that the institutions organising international trade operate to 'exploit' the LDCs. The growing acceptance of this, in spite of such evidence as exists of a positive relationship between growing exports and GNP in the LDCs (Kravis 1970), has led to an intensification of demands by the developing countries for measures to reform international trade. To the date of writing, the UNCTAD IV and North–South Conferences, which were convened to negotiate these major issues, have not achieved their objectives of trade reform. The North–South Conference was especially inconclusive, breaking down in November 1976 and making little progress towards trade reform when it was reconvened in the Spring of 1977. In the case of UNCTAD IV, no final agreement was achieved in 1976 on the measures to be implemented, but a moderately encouraging consensus was achieved in favour of some reform and a time-table was agreed for further negotiations. It was agreed that by the end of 1978 negotiations were to be completed relating to trade in 18 separate primary commodities, and that a negotiating conference be held no later than March 1977 to consider details for a Common Fund to finance buffer stocks of ten key commodities. Experience suggests, however, that whatever measures of reform are agreed in these negotiations, they are unlikely to re-order substantially the hierarchy of rich and poor nations, or to greatly reduce the wealth gap between them. Trade liberalisation measures plus special stabilisation measures are helpful to the developing countries, especially the better-off ones, but are unlikely to lead to large resource transfers. What is needed to accomplish this is acceptance by the rich countries of a high level of taxes for redistribution to the poor nations. This cannot be achieved on any scale by marginally adjusting the rules governing the forces of economic competition which generate international trade. In the case of most of the poorest LDCs trade liberalisation cannot be used as a substitute for grant aid. Moreover, expressions by the developed countries in support of trade agreements and liberalisation should not be interpreted as expressions of the necessary political will to radically alter the relationship between rich and poor countries.

## Notes

1 The expression 'New International Economic Order' emerged into everyday use from the sixth special session of the UN General Assembly in April–May 1974.

2 The data presented by Barratt Brown (1974, table 26, pp. 246, 247) confirm Bairoch's conclusions, but also, most interestingly, indicate that from 1796 to 1870 the net barter terms of trade of primary for manufactured goods almost doubled.

3 The normal operation of market forces will naturally lead to the substitution of export effort into more profitable lines thus partially offsetting adverse terms of trade effects. This process will lead not only to a switch to manufactured exports, but also to higher priced primary commodities.

4 A fuller discussion of the NIEO is given by Kirkpatrick and Nixson (1977).

5 Because sales and purchases of wheat by signatory nations were only partially covered by the quotas, and because the prices of the remaining transactions could take place outside the agreed range, the average price for all traded wheat could lie outside the price range for quota trade.

6 For a detailed examination and critique of the Lomé Convention see Wall (1976), from whose paper most of the details referred to here have been obtained.

7 For a good appreciation of compensatory finance schemes see Brown (1975, pp. 175–180).

## Bibliography

Ady P. (1969), 'International commodity policy', in Stewart I.G. (ed.) *Economic Development and Structural Change*, Edinburgh University Press.

Baer W. (1961/2), 'The economics of Prebisch and the ECLA', *Economic Development and Cultural Change*, Vol. 10, No. 2, reprinted in Livingstone I. (ed.) (1971), *Economic Policy for Development*, Penguin.

Bairoch P. (1975), *The Economic Development of the Third World since 1900*, Methuen.

Baldwin R.E. and Murray T. (1977), 'MFN tariff reductions and LDC benefits under the GSP', *Economic Journal*, Vol. 87, No. 345.

Balassa B. and Associates (1971), *The Structure of Protection in Developing Countries*, Johns Hopkins Press.

Beckford G.L. (1972), *Persistent Poverty: Underdevelopment in Plantation Economies of the Third World*, Oxford University Press.

Brown C.P. (1975), *Primary Commodity Control*, Oxford University Press.

Barrat Brown M. (1974), *The Economics of Imperialism*, Penguin.

Clement M.O., Pfister R.L. and Rothwell K.J. (1967), *Theoretical Issues in International Economics*, Houghton Mifflin.

Commonwealth Secretariat (1975), *Terms of Trade for Primary Commodities*, Commonwealth Economic Papers No. 4.

Emmanuel A. (1972), *Unequal Exchange*, New Left Books.

Erb G.F. and Schiavo-Campo S. (1969), 'Export instability, level of development, and economic size of less developed countries', *Bulletin Oxford University Institute of Economics and Statistics*, Vol. 131.

Fels G. and Glisman H.H. (1975), 'Adjustment policy in the German manufacturing sector', *Adjustment for Trade*, OECD Development Centre.

General Agreement on Tariffs and Trade (1974), *International Trade 1973/74*, Geneva.

Helleiner G.K. (1972), *International Trade and Economic Development*, Penguin.

Helleiner G.K. (ed.) (1976), *A World Divided: The Less Developed Countries in the International Economy*, Cambridge University Press.

Johnson Gale D. (1973), *World Agriculture in Disarray*, Fontana/Collins.

Kirkpatrick C.H. and Nixson F.I. (1977), 'The new international economic order: trade policy for primary products', *British Journal of International Relations*, Vol. 3.

Kitamura H. (1968), 'Capital accumulation and the theory of international trade', *Malayan Economic Review*, Vol. 3, No. 1. Reprinted in Livingstone I. (ed.) (1971) *Economic Policy for Development*, Penguin.

Kravis I.B. (1970), 'Trade as a handmaiden of growth: similarities between the nineteenth and twentieth centuries', *Economic Journal*, Vol. 80, pp. 850–872.

Little I., Scitovsky T. and Scott M. (1970), *Industry and Trade in Some Developing Countries*, Oxford University Press.

MacBean A.L. (1966), *Export Instability and Economic Development*, Allen and Unwin.

Maizels A. (1968), *Exports and Economic Growth of Developing Countries*, Cambridge University Press.

Morton K. and Tulloch P. (1977), *Trade and Development*, Croom Helm.

Murray T. (1973a), 'How helpful is the generalised system of preferences to developing countries?', *Economic Journal*, Vol. 83, No. 330.

Murray T. (1973b), 'EEC enlargement and preferences for the developing countries', *Economic Journal*, Vol. 83, No. 331.

Myint H. (ed.) (1971), *South East Asia's Economy in the 1970's*, Asian Development Bank/Longman.

Prebisch R. (1967), 'Commercial policy in the underdeveloped countries', *American Economic Review Papers and Proceedings.*

Schiavo-Campo S. and Singer H.W. (1970), *Perspectives of Economic Development*, Houghton Mifflin.

Stern E. and Tims W. (1975), 'The relative bargaining strengths of the developing countries', *American Journal of Agricultural Economics*, Vol. 57, No. 2.

Streeten P. (ed.) (1973), *Trade Strategies for Development* Macmillan.

Wall D. (1976), *The European Community's Lomé Convention 'STABEX' and the Third World's Aspirations*, Guest Paper No. 4, Trade Policy Research Centre.

Walter I. (1971), 'Nontariff barriers and the export performance of developing economies', *American Economic Review*, Vol. LXI, No. 2.

UNCTAD (1974), *An Integrated Programme for Commodities*, TD/B/C/1/166.

UN IBRD and IDA (1975), *Price Forecasts for Major Primary Commodities*, Report No. 814.

# 5

# The international setting: foreign exchange flows and indebtedness

It will be recalled from Chapter 2 that, according to the 'two-gap' theory, investment and hence growth may be restricted by the shortage of either domestic savings or foreign exchange. This argument rests on the assumption that some proportion of the capital items and intermediate inputs required for economic expansion have to be purchased from abroad using foreign exchange, and cannot be produced domestically. If domestic savings are not sufficient to enable acquisition of sufficient domestic resources to utilise fully the available foreign exchange for investment, a savings gap is assumed to exist. Alternatively, if foreign exchange availability is insufficient to permit all the available domestic savings to be invested then a foreign exchange gap is said to exist. If either of these gaps were to exist one of the two factors would be restricting investment and growth below the potential level permitted by the other factor. Note that either gap can only exist *ex ante* with respect to what might be achieved if more domestic savings or foreign exchange were available. There can be no gaps in an *ex post* sense, in that the necessary savings and foreign exchange flows must by definition have been available to permit whatever actual level of investment occurred. Thus the gaps can only be envisaged in terms of what could have been, rather than what has been the case.

In the literature (see, for example, Chenery and Bruno 1962, McKinnon 1964 and Chenery and Strout 1966), and by such international bodies as the World Bank, use has been made of the possible existence of a foreign exchange gap in LDCs to argue the need for official aid and other exchange flows from the developed countries, and to argue that increasing such flows would accelerate development in many countries. In the light of such advocacy, this chapter is devoted to examining some of the doubts which have emerged about the value of aid and foreign exchange flows to underdeveloped countries, and to the related issue of the external indebtedness of some countries in the wake of these flows. While inevitably this involves some reference to the role of official aid, as opposed to other types of foreign exchange flow, it must be emphasised that this is not a chapter about aid as such. Indeed, reasons of emphasis and space have dictated omission of detailed consideration of the efficacy and impact of specific forms of aid – only brief reference is made to them here.

## 5.1 Alternative Forms of Foreign Exchange

In examining the productivity to the underdeveloped countries of foreign exchange flows which are additional to export earnings, and which are therefore on the capital account of the balance of payments, a distinction needs to be made between (1) economic aid (which excludes military assistance) and (2) commercial loans and transfers. What distinguishes aid from commercial flows is that the former has a concessional element, either because it is given in the form of grants which are not required to be repaid, or because it is lent at below market interest rates, with long repayment periods, and often with a so-called 'grace period' which waives interest payments in the first few years after the loan. Flows in both categories may emanate from the government of the donor countries and be of an 'official' nature, or they may arise from the commercial activities of banks and firms and be 'private'. In fact, however, economic aid forms a relatively small proportion of private flows and is exclusively confined to the private grants of voluntary organisations (see table 5.1). After discounting grants, private flows are almost equally divided (see table 5.1) into (1) commercial loans and export credits by private banks and firms, to be repaid over typically short repayment periods at market rates of interest – often at variable interest rates in the current situation of fluctuating commercial rates, and (2) direct investment by firms. Both these types of flow have to be paid for by recipient countries. Loans have to be serviced by payment of interest and repayment (amortisation) of the principal, and direct investment is usually undertaken against the repatriation of profits and management fees. Thus both of the major private sources of foreign exchange tend, with a time lag, to have offsetting negative effects on the balance of payments of LDCs, and loans and credits (both public and private) are the source of their indebtedness.

Of course the concessionary loans which form part of official resource flows also add to indebtedness but, because of the concessionary element and the significant proportion of grants, official flows have a smaller impact upon indebtedness and have a lower cost to the recipient countries. For this reason, considerable importance attaches

**Table 5.1**: *Composition of net flows of resources from DAC to developing countries ($ billion)*

| | 1970 | 1971 | 1972 | 1973 | 1974 | 1975 | 1976(P) |
|---|---|---|---|---|---|---|---|
| (A) Official flows | 7.93 | 8.95 | 10.08 | 11.81 | 13.50 | 16.61 | 17.17 |
| (B) Private flows | 7.74 | 8.89 | 9.61 | 12.81 | 14.49 | 23.33 | 22.45 |
| (A) + (B) = (C) + (D) TOTAL | 15.67 | 17.84 | 19.69 | 24.62 | 27.99 | 39.94 | 39.62 |
| (C) Bilateral flows | | | | | | | |
| (C.1.1) Official development aid grants | 3.31 | 3.63 | 4.36 | 4.46 | 5.34 | 6.26 | 6.47 |
| (C.1.2) Private grants | 0.86 | 0.91 | 1.04 | 1.36 | 1.22 | 1.34 | 1.39 |
| (C.2) Official development aid concessional loans | 2.36 | 2.71 | 2.27 | 2.62 | 2.92 | 3.55 | 3.02 |
| (C.3) Direct investment | 3.54 | 3.63 | 4.47 | 6.71 | 7.06 | 10.33 | 8.02 |
| (C.4) Export credits and other lending | 4.00 | 4.84 | 4.98 | 6.95 | 8.46 | 12.40 | 13.42 |
| (D) Multilateral flows | 1.59 | 2.12 | 2.59 | 2.53 | 2.99 | 6.05 | 7.31 |

*Notes:* (1) P. signifies preliminary. (2) Items may not add up due to rounding. (3) Private grants are from voluntary organisations. (4) A high proportion of export credits are guaranteed by governments and are therefore official flows. (5) Nearly all the multilateral flows are official and can be classed as aid.

*Source:* World Bank Annual Report 1976, taken from table 3, p. 100.

to the growth in official, relative to private, flows. But from table 5.1, which indicates the magnitudes of these flows from the group of OECD countries which make up the Development Assistance Committee (DAC) that collectively supplies the bulk of aid and loans to the LDCs, it can be seen that since 1970 growth in private flows has greatly exceeded that in official flows. This signifies that the LDCs demand for foreign exchange (in excess of export earnings) has had increasingly to be satisfied at commercial rather than concessional rates. But, irrespective of whether borrowings are commercial or concessionary, unless such funds cause the receiving economy as a whole to generate additional foreign earnings plus savings (through import substitution) at a rate sufficient to leave a surplus after servicing the debt incurred, then they will have a negative effect upon its balance of payments which can lead to debt repayment problems. Precisely because a number of LDCs have encountered serious debt repayment problems and have had to reschedule payments under threat of default, the doubts which are the subject of this chapter have been raised about the effectiveness to LDCs of foreign aid and borrowings, and about the whole rationale of the two-gap theory that foreign exchange availability may be the critical constraint upon development.

Self-evidently, most private lending and the export credit element of official flows is made specifically for certain uses and is negotiated with firms or institutions to facilitate particular investment projects or to finance nominated import contracts. Similarly, much official aid is advanced for specific uses, and the recipient country has little flexibility in its use. This is obviously true of aid in kind, which may take the forms of food-aid (free or concessionary deliveries of products such as grain, flour or milk powder), items of machinery such as tractors, or of technical assistance personnel such as agronomists, engineers, teachers and so on. It is also true of grants and concessional loans which are donated or advanced against agreed projects for road building, harbour improvement, irrigation schemes and the like. In these latter cases the degree of flexibility the receiving country has for using the aid may be further restricted by contract clauses requiring that any import requirements for the assisted project must be purchased from the donor country. This sort of tying is especially common with bilateral aid, that is aid given directly from one country to another; for every donor country has an understandable wish to see that any export orders which may arise are placed with its own industries rather than with competitors, even though this may diminish the spirit of beneficence in giving the aid. By its very nature, aid given multilaterally is less restricted by such nationalistic considerations. Multilateral aid is that channelled through international organisations such as the World Bank, the Food and Agriculture Organisation, or the World Health Organisation, all of which operate under the umbrella of the United Nations. When aid is received through any of these institutions, it originates from all the countries which contribute to them through the United Nations, and hence is a multilateral contribution from many countries to the recipient. Because this eliminates the particular nationalistic pressures from the donors which is associated with bilateral aid, it has often been suggested (e.g. Pearson 1969, p. 215) that donor countries should switch more official aid from bilateral to multilateral channels.[1] There is, however, as table 5.1 indicates, little evidence of change in this direction over recent years, and donor countries have exhibited a strong preference for retaining control in their own hands. In one way this may be no bad thing; for, in so far as different countries have different priorities and attitudes towards the disbursement of aid, it allows for a greater range of experiments with forms of aid than would probably occur if most aid were channelled multilaterally through a few very large international organisations. But the major limitation of the effectiveness of bilateral aid is the tendency of donors to use it as an arm of trade policy, rather than as a straightforward aided transfer of resources.

From the recipient countries' point of view there can be no doubt that their preference is for aid with as few strings attached as possible, and on the cheapest possible terms. Thus their ideal is for financial grants in aid, which are not tied to specific imports or projects, but which are available to support general development programmes, i.e. the preference is for programme rather than project aid. But the desire of donor governments and international agencies to ensure that aid is used productively, and in an accountable way, means that most aid is given in project form. There is only a limited amount of aid which is not tied in some way. One example was the general budgetary aid which was given by Britain to some former colonies after their independence as a form of revenue support to the new governments; there is a limited amount of non-project aid advanced by the World Bank; and any concessionary elements in the compensatory finance schemes operated by the IMF and STABEX (see last chapter) may also be viewed as programme aid. But these do not amount to a very significant proportion of total aid, which consequently must be considered as being largely tied in varying degrees.

## 5.2 The Contribution of Aid and Foreign Exchange Flows to Development

In fact the debate about the benefits of aid and other foreign exchange flows to underdeveloped countries has been somewhat confused by the fact that analytically it is sometimes difficult to disentangle aid and non-aid flows to study their effects separately. Not only is it difficult to disentangle them, but the institutions of developed countries are happy to include private capital flows, and official 'hard' loans in with official aid, since this indicates their contribution to the LDCs to be larger than when aid flows alone are considered. Consequently, all foreign exchange inflows which balance the external accounts tend to be lumped together, and frequently what is referred to as aid is in reality a mixture of aid (grants and concessional loans), private loans, official loans and direct investment. While undoubtedly this has clouded the issue, some significant points have been raised about the contribution of aid/foreign exchange flows to LDCs.

As a starting point, general support might be expected to exist for one of the conclusions of the previous chapter, namely that economic grant-aid can be expected to make a positive contribution to the development of poor nations. For grant-aid would seem to represent an unambiguous addition of resources to the recipient country in the form of additional import-purchasing capacity, and might therefore be expected to increase GDP per capita. There are however those, for example Bauer (1971, Ch. 2) (and Griffin 1970, 1971, whose views are examined more fully below), who argue that the case for aid in general (including grant-aid) is by no means axiomatic and that aid will not automatically lead to greater development. Specifically, Bauer argues that aid may be inimical to greater self-reliance and to desirable structural reorganisation in recipient nations, and thus that aid as charity may be bad for the recipient. However, Bauer does concede that there are situations (not usually found in the poorest countries) in which the right entrepreneurial and institutional setting exists for aid to play a positive role in development and stimulating the economy of the recipient country. Nevertheless, we cannot agree with Bauer's assessment, and instead accept that aid, and more particularly grant-aid, has a positive role. Undoubtedly there are tales (possibly apocryphal) which have passed into the folklore of development studies, of grant-aid dispatched in the form of snowploughs to desert countries, and of tractors sent without implements and spare parts to countries with virtually no mechanics in rural areas. Such gross mistakes are, however, not characteristic, and there seems to be no strong reason to doubt that well thought out grant-aid can promote development.

Given the last assertion it is of interest to refer very briefly to the debate about the contribution of what is possibly the most important form of grant-aid (given that we have excluded military 'aid' from consideration), namely food-aid. Food-aid has been used for two distinctly different purposes. One has been to alleviate the localised effects on food supplies of natural disasters such as floods, droughts or earthquakes, and there is little argument that in such emergencies food-aid has an important role in preventing severe personal hardship and more acute economic disruption. The only queries which have arisen in this connection relate to the problems of deciding whether there is a genuine emergency, and of ensuring that the food reaches those most in need rather than being corruptly handled by those already provided for. The other role for food-aid has been to provide free or (more usually) cheap food, on a longer-term basis to countries with a chronic malnutrition/food supply problem. The main supplier of food on this basis has been the USA through its Public Law 480 programme, under which there have been extensive shipments of grain to India and other Asian countries. The efficacy of this has been seriously questioned (by, for example, Schultz 1960) principally on the grounds that free or concessionary food supplies will tend to depress food prices in the receiving country, which will in turn cause a highly undesirable reduction in domestic supply. Thus the argument is that food-aid designed to overcome domestic supply shortages may end up by making the shortage worse. However, according to Isenman and Singer (1977) such doubts are probably ill-founded, and their review of the evidence suggests that any disincentive effects of food-aid have been small given the scale on which food-aid has been given in the past.

As has already been stated, food-aid (as with all aid in-kind) falls into the more general category of 'tied' aid. The tying clauses in aid contracts involve the receiving country agreeing to place certain business orders in the donor country – obviously nothing is more completely tied in this sense than that the recipient agrees to accept the aid in the form of a shipload of food from the donor. All forms of tying clearly render aid an official arm of the donor country's trade (and in certain instances, foreign) policy, and diminish its status as a gift. There is no doubt, for example, that USA grain shipments of food-aid were not purely and simply the products of benevolence, but that they were influenced in the 1960s by the fact that the USA held large publicly owned stocks of grain as a by-product of her domestic grain price support policy. Similarly, there is little doubt that electorates in donor countries are more willing to support aid policies if they can see that any export orders which arise are passed to them rather than to competitors in other countries. From the recipient's point of view, however, the tying of aid will diminish its effectiveness if it results in the necessity to buy more expensive and less efficient products and services than could be obtained from sources other than the donor. The question which arises therefore is: by how much does the tying of aid reduce its value to the recipient? For reasons well and fully spelt out by Bhagwati (1967) there is no straightforward empirical answer to this question. But, within wide margins for error, attempts have been made to estimate the costs to the receiver of tying aid. For example, analysis by UNCTAD (1967) of some subset of tied credits led to estimates that, as a proportion of the nominal value of the aid, the cost of tying was 12.4% to Chile between 1964 and 1967, 15% to Iran in 1966–67, and 20% to Tunisia in 1965. These were considered to be conservative underestimates in each case, and this limited evidence suggests a cost for the types of project-tied aid studied of on average, at least 10% to 20%.

A more fundamental set of questions, attacking the efficacy of both aid and commercial exchange flows, has been raised by Griffin (1970) who has gone as far as to assert (p. 100) that 'capital imports, rather than accelerating development have in some cases retarded it.'

While Griffin's position provoked a highly critical response (in a collection of three papers in 1971 by Kennedy and Thirlwall, Frances Stewart and Eshag), particularly with respect to the empirical support for his arguments, some of the points he raises command attention, although some of his conclusions should be viewed with caution.

Perhaps the most important observations relate to the effects of foreign exchange inflows on domestic savings and consumption. Certainly the main point of dispute between Griffin and his critics revolves around Griffin's statements (reiterated in 1971, p. 158) that (1) 'given the level of income, the larger the capital inflow the lower the level of domestic savings', and (2) 'the higher is the ratio of aid to income the smaller will be the rate of domestic savings.'

The logic of Griffin's major argument for the first of these conclusions is not wholly sound, and must be seriously questioned. For, as is shown in note 2, there is certainly a basic algebraic flaw in a critical restatement of his views (in 1971) in his use of comparative static equilibrium analysis. This leads him to conclude, erroneously, that there is in theory a negative relationship between the levels of capital inflow and domestic saving when in fact, according to his own stated assumptions and definitions, the relationship is positive. Thus his attempts to prove his first point axiomatically with the conventional elementary assumptions of macroeconomic theory seems to be misconceived, and its formal justification requires a more complex model embodying assumptions, such as (one considered at length in his 1970 paper) that the marginal propensity to consume increases by more than a definable amount when foreign capital becomes regularly available to a country. That is, the first conclusion depends upon the second one holding in a particularly strong form, namely that the savings rate falls by more than a specifiable proportion of the increase in the capital inflow rate. Whether the evidence supports this strong version of the second hypothesis is debatable.

Certainly the evidence reviewed by Griffin, showing an inverse relationship between the saving and capital inflow ratios, has attracted much criticism. With some justification it has been argued that there are inherent biases in the cross-country form of analysis upon which most of the evidence is based. But Kennedy and Thirlwall (1971) and Papanek (1972) have gone further and argued that the causal mechanism may well be the reverse of that claimed by Griffin. Papanek puts forward the fairly convincing argument that, in years of low export prices or crop failures, the tendency is for consumption rates to be maintained and for the domestic saving rate to fall, which can only be accomplished if foreign capital inflows increase; thus it is low savings rates which cause high capital inflow rates. This argument, however, does not appear sufficiently general to prevent us from concluding that the evidence is consistent with the hypothesis that the saving ratio declines as capital inflows increase. This is perfectly plausible in poor societies with a high marginal propensity to consume, and can occur simultaneously with an increase in the level of saving. This behaviour can also be interpreted slightly differently, as indicating that some proportion of the foreign exchange inflow is used to raise domestic consumption and that not all of it is directly invested. That the evidence suggests this happens should engender no surprise, for not only do all societies tend to consume some proportion of the extra resources made available to them, but some types of aid, like food-aid, health and emergency aid, are deliberately designed to permit consumption and are not directly intended to promote investment. Clearly this cannot be deplored, and as Frances Stewart (1971) pointed out, in developing countries some forms of what are typically classed as consumption expenditure, such as nutrition, health and education, represent investment in human capital and may well raise growth rates. However, the essential point is, and this does not seem to be in dispute, that not all foreign capital flows can be treated as net additions to domestic saving and investment in the manner suggested by equation 2.3 in Chapter 2. Consequently, instead of such flows contributing to growth ($g$) at a rate $(A/Y)(1/k)$ they will only contribute $(1-c)(A/Y)(1/k)$ ($A$ = foreign capital inflow, $Y$ = national income, $k$ = the capital–output ratio, $c$ = the proportion of $A$ which is consumed). Futhermore, capital inflows may, as already discussed, influence the savings rate which may change from $s$ to $s'$. Thus the equation 2.3 may need to be restated as

$$g = \frac{s'}{k} + (1-c)\,\frac{A}{Y}\cdot\frac{1}{k} \tag{5.1}$$

and the contribution of capital inflows to growth will be

$$g_A = \frac{s' - s}{k} + (1-c)\,\frac{A}{Y}\cdot\frac{1}{k} \tag{5.2}$$

In Griffin's view, even this may overstate the contribution to growth of aid/foreign capital in so far as it may be used to finance projects and production techniques which have a higher capital–output ratio ($k'$) than those financed by domestic savings.[3] This possibility is envisaged as a consequence of transnational companies importing capital in connection with relatively capital-intensive processes, and because in the public sector aid is often channelled into capital-intensive rural development projects or infrastructure such as roads and railways which show a low direct rate of return but have a long productive life. However, as Chapter 10 makes clear, capital-intensive industrial processes in LDCs are not necessarily 'inappropriate' and may well have low capital–output ratios overall; also, infrastructure and other forms of public investment may well generate sizeable external economies in the form of benefits to private enterprises and individuals, so that the total rate of return to the economy may be higher than it immediately appears to be. Thus, arguably it is not relevant to query the contribution of foreign capital to development simply on the grounds that it is used to promote capital-intensive private and public projects. What is probably of more concern to critics who raise this point is the effects of capital inflows upon the economic and political structure of the recipient countries.

As regards the political effects, it has already been observed in Chapter 3 that the relationship which has emerged in many LDCs between the local power elite and both transnational corporations and major aid-giving bodies has often led to projects and actions which have not seemed to be in the best interests of development in its broader sense. Thus it has sometimes suited local elites, in terms of enhanced electoral appeal, to support the channelling of aid into prestige projects such as the building of large airports, super-highways and large irrigation projects. This has also been acceptable to the donors, who have often in the past (but to a decreasing extent) wished to have something to show for their money. But often, the show-piece projects have had low or negative returns, and the maintenance of the capital and services associated with them has been a major burden to the budgets of LDCs. Similarly, local elites have frequently found association with the activities of foreign companies to be personally rewarding, and so they have encouraged investment by such companies despite the doubts which exist about the developmental impact of penetration by foreign companies. These doubts are more fully aired in Chapter 2, section C and Chapter 9, but there is one aspect of them which deserves comment here. This is an issue which has been raised forcibly by Griffin (1970), and introduces a broader one about the rationale for the *ex ante* existence of a foreign exchange gap.

The specific issue relates to the impact of foreign exchange flows (other than those arising directly from exports) upon the import requirements for the growth of LDCs. Large aid projects and investment by foreign firms may act to raise import requirements in two ways. Firstly, they may, through the employment of predominantly skilled and expatriate labour cause the distribution of income to be tilted towards those with a high propensity to consume imported foodstuffs and luxury goods. Secondly, they may result in investment and production processes which have a high initial imported capital content and a continuing dependence upon imported intermediate goods and replacement capital. Thus foreign exchange flows on capital account may increase the propensity to import and create a long-term dependence of the economy upon imports. How does all this relate to the existence or non-existence of a foreign exchange gap? Well, if an *ex ante* foreign exchange gap is assumed to exist it rests, among other things, upon assumptions about the imports required to achieve target rates of growth. In effect these assumptions reduce to another, which is that domestic resources cannot be substituted for imported ones beyond a certain level. But it is clear that this assumption implies others about the future scale and types of foreign enterprises and aid projects, and about income distribution. Griffin's point (1970, p. 102) is that in the long run all of these are variables which can be adjusted by policy so as to reduce the ratio of imports to GDP. That is, (1) capital goods and import-substituting industries can be developed to reduce import dependence, (2) only projects which are orientated primarily to the use of domestically available inputs need be encouraged, (3) the income distribution can be adjusted in favour of those with a low marginal propensity to consume imports, and (4) imports of luxury goods could be severely restricted. Thus in the long run at least, in Griffin's view an *ex ante* foreign exchange gap has little meaning in that it involves assuming to be fixed things which are variable. This at once raises doubts about the appropriateness of using the concept of an exchange gap to justify increasing foreign exchange flows to LDCs on capital account, and it raises the question of whether the real issues are not about the ways in which such flows are employed in the LDCs to create import dependence, and about their effects upon income distribution and the structures of political power.

From all that has been said, it will be evident that some of the doubts raised about the contribution of aid/foreign exchange to the LDCs have a genuine basis. Certain tying restrictions in the giving of aid undoubtedly diminish its value to the recipient. The long-run consequences of aid and commercial transfers may well be associated with changes in economic and political structures, which may be held to have adverse consequences on certain of the dimensions of development (see Chapter 1) such as income distribution and national independence. There is no doubt also, as discussed in the next section, that some LDCs have encountered serious debt service problems as a result of borrowings made on capital account. But these reservations do not add up to a conclusion that aid and other exchange flows have made a negative contribution to development in a general sense. In any case a clear distinction must be made between alternative types of exchange flow. Most of the major queries must be held to relate to commercial loans and direct investment. But despite unease about long-term consequences of penetration by foreign firms and organisations – and in some cases, such as the extreme one of the British Phosphate Commission's exploitation up to 1970 of Ocean Island, the results have been disastrous for development – it would be foolish to deny that in many cases these have made an important contribution to growth and development of poor countries. Much depends upon the sector of the economy in which the foreign organisation operates, and on local controls over its operation.

In the case of grants and concessional aid there is much less doubt about their positive effects. There is no obvious reason why these should be employed in such ways that a significant proportion is consumed rather than invested, or that serious debt problems should arise. It is, however, true that aid has frequently been used for political ends by donor and recipient countries (governments) – for a full discussion of this see the book by Judith Hart (1973) – and that the full economic implications of many aid projects have not been fully anticipated, so that the economic returns to some projects have been low and in some cases negative. Such distortions are not inevitable concomitants of aid schemes, and there is no intrinsic reason why aid in most of its various forms should have anything other than a beneficial impact upon recipient countries.

## 5.3 The Problem of the LDCs External Indebtedness[4]

Most underdeveloped countries as well as some developed ones (e.g. the UK and Italy) are net debtors to other countries. Thus indebtedness is not uncommon and is not in itself necessarily a major problem. However, it becomes a serious problem when the burden of servicing the debt precipitates a balance of payments crisis and results in severe restrictions upon the conduct of domestic economic policy. Such a crisis occurs when a country, which has been financing a chronic deficit on its current trade account by foreign borrowings over a period of years, finds that additional credit is hard to obtain and its foreign exchange reserves have been exhausted. It is possible that in such circumstances additional credit will be available only at very high interest rates and short repayment periods, or in the last resort that only the IMF will provide external finance, subject to stringent conditions about changes in domestic policy.

The sort of policy changes required by an LDC to correct such a balance of payments crisis include the ordodox ones prescribed by macroeconomic theory, and have the basic objectives of reducing imports and expanding exports. In fact, however, most LDCs acting individually have little prospect of expanding exports in the short run to meet such a crisis, given that these are likely to be mainly of primary commodities for which there is little domestic demand that could be reduced to permit a switch for export. As regards reducing imports there are a number of policies that can be pursued. The standard prescriptions would be to deflate the domestic economy, cutting back demand for both imported consumption and investment goods, and to devalue the currency. General deflation is, however, particularly undesirable in poor countries with low levels of consumption and low rates of growth, especially when the heaviest burden is likely to fall on some of the poorest members of society. (Indeed, the main rationale for extensive foreign borrowing is that it obviates the need for deflation and (hopefully) it promotes the higher rates of growth needed to finance the loans). Also, straightforward devaluation may well not have the desired results: it is unlikely to have much impact upon export receipts, since (because of ready substitutability between supplies from different countries) there is normally a high elasticity of demand for an individual country's exports of primary commodities and unsophisticated manufactured products, and there should be little difficulty in finding markets for any available supplies of such products without needing to devalue. On the import side, devaluation may not have any marked effect either, unless there are suitable domestic substitutes for a wide range of imports. If there are not, devaluation will tend to promote domestic inflation. In any case, reducing imports of investment goods would have undesirable implications in slowing the future growth rate. In these circumstances it is hardly surprising that LDCs tend not to rely entirely upon general deflation and devaluation; they extensively supplement these by selective policies which aim to cut back imports of luxury and consumer goods, but to be more permissive to raw material and investment goods imports. Such selective control is often exercised by means of multiple exchange rates, with different rates for different classes of transaction, and by direct quotas, licensing controls, and tariffs on specific imports.

Given the limited opportunities for solving balance of payment crises by conventional macroeconomic policies, it is natural that the LDCs should have searched for alternative methods. One obvious line of approach has been to seek an increase in grant-aid, since this represents a straight gain to the balance of payments with no resulting indebtedness. The donor countries, however, have not responded with conspicuous energy in increasing grants to LDCs. On the contrary, in response to domestic political pressures against expanding foreign aid, grant-aid as a proportion of total aid has declined somewhat.

**Table 5.2:** *Capital movements in Latin America. Annual average 1961–1968 ($ million)*

| | | |
|---|---|---|
| 1. | Aid grants | 131.4 |
| 2. | Foreign loans | 938.0 |
| 3. | Amortisation of foreign loans | –310.9 |
| 4. | Interest on foreign loans | –186.8 |
| 5. | Net movement of grants and loans | 571.7 |
| 6. | US direct private investment | 360.5 |
| 7. | Profit and repayments on 6 | –1063.5 |
| 8. | Net movement of private capital | –702.6 |
| 9. | Net movement of all capital | –130.9 |

*Source:* Griffin (1970, pp. 99, 100)

Concern, particularly in Latin America, has also focused upon the large flows of repatriated profits from the LDCs to the headquarters of the transnational corporations (TNCs) in developed countries. This has become a major issue on account of allegations of excessive profits by the TNCs (discussed in Chapter 9), and of the total size of such transfers. Griffin (1970), for example, presents figures, shown here as table 5.2, which indicate that for Latin America between 1961 and 1968 annual repatriation of profits and other charges against private foreign investment exceeded the value of such investment by a factor of almost three, and that it exceeded the value of all loans and grants by a factor of almost two. It is hardly surprising that such a large source of strain to the balance of payments of Latin American and other countries should have come under close scrutiny for evidence of excess profits and discriminatory transfer pricing. In the last decade the LDCs have channelled considerable effort into devising contracts and regulations which try to control and monitor excess profits, transfer prices (accounting prices used in transactions between divisions of a transnational company) and management charges. Another line of attack which the LDCs have brought to bear on the problem of their external indebtedness is to seek reforms of the international monetary system. This has been a central objective of the call for a New International Economic Order, which includes demands for additional short- and medium-term trade credits and export guarantees, and for compensatory financing arrangements for any shortfall in export receipts. This question of compensatory finance (schemes for which are discussed briefly in the previous chapter) introduces the main key to the indebtedness problem, namely that it arises from a combination of a chronic failure to expand exports and limit imports and sharp adverse movements in the current account trade gap. For balance of payments crises are a product of a sudden or final loss of confidence by international bankers in a country's ability to cover a trade deficit. A sudden loss of confidence may occur when there is a sharp and unforeseen increase in a country's trade deficit due to, say, a deterioration in its terms of trade – a crop failure leading to a sharp cutback in export volume and earnings is less likely to affect banking confidence since it will usually be discounted as a temporary setback. When export prices fall or import prices rise, this may be seen in the present context as being equivalent to an unanticipated fall in the rate of return to borrowed capital, a fall which may make the initial borrowing uneconomic and its servicing difficult. Conversely, any improvement in the terms of trade makes loan servicing easier and reduces the real value of the outstanding debt. A balance of payments crisis may also arise when a country's repeated and prolonged failure to meet expected and target levels of performance on its trading account finally (and fairly suddenly) results in a loss of credibility in its creditworthiness. Such a situation is likely to occur if there are chronic weaknesses in a country's economic structure of the type discussed in Chapter 11.

Turning now to the scale of the indebtedness problem, one helpful indicator of this is the ratio of debt service charges (for interest and amortisation) to the value of exports. (The ratio of debt service charges to exports should not be confused with an alternative indicator which is referred to later: the ratio of foreign debt to exports. Naturally the latter ratio will always exceed the former.) For the underdeveloped countries as a whole the debt service to export ratio exceeds 15%, for South Asia as a whole and many of the Latin American countries it exceeds 20%, while for Egypt it even exceeds 35%. These figures, which have tended to increase to this level over time, indicate just how high a proportion of the value of the exports of LDCs would be needed to service their external debt. However, it does not appear to have been expected that the LDCs would finance such levels of debt servicing directly out of exports, and they have not been required to run the necessary current account surpluses that this would entail. For it is not in the interests of the richer countries to see their exports to the LDCs cut and their imports increased in order that the LDCs should pay off their debts. Rather, in the interest of full(er) employment and higher industrial activity domestically, the developed countries have preferred to advance extra credit to finance both the debt servicing charges and continued current account deficits of the LDCs. (It is against this background of always expanding credit to repay interest on existing debts that the idea of a debt moratorium gains respectability, since the situation of extending new credit to pay off old debts possesses a distinct air of unreality. This has in fact just recently (in late 1977) been recognised by Canada, Finland, The Netherlands, and Sweden, all of which have unilaterally cancelled the debt outstanding to them from a number of LDCs.) In this situation ever-expanding volumes of credit have to be advanced if there is to be a net flow of funds to the LDCs. For example, the Pearson Report (1969, p. 74) calculated that from 1965 to 1967 debt service costs as a percentage of gross lending were 73% in Africa, 52% in Asia, 40% in South Asia/Middle East and 87% in Latin America; and that if gross lending was maintained constant only at its 1965/67 average level these percentages would by 1977 rise to 121%, 109%, 97% and 103% respectively. To avoid such a situation of net repayment of debt by the LDCs, additional volumes of credit have to be advanced. As table 5.3 shows, this is precisely what has happened; lending to the group of 84 developing countries increased sufficiently to enable their disbursed debt to increase by 2.36 times from 51.3 to 121.2 billion US dollars between 1970 and 1975. The nominal cost of this debt almost certainly rose by more than the 2.36 times over the period when allowance is made for the rise in interest rates and (as also indicated by table 5.3) the increased proportion of private to official credit.

However, the large increase in nominal indebtedness overstates the rise in real indebtedness. This is because, as noted in the last chapter, there was a sharp rise in the prices of the exports of some LDCs, which between 1970 and 1975 did much to keep down the ratio of indebtedness to export value. In fact the IMF (1977) calculated (using an export price deflator with 1970 as the base) that the real value of the outstanding debt (including undisbursed debt) of 84 developing countries rose from US $71.2 billion in 1970 to about $100 billion in 1975, as against a nominal rise from $71.2 to $174.2 billion. However, since 1975 the export price index has fallen steadily for primary commodities and the terms of trade have moved back in favour of manufactured goods, so that the real value of the LDCs indebtedness has again risen sharply.

Needless to say, the extent to which indebtedness presents a problem varies considerably from country to country. Firstly, as indicated by table 5.3, the proportion of official to private debt increases as one moves from the richer to the poorer developing countries. To the extent that it is easier to arrange the rescheduling of official debts, this suggests that the poorest countries are less likely to be forced into a serious foreign exchange crisis. In a different dimension, as must inevitably be the case, recent movements in the terms of trade have been more beneficial to some countries than to others. Thus for example Zaire, heavily dependent for foreign exchange upon exports of copper, has been badly affected by falling copper prices. By 1976, according to estimates by the Bank of International

**Table 5.3:** *External public debt of 84 developing countries ($ billion)*

| | *1970* | *1971* | *1972* | *1973* | *1974* | *1975* |
|---|---|---|---|---|---|---|
| | *Debt outstanding (including undisbursed)* | | | | | |
| *Non-oil exporting countries* | | | | | | |
| Higher-income | 8.4 | 10.1 | 11.6 | 12.5 | 16.6 | 18.7 |
| Official creditors | 4.5 | 5.3 | 5.7 | 6.3 | 7.8 | 8.5 |
| Private creditors | 3.9 | 4.8 | 5.8 | 6.3 | 8.8 | 10.2 |
| Upper middle-income | 24.9 | 28.8 | 34.1 | 41.8 | 54.5 | 65.1 |
| Official creditors | 15.1 | 17.4 | 20.9 | 24.4 | 29.1 | 32.3 |
| Private creditors | 9.8 | 11.4 | 13.2 | 17.4 | 25.5 | 32.9 |
| Middle-income | 7.3 | 8.5 | 9.7 | 11.4 | 15.9 | 21.4 |
| Official creditors | 5.6 | 6.4 | 7.5 | 8.9 | 12.1 | 16.5 |
| Private creditors | 1.7 | 2.0 | 2.2 | 2.5 | 3.8 | 4.9 |
| Lower-income | 19.3 | 21.2 | 23.4 | 27.5 | 33.8 | 36.0 |
| Official creditors | 17.3 | 19.2 | 21.3 | 24.7 | 30.3 | 32.7 |
| Private creditors | 2.0 | 2.0 | 2.1 | 2.8 | 3.5 | 3.3 |
| *Oil exporting developing countries* | 11.2 | 15.0 | 18.1 | 23.8 | 27.1 | 33.1 |
| Official creditors | 7.8 | 10.2 | 12.1 | 15.0 | 16.4 | 16.8 |
| Private creditors | 3.4 | 4.8 | 6.0 | 8.8 | 10.7 | 16.4 |
| *84 developing countries* | 71.2 | 83.6 | 96.8 | 117.1 | 148.0 | 174.2 |
| Official creditors | 50.3 | 58.4 | 67.5 | 79.3 | 95.7 | 106.8 |
| Private creditors | 20.9 | 25.1 | 29.4 | 37.8 | 52.3 | 67.5 |

NB Undisbursed aid represents funds earmarked for lending but not yet called for by the recipient. It attracts a small interest charge, since potential recipients pay something to maintain the facility to borrow.

Settlements,[5] Zaire's total debt amounted to 163% of her average annual export earnings, and creditors have been forced to arrange rescheduling of loan servicing under threat of default. The same source estimated that in 1976 the debt to export value ratio was as high as 408% for Mexico, 298% for Chile (also dependent upon copper, and with a politically disrupted economy), 214% for Argentina and 208% for Brazil. These Latin American countries, which all had per capita incomes estimated in 1975 to exceed US $521, have all accepted large volumes of loans from predominantly private sources to finance extensive industrial, infrastructural and military investment. The result of the rapid monetary expansion caused by foreign capital inflows has been the exacerbation of domestic price inflation in these countries (which as we have argued in Chapter 11

| | *1970* | *1971* | *1972* | *1973* | *1974* | *1975* |
|---|---|---|---|---|---|---|
| | | | *Disbursed debt outstanding* | | | |
| *Non-oil exporting countries* | | | | | | |
| Higher-income | 6.3 | 7.1 | 8.1 | 9.5 | 11.8 | 13.2 |
| Official creditors | 3.1 | 3.4 | 3.8 | 4.6 | 5.3 | 5.8 |
| Private creditors | 3.2 | 3.6 | 4.3 | 5.0 | 6.5 | 7.9 |
| Upper middle-income | 18.0 | 20.7 | 24.2 | 29.5 | 38.1 | 48.2 |
| Official creditors | 10.2 | 11.7 | 13.4 | 15.5 | 18.4 | 20.8 |
| Private creditors | 7.8 | 9.0 | 10.9 | 14.0 | 19.7 | 27.2 |
| Middle-income | 5.5 | 6.3 | 6.8 | 7.7 | 9.2 | 12.8 |
| Official creditors | 4.0 | 4.6 | 5.0 | 5.8 | 6.7 | 9.5 |
| Private creditors | 1.5 | 1.7 | 1.8 | 1.9 | 2.5 | 3.3 |
| Lower-income | | | | | | |
| Official creditors | 12.8 | 14.6 | 16.2 | 18.2 | 21.0 | 23.2 |
| Private creditors | 1.3 | 1.4 | 1.6 | 1.9 | 2.3 | 2.4 |
| *Oil exporting developing countries* | 7.5 | 9.8 | 12.2 | 15.9 | 17.9 | 20.9 |
| Official creditors | 5.3 | 6.7 | 7.7 | 9.4 | 10.7 | 11.5 |
| Private creditors | 2.2 | 3.1 | 4.4 | 6.4 | 7.2 | 9.4 |
| *84 developing countries* | 51.3 | 60.0 | 69.0 | 82.7 | 100.3 | 121.2 |
| Official creditors | 35.4 | 41.0 | 46.1 | 53.5 | 62.0 | 70.9 |
| Private creditors | 15.9 | 18.9 | 22.9 | 29.2 | 38.2 | 50.2 |

*Source: IMF Survey : Supplement on International Lending,* 6 June 1977 p.186.

results from basic structural constraints with the LDC economy) and, with the exception of Brazil, they have all failed to make the necessary economic progress necessary to avert serious difficulties of debt rescheduling. Paradoxically therefore, it is perhaps some of the richer of the less developed countries which seem to face the most serious problems with their external debts.

## Notes

1 It should, of course, be said that multilateral donors also apply various pressures. In making funds available to LDCs such institutions as the World Bank and IMF apply 'leverage' to encourage LDCs into pursuing economic policies which the donor bodies consider appropriate. For a discussion of this issue see Hayter (1971).

2 The form of consumption function used by Griffin (1971, p. 158), is

$$C = d + a(Y + A)$$

where $C$ = consumption, $Y$ = a measure of national income (it is not precisely clear what measure, since the consumption is also assumed to be possible out of $A$), $A$ = capital inflows, $a$ = the marginal propensity to consume, and $d$ is an intercept constant. If one accepts this then the savings identity would seem logically to be

$$S = (Y + A) - C$$

rather than

$$S = Y - C$$

as suggested by Griffin. Using the correct savings identity, the savings function becomes

$$S = -d + (1-a)Y + (1-a)A$$

and not, as Griffin obtains,

$$S = -d + (1-a)Y - aA$$

This is a very significant difference. In contrast to Griffin's result which indicates that capital inflows are associated with a reduction in domestic savings, the correct result shows them to be positively associated with domestic savings.

3 In this case aid/foreign capital's contribution to growth should be formally restated as

$$g_A = \frac{s' - s}{k} + (1-c) \cdot \frac{A}{Y} \cdot \frac{1}{k'}$$

4 A good and fuller elementary analysis of this problem is contained in Chapters 1 and 2 of Payer (1974).

5 Reported on p. 10 of the *Financial Times*, 22 June 1977.

## Bibliography

Bauer P.T. (1971), *Dissent on Development*, Weidenfeld and Nicolson.

Bhagwati J. and Eckaus R.S. (1970) (eds), *Foreign Aid*, Penguin.

Bhagwati J.(1967), 'The tying of aid', *UNCTAD Secretariat: Progress Report*, TD/7/Supp 4, United Nations, 1967. Reprinted as Ch. 10 of Bhagwati and Eckaus (1970).

BOUIES (1971), 'Foreign capital, domestic savings and economic development: three comments and a reply', *Bulletin of Oxford Institute of Economics and Statistics*, Vol. 33, No. 2.

Chenery H.B. and Bruno M. (1962), 'Development alternatives in an open economy: the case of Israel', *Economic Journal*, Vol. 72.

Chenery H.B. and Strout A.M. (1966), 'Foreign assistance and economic development', *American Economic Review,* Vol. 61, No. 4, Pt. 1.
Eshag E. (1971), 'Comment', in BOUIES (1971).
Griffin K. (1970), 'Foreign capital, domestic savings and economic development', *Bulletin of Oxford Institute of Economics and Statistics,* Vol. 32, No. 2.
Griffin K. (1971), 'Reply', in BOUIES (1971).
Hart J. (1973), *Aid and Liberation,* Gollancz.
Hayter T. (1971), *Aid as Imperialism,* Penguin.
IMF (1977), *Survey: Supplement on International Lending,* 6 June.
Isenman P.J. and Singer H.W. (1977), 'Food aid: disincentive effects and policy implications', *Economic Development and Cultural Change,* Vol. 25, No. 2.
Kennedy C. and Thirlwall A.P. (1971), 'Comment', in BOUIES (1971).
McKinnon (1964), 'Foreign exchange constraints in economic development and efficient aid allocation', *Economic Journal,* Vol. 74.
Papanek G.F. (1972), 'The effect of aid and other resource transfers on savings and growth in less developed countries', *Economic Journal,* Vol. 82, No. 327.
Payer C. (1974), *The Debt Trap,* Penguin.
Payer C. (1976), 'Third World debt problems: the new wave of defaults', *Monthly Review,* Vol. 28, No. 4.
Pearson L.B. (Chairman) (1969), *Partners in Development: Report of the Commission on International Development,* Pall Mall Press.
Schultz T.W. (1960), 'Value of US farm surpluses to underdeveloped countries', *Journal of Farm Economics,* Vol. 42. Reprinted as Ch. 12 of Bhagwati and Eckaus (1970).
Stewart F. (1971), 'Comment', in BOUIES (1971).
UNCTAD (1967), *UNCTAD Secretariat: Progress Report* TD/7/Supp 8, United Nations.

# 6
# Agricultural transformation and economic development

During the process of economic development the agricultural sector is transformed, both internally and in its relationship with other economic sectors. The dimensions of this transformation are not only economic, but include formal and informal institutional changes which are sociological or political in character.

Examination of these changes can be pursued from a predominantly historical standpoint by analysing in detail the actual processes of transformation in different societies in the past (Ohkawa and Rosovsky 1960, Boserup 1965). Alternatively, the process may be examined with a pronounced policy orientation by developing simplified models of change to use in posing questions about what should occur for economic development to achieve specified goals, or what might occur in specified circumstances (Lewis 1954, Ranis and Fei 1961, Nicholls 1963, Jorgenson 1970). In fact there is a degree of complementarity between the two approaches, the historical study serving to isolate apparent key changes and their nature as a basis for the specification of the theoretical models. It is apparent, however, that this complementarity cannot be complete as there is no obvious reason why the pattern of historical development of any now rich countries should be closely followed by any of the currently poor nations in their quest for material advance. Not only does an international pool of technology and experience exist which might enable the poor countries to shortcut some of the steps taken by the now rich nations, but the environment facing the poor countries is substantially different in a largely adverse way from that faced by the rich nations before their industrial development; population growth rates are far higher in poor nations today than they were in Europe in the eighteenth and nineteenth centuries; commercial competition for export markets is now more intense; the material expectations of people are higher because of external contacts through different media; and the rate of technological advance in the rich countries gives them a remarkable and seemingly ineradicable edge in economic competition. Nevertheless, it is accepted that there are some general characteristics of the development process which on historical evidence will feature in the transformation of now poor countries as and when their development intensifies. For the agriculture sector, certainly, there is a consensus about the basic pattern of change, and this will be briefly considered below.

The main reason for attempting to identify characteristic transformation patterns is to assist in the formulation of policies to accelerate development. If a clear view can be formed in advance of the required structural change in a national economy, particularly with respect to the changing relationship between sectors, then it should be possible to frame more effective policies to speed up development and to avoid potential bottlenecks and blockages to change. Thus, after considering some general aspects of structural transformation in development, in particular those concerned with agriculture, it is logical to proceed to discussion of the policy choices poor countries face in expediting development. Ideally the links between agriculture and other sectors of the economy require that policy strategies start with an integrated approach in which the choice of agricultural policy is conditioned by the choices made for the public and various industrial sectors of the economy. That such integration is necessary is clearly indicated by the discussion of theories of development (Chapter 2), and from the observation (Balassa *et al.* 1971) that commercial policies pursued by poor countries to foster industrialisation have often had effects which might inhibit agricultural expansion. Nevertheless, for expository purposes agricultural development policies will have to be considered principally from a narrowly agricultural standpoint.

Before proceeding further, qualification is necessary regarding the definition of the 'agricultural sector'. Because of the attempts by analysts to simplify their exposition of development theories and issues, there is a tendency to use the 'agricultural sector' label loosely to describe different concepts. Thus in two-sector theoretical models large-scale commercial agriculture has been classed as part of the capitalist, industrial sector, and the term 'agricultural' is applied to the whole non-capitalist, subsistence sector (Ranis and Fei 1961, Jorgenson 1970). Thus using this definition all people in domestic service, or in the urban informal sector (shoe-shine 'boys', petty thieves, etc.) are lumped together with peasant farmers, rural labourers, village craftsmen and the openly unemployed, as belonging to the agricultural sector. In fact, the number 'employed' in the urban informal sector plus the number of urban unemployed is typically large in the major cities of developing countries and constitutes one of the most serious modern social and political problems in these countries. It may seem highly arbitrary to classify agricultural employment in a way which includes such people. It is often the case, however, that these fringe urban dwellers retain close links with their rural origins, and are supported by relatives in rural areas while seeking to establish an urban economic base. Given their skills and rural contacts they could, if the opportunity were created, probably be drawn back into agricultural (or rural) employment more readily than they could be assimilated into industrial occupations.

In a different set of contexts the terms of agricultural and rural are often used interchangeably, while a similar tendency is followed in equating industrial with urban. In fact the rural sector contains much more economic activity even in poor countries (Colman and Garbett 1976) than just primary agriculture, i.e. farming. In addition to service activities for farming at both the input supply and product marketing ends, the rural areas provide a wide range of employment activities serving basic human needs, e.g. weaving, pottery, house construction, etc. Thus, if rural development is defined as improved living standards for the non-urban population, it must be recognised that success in agricultural development may not be synonymous with that in rural development. Indeed, the latter may be greatly influenced by industrial policy towards small-scale and craft industries (Myrdal/King 1971, Ch. 20). Having remarked upon this distinction it is important to note that the ensuing discussion will largely confine itself to the effects of agricultural policy choices upon output and employment in farming, although in discussing choices of technology reference will be made to the forward and backward linkages from farming which generate a potential source of additional employment in the rural areas.

## 6.1 Key Features of Agriculture's Transformation

One universally recognised feature of structural economic change is that, as countries develop, the proportions of GDP and employment accounted for by agriculture must decline. This stands to reason, for improved living standards entail an increasing personal consumption of goods and services other than food, and this necessitates a concomitant rise in the proportion of human and other resources allocated to non-agricultural production. It has escaped few people's attention that in the rich countries of Western Europe and the USA agriculture accounts for less than 10% of the labour force, while in many of the poorest countries less than 20% of active population are supported by employment outside the agricultural sector (see table 6.1). This observation has been central to the perception of how development

**Table 6.1** *Population engaged in agriculture and income levels per capita in selected countries 1960 and 1970*

| | *Percentage of economically active population involved in agriculture* | | *Income per capita (US $)* | |
|---|---|---|---|---|
| | *1960* | *1970* | *1960* | *1970* |
| Central African Republic | 94.1 | 87.2 | n.a. | 122 |
| Kenya | 85.8 | 80.4 | 81 | 130 |
| Ghana | 61.5 | 54.8 | 182 | 238 |
| Malawi | 92.5 | 87.5 | 36 | 68 |
| Nigeria | 70.8 | 67.0 | n.a. | 125 |
| Tanzania | 89.4 | 85.9 | 52 | 94 |
| | | | | |
| Burma | 68.3 | 63.7 | 57 | 73 |
| India | 74.1 | 67.7 | 69 | 94 |
| Indonesia | 74.8 | 70.0 | 77 | 98 |
| Malaysia | 63.6 | 56.5 | 250 | 293 |
| Nepal | 94.4 | 91.6 | n.a. | 75 |
| Pakistan | 76.0 | 70.5 | 78 | 165 |
| South Korea | 66.4 | 58.0 | 148 | 252 |
| Thailand | 83.8 | 76.5 | 93 | 167 |
| Turkey | 78.2 | 69.1 | 197 | 352 |
| | | | | |
| Egypt | 58.5 | 54.8 | 123 | 202 |
| Iran | 53.9 | 46.3 | 176 | 352 |
| Iraq | 53.2 | 46.6 | 198 | 311 |
| Libya | 55.8 | 42.6 | 137 | 1450 |
| Saudi Arabia | 71.5 | 60.5 | n.a. | 495 |
| | | | | |
| Brazil | 51.9 | 43.7 | 196 | 368 |
| Chile | 29.8 | 25.4 | 245 | 614 |
| Colombia | 51.5 | 45.2 | 225 | 366 |
| Mexico | 55.1 | 46.6 | 315 | 653 |
| Peru | 52.5 | 45.6 | 191 | 293 |
| | | | | |
| Australia | 11.4 | 8.4 | 1438 | 2644 |
| Canada | 13.1 | 8.0 | 1909 | 3364 |
| Ger. Fed. Republic | 14.3 | 9.3 | 1198 | 2708 |
| Japan | 32.9 | 20.7 | 417 | 1636 |
| UK | 4.0 | 2.8 | 1263 | 1972 |
| USA | 6.6 | 4.0 | 2559 | 4294 |
| USSR | 42.1 | 31.9 | n.a. | n.a. |

*Source:* UN, FAO, *Production Yearbook*, 1973, and UN, *National Account Statistics*, 1973 and 1974.

should occur, and of the role the agricultural sector should play in this. The relationship between industrialisation and development led many developing countries to adopt, until recently, rather negative policies towards agriculture (e.g. India in its second 5-year plan, and the USSR until very recently), and to transfer a disproportionate amount of government controlled investable resources into industry. It was anticipated, in line with the historical precedents of the USA and Western Europe, that rapid expansion of industry would create demand for labour on a scale that would require a transfer of labour from the agricultural and handicraft sectors. This in turn would raise rural living standards, and would reduce population pressure on the land in the most populous countries thus paving the way for the re-organisation of agriculture into larger sized holdings. It would also require an increase in agricultural efficiency for a sufficiently large marketable food surplus to be transferred to the burgeoning urbanised industrial labour force and their families. Also, because of the dominance of the agricultural sector in poor countries, it was evident that the capital to finance industrial expansion, at least in the early stages of development, would have to be largely raised from agriculture by taxation, voluntary transfer (savings) or by encouraging the terms of trade to move against agriculture and in favour of industrial goods; apparently in Japan at the end of the 19th century over 80% of the central government tax revenue was contributed by the land tax (Ohkawa and Rosovsky 1960).[1]

Kuznets (1961) has succinctly summarised these changing relationships between agriculture and the rest of the economy in terms of three contributions to development. Firstly, there is the 'product contribution' whereby an increasing amount of food is supplied to the expanding non-agricultural population, and industrial crops are produced as a basis for processing industry. Secondly, there is the 'factor contribution' through which agriculture supplies the rest of the economy with labour and a net outflow of capital; it is perhaps emphasis on these aspects of change which led to some of the more negative aspects of agricultural policy, i.e. those of squeezing as much as possible out of agriculture. Thirdly, there is the 'market contribution' whereby agricultural revenue from cash sales (domestically and for export) creates a demand for products of the industrial sector; agricultural exports also create a flow of foreign exchange which can be used to purchase capital items from abroad. Inadequate allowance for this third factor may partially account for the under-utilisation of the industrial capacity created by India in the 1950s.

With hindsight there is no doubt that in the 1950s and 1960s economists and others were over-optimistic in their assessment of the time scale within which industrial expansion would bring about a reduction of the labour force in agriculture. To a large extent this must have been due to a failure to appreciate just how much more rapidly the populations of poor countries are growing than was the case in rich countries at a comparable stage in development; it was also due to a failure to anticipate just how capital-intensive industrialisation has been. As indicated in table 7.1 in Chapter 7 the annual population growth of the poorest areas of the world in the last decade varied between 2.5% for the Far East and 2.9% for Latin America. This compares to population growth rates for the Western European countries during the 18th and 19th centuries, in the 40 to 60 years preceding the start of their industrial development, of 0.5% to 0.7% per annum (Bairoch 1975, p. 8).

It is a simple matter to calculate (following Dovring 1959) that, if the total labour force of a poor country is growing at 2.5% annually and agricultural employment accounts for 80% of the total (as it does in several of the poorest countries, e.g. Tanzania), then non-agricultural employment must increase at 12.5% annually if the agricultural labour force is not to expand.[2] The higher the rate of population growth and the smaller the initial size of the non-agricultural sector the greater must be the rate of growth in the non-agricultural labour force to prevent expansion of the agricultural population.

Even though, as indicated by table 8.1 in Chapter 8, the rates of industrial growth in poor nations have recently been high by the historical standards of the now rich countries, they have not in most poor countries proved high enough to forestall an increase in the numbers who have had to be absorbed into the agricultural sector. As Bairoch's interesting table shows (reproduced here as table 6.2), even in the recent period from 1950 to 1970, in the less developed countries agriculture absorbed 131 million out of an estimated increase of 235 million in the economically active population. True, over the same period, the overall proportion of the active population in agriculture is estimated to have fallen from 73.3% to 66.0% of the total, which conforms to the broadly expected pattern of transformation.[3] Nevertheless the large recent increase in the numbers primarily dependent upon agriculture presages yet further increase at least until the end of this century. For many poor countries this invalidates entirely strategies based on the assumption that industrial expansion will cause a reduction in the agricultural labour force. It also complicates the issue of how a large and increasing marketable surplus of food is to be produced. Note in this connection that (a) if the non-agriculturally employed population is increasing at 10% annually the marketed food surplus will, to avoid increased food imports, have to rise faster than this to allow for the additional demand created by any growth in the incomes of urban dwellers, (b) for there to be any increase in the marketed surplus the rise in productivity per acre devoted to food will need to exceed the rate of growth in food demand from the

**Table 6.2** *Changes in the structure of the active population of the less-developed countries between 1900 and 1970, according to type of employment*

| | *1900* | *1920* | *1930* | *1950* | *1960* | *1970* |
|---|---|---|---|---|---|---|
| *Percentages:* | | | | | | |
| Agriculture | 77.9 | 77.6 | 76.6 | 73.3 | 70.7 | 66.0 |
| Extractive industries | | 0.4 | 0.4 | 0.6 | 0.6 | |
| Manufacturing industries | 9.8 | 8.5 | 8.5 | 7.6 | 8.9 | 13.0 |
| Construction | | 1.0 | 1.1 | 1.8 | 2.0 | |
| Trade, banking | | 5.4 | 5.4 | 5.8 | 5.9 | |
| Transport, communications | 12.3 | 1.6 | 1.8 | 2.0 | 2.2 | 21.0 |
| Services | | 5.5 | 6.1 | 8.9 | 9.6 | |
| Total | 100.0 | 100.0 | 100.0 | 100.0 | 100.0 | 100.0 |
| *Absolute figures (millions):* | | | | | | |
| Agriculture | 213.0 | 238.0 | 249.0 | 304.0 | 366.0 | 435.0 |
| Extractive industries | | 1.1 | 1.3 | 2.5 | 3.2 | |
| Manufacturing industries | 26.5 | 26.0 | 27.7 | 31.5 | 46.0 | 85.0 |
| Construction | | 2.9 | 3.6 | 7.2 | 10.6 | |
| Trade, banking | | 16.4 | 17.6 | 24.2 | 30.8 | |
| Transport, communications | 33.5 | 4.9 | 6.0 | 8.3 | 11.4 | 140.0 |
| Services | | 16.9 | 19.9 | 37.0 | 49.9 | |
| Total | 273.0 | 306.0 | 325.0 | 415.0 | 518.0 | 660.0 |

*Source:* Bairoch (1975, p. 160).

increasing number of people engaged in agriculture, (c) that any tendency of the prices of export crops to rise more rapidly than domestic food prices will lead to a diversion of acreage from food production for the domestic market, but (d) that if non-agricultural population is proportionately small it should be comparatively easy to expand the marketed surplus since it will be only a small proportion of total food production. Of course, there is always the possibility that the urban population's food requirements can be met by imports rather than from domestic sources, but that reduces the capacity to import capital goods and acts as a brake on development.

Indeed, one thing on which there is wide agreement is that a large and increasing domestically produced agricultural surplus is a necessary condition for successful economic development (see the section on dual economy models in Chapter 2), and it is instructive to observe that the currently rich countries were favoured with access to ample cheap food supplies during the 18th and 19th centuries at the start of their industrialisation.[4] To generate such a surplus in the now poor countries with low agricultural productivity and rapidly increasing populations requires positive policies involving substantial investment in agriculture. And the key issue in most poor countries is to find policy strategies which can simultaneously raise agricultural output and create sufficient jobs to prevent massive growth in the numbers of the landless unemployed[5] – it is accepted that in many less developed countries unemployment exceeds 15% and that the rate of growth of unemployment may well be rapid.

If agricultural output and productivity are to increase, it is necessary to increase the supply of both traditional and unconventional factors of production. To the extent that additional supplies of the main traditional factor, land, are small in most countries, expansion rests mainly on increasing supplies of non-conventional inputs, e.g. improved and hybrid seeds, inorganic fertilisers, pesticides, irrigation equipment, and machinery. Many of the central issues of agricultural development revolve around what combination of these factors should be adopted, and by which farmers. The choice, as we shall see in more detail below, affects not only the extent of new job creation within agriculture, but also the extent to which agriculture's input needs can be met by local industrial development as opposed to imports. Governments in poor countries are typically involved in accelerating and steering technological change in agriculture (although often without directly perceiving this), and they actively participate in organising the delivery of new inputs to the sector.

There are other features of agricultural transformation which, although possibly less important than those mentioned above, have significance for policy formation. As per capita incomes rise not only does aggregate food demand increase, but there is a shift in the types of food demanded. In particular, consumption of staple grains and starchy roots tends to decline while that of sugar, meats, dairy products and vegetables increases. To cater for these changes requires, among other things, mounting emphasis on technical improvement in the livestock sector, plus development and improvement of the marketing system for highly perishable foodstuffs. Such changes typically require detailed involvement by government agencies, especially in developing road and rail infrastructure to carry the increasing volume of interregional trade.

## 6.2 The Scope of Agricultural Planning

Before proceeding to examine policy strategies for agriculture it is appropriate to consider, briefly and in only the most general terms, how the prevailing philosophy about planning may influence such strategies and more particularly the tactics employed to execute them. For, with the exception of policies of complete laissez-faire, development strategies imply intervention to alter the course of events, which in turn presupposes the existence of plans with targets, and of organisations to execute the plans. Planning however, is not just an economic activity. It is carried out by political authorities and, inevitably, political considerations influence most aspects of plan formulation and implementation. Indeed, as Wallerstein observes (in Bernstein 1973, pp. 279-280), 'the political institution of the state was critical to the process of economic development whether under a capitalist or a socialist mode'. To him, 'the essential problem of economic development can be posed as follows: How is it possible to install and maintain in power a regime with the will and the possibility to transform the social structure in such a way that would make possible a dramatic rise in productivity and investment, when the possibility is based on somehow insulating government from the various pressures to consume its surplus immediately.' This element of controlling the investable surplus and directing it to appropriate productive use is the key economic feature of planning. In countries with socialist or national revolutionary governments, planning is clearly more comprehensive, in the sense of the extent of reliance upon detailed directives for action, than in mixed economies with large private sectors. For as Lange (in Bernstein 1973, p. 214) says, 'with regard to the private sector, the plan has not the power of directive, but is a desire expressed which must be followed by creating such incentives as will induce producers to do exactly the things which are required of them in the plan.'

Central coordination of activities implies suspension or the overriding of some traditional market institutions, and their substitution or augmentation by state institutions to perform similar roles. In fact the justification for planning lies in the observation that there are inherent weaknesses in many of the traditional market institutions. Amongst what he calls a considerable list of such market defects, Cochrane (1974, p.49) includes that (a) income is not fairly distributed under a laissez-faire system, (b) the market mechanism is oblivious to the basic rights of each worker, (c) the market economy is unstable, (d) the market economy is ineffective in coping with major changes, and (e) the market economy is wasteful. While it is not necessary to amplify all of these points, it should be noted with respect to point (b) that in the agricultural sector the market allocates the returns from output in conjunction with what are often very complex systems of land use rights. Hence the effects of the market system cannot be examined independently of the systems of land ownership and tenure, and agricultural policies usually reflect concern that these systems give rise to large inequalities in agricultural incomes. Also, in respect of point (d), it is worth observing again that the slow natural rate of evolution of traditional market institutions is unlikely to meet the demands of rapidly growing trade in agricultural products and inputs.

Despite widespread acceptance of various weaknesses in market institutions, particularly in poor countries, the case for government intervention needs to be qualified by consideration of the efficiency of public institutions, and as Arthur Lewis has argued there is

> no *a priori* case for using the State in place of other social institutions which serve the same purpose ... The issue between planning and laissez-faire is whether we can use the visible controls of state action to improve on the invisible social controls exercised by the market ... The principal objective of planning by direction should be to overcome immobilities, and the speed with which this is achieved is the true measure of the quality of planning.
>
> (Lewis 1949, p. 28)

In fact, of course, there is little disagreement that there are some functions requiring the intervention of the state, e.g. in providing agricultural extension services to farmers, or that there should be some state planning. In any case argument has been pre-empted by the fact that the governments of all nation states have accumulated and adopted various powers of economic management. Where there is room for dispute is over the desirable extent of planning and the form which it should take. These issues have strong and undeniable political overtones. At the one extreme we have those who propose as models for the poor countries either the Chinese or the Russian agricultural systems in which private land ownership is all but abolished and where allocation of inputs and outputs is largely centrally controlled.[6] Simultaneously there are those who propose that the poor highly populated countries would do well to emulate Japan and Taiwan, where dynamic results have been achieved through extensive planning without abandonment of private property rights or usurpation of the allocative functions of markets. At the same time there are minimalists like Bauer (1971) who feel that often planning organisations perform with no greater efficiency than the institutions they supplant, and that reliance upon them should be restricted.

The issues raised by these alternative viewpoints are far too extensive to be dealt with comprehensively here. For example, it is not possible to do more than consider the significance of certain broadly defined policy strategies and some of the main groups of policy instruments which may be used to pursue them. Those readers interested in a greater depth of treatment of agricultural development policy should consult such specialist texts as Griffin (1974), Johnston and Kilby (1975), Hayami and Ruttan (1971), Southworth and Johnston (1967), Eicher and Witt (1964).

Nor is it possible to explore here the question of appropriate organisational structures for the implementation of agricultural policy. In fact this is a very important topic, which increases in significance as planning becomes more comprehensive and requirements increase for experienced and trained administrators and specialists, resources which are especially scarce in most poor countries. Many criticisms of comprehensive planning arise precisely because of shortcomings in administrative and organisational capacity. Thus the significance in planning of effective manpower utilisation and appropriate organisational structure is almost as large as that of formulating the broad plan objectives. It is a topic which is increasingly prominent in the development literature (Cochrane 1974, Chs 4,7; Hunter 1969, Chs 3, 7, 8; Helleiner 1968).

## 6.3 The Attributes of Peasant Farmers

In poor countries a relatively small number of large or modern agricultural holdings, which provide a large proportion of the marketed output, exist alongside a vastly larger number of subsistence or peasant holdings on which the primary activity is producing basic foods for home consumption, with surplus land and labour resources devoted to producing crops and livestock products for sale (cash crops).[7] The peasant holdings may be very small, no greater than four acres on average in some parts of Africa, and they provide a meagre livelihood for up to 60% of the world's population. Inevitably, therefore, agricultural development economics tends to be dominated by consideration of how to modernise the subsistence sector and increase its orientation to producing for the market, while the problems of the large-scale sector of agriculture are relegated to second place on the assumption that they are easier to handle.

The problems of modernising subsistence agriculture are undeniably great. In the first place most poor countries lie in the tropics, which poses agricultural and other difficulties of far greater dimensions than those of temperate climates. A good catalogue of these problems is presented by Dumont (1966, Ch. 1), who is moved to note that 'none of the great modern economic powers . . . has developed under tropical conditions' and to further quote others who question whether such achievement is possible. This may be over-pessimistic as the recent rapid economic growth of Brazil suggests, but they do highlight the special problems of development in the tropics.

From the purely human point of view the problems have appeared not much less formidable. Subsistence cultivators employ rudimentary farming techniques. In much of Africa the only traditional source of cultivation power is human, and the cultivation implements are often no more sophisticated than a hoe and slasher. True, in Asia bullocks have long been harnessed for draft and transport power, but basic techniques are simple. Everywhere in traditional agriculture fertiliser use is minimal and seeds are of local origin, kept back from one season's harvest for planting in the next. Crop yields employing this technology tend to be very low, and for unirrigated grain crops yields may average as little as 20% to 30% of those obtained in Western Europe. Livestock husbandry in the traditional setting tends to be even less effective, with low rates of productivity and high rates of mortality.

A typical caricature of the operators of subsistence holdings in whatever continent, is that they are illiterate, poorly nourished, probably debilitated by endemic disease, and bound by a set of traditional beliefs which are counter-productive to efforts of modernising the sector.[8] The task of converting such cultivators into highly productive 'modern' farmers with an improved standard of living is obviously a daunting one. To some it is so daunting that an alternative strategy should be pursued. This might involve either concentrating resources in the large-farm sector coupled with policies to encourage the formation of larger capitalistic farming units, or it might involve the amalgamation of small subsistence holdings into large cooperatively or communally managed units with a non-traditional administrative structure. There is, in principle, no reason why these strategies should not create as much employment for the increasing rural population as the alternative of modernising small individually owned (or rented) and operated holdings. However, in practice, there appears to be a tendency for them not to do so for reasons elucidated below, and there exists strong support for development based on small owner-occupied family holdings.

The picture of the economic performance of subsistence cultivators is, however, not entirely negative and discouraging. In many different farming conditions where subsistence cultivators exist, there are always individuals or groups of small farmers who have demonstrated a progressive and innovative spirit in searching out new products and techniques without waiting for the specific intervention of public officials. The existence of such progressive farmers is recognised in various countries by allotting them priority in the allocation of scarce public resources; this type of policy leads to dualistic agricultural development in which the position of the large and more progressive farms steadily improves relative to that of the mass of small subsistence holdings and the problems of this dualistic or bimodal strategy are returned to below.

Further encouragement has been created by the successful response of some peasant producers to well thought out official smallholder projects, e.g. the smallholder tea growers in Kenya, smallholder sugar growers in Swaziland, and rice farmers in the Philippines and Taiwan.

Theoretical and empirical research into the economic behaviour of peasant families has also served to create a more positive picture of them as rational economic actors, and to counter the ultra-conservative, anti-progressive image. Chayanov's theory of peasant farm family production as developed by Mellor (1966, Ch.9) and Nakajima (in Wharton 1969, Ch. 6) presents peasant farm families, not as profit maximising units, but as units whose production decisions (constrained by land and labour availability) are influenced directly by the family's desire for consumption goods (retained and marketed output) and leisure.[9] Where the peasant family does not hire or supply labour in the local labour market this theory implies different family resource allocations from those which would satisfy the profit maximisation rule; although these differences are mainly of degree rather than of character. The theory explains why subsistence households with large families and little land are likely to employ their labour at higher levels per acre and at lower marginal productivity per acre than capitalistic farms hiring labour at the going wage rate. It therefore also explains why output per acre on such subsistence holdings is likely to exceed that on larger farms using the same basic technology. There is ample empirical evidence that this is in fact the case, e.g. the high productivity of private plots in Eastern European agriculture, and evidence presented by Griffin (1974, Ch. 2) and Chayanov (1966, p. 98). Acceptance of this point provides a key plank in the argument, put forward by economists such as Griffin (1974), that total agricultural output will be higher if development is based on small labour-intensive units.[10]

Empirical evidence also supports another implication of the theory which is that, in cases where families neither hire-in or supply labour, land has a higher opportunity cost to peasant farm households with a high labour-to-land ratio and that they will outbid larger farmers to buy or rent small parcels of land.

The Chayanov–Mellor–Nakajima (CMN) theory contains nothing which explains the conservatism of peasant farmers. In the case where households neither hire or supply labour the theory does provide for the possibility that the aggregate supply of agricultural produce by volume (not value) may decline as prices increase – a possibility not envisaged by the conventional profit-maximising theory of the competitive firm. It must be emphasised, however, that the theory does not suggest that this negatively sloping supply curve of output or labour is a likely outcome, and there is no reliable statistical evidence to suggest that it occurs in peasant societies. That such an outcome is possible at all is largely attributable to the comparative static nature of the theory, and it is a possibility which would be diminished within the model if dynamic increases in wants were adjusted for, and if allowance were made for the fact that the value of the minimum subsistence requirement itself shifts upwards with increased food prices. But more significantly it should be noted that there is nothing in the theory to suggest that peasant producers do not respond to changes in the price of one product relative to another by shifting resources to increase output of the product with the higher price. Indeed, there is no rational economic strategy under which such a response would not occur. It is therefore hardly surprising that (after allowing for difficulties in statistical analysis) there is considerable evidence that peasant producers do respond positively to price signals by switching resources to higher price crops (Wharton 1969, Ch. 8). This evidence has been interpreted as having significant policy implications in that it suggests that planners can influence change in subsistence agriculture through generalised price instruments and the market mechanism, and it obviates the need to rely entirely on direct controls which require personal contact between officialdom and the farmers.

The image of the peasant farmer as a conventional economic entrepreneur has been furthered by yet another line of empirical investigation which purports to show that peasants allocate different farm inputs (labour, land, animal power, fertiliser, etc.) to alternative products in such a way that their marginal productivity is approximately equal in each case, e.g. Hopper (1965), Chennareddy (1967), Yotopoulos (1967), Sahota (1968). The conclusions drawn from this type of evidence by Schultz (1964) and others, have been influential in formulating development strategies. They argue that this evidence about peasant farmers, coupled with that of their positive responsiveness to price and their innovative reaction to exposure to new technology, demonstrates the ability of the subsistence sector to modernise with only minimal changes of institutional structure. It is argued that if new technology (improved seeds, inorganic fertiliser, pesticides, water pumps and wells for irrigation, veterinary services, etc.) is made available cheaply, farmers will respond by adopting it and will modernise to become increasingly market orientated. What is needed, according to this line, is a policy (a) to promote research into agricultural technology, particularly for testing imported technology (new seeds, crops, chemicals) and modifying it to suit local conditions, (b) to develop industries supplying farm inputs, and (c) to provide farm advisory services and marketing facilities. The minimum of reorganisation of land ownership is needed since the subsistence sector has the latent potential to accept and exploit new techniques to expand production.

A substantial question exists as to whether such conclusions are warranted by the facts. It is quite possible to accept that the production decisions of peasant farmers as a group do display many of the characteristics of the competitive, profit maximising firm, i.e. that (a) they allocate resources so as to equate their marginal productivity, (b) they expand output if prices increase, and (c) they introduce new inputs into production if their marginal value product exceeds their marginal cost. It is, however, a large step in logic to infer from the evidence that the subsistence sector responds at an adequate or socially optimal rate, or that responses will occur outside the very limited range of historic experience. There must exist a possibility of even more rapid and socially desirable development if the modernisation of agricultural technology is accompanied by land reform or other radical institutional changes to the agricultural system, and by significant changes in the mentality and aspirations of farmers.

It seems clear that it is quite possible for the subsistence sector to react in what are accepted as economically rational ways, but at the same time for it to be conservative and react slowly. For example, when it is observed that the supply of wheat tends to be higher following an increase in its price relative to that of other crops there is no inference that all or even a majority of farmers have reacted to the price change, or that those who have reacted have done so 'optimally'. A positive reaction by a minority of farmers may be sufficient to produce a statistically significant response. Similarly, while a reduction in the real price of fertiliser may stimulate an increase in total agricultural output, a large number of subsistence cultivators may not buy any fertiliser or increase their production. Most, but probably not all, of these non-reacting farmers may be behaving rationally. Production systems involving applications of inorganic fertiliser may have higher risks of loss (as well as gain) than traditional methods, and it is accepted that households producing no more than a small excess above subsistence needs may resist such innovations, because they are highly risk averse (see for example Lipton 1968). They have to be, for any failure of output might mean acute hunger, or even the loss of their holding which might be mortgaged against credit, the repayment of which depends upon a small output surplus.

It is clear that to be risk averse is entirely rational and, of course, risk aversion is not confined to the smallest farmers, nor even to farmers in developing countries. It is also apparent that behaviour to avoid risk will not generally lead to 'perverse' aggregate economic responses but will tend to damp down reactions below the levels which would occur in a risk free environment – crop insurance schemes are often proposed as a means of accelerating innovation.

But riskiness is not the only reason why farmers may not respond rapidly to a fall in fertiliser prices. For some tenant cultivators the major share of the additional output from using fertiliser might be appropriated by the landlord, thus eliminating much of the incentive for the cultivator to innovate. Yet for others there may be constraints arising out of the extended family system, or other social obligations which impede a positive response to lower fertiliser prices.

It is therefore apparent that, even if one accepts the validity of the statistical evidence showing that in the aggregate peasant agricultural societies respond in a manner similar to that implied by the neo-classical theory of the firm, the possibility exists that larger reactions of the same type might be achieved if public policy were directed to eliminating constraints believed to originate from the structure of agriculture and the institutions serving it. It cannot be argued automatically from the empirical evidence, as Schultz (1964) and Hayami and Ruttan (1971) do, that the latent entrepreneurship of subsistence cultivators will ensure rapid agricultural modernisation, provided that governments take steps to ensure adequate farm prices, an increased flow of cheap new technology, expanded marketing facilities, plus a general educational campaign. That prescription may work, although even in Japan and Taiwan, which are examples of successful agricultural development of a non-socialist type, firm measures have been taken to control the distribution of land rights.

## 6.4 General Agricultural Development Strategies

It is obvious that the choice of agricultural development strategy depends upon the desired contribution of this sector to the development of the economy as a whole. It is equally obvious that the detailed nature of this desired contribution will vary from one country to another depending upon the state of 'modernisation', resource endowments, and the prevailing politico-economic philosophy. In our view, as stated above, the key contributions are to raise agricultural output and create sufficient jobs. The objective of increasing output is in all developing countries accepted as of high priority in view of the recognised need for an agricultural surplus. However, there is no consensus as to what the desired composition of the output should be. There are two major classes of choice to be made in this connection. One of these concerns the balance between products (a) primarily for export, (b) crops which are industrial raw materials, and (c) basic foodstuffs. The precise combination of these three types of output which will maximise the value of agriculture's contribution over time is not uniquely determinable, but depends upon such things as the expected terms of trade for agricultural exports and processed agricultural raw materials, and upon differences in anticipated changes in production efficiency in each of these product areas.[11] The second major area of choice is between whether it is marketed surplus or total output which is the focus of attention. The main problem here is that there may be a conflict between employment creation in agriculture and the objective of maximising the marketed surplus, but not necessarily with that of maximising total output. The explanation of this is simply that the larger the agricultural labour force the greater the proportion of agricultural output consumed within agriculture and the smaller the proportion marketed to other sectors. Of course, if there are fewer people to feed in the non-agricultural sectors it might be argued that this is not too serious; but a smaller marketed surplus also implies a lower tax and savings base from which to extract resources for non-agricultural development. As discussed more fully below, this conflict between marketed output and employment generally appears to have been resolved in favour of the former. Suffice it to say at this stage that it is not possible to be dogmatic about what balance should be achieved between these objectives in the short run, and it is possible to do no more than evaluate potential strategies with regard to their impact upon them. Whatever the output, employment and resource transfer objectives set for agriculture in national development plans, a number of broad classifications of agricultural development strategy can be discerned each of which places different emphasis on the various objectives.

In the terminology of a World Bank mission to Tanzania (then Tanganyika) (IBRD 1961), approaches to agricultural development may be classified as being either *Improvement* or *Transformation.* The Improvement approach is essentially the minimalist one in which an attempt is made to upgrade the productivity of the existing farm system. It accepts the pattern of land ownership and farming rights and attempts to stimulate rather than coerce subsistence farmers into adopting new methods. The main policy instruments of such a strategy would be (a) to increase the effectiveness and coverage of the farm advisory service, (b) to upgrade the marketing system so as to make it easier for farmers to sell their produce and to obtain price and other market information, (c) possibly to extend credit to help small farmers purchase inputs, and (d) certainly to take measures to improve supplies of fertiliser, improved seeds, and knowledge about the cultivation techniques for non-traditional crops. These we may term the 'minimalist policy package'. In identifying the Transformation approach the IBRD mission recognised that more fundamental changes might be necessary to maintain or accelerate the rate of progress. In the context of Tanzania the mission foresaw the need for the creation of farming systems based on more intensive use of the land by efficiently run, planned farms of economic size. More specifically, in this instance, transformation was seen as the creation of settlement schemes, particularly irrigated ones, in which the major part of the capital investment is provided by the public sector, and where farmers in return for the right of access to this public capital submit to a degree of discipline regarding the crops they may grow and the husbandry standards they must achieve.[12] Transformation schemes of this type have been extensively adopted in Africa and Asia, and because of their definable limits and the possibilities these create for monitoring and control they have often attracted support from international aid agencies. Such schemes tend to be very capital-intensive and to absorb large numbers of skilled administrators, accountants and agricultural specialists. Very rapid rates of progress and response are required to justify such intensive concentrations of investment and (more crucially) skilled manpower when using conventional economic criteria. While good progress is often achieved in comparison to historical rates of innovation and output expansion, the rates of economic return on these large projects are often rather low, i.e. less than 10% per year. Of course, where the financial capital is provided at very cheap concessionary rates through international aid, low rates of return on the investment do not preclude the possibility of significant gains to the underdeveloped country. This is especially so where these large projects are the means of attracting aid which would not otherwise be available. For it has to be admitted that large public projects may permit aid and domestic resources to be pumped into the rural areas on a scale which could not otherwise be achieved; although small projects may (as, for example, Ruthenberg 1966 suggests) tend to show higher economic rates of return than large projects, it may be difficult to devise sufficient of them to absorb large amounts of aid.

There is, however, no reason why the transformation approach should be defined restrictively as applying to capital-intensive projects. It is also a label well-suited to describing strategies which involve land reform and wholesale redistribution of rights in the land. In China, for example, following the end of the Civil War in 1949, an Agrarian Reform Law was published in 1950, and policy was directed towards 'the elimination of landlords, land distribution and the creation of mutual aid teams as the operational units in agriculture, and of peasants' associations as the political and social channels for rural reorganisation. At the same time, the state abolished private money-lending and took a firm grip on the trade and the rural credit system' (Henle 1974, p. 127).[13] After a period of reorganisation and experimentation 76,000 communes were established as the main organisational units in agriculture, and ownership of land was transferred to the village level, except for up to 5% of the land which was allowed to remain in small private plots. Free markets in products were restricted and a system of delivery targets enforced. A most interesting aspect of Chinese agricultural development is the extent to which the communes have been required to provide the labour and materials for the construction of roads, irrigation projects, re-afforestation schemes and other public works. In this way considerable capital investment has been achieved at small cost to the central government and without needing much expensive equipment. The Chinese case is thus an example of an extremely radical transformation strategy executed without great financial expense. It is an experience shared to some extent by the agricultural development strategies of such countries as Cuba and Tanzania.

A classification of strategies which is different from, but not entirely incompatible with, the transformation-improvement categorisation, is that which distinguishes policy emphasis at the so-called *extensive margin* from that at the *intensive margin.* In this, attention is directed not so much to the form and content of the policy package, as to which should be the target groups and geographical areas. The question posed by this taxonomy is whether or not efforts should be concentrated on the best growers and areas (the intensive margin) or applied more evenly across the board. On the face of it, it seems entirely rational to direct scarce public resources to the intensive margin. The returns to the small cadre of trained specialists, to credit funds, to limited supplies of improved seeds from government seed-bulking stations, to capital invested in irrigation schemes, etc. are likely to be highest when these are allocated to the best farmers and the most fertile areas. While in terms of maximising the growth of marketed output (and hence benefiting the urban sector) such a policy may be optimal, it tends to concentrate rural economic power in an elite group, to create pressures for the development of larger capitalistic farm units, and to progressively increase the numbers of landless unemployed.

This conflict between the objectives of maximising the marketed surplus and of creating jobs in agriculture constitutes a serious dilemma in planning agricultural development. The main argument which may be deployed to support the concentration of effort at the intensive margin in order to maximise the marketed surplus is that, although this fails to improve the lot of the majority of peasants in the short run, it is in their long-run benefit since it is this strategy which maximises the rate of capital accumulation and hence job creation in the long run, that is, the effects will 'trickle down' from the top. Proponents of this line reinforce it with the often reiterated view that, because the mass of farmers are more difficult to manage and are slower to respond than the elite, the rate of return on investment must be higher at the intensive than the extensive margin. Although the empirical evidence does not fully support this view, the urban bias (Streeten and Lipton 1968, Ch. 4; Lipton 1977) of the political establishment in developing countries creates strong pressure for policies which increase the marketed surplus for the benefits of the urban and industrial sectors, even though this is not in the interests of the rural poor. In opposition are those who see this sort of outcome as negating much of the benefit of development, where development (in contrast to economic growth) is seen as an improvement of living standards for all and most particularly for the poor; this position is strengthened by the lack of evidence that industrial development is displaying the required capacity for job creation, or that the 'trickle down' effects are at all substantial. Thus intensive-margin schemes in agriculture have come under criticism for failing to improve the lot of the peasants most in need.

While granting its contribution to marketed and aggregate output, precisely the class of criticism just outlined above has been extensively levelled against the 'Green Revolution' in Asia. The name 'Green Revolution' is applied to the complementary package of technological innovations surrounding the introduction of new high yielding varieties (HYVs) for wheat and rice. The chief characteristics of the HYVs is that with an ample supply of irrigation water they are much more responsive to inorganic fertilisers than traditional varieties, and so they greatly increase productivity of land and to a lesser extent of labour. However, the new varieties are also less disease-resistant than traditional varieties and so require insecticides and fungicides for optimal husbandry. The need for adequate water supplies restricts the areas where the new package of technology can be applied so that growers in other areas are excluded from the benefits. And also the new technology has so shifted the supply curve that there is downward price pressure on growers using traditional methods in non-irrigable areas. However, even in the irrigable areas, as Griffin (1974) argues, the benefits have been unequally distributed in favour of the larger farmers and landowners. His well-supported argument is that, even if there was no deliberate policy of channelling resources to the biggest farmers, markets in agricultural factors of production would tend to achieve precisely that. Possibly the main factor market imperfection Griffin identifies as responsible for this is that credit for the purchase of inputs such as tubewells, fertiliser and seed is much easier and cheaper to obtain for large farmers than it is for small peasants. Such is the profitability of this new technology that their easier access to the resultant earning capacity provides the incentive to landlords to displace their tenants, to increase the scale of their own farming operations and capture the full return to innovation. At the same time, access to the new technology provides large innovating farmers with the means to expand by buying land from, or renting it in competition with, those small farmers unable to raise credit to gain full access to the new technology package, and in particular to its irrigation and mechanical components.[14] Griffin argues that

> the new technology for producing food is not characterised by important economies of scale and the growth in inequality which has in practice accompanied technical change is not a necessary consequence of attempts to raise yields. The problem arises not from the nature of the most appropriate technology but from the bias of government policy (emphasis at the intensive margin) and the fact that public institutions are not scale-neutral.
>
> Griffin (1974, p.69)

Because of this situation, and because for Griffin (as for many others, e.g. Myrdal 1970) rural welfare and hence general welfare would be increased more by de-emphasising higher marketed output and the placing of more stress on the need to spread the new technology to the maximum number of small labour-intensive farms, institutional reform is seen as a necessary concomitant of modernisation. In Griffin's assessment of the Indian and Pakistan situations, change to reduce policy and factor market bias towards the better-off is unlikely to emerge from the existing political and social systems, and therefore these latter themselves need to be radically altered in pursuance of an appropriate agricultural development strategy.

There is an obvious relationship between the two previously discussed classifications of agricultural development strategies and that in which Johnston and Kilby (1975, Ch. 4) distinguish between what they call *unimodal* and *bimodal* strategies. The main difference is that in this classification the emphasis is on the technological characteristics of the development strategy. Thus Johnston and Kilby define as unimodal the Japanese–Taiwanese development patterns in which development has centred on small-scale farming units using primarily the biological technology package of high yielding crop varieties, multiple cropping, with irrigation and intensive fertiliser use. In contrast, the bimodal strategy is defined as that followed by Mexico and Colombia in which attempts have been made to develop large-scale mechanised agriculture simultaneously with small-scale labour-intensive farming. In their view the bimodal strategy is not appropriate since, as in Mexico, the main development will tend to occur in the large-scale sector, with the small-scale sector taking a very much secondary role. Failure to expand the horizons and living standards of the mass of rural poor may be consistent with maximising marketed output from agriculture, but in the long run it is likely to act as a brake on development, primarily because the slow growth in rural demand will restrict the capacity for industrial growth. Not only will industries producing consumer goods prosper if the demand for their product is increased as a result of the unimodal strategy of distributing additional purchasing power over a larger number of families, but industrial expansion will be accelerated because of increased demand for factors of production and marketing services. Johnston and Kilby argue, very reasonably, that the agricultural technology required for the unimodal strategy is better suited to the embryonic industrial skills of many poor countries, and is therefore more likely to provide a stimulus for domestic industrial growth based on local entrepreneurship. This is because in the unimodal strategy emphasis is on biological technology plus small tools and simple implements which can be easily fabricated and serviced, whereas the technology required for larger-scale farming in the bimodal strategy contains a large element of sophisticated machinery, e.g. tractors and combine harvesters, which is more likely to be imported than locally manufactured.

A most significant element of the views of Griffin and Johnston and Kilby is that they see the choice of strategy for agricultural development as revolving round the selection of the appropriate technology, where appropriateness is defined with respect to the political and sociological as well as the economic goals of society. This approach seems to be correct in the view of the present authors, as also does their view that a scale-neutral technology is the appropriate one.[15] There is, however, a difference of views as to what policies are required to disseminate this technology and promote its general acceptance. Both Griffin and Johnston and Kilby are agreed that all the elements of the 'minimalist policy package' are needed. Given active policies of this type Johnston and Kilby believe that the invisible hand of market forces will bring about wide diffusion of the scale-neutral technology and a general improvement of rural living standards. Griffin's view is that the minimalist policy on its own is insufficient, that the anti-small farmer bias of the factor markets represents an impediment to the rapid adoption of such a new technology by small producers, and that policies to create new institutions of land ownership and for factor distribution are needed for successful development. This observation provides a key to answering a central problem in the choice of agricultural development strategy, which is whether or not the more egalitarian type of strategy (extensive margin, unimodal or improvement) is inherently slower in producing the desired output results than the alternative (intensive margin, bimodal, transformation). The answer, in the Griffin mould, is that it is not intrinsically slower, but will be so if the institutional structure is biased against it. Where this bias exists, opting for the more egalitarian strategy involves a commitment to institutional change. This may involve large-scale mobilisation of administrators, specialists and groups in the rural areas, a process which absorbs scarce resources, and it may disrupt the smooth flow of agricultural output for some time (see the section on Land Reform below). Unless the political commitment to equalising incomes is fairly strong it may require only modest short-run costs of this type to persuade those responsible to soft-pedal the egalitarian strategy in favour of policies directed towards large-scale farming units and capital-intensive agriculture. These latter have the advantage from the planners' point of view of being easier to control, both with regard to achieving output targets and to minimising the number of people to be organised.

## 6.5 The Appropriate Agricultural Technology

In fact there is no such thing as the appropriate technology for the agricultural sector of any one country, let alone for the collectivity of poor countries. Ecological and demographic factors, as well as the location of transport systems, dictate substantially different resource combinations for different regions. In some developing countries there are large developable areas of forest (e.g. the Amazon forests of Brazil) or uplands and sparsely populated arid areas (e.g. North Africa). These demand different technological solutions from the river basins and savannah grassland areas which support the majority of the world's rural poor. It is therefore on these latter areas that the success of agricultural development in the poor countries largely depends, and it is to the technical possibilities for transforming them that the current section is primarily addressed.

In the previous section it was accepted that for the highly populated rural areas what is required is scale-neutral technology, that is methods which are suitable to any size of holding and most particularly the smallest. Essentially, therefore, we are considering technology which is embodied in inputs which are readily divisible into small lots.

It is immediately obvious that there are many important agricultural inputs which are in fact readily divisible. These include most inputs of biological and chemical origin. Easily divisible biological inputs include improved and hybrid seed, improved livestock, and veterinary services, while chemical inputs such as fertiliser and insecticide can also be dispensed easily in small quantities. It is worth noting that application of these inputs, separately or in combination, increases land productivity and the demand for labour, thus simultaneously permitting output and employment to expand. It is also interesting to note that most of these scale-neutral elements of technology figure prominently in all areas which have achieved rapid expansion of output per acre, e.g. China, Japan, Taiwan, the Punjab and Mexico. They are also major constituents of the technology promoted by agricultural development strategies everywhere.

Another input which, in combination with fertiliser and high yielding crop varieties (particularly of wheat and rice), is of critical importance in Asia and tropical areas generally is irrigation. While water itself is undoubtedly highly divisible, the means for delivering it are usually 'lumpy'. Dams, irrigation feeder canals and large pumps can only be installed to serve comparatively large areas, while the tubewells (boreholes) with diesel pumps which feature in Indian and Pakistani schemes are best suited to areas of 10 acres or more. Clearly these elements of irrigation technology are not scale-neutral. They are only economical on larger farming units. But there is no reason why these larger units should comprise single owner-occupied farms. On irrigated settlement schemes run by governments dams and canals can be used to deliver irrigation water to a large number of settlers with very small holdings – they may not exceed 2 acres in some schemes. Alternatively, cooperative forms of ownership and management may permit wells and small irrigation schemes to serve a number of farmers. It is clear, therefore, that there is no fundamental scale problem for small farmers arising from the lumpiness of irrigation works and equipment, except under conditions where each farm is privately owned and is managed in isolation. Where land is owned collectively, or cooperative management is imposed (or voluntarily espoused by owner-occupiers) the problems of input lumpiness can be overcome by collective action. It is presumably this point that Griffin is making when he says that the technology of the Green Revolution is inherently scale-neutral but that it is public institutions and policy which create its scale effects (1974, p. 69).

While discussing irrigation it is important to note its substantial capacity for employment creation, which explains why irrigated Japanese agriculture succeeded in generating a rapid increase in rural incomes while maintaining its structure of small farms. Irrigation can transform land use in the tropics from the growing of one poor crop a year using the highly uncertain rains of the wet season, into a multi-cropping system of two and even three crops a year. The potential for expanding output and labour use simultaneously is obvious and has been seized upon by agricultural planners everywhere.[16]

From the development standpoint most of the problems of technological indivisibility arise with machinery, for it is in this category that there are innovations designed specifically to substitute for human labour. Not all mechanical innovations have this effect; static power sources like diesel pumps and electric motors are used to move water on a scale not possible with human and animal power and they lead directly to job creation through the increase in crop output they facilitate; similarly, knapsack sprayers for insecticide perform a productive task which would not be undertaken without the innovation. It is through the introduction of large tractors in some areas that jobs have been destroyed and economic benefits channelled mainly to the already better off (e.g. McInerney and Donaldson 1975).

It must be recognised, however, that it is not necessarily the tractors as such which are responsible for these effects, but that in some cases they are shaped by the biased institutional setting for the adoption of tractors. Undoubtedly there are cases where the introduction of large tractors has been basically inappropriate; where they have been introduced with generous subsidies in conditions where the essential cultivation services required might have been provided adequately by small, mechanical hand-tillers without any adverse social or employment effects. But there are other situations in poor countries where the introduction of large tractors can readily be justified: where they permit the cultivation of land which is not otherwise manageable, where they remove labour bottlenecks which otherwise restrict successful implementation of more intensive farming systems, or where land is plentiful and labour scarce. If, where these conditions exist, there are institutions for cooperative or collective ownership of tractors, there is no reason why the benefits of tractor power should accrue principally to large farmers, since such institutions permit a tractor's services to be fairly divided among a number of small farms. Such institutions would be capable of matching large farmers in providing the collateral required to obtain credit to purchase a tractor, but in their absence tenant farmers and owners with little land are likely to find themselves denied access to this technology.

It is, therefore, evident that there are few inherent properties of biological, chemical, or even mechanical agricultural technology which render them unsuitable for use on small farms. Policies can always be devised in principle to ensure that the agricultural technology adopted is scale-neutral, and in some socio-political situations (such as the often referred to ones of Japan and Taiwan) these policies do not necessarily require abandonment of private land ownership. An inappropriate technology is one that has effects which conflict with the avowed goals of society (or of an individual, if it is a personal judgement). If such a situation arises it is because the policies followed are not consistent with the goals laid down.

It would be wrong from the foregoing to infer that the identification and selection of appropriate technology is a straightforward matter. If it were there would be few problems in agricultural development. The suitable combination of seed variety and fertiliser requirement may change over comparatively short distances as altitude and soil type change. Rarely therefore can the biological–chemical input package just be plucked off an international shelf. Generally, local crop trials have to be organised to select plant varieties and a husbandry system which can be recommended to farmers without high risk of failure. The necessity for this is compounded by the fact that disease organisms rapidly mutate to break down the inbred disease resistance of hybrid and improved seeds, so that new varieties must be continuously produced to contain disease damage. The setting up of agricultural research establishments at a national level to supplement the internationally funded centres (e.g. the International Maize and Wheat Improvement Centre in Mexico, and the International Rice Research Institute in the Philippines) has therefore played a vital role in promoting agricultural expansion.

## 6.6 Two Central Issues

There are two issues which have been mentioned in the preceding pages which deserve brief amplification. These relate (a) to the way in which development policies have tended to squeeze the agricultural sector and (b) to the nature and effects of land reform.

### *The Policy Squeeze on Agriculture*

As has already been stated, there has been increasing recognition that in the 1950s and 1960s many poor countries adopted policies which were too negative towards the agricultural sector, and that this resulted in the virtual exclusion of large numbers of poor people in these countries from the benefits of development. It is important to explore briefly the reasons for this neglect, especially because in some cases it appears to have been unintentional.

It is inevitable that in the early stages of industrial and public sector expansion the major proportion of the required investable funds must be extracted from the dominant agricultural sector by either voluntary savings or taxation. There is thus the classic question of social choice as to how much current consumption should be forgone by agriculturalists to provide for expanded consumption for all in the future. In the absence of any government policy to enforce or encourage saving, this choice would be produced by the sum of individual saving decisions – made by farmers and landlords. In all countries, however, it is obviously judged that the sum of privately made decisions provides less than the socially optimal rate of capital accumulation, since all governments employ various forms of taxation to increase the rate. In such countries as the USSR and China where product delivery targets and input allocation controls are imposed on the agricultural sector, it may be assumed that government targets for the level of agricultural surplus to be extracted are approximately met.[17] In other countries without the same degree of direct control there may be less correspondence between the target (if this is specifically stated at all) and the achieved level of forced plus voluntary savings. This may arise because there is no comprehensive understanding (model) of the relationship between policy instruments and objectives. In particular, policies may be implemented to pursue specific objectives without full recognition being given to their influence on other goals. What is suggested here is that many countries may have squeezed their agricultural sector more than was planned because of a failure to recognise that certain policies would have that effect. In particular it appears that (a) industrial policies may have been pursued without proper account being taken (until more recently) of their impact on agriculture; (b) price intervention policies in agriculture have in some notable cases had effects other than those expressly stated as intended, and (c) a combination of factors has favoured expansion of the more readily taxed export crops at the expense of foodgrain production.

The emphasis laid by poor countries on industrial expansion through import substitution (ISI) (see Chapter 8) has had side effects on agriculture which may be assumed in many cases to be unintended. Important elements of the policy to foster ISI have been the adoption of high import tariffs and various direct import controls on products competing with those of domestic industry. These have produced a situation in many developing countries (Balassa 1974, Ch. 4) of negative protection for agriculture; that is, one where returns to agriculture have been squeezed and resources have been transferred to industry. This results for two main reasons: one, that farmers have had to pay more for those inputs and consumption goods which are domestically produced than they would have done without the tariffs and import restrictions; and two, that the reduction of imports due to these policies is accompanied by a situation where the domestic currency is overvalued, in which foreign currencies buy fewer units of domestic currency than would otherwise be the case, so that farmers receive fewer units of domestic currency for their exports. In these ways the policies of ISI have squeezed resources out of agriculture and this may have been unplanned.

It is not possible to explore the full complexities of farm price intervention policies here. Such policies have a variety of forms and have been directed at several objectives. In the case of the Indian and Sri Lankan schemes for delivery of grain at low prices the intention to transfer resources out of agriculture is undisguised. In other cases, however, this effect is either disguised or unintended. The notion that stability of prices and/or incomes is desirable in agriculture is widely accepted, and it appears that simply for it to be claimed that a policy measure is likely to achieve stability is a guarantee of strong political support. Unfortunately, the issue of stability seems to be open to much misunderstanding. Firstly, and most elementarily, stabilisation of both prices and incomes is not usually achievable by a single policy instrument. To fix (stabilise) producer prices in the face of fluctuating supplies will destabilise farmers incomes. More importantly, in this context, price stability – which is much easier to achieve than income stability, although possibly not as desirable for the purpose of eliminating the risks of agricultural production and modernisation – may be achieved in a variety of ways. Complete stability, for example, may be achieved either by setting a price payable to farmers which is consistently above the 'free' market equilibrium level, or alternatively by devising a system to enforce delivery at a level consistently below this. These alternatives are equivalent to price stabilisation through subsidisation and taxation respectively. It appears that a number of countries, for example, Nigeria and Ghana (see Bauer and Yamey 1968, Ch. 9), instituted policies to promote price stability for certain export crops, which were applied in a way which achieved a high rate of taxation. This arose because in West Africa, as elsewhere, the Marketing Boards which administered the policies were set up by governments. Because of shortages of government revenues, the Boards were required to maintain positive balances which could only be done if receipts from sales exceeded payments to farmers; the same revenue shortages led governments to appropriate the stabilisation scheme balances to finance development and to come to rely on this source of funds. Hence, whether anticipated or not, stabilisation schemes have tended to become instruments of taxation in underdeveloped countries.

In relation to this last conclusion, it should be noted that taxation of export crops is one of the easiest ways for governments to extract revenue from the agricultural sector. This is so because export crops have to pass through a (usually) small number of ports, so that taxes do not have to be levied at the farm-gate which is extremely costly in manpower with so many small farmers, but can be imposed on licensed exporters, or on a marketing board at small administrative cost. Moreover taxing export crops avoids the need to tax and hence increase the price of domestic food crops. Indeed, the price of food crops may decrease because the tax causes a switch of resources from export crops to untaxed domestic food production. Clearly, any policy which has the effect of increasing export crop production will also tend to increase the tax offtake from agriculture. It is argued that the systematic biases towards export products in agricultural research and in the development of marketing systems, which were a feature of the colonial era, still persist or at least have done until very recently. This institutional orientation plus the weak demand for domestic foodstuffs due to inadequacies in market institutions has tended to channel inputs into export products which are easily taxed, thus tightening the resource squeeze on agriculture.

*Land Reform*

From the discussion above it is apparent that land reform is potentially the most powerful weapon in the armoury of institutional reforms for adjusting the pattern of technological change. The more sweeping the reform the greater its impact upon the chosen agricultural techniques and upon the distribution of incomes from agriculture. Large-scale land reforms epitomise radical political change and are, as in China, Russia and Cuba, an integral part of political reforms to which the redistribution of income and economic power is central, and to which the agricultural output and technological consequences are an important but secondary consideration.

The primacy of political factors is reflected in a widely accepted definition of land reform whereby 'land reform means the redistribution of property rights in land for the benefit of small farmers and agricultural labourers' (Warriner 1969, p. xiv). Such a narrow definition excludes actions like land amalgamation in conditions where there is fragmentation of holdings, the fostering of cooperative ownership, or modifications of legislation affecting the rights of existing tenants. These types of policy as well as those of land redistribution are all embraced by the politically more neutral United Nations definition which sets land reform as equivalent to agrarian institutional reform, which includes changes in land tenure plus a variety of complementary changes in credit, research, marketing and other institutions (UN 1962, p. iv).

It is, however, true that most important land reforms are of the redistributive type in which land is taken from existing owners and farming rights distributed to the less wealthy. Indeed, it is arguable that in underdeveloped countries failure to institute land redistribution measures betrays a lack of genuine political commitment to improving the lot of the poor. The level of this commitment is, however, not revealed simply by the passing of legislation, but by the scale on which land reform is implemented. In some cases (China, USSR) all private land ownership rights, except to garden plots, have been abolished and effectively appropriated for all the people through the State. In other less radical cases, such as southern Mexico, latifundia were compulsorily purchased and the land reallocated in minifundia to previously landless people. Similarly in Kenya, some land which was formerly in white-owned estates or farms has been purchased or taken over to be settled by tenant farmers operating under government supervision. But in both Mexico and Kenya the unequal pattern of land holdings persists, partly because not all large holdings are broken up – in Kenya some were merely transferred to new owners – and because the market in land continues to exist, enabling new large landholdings to be amassed. On an even less radical scale India has passed ineffective legislation to limit the maximum holding size in order to release land for smaller holdings.

The reason for citing these few different examples is to emphasise that redistributive land reform is not an all-or-nothing policy but can occur on a variety of scales. Where private ownership is abolished completely the scale of reform is greatest, as also is the potential short-run disruption of production since political and social development objectives override economic ones. In other cases, where private ownership and tenancy rights are retained subject to limitations of size of holding, a more gradual reform is possible with less disruption of output – indeed, given that output per acre may be higher on small farms, limited production increases may accrue very quickly. In such cases, however, it is not simply that reform may be gradual, but where (as often happens) large landowners are compensated for their loss of land the limited financial allocation for the reform programme usually dictates a slow rate of change. Inevitably, such gradual and limited reforms have a relatively small impact upon income distribution, since they do not guarantee all the rural poor access to land or work, and they probably fail to ensure a unimodal pattern of development.

Although we can agree that the key element of most land reform programmes is the redistribution of land, a successful outcome typically requires the adoption of ancillary measures. For even if the objectives of reform are mainly political, the aim of achieving a redistribution of power and income will only be attained if the new holdings provide incomes adequate to support their new occupiers and to induce them to remain and develop as farmers. This cannot be achieved by mere transfer of title alone, but requires that the new farmers have access to inputs and credit, have opportunities for the sale of their products, and have access to advice (most of them will not have farmed on their own account before). Because land reform may be creating a large number of small new farms in areas where only a few large ones previously existed, it is unlikely that existing market and advisory institutions are adequate to supply the new farmers' needs in these respects; and therefore public policy intervention may be required to create new institutions. If so, the specific institutions required will be those of the 'minimalist policy package' detailed above. This explains why those economists who demand a more radical policy for agricultural development also accept the elements of the minimalist strategy. It also explains why land reform is such a powerful tool for technological change in agriculture, because it demands the setting up of new institutions to promote a shift to the chosen production techniques in the areas affected by the reform policy.

## Notes

1 As has been discussed already in Chapter 5, not all saving need be from domestic sources, and development aid can provide an additional source of funds for investment in industry and the public sector. Aid cannot, however, entirely or even largely supplant domestic saving and the need for the agricultural sector initially to contribute much of it.

2 If one assumed a country to have a workforce of 1 million of whom 20% were employed in industry, a 2.5% population growth rate would imply an addition of 25,000 people to the workforce. If all of these were to be absorbed into industry, employment in that sector would have to grow from 200,000 to 225,000, that is by 12.5%.

3 One feature of the pattern of employment in less developed countries which is perhaps surprising is the high proportion of the active population engaged in the trade, transport and service (including government) sectors. This highlights the weakness of classifying any employment which is non-agricultural as being industrial. Also as Bairoch points out, the proportion employed in the trade, transport and service sectors is far higher than in the rich countries at a comparable stage of development and it may be excessive for the needs of poor countries.

4 In England the Industrial Revolution which started in the 18th century was preceded by an Agricultural Revolution in which marked advances were made in crop and animal husbandry. This had its origins in the enclosure movements of the 17th century, and made available the necessary food surplus, while at the same time releasing labour from the land. European countries industrialising later were doubtless assisted by the spread of the same improved technology. Also, significantly, in the latter half of the 19th century the European countries began to benefit from the increasing supplies of food from the newly opened lands of N America, Argentina and Australia, which these countries supplied in exchange for manufactured goods.

5 Of course not all the burden of responsibility rests with agricultural policy.

There is increasing recognition that industrial development has tended to be too capital-intensive and has created too few jobs.

6 Of course, in other fundamental respects these two systems are markedly different, the large-scale mechanised technology of Russian collective and state farms contrasting sharply with the labour-intensive technology of the Chinese 'village' farms.

7 The terms 'subsistence' and 'peasant' are not used in any precise way here. Consideration of how to define them is given by Wharton (1970, Ch. 2).

8 Extensive lists of the alleged negative qualities of peasant societies are presented by Rogers (in Wharton 1970, Ch. 5) and Brewster (in Southworth and Johnston 1967, Ch. 3).

9 In the neo-classical theory of the firm the intra-household trade-off between work (goods) and leisure determines the supply price of labour to the firm and is external to the decision making of the firm. Nakajima's extension of the Chayanov—Mellor model, to permit the farm family to trade labour, produces an exact equivalent of the neo-classical theory since it allows the wage rate at which the family can exchange labour to be determined not by the family but externally by the market. In this case peasant farms are postulated to behave no differently from profit maximising farms.

10 It is not entirely clear, however, that this empirical evidence can support this conclusion. For, while it may be true that the smaller farms in a group employing the same basic production methods apply certain inputs to the land more intensively than large farms, it does not follow that as technology changes there will not be differences in the rates at which large and small farms adopt it. Indeed, as is discussed later in relation to the 'Green Revolution' type of technology, large farmers have tended to adopt what is a more land intensive technology more rapidly than small farmers. As is discussed later, one explanation (put forward by Griffin 1974) is that it is the institutions governing the uptake of technology, rather than any intrinsic properties of the technology, which are biased in favour of adoption by large farmers. Accepting this explanation then there is no technological reason why, in the case of the Green Revolution, land in large holdings should be more productive than that in small ones. However, as Bell (1972) observes, there are risks associated with the new technology, and to the extent that small farmers are more risk averse than large ones they may quite rationally lag behind large farmers in adopting it.

11 It should probably be noted that traditionally there has been a tendency by both governments and private commercial agriculture to concentrate efforts on exportable crops and to put relatively little effort into improving local food crop production. This bias has resulted from a number of factors. (1) The existence of well organised international commodity markets contrasts in many LDCs with weakly organised local foodstuffs markets which exhibit great variability and seasonality of demand. Investable resources naturally tend to gravitate to export production in these circumstances. (2) International private (and, in the colonial era, public) capital, aware of export possibilities, has been available to LDCs to exploit such opportunities, but has not been similarly tempted to invest in producing food for the local market. (3) From LDC governments' points of view export crops, unlike local food crops, are a taxable flow and provide a much needed source of government revenue; they also generate much needed foreign exchange and therefore, understandably, there is strong official support for

their expansion. These pressures on LDC governments have not eased greatly, and if in recent years more emphasis has been placed on local food production some credit must go to international initiatives by the Rockefeller Foundation, Ford Foundation, World Bank, and the other sponsors of the Consultative Group on International Agricultural Research which funds the various international research centres such as IRRI, CIMMYT and ICRISAT.

12 This type of settlement scheme proposed by the World Bank should not be confused with the more radical Villagisation (Ujaama) schemes which evolved as a purely Tanzanian initiative at a later date.

13 This monograph provides a most interesting account of Chinese agricultural policy.

14 The scale on which these effects can occur is shown by the World Bank study of a project in Pakistan which combines tractor mechanisation with irrigated farming of the new high yielding varieties of wheat and rice (McInerney and Donaldson 1975). The study found that farms which had bought tractors with the subsidised credit provided in this project expanded from an average of 45 acres to 109. Twelve percent of the increased acreage was attributable to purchases of land, 24% to increased rental, 42% to reduced renting out (removal of tenants), and the balance to reclamation and improvement. Another very significant and interesting estimate of the study is that as a result of the project a net 2,203 full time jobs were eliminated on the survey area of 22,025 acres, i.e. one job lost for every 10 acres introduced to the new technology. This loss was equivalent to between 7.5 and 11.8 jobs per tractor purchased.

15 This judgement is predicated on acceptance that a high weight must be assigned to the employment objective of agricultural policy, and that emphasis on this objective need not prejudice that of expanding total farm output.

16 The note of caution attributable to Borgstrom (1969) which is sounded in Chapter 7 should possibly be reiterated here. It is that there is a distinct possibility that water scarcity in future may limit the extent of irrigated agriculture in many parts of the world. Without the opportunities that irrigated agriculture provides, the prospects for many poor countries would be bleak.

17 India and Sri Lanka have also instituted schemes for compulsory foodgrain delivery at fixed prices. Note that it is through the capacity to enforce a delivery price lower than that charged to consumers that some surplus is extracted by government.

## Bibliography

Bairoch P. (1975), *The Economic Development of the Third World since 1900*, Methuen.

Balassa B. *et al.* (1971), *The Structure of Protection in Developing Countries*, Johns Hopkins Press.

Bauer P.T. (1971), *Dissent on Development*, Weidenfeld and Nicolson.

Bauer P.T. and Yamey B.S. (1968), *Markets, Market Control and Marketing Reform*, Weidenfeld and Nicolson.

Bell C. (1972), 'The acquisition of agricultural technology: its determinants and effects,' *Journal of Development Studies*, Vol. 9, No. 1. Reprinted in Cooper C. (ed), *Science, Technology and Development*, Frank Cass, 1973.

Bernstein H. (ed.) (1973), *Underdevelopment and Development; The Third World Today*, Penguin.

Borgstrom G. (1969), *Too Many: A Study of Earth's Biological Limitations*, Macmillan.

Boserup E. (1965), *The Conditions of Agricultural Growth*, Allen and Unwin.

Chennareddy V. (1967), 'Production efficiency in South Indian agriculture', *Journal of Farm Economics*, Vol. 49, No. 4.

Chayanov A.V. (1966), edited by Thorner D., Kerblay B. and Smith R.E.F. *The Theory of Peasant Economy*, Irwin.

Cochrane W.W. (1974), *Agricultural Development Planning*, Praeger.

Colman D.R. and Garbett G.K. (1976), *The Labour Economy of a Peasant Community in Malawi*, Overseas Development Administration.

Dovring F. (1959), 'The share of agriculture in a growing population,' *Monthly Bulletin of Agricultural Economics and Statistics*, FAO, Vol. 8. Reprinted in Eicher and Witt (1964).

Dumont R. (1966), *False Start in Africa*, Andre Deutsch.

Eicher C.K. and Witt L.W. (1964), *Agriculture in Economic Development*, McGraw-Hill.

Griffin K. (1974), *The Political Economy of Agrarian Change*, Macmillan.

Hayami Y. and Ruttan V.W. (1971), *Agricultural Development: An International Perspective*, Johns Hopkins Press.

Helleiner G.K. (ed.) (1968), *Agricultural Planning in East Africa*, East African Publishing House.

Henle H.V. (1974), *Report on China's Agriculture*, UN Food and Agriculture Organisation.

Hopper D.W. (1965), 'Allocation efficiency in traditional Indian agriculture', *Journal of Farm Economics*, Vol. 47, No. 3.

Hunter G. (1969), *Modernizing Peasant Societies*, Oxford University Press.

International Bank for Reconstruction and Development (IBRD) (1961), *The Economic Development of Tanganyika*, Johns Hopkins Press.

Johnston B.F. and Kilby P. (1975), *Agriculture and Structural Transformation*, Oxford University Press.

Jorgenson D.W. (1970), 'The role of agriculture in economic development: classical versus neoclassical models of growth.' Ch. 11 of Wharton (1970).

Kuznets S. (1961), 'Economic growth and the contribution of agriculture: notes on measurement,' *International Journal of Agrarian Affairs*, Vol. 3. Reprinted in Eicher and Witt (1964).

Lewis W.A. (1949), *The Principles of Economic Planning*, Allen and Unwin.

Lewis W.A. (1954), 'Economic development with unlimited supplies of labour,' *The Manchester School*, Vol. 22.

Lipton M. (1968), 'The theory of the optimising peasant,' *Journal of Development Studies*.

Lipton M. (1977), *Why Poor People Stay Poor*, Maurice Temple Smith.

Mellor J. (1966), *The Economics of Agricultural Development*, Cornell University Press.

McInerney J.P. and Donaldson G.F. (1975), *The Consequences of Farm Tractors in Pakistan*, World Bank Staff Working Paper No. 210.

Myrdal G. (abridged by Seth King) (1971), *Asian Drama: An Inquiry into the Poverty of Nations*, Pantheon Books.

Myrdal G. (1970), *The Challenge of World Poverty*, Penguin.

Nicholls W.H. (1963), 'Development in agrarian economics: the role of agricultural surplus, population pressure, and systems of land tenure,' *Journal of Political Economy,* Vol. 71. Reprinted in Wharton (1970).

Ohkawa K. and Rosovsky H. (1960), 'The role of agriculture in modern Japanese economic development.' *Economic Development and Cultural Change,* Vol. 9, Pt. 2. Reprinted in Eicher and Witt (1964).

Ranis G. and Fei J.C. (1961), 'A theory of economic development.' *American Economic Review,* Vol. 51. Reprinted in Eicher and Witt (1964).

Ruthenberg H. (1966), *African Agricultural Production Development Policy in Kenya, 1952-65.*

Sahota G.S. (1968), 'Resource allocation in Indian agriculture,' *American Journal of Agricultural Economics,* Vol. 50, No. 3.

Schultz T.W. (1964), *Transforming Traditional Agriculture,* Yale University Press.

Southworth H. and Johnston B.F. (eds) (1967), *Agricultural Development and Economic Growth,* Cornell University Press.

Streeten P. and Lipton M. (eds) (1968), *The Crisis in Indian Planning,* Oxford University Press.

Turnham D. (1971), *The Employment Problem in Less-Developed Countries,* OECD Development Centre.

United Nations, Department of Economic and Social Affairs (1962), *Progress in Land Reform,* Second Report.

Warriner D. (1969), *Land Reform in Principle and Practice,* Oxford University Press.

Wharton C.R. Jr. (ed.) (1970), *Subsistence Agriculture and Economic Development,* Aldine Publishing Co.

Yotopoulos P.A. (1967), *Allocative Efficiency in Economic Development,* Centre of Planning and Economic Research, Athens, Research Monograph 18.

# 7

# The world food problem: a classic syndrome of underdevelopment

One of the most pressing concerns of the present age is with what is often referred to as the world food problem (WFP). While this is undoubtedly a complex, multifaceted problem, its 'essential feature is quite simply that there is not enough food produced or available – certainly at reasonable prices – in the developing countries of the world which together account for more than two thirds of the human population' (Boerma 1975, pp. 3, 4). Examination of this proposition using elementary economic analysis reveals that this essential feature is an inevitable consequence of underdevelopment, probably its most serious one. It will also be seen that the existence of international markets in agricultural products may well exacerbate the food problem in the poorest countries.

These conclusions appear to have been clearly understood as long ago as 1800 by Malthus, a political economist and cleric. His view of the world was that the capacity of the human race to reproduce itself was potentially much greater than the capacity of the economic system to expand food production. From this he concluded that the size of the human population would, if not limited by preventive checks (of late marriage and various forms of birth control, some of which Malthus termed 'vice') be restrained by the positive checks resulting from malnutrition and starvation. Malthus also saw clearly that the more affluent societies were more likely to employ preventive checks to population growth and that it was poorer countries and people who were more likely to reproduce rapidly and suffer the positive checks from hunger.

In formulating his theories Malthus failed to anticipate the extent to which technology could expand the capacity for food production; nor did he foresee the capacity of modern medicine to limit the force of the natural, positive checks to population growth. Despite these and other legitimate criticisms of the relevance of his theories,[1] Malthus' vision has in many basic respects proved to be an accurate one. Certainly preventive measures (of birth control) have caused population growth in the richest countries to fall to a low level, whereas in the poorest countries these rates are high and in some, but not all of them, are a cause for concern. It is also in the poorest countries that the operation of the positive checks are most clearly evident; their main expression being the appallingly high rate of child mortality – in the poorest areas of underdeveloped countries as much as 40% of live-born children typically die before the age of five – and the generally low life expectancy of the survivors from childhood. Malthus, then, was basically correct in foreseeing that the burden of any limitations on the capacity of food supplies to grow at the same rate as food demand would fall mainly upon the poor, who comprise a high proportion of the populations of underdeveloped countries.

## 7.1 The State of the World Food Problem (WFP)

Quite how many or what proportion of the world's population is seriously undernourished is unknown with any degree of certainty, and is a subject of heated debate (Clark 1967, Ch. 4). Dependent upon what assumptions are made about the physiological nutrient requirements of different human types, and about the distribution of available foodstuffs within any given population, widely different estimates can be produced for the proportion of people seriously affected by malnutrition. Whatever the disagreement about exact numbers, there is no disputing that many people are seriously handicapped by food shortage. By way of illustration, the World Health Organisation has estimated (as an indicator of the extent of malnutrition) that in low-income countries 25% of children aged less than five are below 75% of normal bodyweight and that as many as 45% are below 90% of normal bodyweight (Berg 1971, p. 5). What does not appear to have been estimated is in what direction these proportions or those of other malnutrition indicators are changing. If they were increasing proportionately the WFP would be worsening unambiguously. If the proportions were declining but the absolute numbers of the disadvantaged were growing as world population grows, then it is a moot point as to whether the situation is improving or worsening. Only if the absolute number of the malnourished were declining could it definitely be judged that the WFP was a diminishing one.

Comparison of the rapidly increasing world population, which in 1962–72 exhibited an annual growth of 1.9%, with the growth rate of production (see table 7.1) suggests that since 1962 there has not been a definite diminution of the WFP when assessed by the third

**Table 7.1:** *Rate of growth of food production[a] in relation to population, world and main regions 1952–62 and 1962–72 (percent per year)[b]*

| | *1952–62* | | | *1962–72* | | |
|---|---|---|---|---|---|---|
| | | *Food production* | | | *Food production* | |
| | *Population* | *Total* | *Per cap.* | *Population* | *Total* | *Per cap.* |
| Developed market economies | 1.2 | 2.5 | 1.3 | 1.0 | 2.4 | 1.4 |
| Western Europe | 0.8 | 2.9 | 2.1 | 0.8 | 2.2 | 1.4 |
| North America | 1.8 | 1.9 | 0.1 | 1.2 | 2.4 | 1.2 |
| Oceania | 2.2 | 3.1 | 0.9 | 2.0 | 2.7 | 0.7 |
| Eastern Europe and USSR | 1.5 | 4.5 | 3.0 | 1.0 | 3.5 | 2.5 |
| Total: developed countries | 1.3 | 3.1 | 1.8 | 1.0 | 2.7 | 1.7 |
| Developing market economies | 2.4 | 3.1 | 0.7 | 2.5 | 2.7 | 0.2 |
| Africa | 2.2 | 2.2 | nil | 2.5 | 2.7 | 0.2 |
| Far East | 2.3 | 3.1 | 0.8 | 2.5 | 2.7 | 0.2 |
| Latin America | 2.8 | 3.2 | 0.4 | 2.9 | 3.1 | 0.2 |
| Near East | 2.6 | 3.4 | 0.8 | 2.8 | 3.0 | 0.2 |
| Asian centrally planned economies | 1.8 | 3.2 | 1.4 | 1.9 | 2.6 | 0.7 |
| WORLD | 2.0 | 3.1 | 1.1 | 1.9 | 2.7 | 0.8 |

*Source:* FAO (1974).

*a* Crop and livestock component of food production only (i.e. excluding fish production).

*b* Exponential trend.

criterion stated above. The most likely underlying trend is that the proportion of malnourished in the world is declining, but that the absolute number of such people is increasing. This conclusion is based on the following casual empiricism. It appears from the evidence of table 7.1 that per capita food production in the developing countries has averaged a low positive rate of growth in each of the two decades from 1952. It follows that if the increments in food production during this period had been equally distributed among the population, everybody would have had more to eat and the absolute number of underfed people would have declined.[2] However, this period also witnessed an appreciable growth in real per capita incomes in less developed countries. Consequently, in view of the high income elasticities of demand for food in poor countries, the growth of food demand (at constant real prices) almost certainly outstripped the growth of per capita production in such countries. Bearing this in mind, it seems most probable that, because of the unequal distribution of the growth of income, the rate of growth of food consumption by better off families in poor countries must have exceeded the growth rate of supplies (production plus net imports), and that an increasing number of poor families must have found it impossible to purchase adequate supplies.

This conclusion is reinforced when allowance is made for the fact that the rate of growth of food supplies between 1952 and 1972 failed even to match that of population in some highly populated developing countries, e.g. Bangladesh, Indonesia and Nigeria. Furthermore, FAO has calculated that during this period food production increased by less than demand in as many as 54 out of 85 developing countries (FAO 1971).

Thus there are a number of large countries, mainly in Asia, where population growth does appear to be pressing against the capacity for food supply growth; and Bangladesh, China and India all have extensive programmes to introduce methods of birth control. But for those worried that this confirms the more pessimistic assessments of the world's maximum sustainable population, it should be emphasised that the general condition has been one of increasing per capita food supplies in all continents. Moreover, since 1900 these increases have in the African, Asian and Latin American continents as whole units managed to keep ahead of steadily increasing population growth rates. Thus, to the extent that food supplies have not generally exerted a tight constraint on global population growth in the recent past, there is no compelling reason to believe that they will do so in the near future; as Sinha (1976, p. 5) states 'the unprecedented rate of population growth which has been experienced by the developing world is itself partly a sign of the success of developmental efforts and not of failure.' However, as already stated, a large number of the additional population is undernourished, and there is likewise no reason for optimism that this condition will disappear.

While the most important dimensions of the WFP are to be observed in the long-run underlying trend of chronic malnutrition, it appears to be the periodic worsening of the problem arising from the inevitable fluctuations around the trend which does most to focus attention upon it. In particular, the food shortages of 1972–75 caused a sharp upsurge of concern about present and future food supplies, and led to questioning as to whether sufficient priority has been attached to agricultural expansion by both developing and developed countries.[3] In periods such as this, increases in food prices, which are the natural indicators of shortages, seriously affect people in the richer nations and cause them to have heightened awareness of the scarce economic nature of food. More critically, an undoubted consequence of this period of global high prices must have been an increase in the number of poor people, predominantly in developing countries, whose nutritional intake fell below the prescribed standards. Such periods of aggravation of the food problem are rightly a matter of deep concern, but they should not be allowed to obscure the fact that the true nature of the WFP is the chronic, deep-seated one that at any time a substantial proportion of the world population is too poor to purchase sufficient nutrients to feed itself adequately at prevailing prices. For the most part these hungry people will be the families of landless-workless men, families with farm holdings too small to generate even subsistence needs, or families of the working poor. Inevitably, most of these people live in poor countries which cannot afford and do not provide welfare benefits so that, by definition, the world food problem can be seen to be directly attributable to, and the most serious consequence of, underdevelopment.

In order to fully comprehend the significance of underdevelopment it is vital to explore, however briefly, the human implications of what we have stated to be its most serious feature, biological food shortage. Reference has already been made to high infant mortality and low child bodyweight which are endemic characteristics in hungry societies. These are alarming factors, but when stated in cold statistical terms will probably not excite the feeling of concern which is due to societies with a chronic hunger problem among the poor. It is in the conditions of survival of the undernourished children that the true awfulness of the situation is revealed.

Being poor increases the likelihood of living in insanitary conditions which increases the risks of infection and of chronic parasite infestation. Being undernourished weakens resistance to both microbes and parasites and greatly increases the probability that infection will be fatal – note that few deaths are recorded as being from starvation as such, but most are attributed to various diseases. In such conditions children are likely to survive into adolescence suffering from some serious disability. Continuous exposure to general calorie or protein deficiency[4] and to illness weakens adults so that men are often unable to sustain hard physical endeavour at expected levels for long periods, and so that pregnant women are seriously at risk from death in childbirth or are unable to provide adequately for the foetus. Thus adults who have suffered a regime of recurrent malnutrition are likely to perform at physical levels much below their well-fed equivalents. This represents a serious economic loss to poor countries through a reduction in the effective capacity of the labour force.

Even more serious, perhaps, than the effects upon physical strength and capacity, are the possible effects of malnutrition upon mental capacities. There is increasing evidence that malnutrition can substantially reduce brain weight, and can reduce learning rates and abilities in children (Berg 1971, pp. 9–12). Since a reduced capacity to benefit from education in childhood has permanent effects into adulthood, it is probable that undernourishment may seriously affect the ability of people to take rational decisions. This is likely to be particularly true with respect to long-run economic decisions, and if so the economic losses from this effect of malnutrition may well be considerable.

## 7.2 Some Elementary Analysis

In analysing the WFP it is of critical importance to distinguish between biological and economic concepts of food shortage. The notion of biological shortage is conceptually straightforward in the human context – it is that there are insufficient nutrients available to supply the physiological needs of some person or group of persons. The economic notions of demand and shortage are entirely different, and to illustrate this we need no more complicated a tool than the elementary demand curve.

The market demand curve for a commodity is conventionally defined as the amounts of that commodity which would be purchased during a specified time interval at alternative prices of the commodity by a group of people with a fixed disposable income, the prices of all other commodities being held constant. It is generally assumed that such a curve will be negatively sloping so that at lower prices more will be consumed, as in figure 7.1

Consider then the alternative forms of individual family behaviour which might underlie the increase in demand which accompanies a fall in price (from $P_1$ to $P_2$) along a market demand curve defined for food. (1) Some families already consuming sufficient food at $P_1$ will increase their consumption further as prices fall to $P_2$. (2) Other families consuming insufficient nutrients at $P_1$ will be able to afford to satisfy their biological needs at $P_2$. (3) Some families consuming insufficient nutrients at $P_1$ will increase their consumption at $P_2$ but still have inadequate diets. Within this category would lie those who produce insufficient food for their own needs, and who can purchase very little at the higher price of food, $P_1$. (4) There may be other families who purchase no food at either $P_1$ or $P_2$ within a given time period. Two types of people will fall into this category, those who produce more than sufficient for their own requirements, and more

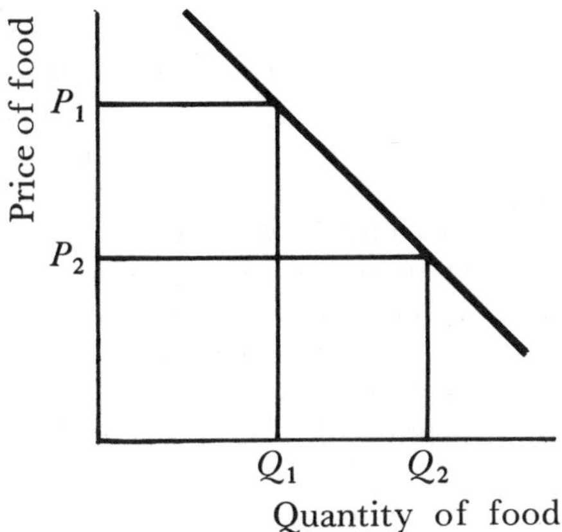


**Figure 7.1** Demand curve

importantly those who neither produce enough nor have money income with which to buy food.

The main reason for the existence of these four different types of reaction to lower food prices is the unequal distribution of income, which dictates that some people can afford sufficient food even at very high prices, while others have insufficient income to satisfy their needs even at low prices. It is evident from the possible existence of behavioural types three and four above, that even at very low food prices there can be no guarantee that hunger and malnutrition among the poor will be eliminated. It is in the nature of the market system that nearly everybody has less than they want, and that some people may have less than they need, whatever the prevailing price. Provided that income continues to be unequally distributed it seems inevitable that hunger and malnutrition will continue as long as we rely upon the competitive market system to allocate available food supplies.

This last conclusion is reinforced upon consideration of the elementary economics of supply. This theory suggests that the higher the price the greater will be supply. But at higher prices the poor are increasingly unable to feed themselves adequately. Of course, technological change does shift the food supply curve to the right over time. The future of the world food problem depends greatly upon the rate of such shifts in relation to corresponding shifts in the demand curve (arising from population and income growth). If, as in the past, technological change shifts agricultural supply curves to the right more rapidly than the demand curves, the real price of food will fall and an increasing proportion of productive resources can be deployed for non-food production. If, however, supply shifts exactly match demand shifts then food prices will remain constant. Any tendency of supply shifts to lag behind those in demand will cause prices to rise, and it is this condition which can be defined as a situation of increasing economic shortage.

The theory also provides a basis for assessing the prospects for future growth of food supplies in the face of ever increasing demand. Supply curves slope upwards because, it is argued, higher prices will make it profitable to allocate new resources to production. With this principle in mind it seems feasible to argue that the world economic *potential* for supply growth is more than adequate to cope with the expected doubling of the world population to seven billion by AD 2010. This is based on the reasoning that, even making no allowance for new technological innovations, if prices were sufficiently high it would be possible to switch a massive amount of resources from industrial production into intensive agriculture. Such a process would represent a reversal of the historic process of development, whereby food expenditure and agricultural employment have fallen as proportions of the relevant totals. Control of the ecological consequences of such an intensification of agricultural production would itself demand substantial resources thereby increasing production costs and agriculture-related employment still further.[5]

This extreme scenario highlights several important aspects of the world food problem and of underdevelopment. It is not limitation on the technical capacity to produce food which is the prime cause for concern about hunger and malnutrition in poor countries. It is lack of income by the poor in underdeveloped countries, which is a necessity for them to convert their biological food demand into effective economic demand, and for them to pay the higher prices needed to stimulate food production or encourage importation of food. The question of how such incomes are to be obtained by the poor is the key issue of underdevelopment. Another highlighted aspect is the central role of agricultural technology, in that large-scale mobilisation of resources and changes in farming technique are required in some, mainly developing countries if the massive technical potential for increasing world food production is to be realised. Unless cost-reducing, yield-increasing technological change in agriculture continues at a rapid rate, it is inevitable that world food prices will rise and cause the underdevelopment problem to be more intractable than it is now.[6] High-priority for agricultural development is essential in the economic plans of poor countries and in international policies to assist these countries to ensure that rates of technological changes do not fall below the levels which have been achieved historically.

Simple economic analysis also illuminates the existing and prospective pattern of world trade in foodstuffs. A direct implication of the conclusion that the rich will always be able to purchase as much food as they need (and often more) is that the wealthier nations are always likely to be able to acquire food supplies on an adequate scale for their population, whereas the poorer ones may not find themselves in such a favourable position.[7] In fact the action of commodity exporters and brokers may well result in food being exported from poor countries with a chronic malnutrition problem to countries which on average are overfed. Such exports will occur if the export price obtainable by traders exceeds the price which food commodities command in domestic markets – such action will of course bid domestic prices up to the international level. This situation is most likely to occur with concentrated protein sources, for which transport costs to the final destination are a smaller percentage of export (f.o.b.) value, than for bulky starchy foods. In some cases it may be commercially profitable for poor countries to export high-quality protein foods and to import cheaper, low-quality (in terms of protein) foods such as grains and, in a subset of these, the nutritional position may be improved by such trade; but in some instances it may even pay private traders to export basic grains from countries with serious malnutrition problems. Typical examples of the sort of trade that arises in foodstuffs are the export to developed countries of beef from Kenya and Brazil, of fishmeal from Peru for use as animal feed, and oilseeds from a number of tropical countries (Abbott 1972). At the same time there has been a major trade in wheat and other grains from the USA, Canada and Australia to various developing countries, particularly to India.

Food exports from poor countries are, of course, more likely to occur in periods of global food shortage and high prices, such as that occurring from 1973-75, which is when the capacity of the rich to outbid the poor for food supplies becomes most evident. That this capacity has been heightened by economic development is one of the paradoxes of development. For as rail, road, telephone and port facilities in poorer countries have been improved, and as their professional expertise in organising international trade has grown, so increasingly have separate regional markets in agricultural products coalesced into a single global market in which price signals emanating from North America, Europe and Japan directly influence food prices in Central Africa, Asia and South America, and can induce the export of food from these countries.

## 7.3 Future Prospects and Policy Options

At the beginning of the 1970s there was a measure of optimism about the world food supply situation. Even allowing for the large increase in world population, FAO projections made in 1971 suggested that by 1980 there would be a tendency of world cereal supply growth to outstrip growth in demand with a consequent downward pressure on food prices (FAO 1971). It was further projected that net annual cereal imports to the low income countries might fall from 12.9 to 3.5 million tonnes between 1970 and 1980. The largest part of this reduction was expected for Asia and the Far East with a projected decline in cereal imports to them of almost 6 million tonnes. To a substantial degree this encouraging assessment was based upon an optimistic view of the potential for the Green Revolution in Asia and its counterparts elsewhere. Subsequent events, however, have cast a shadow over this optimism and it must now appear questionable as to whether food supply growth is going to be sufficient to exert downward pressure upon prices and so to alleviate the poverty–hunger problem in underdeveloped countries. The main shadow which has emerged is due to the sharp rise in energy prices initiated in 1973. While in real terms energy prices have (by 1977) fallen back from their peak 1974 levels, their future level is uncertain. Should their real level again rise to, or surpass, that of 1974 a further check may be expected to the rate of adoption of that agricultural technology based on more intensive use of fertiliser, machinery and insecticides, all of which are expensive to produce in terms of fossil energy.

In addition, growing problems of supplying water for irrigation are imposing limitations upon the rate at which agricultural intensification can proceed in some of the poorest countries.[8] Thus later projections suggest that, although world food supplies may grow faster than demand at constant prices, in the low- and medium-income countries production growth will not keep pace with demand (Blakeslee, Heady and Framingham 1973). Hence it is projected that the developing countries will become increasingly dependent upon the rich countries (the USA, Canada and Australia in particular) for their food supplies. From the developing countries' viewpoint this is an extremely depressing prospect, implying as it does increased food prices, no alleviation of the extent of hunger and malnutrition, and a severe, deteriorating balance of payments situation.

Even if food supply prospects were less gloomy than the preceding statement suggests – and for some individual developing countries the outlook is relatively promising – there can be no doubt that as long as underdevelopment and accompanying poverty persist hunger and malnutrition will exist. The international community appears to have become increasingly aware of this, and public policy statements by international bodies have begun to accord high priority to overcoming the hunger aspect of underdevelopment. Evidence of this heightened concern is to be found in the convening of the World

Food Council in 1974 and 1975, and in the enormously increased volume of literature and discussion about world food policy, but not as yet in any major new policy measures.

Although no attempt is made here to classify policies for tackling the food problem of the poor countries according to whether they originate within these countries, rather than at an international level with the support of the rich countries, it has to be recognised that the distinction between policies at the two levels is significant. International level policies reflect not purely humanitarian or imperialistic considerations, but also acceptance that some major irritants of the problem arise from demand–supply conditions in world markets which are outside the control of the poor countries. It is considered appropriate that the rich countries should at least partially compensate the poorer ones for certain adverse external effects of the fluctuations in economic activity in the industrial nations. Nevertheless, the main attack on the nutrition problem of poor countries must be managed directly through the policies of the countries themselves. This is especially true in relation to expanding domestic food supplies and taking steps to adjust income distributions. Individual countries may wish, and be able, to enlist international support for their domestic policies, but while considering the policy options discussed below it should be remembered that the initiative lies primarily with the developing countries.

The types of policy which might be pursued to reduce the incidence of malnutrition are characteristic of the policy options for promoting economic development generally. Broadly there are three groups of policies: those which aim to accelerate change without modifying institutional structure or materially interfering with the 'free' operation of markets; those which require the introduction of new major institutions to modify either the operations or outcomes of existing market systems; and policies which aim to bypass normal market operations. The majority of the commonly applied policies of agricultural development fall within the first two of these groups. Since these are extensively discussed in the previous chapter no further consideration is given here.

However, there are aspects of the third policy category which have not been discussed hitherto, and which merit a brief mention here. This third category of policies recognises the inherent weaknesses of market systems (particularly in developing countries), and represents the most direct means of tackling the food problem. It should, therefore, in principle be both the cheapest and most effective approach to the problem. Basically it entails making direct transfers of food to those unable to purchase their needs in open markets — direct transfers of income would represent the same direct type of policy, but have not been employed in developing countries for obvious fiscal reasons.[9] On an international basis, food transfer programmes have been and are employed to provide cheap or free food to those who would otherwise suffer calorie- and possibly protein-deficient diets. These transfers from developed to underdeveloped countries have taken the form either of regular food-aid, that is of continuous flows of food such as of wheat from the USA to India under the Public Law 480 programme, or of emergency food-aid.

Emergency relief schemes deal with temporary food shortages arising from localised man-made or natural disturbances, and they provide free food to those in need. Regular international food-aid programmes on the other hand are directed at the chronic, persistent aspect of malnutrition in developing countries. There are, however, reservations about their effectiveness; there are many administrative difficulties in large-scale distribution of free food, and food received on concessionary terms is often sold by recipient governments on commercial terms. Where this is done the most needy, those with low incomes, are not greatly helped, except in so far as the extra food supplies depress prices. This is, however, a source of much criticism levelled at food-aid schemes; that the reduction of food prices in the recipient countries leads to cut-backs in local food production, and aggravation of the long-run food problem in poor countries (Bhagwati and Eckaus 1970). Recent empirical evidence for India (Rogers *et. al.* 1972; Isenman and Singer 1977) does not lend empirical support to this criticism, and suggests that a relatively high proportion of food aid may bypass the normal market and be allocated on concessional terms to those in need. Despite this evidence the view that food-aid depresses food prices and locally produced supplies in receiving countries has been widely held and used to argue that food-aid programmes are an inappropriate way of fighting the food problem.

Clearly there are great difficulties in applying ability-to-pay criteria to assess those eligible for free supplies. This is especially so in view of the need to avoid (a) the build up of new communities completely dependent upon free supplies and (b) restricting labour mobility. Further difficulties in expanding food distribution schemes and building strategic food reserves arise in devising criteria to distinguish disaster conditions from those of chronic and typical shortage (Sinha 1976). The distinction is important in that different distribution systems are appropriate to the different circumstances. In a disaster situation most people in an affected area are eligible for relief. In a situation of persistent shortage only some people may be eligible, and relief should probably be contingent upon the institution of other measures in the recipient country. There are also other problems, such as where should food stocks be held and who should finance and administer them, all of which consume much time in negotiations.

It is not possible to review all the specific policies which involve the creation of new institutions to moderate the impact of market forces upon the malnourished. But perhaps the most discussed and favoured policy of this type is the creation of buffer stock schemes either at national or international level. At national level such schemes may greatly augment food storage capacity and reduce food losses from on-farm storage, thus creating both long- and short-term benefits. In the short term, such schemes help ensure that food supplies last from one harvest to the next,[10] while in the longer run they should help eliminate the extreme high prices in years of poor harvests and can provide emergency food reserves. With regard to these latter functions it is argued that they could be more efficiently performed by an internationally controlled stock policy covering many food products, rather than by independently operated national stocks. This follows from the lower probability of simultaneous shortfall in supply of many crops in many countries than of one commodity in one country. This thinking is one of the factors underlying the UNCTAD negotiations started in 1976 relating to the establishment of a multilateral, multicommodity scheme embracing buffer stocks for a possible 18 commodities (Sinha 1976). It must be stated, however, that buffer stock schemes, except in so far as they include provision for emergency food relief, do not frontally attack the hunger problem. To the extent that they help poor consumers in some years by holding down prices, and poor peasant producers in others by supporting prices, such schemes may alleviate the food problem at the margin; but their effectiveness in this is constrained by the fact that price stabilisation rather than solving the food problem is their main objective. This criticism is also true of the other proposed components of the New International Economic Order (NIEO), except in so far as they might increase export earnings in developing countries and transmit these increases to the poor. (For further more detailed consideration of the NIEO see Chapter 4.)

One policy of institutional change which must be mentioned in this context is redistributive land reform. As is more fully discussed in Chapter 6, one of the most critical issues in agricultural development strategy is whether it is more efficient to distribute land in small parcels to peasants, or to create larger holdings on which there is a tendency to substitute machinery and other inputs for labour. There can be little doubt that where the latter strategy increases the number of landless-workless people it exacerbates the food problem of the rural poor, whereas distributive land reform, although it may reduce the rate of growth of marketed surplus, puts either food or income directly into the hands of some of the poorest families. This highlights once again the links between unequal income distribution and the food problem.

As to the other set of policies which may exert beneficial influence upon the food problem – those which neither create new institutions nor explicitly interfere with the operation of markets – it includes all those aspects of policy which improve efficiency in the production and distribution of foodstuffs and exert a downward influence on prices. Its principal component is the set of national policies typically operated by Ministries of Agriculture via the extension services, parastatal marketing organisations, rural development agencies and research organisations. These have been discussed extensively in Chapter 6 and it would be superfluous to consider them further in detail here. But what should be pointed out is that these policies, which form the core of agricultural policy, are not specifically intended to tackle the food problem as we have defined it. Their main objectives are in increasing agricultural supply rather than in reducing the gap between the biological need for food and the expressed economic demand for food in the market place. Such general measures cannot therefore be expected to have a dramatic impact upon the food problem, and will only help alleviate it to the extent that the development benefits they produce trickle down to the poorest (unemployed and underemployed) members of society. This observation also extends to general (non-radical) development policies directed at sectors other than agriculture. Their contribution to solving the food problem (as a key symptom of the deprivation associated with underdevelopment) rests more upon the extent to which the benefits are distributed to the poor than upon simply increasing the rate of economic growth. However, because general development policies by definition are not specifically aimed at the poorest people, it is doubtful whether, except in the very long run, they can have a major impact upon the problem of malnutrition. It is for this reason that we have argued that specifically designed food distribution policies or radical redistributive measures are best suited to overcoming this 'food problem' syndrome of underdevelopment.

## Notes

1 For a helpful appreciation of Malthus and his critics see T.H. Hollingworth's introduction to the recent edition of Malthus' work published in 1973 (Malthus 1973).

2 To the extent that food has been increasingly imported by the developing countries from the developed ones this decline in numbers would have been greater than that implied by examination of production growth alone.

3 For a fairly complete account of the factors contributing to the 'food crisis' of 1972-75 see Allen (1976).

4 It should be recognised that malnutrition may occur only in the sense of a deficiency in some minor element or nutrient, such as iodine or vitamin D. Such deficiences may have serious long-run consequences but are amenable to solution cheaply by including additives in diets. The problem which cannot be solved cheaply is that of gross calorie or protein deficiency. Note that, as Joy (1973) has forcefully pointed out, protein deficiency is seldom found when calorie intake is adequate. Accepting this, the cheapest and most effective solution to protein deficiency is to increase intake of highly calorific foods such as grains, in preference to concentrating on supplying expensive animal protein.

5 For a more than usually balanced account of the ecological and resource implications of substantially increasing world agricultural output see Borgstrom (1969).

6 Of course it is true that high food prices may increase the GDP per capita in poor countries. But the benefits of this will primarily go to those with land and the poor will be further disadvantaged.

7 Referring to countries as if they were indivisible consumer units is a useful form of shorthand. It is not used to imply that the food balance is not the outcome of independent decisions taken by producers, middle-men, and consumers.

8 In the light of Borgstrom's (op. cit.) concern expressed in 1969 about the likelihood that water supplies would prove the most critical constraint to all forms of economic activity, it is also particularly interesting and worrying to note the problems of dwindling water supplies in the irrigated grain producing regions of the USA which supply much of the grain imports of developing countries.

9 Income transfer schemes have been adopted in the USA Food Stamp Scheme, in which poor families are eligible to purchase stamps for less than their exchange value into food. The subsidy involved is Federally financed.

10 It should be recognised that, for many, hunger and malnutrition may be a seasonal phenomenon, where supplies are plentiful and cheap immediately after harvest but scarce and expensive immediately before harvest. Evidence of such a pattern is presented by Haswell (1975, Ch. 4).

## Bibliography

Abbott J.C. (1972), 'The efficient use of world protein supplies', FAO, *Monthly Bulletin of Agricultural Economics and Statistics*, Vol. 21, No. 6.

Allen G.R. (1976), 'Some aspects of planning world food supplies', *Journal of Agricultural Economics*, Vol. 27, No. 1.

Berg A. (1971), *The Nutrition Factor*, The Brookings Institution.

Bhagwati J. and Eckaus R. (eds) (1970), *Foreign Aid*, Penguin.

Blakeslee L.L., Heady E.O. and Framingham C.F. (1973), *World Food Production, Demand and Trade*, Iowa State University Press.

Boerma A.H. (1975), *Political Will and the World Food Problem*, UN Food and Agricultural Organisation, Rome.

Borgstrom G. (1969), *Too Many: A Study of Earth's Biological Limitations*, Macmillan.

Clark C. (1967), *Population Growth and Land Use*, Macmillan.

FAO (1971), *Agricultural Commodity Projections 1970-1980*, Vol. 1, Rome.

FAO (1974), 'Population, food supply and agricultural development', *Monthly Bulletin of Agricultural Economics and Statistics*, Vol. 23, No. 9.

Haswell M. (1975), *The Nature of Poverty*, Macmillan.

Isenman P.J. and Singer H.W. (1977), 'Food aid: disincentive effects and their policy implications', *Economic Development and Cultural Change*, Vol. 25, No. 2.

Joy L. (1973), 'Food and nutrition planning', *Journal of Agricultural Economics*, Vol. 24, No. 1.

Malthus T.R. (1973), *An Essay on the Principle of Population*, Dent.

Rogers K.D., Srivastava U.K. and Heady E.O. (1972), 'Modified price, production and income impacts of food-aid under differentiated distribution', *American Journal of Agricultural Economics*, Vol. 54, May.

Sinha R.P. (1976), 'World food security', *Journal of Agricultural Economics*, Vol. 27, No. 1.

Sinha R.P. (1976), *Food and Poverty*, Croom Helm.

# 8
# Industrial development in LDCs

## 8.1 The Desire for Industrialisation

In its broadest sense, the term 'industrialisation' denotes the organisation of production in business enterprises, characterised by specialisation and the division of labour, and involving the application of technology and mechanical and electrical power to supplement and replace human labour. Conceived of in this way, all sectors of the economy (the production of consumer goods and capital equipment, agriculture and service activities) can be 'industrialised' and thus it is the rational approach to the production process itself that is of significance, not merely the production of commodities considered to be 'industrial'.

In this chapter, however, we are concerned with a much narrower concept of industrialisation – the development of manufacturing enterprises, producing commonly accepted industrial goods, within the so-called 'modern' sector of the economy. Lip-service is paid to the need for the establishment of small-scale, rural industries by the majority of LDCs but only China has made real progress in this field and, in general, industry is large-scale, capital-intensive and urban-based. The past few years have seen the 'informal sector' of the economy (sometimes referred to as the 'low productivity urban sector' or the 'traditional urban sector') emerge from obscurity, with emphasis placed on the need for its development in order to absorb at least partly the rapidly growing urban populations of LDCs (ILO Report on Kenya, 1972). But as a broad generalisation, in the absence of radical political and social changes within LDCs, a shift of emphasis in development priorities is unlikely and attention will remain focused on modern, urban-based manufacturing enterprises.

For many politicians and planners in LDCs, industrialisation (narrowly interpreted) and development have been synonymous with one another. The industrialisation of a basically agricultural, primary export-oriented economy was seen as the means by which the chains of dependence forged during the colonial period could be broken, matching the newly acquired political independence with economic independence. Industry would create extensive employment opportunities, absorbing excess labour leaving the rural sector, it would raise output per head and living standards throughout the economy and, significantly, it would induce necessary and desirable changes in social and cultural attitudes and institutions through the 'modernising' impact of imported organisational methods and technologies. In some LDCs, industrialisation was seen as the means by which specific socialist objectives could be achieved (with the experience of the Soviet Union very much in mind); in others, economic planners were more concerned with the role of industry in alleviating the balance of payments constraint, diversifying the economy and reducing excessive dependence on the export of a few primary commodities, the prices of which were allegedly subject to a long-run secular deterioration and which, in the short run, exhibited substantial year-to-year fluctuations around the trend.

## 8.2 Industry versus Agriculture

Industrial development and agricultural development have too often been viewed as conflicting objectives and a largely unproductive debate has flourished over the relative priority to be afforded to the expansion of the two sectors. Sutcliffe (1971, Ch. 3) has argued that conflict is not inevitable and that the concept of 'priority', as used in the debate, is a misleading one:

> To give priority to something does not necessarily involve the expenditure of more than a very small amount of time or money. Matters of priority can be small or large. To give 'priority' to agriculture does not imply that investment, employment, output or productivity in agriculture should grow *faster* than in industry or that public investment in agriculture should be greater than that in industry ... It is quite possible that if the aim of a government was to encourage the maximum growth of industry within ten years, then for the first five years most attention would be devoted to agriculture, which could thereby more effectively provide raw materials for industry and demand for its products ... 'Priority' to industry here appears to imply 'priority' for agriculture; 'priority' is thus robbed of any operational meaning.
>
> (Sutcliffe 1971, p. 72, emphasis in original.)

It is now generally accepted that, for the majority of LDCs, industrial and agricultural development should, as far as possible, proceed simultaneously. Agriculture provides the market for manufactured goods, satisfies the food requirements of the urban population, releases labour and capital for the industrial sector and earns the foreign exchange required for the importation of machinery and raw materials. Industry in turn supplies the inputs (tractors, fertilisers, etc.) required for the modernisation of the agricultural sector and the consumer goods demanded by the rural population and provides a market for a part of agricultural output through the processing and manufacture of foodstuffs for both domestic consumption and export.

These are essentially arguments for 'balanced growth' between the two sectors but not all the arguments are equally valid for all LDCs. An overpopulated country with a poor agricultural resource endowment may have no alternative but to attempt to industrialise and export manufactured goods with which to import essential foodstuffs. In open economies, the concept of 'balanced growth' loses a great deal of its meaning and in any case it does not indicate which sector should be made the 'spearhead' of the development effort.

Paul Baran, with the experience of the Soviet Union in mind, has argued that, under conditions of socialist planning,

> ... there can be no question as to whether development should proceed through industrialisation or through improvement of agriculture. It can take place only by a *simultaneous* effort in both directions ... the investment policy has to place its main accent on the development of industry – lifting agriculture at the same time high enough to support the industrialisation process – so as to be able eventually to turn around and give agriculture a major boost with the help of the expanded resources of industrial production.'
>
> (Baran 1957, pp. 282-83)

Baran's recommendation partly reflects the Soviet Union's decision that agriculture was to serve industry even though, as already indicated, the development of the two sectors is closely interrelated. The other important characteristic of the Soviet Union's industrialisation experience was the emphasis placed on the establishment of producer goods industries (especially producer goods that manufactured other producer goods). It is of interest to contrast this with the current Chinese strategy. Since 1966, the Chinese have attempted to develop heavy industry, light industry and agriculture simultaneously. Heavy industry remains the focus of the development effort but it is not promoted at the expense of the other two sectors. Light industry is expanded in order to raise the living standards of the mass of the population and has permitted a reduction in agriculture's contribution to state revenues (the source of finance for industrial expansion) from approximately 70% at an earlier stage to 10% at the present time (the remaining 90% is raised by taxes and the profits of industry) (Magdoff 1975, p. 44).[1]

The above discussion should make it clear that the categories that are conventionally used for the classification of activities must be treated with caution. Some activities, for example the processing of foodstuffs, are an integral part of both the industrial and agricultural sectors, thus making nonsense of the 'industry–agriculture' dichotomy. In the industrial sector itself, we must clearly distinguish between producer (or capital) goods industries and consumer goods industries. (The Marxist tradition in particular has always made a sharp distinction between capital goods (Department I) and consumer goods (Department II).) The more common distinction between heavy and light industries is less satisfactory as it gives no indication of the destination of the output of those industries. Capital goods industries (machines that make machines) need not, of necessity, be 'heavy'. Intermediate goods (iron and steel) could fall into either category and so presumably could consumer goods. Although definitional problems exist, we assume, with Stewart (1976, p. 121) that the distinction between capital and consumer goods is 'unproblematic'. The importance of different types of industries will be made clearer in later sections of this chapter.

## 8.3 The Growth of Industry in LDCs

The majority of LDCs in the post-World War II period have made substantial progress in the establishment of domestic manufacturing industries. Chenery (1971) identified eleven LDCs which had an annual average growth rate of manufacturing production for the period 1951–1969 of above 10% (Taiwan, Jordan, Republic of Korea, Panama, Trinidad and Tobago, Iran, Venezuela, Zambia, Turkey, Pakistan and Singapore), an impressive performance judged by any historical comparison.

Table 8.1 presents a global picture and includes both the centrally planned economies and the developed market economies (to use United Nations terminology) by way of comparison. The industrial sector in general and manufacturing in particular grew rapidly in all the major regions of the less developed world, outpacing the growth of total GDP and growing much faster than the agricultural sector. In the period 1970–73, all regions except Africa showed a quite substantial increase in the rate of growth of manufacturing.

Table 8.2 presents data on the growth of manufacturing for a representative group of 36 LDCs, demonstrating considerable differences between individual LDCs. Care must be taken in interpreting the data as the high growth rates recorded for some of these economies (for example Nigeria, Jordan, Tanzania and Malaysia) are merely a reflection of the restricted size of the industrial sector that existed in these economies at the beginning of the period. The final column of table 8.2 illustrates the relatively low share of manufacturing in GDP in these countries even after a decade of rapid industrial growth. Nevertheless, the share of manufacturing in total GDP for some of

**Table 8.1** *Average annual percentage rates of growth of GDP at constant prices*

| Region | Period | GDP Total | GDP Per cap. | Agriculture | Industrial activity Total[a] | Industrial activity Mfg. |
|---|---|---|---|---|---|---|
| World[b] | 1960–70 | 5.6 | 3.5 | 2.2 | 6.7 | – |
| | 1970–73 | 5.8 | 3.9 | 1.0 | 6.7 | – |
| Centrally planned economies | 1960–70 | 6.8 | 5.7 | 1.6 | 8.7 | – |
| | 1970–73 | 6.2 | 5.2 | 0.2 | 7.2 | – |
| Developed market economies | 1960–70 | 5.2 | 4.0 | 2.4 | 6.0 | 6.3 |
| | 1970–73 | 5.1 | 4.1 | 1.7 | 6.3 | 6.6 |
| Developing market economies[c] | 1960–70 | 5.3 | 2.7 | 2.7 | 7.5 | 7.0 |
| | 1970–73 | 6.0 | 3.2 | 1.1 | 8.5 | 8.6 |
| Africa (excluding South Africa) | 1960–70 | 5.0 | 2.4 | 1.7 | 10.2 | 7.1 |
| | 1970–73 | 5.1 | 2.2 | 0.8 | 4.7 | 6.3 |
| Caribbean and Latin America | 1960–70 | 5.5 | 2.6 | 3.4 | 6.6 | 6.8 |
| | 1970–73 | 6.9 | 3.9 | 2.9 | 8.2 | 9.0 |
| Asia – Middle East | 1960–70 | 7.4 | 4.4 | 3.7 | 9.7 | 10.1 |
| | 1970–73 | 9.6 | 6.6 | 0.6 | 13.6 | 13.3 |
| Asia – East and South East (excluding Japan) | 1960–70 | 4.5 | 2.0 | 2.6 | 7.1 | 6.9 |
| | 1970–73 | 4.0 | 1.5 | 0.6 | 7.6 | 7.4 |

*Source:* UN, *Year Book of National Accounts Statistics, 1974,* Vol. III, *International Tables,* New York, 1975, Table 4b.

[a] Mining, manufacturing, electricity, gas and water. Includes also sanitary services in a number of market economies.

[b] Excludes China, Democratic People's Republic of Korea, Democratic Republic of Vietnam and Mongolia.

[c] Countries in Africa (except South Africa), Caribbean and Latin America, East and South East Asia (except Japan) and Middle East (except Israel) and Fiji.

the more advanced LDCs (for example Brazil, Mexico, Argentina, Chile and Iran) is becoming comparable to the contribution of that sector to the GDPs of the advanced capitalist economies. We return to this point below.

The rapid growth of manufacturing output has not been matched by an equally rapid growth of employment in modern manufacturing establishments in the majority of LDCs. Population growth has been rapid, but the rate of growth of urban populations has been even higher, largely owing to the massive migration of labour from rural to urban areas (see table 8.3). The data in table 8.3 also show that during the 1960s, the total labour force (employed and unemployed) in LDCs increased at an annual average rate of 2%, but that the annual average rate of increase of the industrial labour force (those employed

**Table 8.2** *Expansion of value added in manufacturing activity and of gross domestic*

| *Country* | *Average annual rate of increase*(b) | | *Increase in value added in mfg. as % of increase in GDP* | *Value added in mfg. as % of GDP* | |
|---|---|---|---|---|---|
| | *Mfg. activity* | *Gross domestic product* | | *Early 1960s* | *Early 1970s* |
| *Annual rate of increase in manufacturing activity of 8% or more:* | | | | | |
| Singapore | 19.3 | 9.7 | 30 | 9.3 | 21.5 |
| Republic of Korea | 17.3 | 9.0 | 31 | 10.8 | 22.6 |
| Iran | 12.5 | 9.1 | 27 | 17.5 | 22.4 |
| Nigeria | 11.3 | 5.4 | 14 | 4.8 | 8.4 |
| Thailand | 10.9 | 7.9 | 21 | 13.2 | 17.5 |
| Malaysia | 10.9 | 5.5 | 20 | 8.3 | 12.6 |
| Panama | 10.6 | 7.7 | 21 | 13.2 | 17.2 |
| United Republic of Tanzania | 10.3 | 5.7 | 15 | 7.4 | 9.5 |
| Mexico | 9.5 | 7.3 | 27 | 19.3 | 23.1 |
| Jordan | 8.8 | 4.8 | 16 | 7.4 | 10.0 |
| Brazil | 8.3 | 6.7 | 29 | 21.6 | 25.1 |
| El Salvador | 8.3 | 5.9 | 23 | 14.9 | 18.2 |
| Honduras | 8.0 | 5.3 | 21 | 12.8 | 15.5 |
| *Annual rate of increase in manufacturing activity of 6% to 8%:* | | | | | |
| Kenya | 7.9 | 7.2 | 12 | 10.7 | 11.2 |
| Pakistan(c) | 7.7 | 4.9 | 18 | 10.1 | 13.0 |
| Uganda | 7.6 | 4.8 | 10 | 6.0 | 7.0 |
| Guatemala | 7.6 | 5.6 | 20 | 13.0 | 15.8 |
| Ecuador | 7.5 | 5.4 | 24 | 15.5 | 18.6 |
| Bolivia | 7.2 | 5.6 | 16 | 12.0 | 13.9 |
| Sri Lanka | 7.1 | 4.2 | 15 | 7.5 | 10.0 |
| Peru | 6.7 | 4.5 | 28 | 16.6 | 20.4 |
| Dominican Republic | 6.6 | 5.7 | 19 | 15.6 | 17.1 |
| Venezuela | 6.5 | 5.5 | 25 | 19.7 | 21.7 |
| Syrian Arab Republic | 6.1 | 4.9 | 19 | 14.8 | 15.9 |
| Colombia | 6.1 | 5.2 | 22 | 17.9 | 19.5 |

and seeking employment in mining, manufacturing, construction, electricity, gas and water) was more than twice as great. The inability of the 'modern' industrial sector to provide sufficient job opportunities for the growing labour force has meant that large-scale urban unemployment (ranging between 15–25% of the labour force for many LDCs, with often higher percentages for young people) has become a characteristic feature of the pattern of development experienced by the majority of LDCs.

Some LDCs have achieved high rates of growth of manufacturing *product in constant prices, early 1960s to early 1970s*[a] *(percentage)*

| *Country* | *Average annual rate of increase*[b] *Mfg. activity* | *Gross domestic product* | *Increase in value added in mfg. as % of increase in GDP* | *Value added in mfg. as % of GDP Early 1960s* | *Early 1970s* |
|---|---|---|---|---|---|
| *Annual rate of increase in manufacturing activity of less than 6%* | | | | | |
| Jamaica | 5.7 | 4.9 | 16 | 13.8 | 14.7 |
| Chile | 5.7 | 4.5 | 30 | 23.1 | 25.7 |
| Egypt | 5.6 | 4.7 | 24 | 19.6 | 21.2 |
| Paraguay | 5.5 | 4.2 | 19 | 15.3 | 16.6 |
| Tunisia | 5.4 | 4.0 | 20 | 13.7 | 15.6 |
| Argentina | 5.4 | 4.0 | 45 | 31.5 | 35.4 |
| Philippines | 5.4 | 4.9 | 21 | 18.8 | 19.8 |
| India | 5.2 | 3.7 | 22 | 14.6 | 16.6 |
| Iraq | 5.1 | 5.9 | 8 | 9.7 | 9.1 |
| Morocco | 4.4 | 4.3 | 15 | 13.9 | 14.1 |
| Indonesia | 4.1 | 4.0 | 11 | 7.5 | 8.4 |

*Source:* Centre for Development Planning, Projections and Policies of the Department of Economic and Social Affairs of the United Nations Secretariat (1975).

*(a)* Data are at constant factor cost except for the following countries where they are at constant market prices: Bolivia, Chile, Colombia, Dominican Republic, El Salvador, Guatemala, Indonesia, Mexico, Morocco, Paraguay, Peru, Republic of Korea, Syrian Arab Republic, Thailand, Tunisia and Venezuela.

*(b)* Annual compound rate calculated from average of two consecutive years in early 1960s and average of two consecutive years in early 1970s.

*(c)* Including data for Bangladesh.

employment. According to the United Nations (1975), between 1963 and 1970, Singapore, Sri Lanka, Republic of Korea, Honduras and Malaysia (West) all achieved rates of growth of manufacturing employment exceeding 11% per annum (the figure for Singapore was 17.6% per annum). The figure for Hong Kong between 1963–1969 was 9.2% per annum (Morawetz 1974, table 1). But others were less successful. For India the figure was 2.3% per annum, and for Brazil 1.6%. The Dominican Republic recorded a growth rate of –2.9% per annum.

**Table 8.3** *Average annual rate of increase (percentage) of population and labour force, 1960 – 1970*[a]

| *Region* | *Population* | | | *Labour force*[b] | |
|---|---|---|---|---|---|
| | *Total* | *Urban* | *Rural* | *Total* | *Industrial*[c] |
| Latin America | 2.9 | 4.5 | 1.1 | 2.3 | 3.7 |
| Caribbean | 2.3 | 4.5 | 1.1 | 1.5 | 2.6 |
| Africa | 2.6 | 5.1 | 2.1 | 2.1 | 4.6 |
| South and East Asia | 2.6 | 3.9 | 2.3 | 2.0 | 4.7 |
| West Asia | 3.0 | 5.1 | 1.8 | 2.3 | 4.2 |
| Total (57 developing countries) | 2.7 | 4.3 | 2.1 | 2.0 | 4.4 |

*Source:* Centre for Development Planning, Projections and Policies of the Department of Economic and Social Affairs of the United Nations Secretariat (1975).

(*a*) Data are for 57 LDCs that account for 75% of the population of all developing market economies.

(*b*) Economically active population.

(*c*) Mining, manufacturing, electricity, gas, water and construction.

Employment data have to be interpreted with caution. The creation of employment opportunities in modern manufacturing industries may be partially offset by the destruction of employment opportunities in handicraft and artisan activities. Part of the increase may result from a more comprehensive statistical coverage. The United Nations is at pains to point out that the data include not only employed workers in manufacturing production but also working proprietors, business partners and unpaid family workers, and thus the data do not provide an adequate basis for the precise examination of the relationship between employment and manufacturing production.

What is not in doubt is that employment in the modern (or 'organised') sector of manufacturing industry accounted, at the end of the 1960s, for less than 10% of the total labour force of many LDCs, and that, other things being equal, this proportion was not likely to change radically in the immediate future. The apparent inability of modern manufacturing industry to create extensive employment opportunities has led to attention being focused on a number of wider issues: alternative or 'appropriate' technologies, the encouragement of the so-called 'informal' sector of the economy, agrarian reform, income redistribution, the reform of the educational system, and so on. Many of these issues are touched on in this and other chapters.

Unemployment is a massive economic, social and political problem in the majority of LDCs and its elimination must be one of the major objectives of development planning (indeed, as we argued in Chapter 1, the move towards the fuller utilisation of available labour is an integral component of the concept of 'development' that we are using). But the immediacy of the issue should not blind us to the very real problems of measurement (referred to above) and conceptualisation that exist. For example, the terms 'unemployment' and 'underemployment', as used within the context of LDCs, are difficult both to conceptualise and quantify with any degree of accuracy. In Africa, to take one example, many of those registered as unemployed (that is seeking a job in the modern sector of the economy) will in fact be fully employed in the informal sector (street hawkers, illegal beer brewers, etc.), working very long hours for a very low income. In Nairobi it has been estimated that 20% of the income-earning opportunities in 1969 were provided by the informal sector (the equivalent figure for Mombasa was 35%, and for the smaller urban centres the figure may have been as high as 50% – see ILO 1972, pp. 54-57).

It is misleading to apply the term 'unemployed' (with its advanced economy connotations) to such people. Weeks has gone so far as to argue that '... it has not been established that "unemployment" is in fact a general problem in less developed countries' and that '... it is absurd to define the employment norm in terms of the conditions enjoyed by a tiny minority of the labour force' (that is, wage employment in the 'modern' sector) (Weeks 1971, p. 62). It must be stressed that the 'unemployment' problem and its associated symptoms are the *consequences* of the particular type of development occurring in LDCs. It is to a consideration of the strategies which underlie these patterns of development, with particular reference to the drive for industrialisation, that we now turn.[2]

## 8.4 Strategies of Industrial Development 1: Import Substituting Industrialisation (ISI)

In principle, although there are a number of different strategies that LDCs can follow in their pursuit of industrial development, it is essentially a choice between producing goods for overseas markets (export-led growth) or for the domestic market (import substitution), although the two strategies are not mutually exclusive. But even if the LDC decides to pursue a policy of ISI, it still has a number of options open to it:

(a) it can use its foreign exchange to import investment goods (for example looms), raw materials, fuels, etc. to manufacture consumer goods (cloth);

(b) it can use its foreign exchange to import capital goods (machine tools) to make both investment goods (looms) which in turn produce consumer goods (cloth), and to make intermediate goods and develop domestic raw material supplies;

(c) it can use its foreign exchange to import capital goods (machine tools) to make capital goods (machine tools). (This classification is based on Raj and Sen 1961.)

The great majority of LDCs, almost irrespective of their economic size or natural resource endowment, have pursued variation (a) of the ISI strategy (that is, the importation of investment goods to produce consumer goods, previously imported, for the domestic market). The more advanced, semi-industrialised LDCs, have moved on to variation (b). More broadly, ISI has been conceived of as a wider development strategy, rather than as merely an industrialisation strategy.

The exceptions to this generalisation are generally taken to be Hong Kong, Singapore, South Korea and Taiwan, all of which are regarded as having pursued, at least in recent years, 'outward-looking' development strategies (the concept of which we will criticise below). Countries such as Mexico, India, Brazil, Argentina, Pakistan and the Philippines are becoming of increasing importance as exporters of manufactured goods, but it is still true to say that their basic development policy is (or was until very recently) one of ISI.

*The Origins of ISI*

The impulses underlying the process of ISI are diverse. ISI was initiated in many Latin American countries as a response to the disruption caused by World War I, the economic depression of the 1930s and World War II, when either imports were not generally available, or there was insufficient foreign exchange to pay for them and thus domestically produced goods had to be substituted for those previously imported.[3] But ISI became more widespread in the post-1945 world. In some cases it was stimulated by balance of payments difficulties (import substitution was seen as being 'easier' than export promotion); in other cases, newly independent governments wishing to stimulate industrial development would impose protective tariffs on imports of manufactured goods and force international corporations (or local enterprises previously engaged in the import of the goods) to establish domestic production facilities if they wished to protect their market position. Kilby's (1969) study of Nigeria's industrialisation provides support for this 'market protection' hypothesis. In Latin America, the UN Economic

Commission for Latin America (ECLA) early on gave greater intellectual respectability to the pressures from various social groups for accelerating industrialisation (Felix 1968) by stressing the need for ISI based on protection, to stimulate employment, alleviate the balance of payments constraint and secure the benefits of technical progress. In other words, ISI was pursued as a conscious national development strategy.[4] In addition, Hirschman (1968) has pointed to the process of 'import swallowing' that occurs as an economy grows along an export-propelled path. As the domestic market expands as the result of export-led growth, certain industries with locational characteristics that give them a high degree of natural protection against imports (industries producing heavy, bulky final products which are costly to transport – for example, cement and brewing) become economically viable and can be established without deliberate government protection or intervention.

We must note here the importance of foreign private investment in the ISI process in most LDCs. Indeed, private direct foreign investment can be said to be part cause and part effect of the ISI process. An important feature of the post-war period has been large-scale direct investment (that is, the establishment of productive facilities) in manufacturing industries by transnational corporations (TNCs). Direct investment is becoming of increasing importance as a proportion of the total net private capital flow to LDCs and manufacturing investment accounts for approximately 50% of total direct investment. Barratt Brown (1974, Ch. 9) presents data which suggest that by 1966, approximately one-third of all manufactured output in LDCs, and nearly one-half of the growth of the previous decade, came from foreign firms.

The quantitative aspects of direct foreign investment hide its qualitative significance. Within manufacturing, direct investment has tended to concentrate in industries characterised by rapidly changing, advanced technology, a high degree of product differentiation and capital intensity. The concentration of foreign investment in the modern, rapidly growing sectors of the LDC economy has permitted it to exert an influence greater than that to be expected judged only by its quantitative measure.

We return to these issues in Chapter 9. For the time being, it is relevant to point out that the process of decolonisation amongst LDCs and the increasingly oligopolistic structure of the developed capitalist economies, together resulting in the changed structure of capital exports to LDCs, have produced a new international division of labour. On the one hand, we have the centres of industrial technology and scientific research within the developed capitalist economies and, on the other hand, we have the international periphery, consisting of those countries importing the achievements of technological advance (the LDCs). The implications of this process for the LDCs and the problems of technological dependence are dealt with below and in Chapters 9 and 10.

*The Concept and Measurement of ISI*

Attention has been focused on the problems of measuring the amount of ISI that has actually taken place within any one country or group of countries, but relatively little attention has been devoted to the critical examination of the concept of ISI itself. In particular, the distinction between ISI as a historical phenomenon (an *ex post* concept) and as a development strategy (an *ex ante* concept) has not always been clearly made and this confusion has had an adverse impact on the planning of industrialisation strategies.

For Chenery (1960) and others, ISI is a 'cause' of economic growth and it thus recommends itself as a development strategy. Historically, import substitution has always accompanied economic growth (Maizels 1963 shows that the import content of supplies declines with the progress of industrialisation, at least up to the point where a fairly mature level has been reached), but it could equally be a cause or a concomitant of that growth. Studies based on historical data do not tell us whether a deliberate ISI strategy is of relevance to today's LDCs and will provide the basis of a long-run development strategy.

Chenery's influential study published in 1960 seemed to indicate that ISI was responsible for perhaps 50% of industrial growth in a large number of countries. His analysis was based on a cross-section regression equation in which per capita value added in each industrial sector was regressed on per capita income and population of the economy concerned. He found that, as income grew, the industrial sector grew more rapidly than the rest of the economy and he distinguished the existence of a fairly uniform pattern of change in the production and import of industrial products. For each industry the positive deviation from proportional (or 'normal') growth was calculated. For example, if the economy grew by 10% and the textile sector grew by 16%, it was the 6% (non-proportional) growth that needed explanation.

Non-proportional growth could be attributed to:

(a) the substitution of domestic production for imports (that is, import substitution, defined by Chenery as the difference between growth in output with no change in the import ratio and the growth that actually took place);

(b) the growth in the final use of industrial products;

(c) the growth in intermediate demand arising from both import substitution and final demand changes.

Chenery concluded that:

> ... the effect of income growth on final demand accounts directly for only 22% of industrialisation. To this should be added the intermediate demand deriving from the growth of final demand, which increases the pure demand effects to 32% of the total deviation from proportionality.
>
> The increased share of domestic production in total supply, defined here as import substitution, is more important than the pure demand effects, since it accounts for 50% of industrialisation.
>
> (Chenery 1960, p. 641)

For Chenery, import substitution arose largely out of changes in supply conditions, that is changes in comparative advantage, rather than from changes in demand.

Chenery's concept of import substitution and his empirical analysis have been subject to many criticisms, only the more important of which can be mentioned here. The results are obtained from cross-section data which represent the relative position of a large number of countries at one point in time, but not necessarily the trend that will be followed by one country over a long period of time. Indeed, a study by Steuer and Voivodas (1965) reruns Chenery's model using time series data and obtains results inconsistent with the 'normal' pattern. Chenery's definition and measure of import substitution is very sensitive to the levels of income between which it is measured and the time periods chosen.

Furthermore, Sutcliffe (1971) maintains that the phenomenon actually measured by Chenery should be referred to as 'the reduction in the import content of manufactured supplies' and suggests that the term 'import substitution' should be used to cover '... only the direct substitution of domestic production for the import of the same product' (p. 255). This definition appears to be of greatest relevance to policy issues since it relates to the identification of import substitution opportunities (see following section), but it is still open to criticism.[5] There is no one generally accepted and consistent measure of import substitution; different measures can produce different and often conflicting estimates of the quantitative importance of ISI[6] and thus great care must be taken when interpreting and using the results.

### *The Estimation of the ISI Potential*

Under a regime of ISI, the development planner will usually consider a product suitable for domestic production if the domestic market, as given by the value or volume of imports of that product, is equal to or greater than the minimum economic output of a manufacturing unit. Protection will be given to the domestic producer so that the price of the imported product is equal to or greater than the price of the domestic product (assuming that imports are permitted after domestic production has commenced). Examples of this approach to the estimation of ISI potential can be found in the work of Maitra (1967) and Van Arkadie (1964), both of whom are concerned with estimating the potential for ISI in East Africa.

A number of criticisms must be made of this approach. Trade data may not be sufficiently disaggregated to permit the identification of specific products, especially in the case of consumer goods where product differentiation is important. Furthermore, if tariff protection is required, there will be a reduction in market demand as a result of the higher priced domestic product, unless the price elasticity of demand is zero (Helleiner 1972). But at a more general level, it is not necessarily the case that products that do not enter the country (or enter in only small amounts) do not merit investment and, conversely, because certain products are imported in large amounts, this does not mean that domestic production is desirable. In other words, it may be beneficial for a country to produce a product domestically which it did not previously import (for example, insecticides).

Under the ISI strategy, the production of consumer goods (often of a luxury or non-essential character) is likely to take priority and this may lead to a timid and conservative industrialisation policy. In general, criteria based on import data say nothing about the suitability of the product for domestic production and there is the need for full project appraisal, taking into account the factor endowments and development objectives of the LDC and the engineering and technological characteristics and demands of the project in question. But once we admit the importance of these other variables, we no longer have a policy of ISI in any meaningful sense.

Another important point is that the market for imported goods is unlikely to be representative of the demands of the population as a whole. ISI is more likely to cater for the demands of urban dwellers in general and middle and upper income groups in particular, rather than cater for the great mass of the population in rural or semi-urban areas. ISI accepts the pattern of demand, and the underlying pattern of income distribution, as given, whereas it may be both necessary and desirable to change both consumption patterns and distribution structures, which are aspects of a social and economic structure which industrialisation should radically change. This is more than an attack on ISI *per se*, but that does not destroy the validity of the criticism.

We return to the question of ISI and the distribution of income below.

*Alternative Critiques of ISI*

In this section, we attempt to outline two alternative ways of analysing the ISI process, the neo-classical critique and the structuralist/Marxist critique. The neo-classical approach can rightly be called a school of thought as it presents a coherent and logically consistent theoretical critique of the ISI process, but this is not the case with the structuralist/Marxist 'school' and we use that term simply for convenience. This will be elaborated below.

At a purely descriptive level, both 'schools' exhibit some similarities. It would be generally agreed that the majority of LDCs have relatively small, inefficient industrial sectors, highly protected and unable to withstand foreign competition, monopolistic in structure, over-diversified and with substantial excess capacity, utilising complex capital-intensive technologies, with low levels of productivity and low employment-creation potential. Furthermore, the incentives for the establishment of, and government preoccupation with, the manufacturing sector have led to the serious neglect of other areas of the economy, especially agriculture. It might even be agreed that industrialisation has given rise to an excessive dependence on foreign capital and technology, with a consequent diminution of domestic ownership and control; that such development has hampered the emergence of export industries; that it has produced a rigid, inelastic import structure and that the bottlenecks and distortions that have arisen as a result of ISI have aggravated already existing inflationary pressures. Most critiques of ISI would agree that it has not alleviated the balance of payments constraint on development.

*The Neo-classical School.* A growing body of literature in recent years has attempted to explain the persistence of underdevelopment as the result largely of distorted and inefficient factor and goods markets in the LDCs. The major source of these alleged imperfections is government intervention in the economy aimed especially at the rapid promotion of industrialisation (usually ISI) via the imposition of tariff barriers and other protective devices. The central problem of economic development is seen as the promotion of efficient resource allocation through the elimination of divergencies between market and social prices.

The apotheosis of this approach is to be found in the study of Little, Scitovsky and Scott (1970) (hereafter referred to as Little *et al.*). The burden of their message is that excessive protection, permitting or encouraging the overdevelopment of ISI, violates the principle of comparative advantage and gives rise to distortions in domestic factor and product markets. Labour is overvalued, the domestic currency is overvalued in terms of foreign currencies and capital is undervalued. Industrial development has been based on capital-intensive technologies because of factor market imperfections and this has exacerbated employment problems, led to the rapid growth of urban centres and has accelerated rural–urban migration. ISI has aggravated existing inequalities in the distribution of income and, in particular, the high protection given to industry has turned the domestic terms of trade against the agricultural sector, thus discouraging agricultural output and exports. Excess capacity within the industrial sector is a general problem and the ISI process generates inflationary pressures throughout the economy.

Little *et al.* argue the case for the promotion, rather than the protection of industry (that is, subsidisation of labour costs, provision of training facilities, etc.), in general policies designed to eliminate the disadvantages under which industry suffers, rather than offsetting them by policies with allegedly undesirable side-effects. Protection should be lowered and rationalised, import controls removed, the exchange rate devalued and the free play of market forces encouraged. As a result, domestic industries would either have to face foreign competition or perish, exports (especially of manufactured goods) would be encouraged, industry would not be over-encouraged at the expense of other sectors and more intensive employment opportunities would be generated through the use of labour-intensive (or appropriate) technologies. Sutcliffe (1973) has noted that '... the neo-classical approach, empasises – indeed is often obsessed by – the question of the efficient allocation of resources in the short-run, while it pays little attention to the economic determinants of long-run growth and none at all to the socio-political aspects' (p. 60). Specifically, it is an oversimplification to assume that a total structural transformation can be brought about by the free play of market forces while underestimating (or ignoring) the problems associated with foreign penetration of the economy, economic and political dependence and the disintegrated nature of the LDC economy.

*The Structuralist/Marxist Critique.* Writers within this broad analytical framework focus attention to differing degrees on the question of the ownership and control of the means of production and the social relations arising out of differing ownership patterns. They are concerned with the problems that arise from the distorted structure of production inherited from the colonial period, the contemporary foreign penetration of the economy, the importation of an 'alien' technology, the operations of transnational corporations (TNCs) – especially the repatriation of profits, the use of transfer pricing (non-market prices used for transactions within the TNC), etc., discussed in greater detail in Chapter 9 – the distribution of income and the balance of social forces within the economy. Many structuralist critiques of the industrialisation process are avowedly non-Marxist, but apart from a similar descriptive content, they have little in common with the neo-classical position.

At a more general level, Marxist analysis has focused attention on the nature and characteristics of the development process and has raised the question as to whether capitalism can be regarded in the contemporary developing world as a progressive force and can thus be expected to lead to independent capitalist industrialisation (a problem discussed in greater detail in section 8.7). With regard to policy prescriptions, structuralists, as the name implies, place great emphasis on the need for radical changes in the economic structure of the economy (land redistribution, agrarian reform, a more equal distribution of income) while Marxists emphasise the necessary, radical political changes that must take place before genuine economic restructuring is possible. Our critique of the ISI process that follows will be largely within the structuralist/Marxist framework of analysis within which much of the neo-classical analysis (excluding its policy prescriptions) can be subsumed.

*The Impact of ISI on Imports and the Balance of Payments*

Attention has been focused in the past on the behaviour of the import coefficient (the ratio of total imports to GDP) during ISI. In general, the import coefficient falls as ISI proceeds, although this does not imply either a reduction in absolute value or quantity of imports. It is also likely that some minimum limit on imports will exist, determined, *inter alia,* by the country's resource endowment, technological trends affecting the utilisation of resources, the size of the country and its level of development and rate of growth (Robock 1970).

Of greater importance is the change in the composition of imports that occurs as ISI proceeds. Typically the process begins with the domestic manufacture of consumer goods (the highest tariffs are imposed on consumer goods imports and so we get the perverse result that the 'least' essential imports are given the greatest incentive for domestic production). Thus as domestic consumer goods production increases, the commodity composition of imports changes, with consumer goods imports becoming less important and imports of machinery, equipment, raw materials and other inputs and fuels becoming of greater significance. In other words, 'non-essential' consumer goods imports are converted into 'essential' imports needed to maintain domestic output and employment. ISI increases the proportion of domestic value added supported by imports, and in these circumstances, any decline in export proceeds not counterbalanced by a net inflow of foreign capital will lead to forced import curtailments and industrial recession. In general therefore, the economy becomes more dependent on foreign trade and more vulnerable to fluctuations in foreign exchange receipts. ISI, originally conceived of as lessening external dependence, is more likely to have the opposite effect and Baer notes that:[7]

> ... the net result of ISI has been to place Latin American countries in a new and more dangerous dependency relationship with the more advanced industrial countries than ever before.
>
> (Baer 1972, p. 106)

The inflexibility or rigidity of the post-ISI structure is not total, however. There is always likely to be some margin of 'non' or 'less essential' imports of finished goods which can be varied with little impact on income or employment, although this margin does become narrower over time.

Turning to the wider problem of the impact of ISI on the balance of payments, there is no evidence that convincingly shows that ISI actually saves foreign exchange. Analytically, we can separate out a number of different aspects of the relationship between ISI and the balance of payments although, in reality, such effects will interact with one another in a complex way and are unlikely to be individually identifiable.

Leff and Netto (1966) constructed a sequential model to show the national income and balance of payments effects of an ISI programme. Applying the model to Brazil, they found that massive ISI policies and foreign capital inflows did not eliminate the balance of payments deficit. On the contrary, the deficit was larger at the end of the sequence than it was at the beginning, largely because of the dynamic income-creating effects of ISI; that is, the generation of additional income through investment in ISI activities and the consequent creation of additional demand for new imports. The authors assume a high marginal propensity to spend, an inelastic demand for exports, a low marginal propensity to import (available foreign exchange earnings forcibly limit the volume of imports, reducing the leakages from the income generation process thus giving rise to a high multiplier) and an import coefficient which no longer declines, once a country has passed a given stage.

They conclude:

> ... the conditions of many underdeveloped countries approximate those of our model, and its conclusions have a validity going beyond the Brazilian experience: import substitution cannot be relied upon to end the international disequilibrium of most underdeveloped countries.
>
> (Leff and Netto 1966, p. 229)

In this case, therefore, imports stimulated by growing national income are greater than the foreign exchange saved by the domestic production of the goods formerly imported.[8]

A second aspect of the relationship between ISI and the balance of payments is the import intensity (or import content) of ISI industries. This feature in itself does not explain the continuation or aggravation of the external deficit (except perhaps in the short run – in the longer run, once a given rate of growth is attained and maintained through time, the direct impact of current investment on demand for imports should be more than offset by the previous year's investment in ISI currently coming to fruition (Diaz-Alejandro 1965)), but it does add to the problem. Different domestically produced commodities will have different import contents. In Colombia, for example, the ILO (1970) estimated that basic industrial consumer goods (clothing, footwear, furniture, beverages, etc.) had an import content of less than 5% while other goods (for example, electrical consumer durables, bought very largely by the rich) had an import content of about 30%. The choice of industries in an ISI programme, itself partially determined by the distribution of income within the ISI economy, will thus influence the balance of payments impact of the industrialisation programme.

In the Leff and Netto model, profit remittances arising from private foreign investment have only a negligible effect on the balance of payments deficit, but it is unlikely that this conclusion could be generalised (even assuming that it is valid for Brazil). Where TNCs have been heavily involved in the ISI process, profit remittances, royalty payments, the effects of transfer pricing, etc., are likely to have a significant balance of payments effect and should not be neglected. We return to these issues in Chapter 9 on TNCs.

Two further related effects on the balance of payments must be mentioned. Little *et al.*, among others, argue that ISI leads to a redistribution of income, from agriculture to manufacturing (because of agriculture's deteriorating terms of trade vis-à-vis industry) and that within manufacturing itself there is a redistribution from wages to profits (because of the capital-intensity of techniques employed). Income is thus redistributed in favour of those groups (the urban sector and middle and upper income groups) which are likely to have a higher marginal propensity to consume imported goods (and services) or domestically produced import-intensive products, thus further aggravating the balance of payments problem. We discuss in greater detail the relationship between income distribution and development in Chapter 3.

The second effect involves the concept of the effective rate of protection, defined as the percentage excess of domestic value added, obtained through the imposition of tariffs and other protective devices on the product and its inputs, over foreign or world market value added. In other words, the effective rate of protection shows the percentage by which value added at a stage of fabrication in domestic industry can exceed what this would be in the absence of protection (Little *et al.* 1970). In certain cases, protection is so high that domestic value added, measured at world prices, is negative; that is, the value of the industry's inputs at world prices is higher than that of its output and thus the activity costs the country foreign exchange.

In a study of 48 manufacturing industries in Pakistan, Soligo and Stern (1965) found that in 23 industries, value added measured at world prices was negative. Fourteen of these industries were in the consumer goods sector. The authors concluded that investment had either been premature or over-extended, primarily in consumer goods industries (although some of these industries may have been genuine 'infant' industries) and that, in general, investment made on the basis of ISI potential too often ignored comparative advantage considerations. The use of world prices in this type of calculation is not without controversy, but Soligo and Stern's and similar studies highlight the extreme inefficiency that exists in the manufacturing sectors of many LDCs which have pursued the ISI strategy.

The actual experience of ISI thus seems to suggest that the economy will not experience a lessening of the balance of payments constraint. It will become increasingly dependent on inflows of foreign capital (private and public) to maintain the real capacity to import if export earnings cannot be significantly increased. ISI may successfully create income and employment but the redistribution of income towards sectors and groups with high marginal propensities to import and the establishment of highly import-intensive industries will have a detrimental effect on the balance of payments position.

### *ISI and the Rate of Saving*

Many authors have argued that ISI will reduce the rate of saving. The establishment of a domestic consumer goods sector and the development of an ISI-based business community will lead to pressures to minimise constraints on consumption, especially if excess capacity exists (which is likely to be the case), thus reducing the rate of saving below that which could have been achieved. This phenomenon would not be present, of course, if industrialisation concentrated on the establishment of capital goods, rather than consumer goods industries.

Khan (1963) introduced the concept of 'consumption liberalisation'. When ISI occurs, domestic absorption often exceeds what would have been absorbed or demanded if the good had continued to be imported, and when the good concerned is a consumption good, the effect is to liberalise consumption and reduce aggregate savings and the development effort. Khan calculates that for cotton cloth, for example, during the period 1955/56 to 1959/60, 46% of increased production (in Pakistan) was due to consumption liberalisation; for sugar during the same period, consumption liberalisation accounted for 49–51% of increased production.

Actual consumption exceeded 'normal' consumption (determined by the aggregate consumption constraint necessary to achieve the planned rate of saving and consumer preference as to the distribution of expenditure between different commodities within the overall constraint) for three main reasons: (1) high levels of protection led to excessive investment in ISI industries which in turn led to attempts to utilise capacity through sales campaigns, etc., aimed at raising consumption; (2) if the only control over consumption consisted of import licences, then the 'decontrol' of consumption would automatically occur as ISI took place; (3) the shift in the distribution of income in favour of the urban sector would create upward pressures on the consumption function. Khan's general conclusion is that the liberalisation of consumption of import substitutes means the liberalisation of consumption in general and hence a reduction in saving.

*ISI and Long-Run Growth and Development*

Perhaps the most crucial problem of the ISI process is its apparent inability, in the long run, to sustain a growth rate of GNP in excess of the growth in the capacity to import. In other words, ISI generates a high rate of growth in its initial stages but such growth is short lived (perhaps 10 to 15 years) and the economy experiences stagnation at a low level of development once ISI opportunities appear to have been exhausted and the foreign exchange constraint once again becomes dominant. Broadly, we can distinguish between those writers who believe that stagnationist tendencies are inherent within the ISI process itself and those who believe that poor planning and implementation of the ISI strategy, rather than the strategy itself, is at the root of the problem.

The latter school has already been referred to above in our discussion of the neo-classical critique. Bruton (1970) lists three general features arising from ISI: the distortion of the economy, the creation of activities alien to the economic and social environment of the community and the creation of conditions which dampen productivity growth. He argues that government policies should concentrate on these issues and, like Little *et al.*, recommends promotion rather than protection – uniform tariffs, currency realignments, subsidies to firms doing research, tax advantages or subsidies aimed at correcting market imperfections, provision of market information, etc.[9]

There are a number of important structuralist/Marxist models of stagnation which must be briefly considered, but before doing so we must look at the ISI 'model' itself. Hirschman described the ISI process as 'industrialisation by tightly separated stages' and as a 'highly sequential' affair (Hirschman 1968). ISI typically begins with the establishment of consumer goods industries (the technology required may be less complicated and the cost differential lower than for capital goods) and then, in principle, moves on to intermediate and finally to capital goods. The influential ECLA (1964) study of Brazil asserts that, in practice, this is virtually impossible to achieve. Rather, the substitution process 'might be regarded as a building of which every storey must be erected simultaneously, although the degree of concentration on each varies from one period to another' (pp. 6-7).

The transition from consumer to intermediate goods is difficult to achieve (greater capital requirements, more complex technologies, lack of TNC cooperation, etc.) and thus the first stage of the process is pushed to the maximum possible extent – what Felix (1964) has referred to as the 'premature widening' of the productive structure. The problems associated with the tendency of ISI to get 'stuck' at the stage of consumer goods substitution are not, of course, insuperable and to a certain extent are related to the particular kinds of consumer goods industries established. For example, modern sophisticated luxury consumer goods industries are likely to require equally sophisticated capital goods which, to say the least, will prove very difficult to produce locally.

Determined government action in some of the larger LDCs (for example, Brazil and India) has led to the establishment of intermediate (iron and steel) and capital goods (machine-making) industries. But it could be argued with some validity that these industries would not have been established in the absence of specific government intervention, that is, if the ISI process had been purely unplanned and spontaneous, completely determined by the free play of market forces. We discuss this problem in greater detail in Chapter 9 on TNCs.

The ECLA (1964) study of Brazil focuses attention on the economic and social characteristics of the ISI model of development and argues that stagnation arises from a number of specific imbalances or disequilibria that arise during ISI. These take the form of sectoral imbalances (between industry and other sectors of the economy and within the industrial sector itself, between consumer and capital goods); regional imbalances (a large part of the population lived in very underdeveloped areas which had not benefited from the economic transformation taking place within the Centro-Sur region); social imbalances (unequal distribution of income and increasing social inequalities)[10] and financial imbalances (the generation of inflationary pressures).

The authors of the report argued that Brazil had to move from the ISI model to a self-sustaining growth model, by means of the reduction in the duality of the system and the expansion of the market. Government action would be required to improve infrastructure facilities, encourage investment to intermediate industries, the primary sector and underdeveloped areas, and to achieve a better distribution of income. We shall see in the concluding section that the 'Brazilian model of development' has turned out to be rather different from that envisaged by ECLA.[11]

Felix (1968) accepts the view that for many Latin American countries ISI has lost its capacity to lower the import coefficient and that ISI becomes progressively harder to sustain with the attempt to establish intermediate and capital goods industries. He argues that insufficient attention has been paid to the changing composition of final demand under ISI and he maintains that only by postulating a persistent import bias to changes in the final demand mix can a levelling-off of the import ratio be adequately explained. Rising incomes shift demand towards products with high income elasticities of demand and higher import intensities (than products with slow-growing demand). But he further argues that import-biased demand shifts occur independently of income changes, through the international demonstration effect:

> ... the import bias of consumer demand is positively related not merely to rising income but also to the rate of product innovation in advanced countries, to factors reducing information lags concerning such products in borrowing countries, and to the trend towards greater technological complexity of these products and their components.
>
> (Felix 1968, p. 67)

Felix tests his model with data for Argentina and finds that the intermediate import requirements per composite unit of Argentine output were higher in 1960 than in 1953, even though there had been considerable ISI in the intervening years. The reason for this is attributed to the shift in demand to 'dynamic' industries (income elasticity of demand greater than one) with above-average import coefficients.

The final stagnationist model we consider is that of Merhav (1969). He argues that the importation of technology developed in industrialised countries makes monopoly (used in a broad, generic sense) inevitable at a very low level of development in LDCs. The application of monopoly theory to the problem of development leads to the conclusion that monopoly, after the initial spurt of growth in which it establishes itself, is likely to halt, or seriously retard, further growth. The monopolistic structure is likely to be strongly resistant to change and will be characterised by relatively inefficient techniques, smaller plants, lower output and higher prices as compared to the industrialised economies. In the latter, Merhav argues that monopolies grow via diversification, but in LDCs:

> ... the investment opportunities presented by diversification are not only narrow from the outset, but tend to shrink rapidly in consequence of the market restrictions engendered by oligopoly and monopoly, and as a result of the dependence upon imports of capital goods.
>
> (Merhav 1969, p.82)

Thus in LDCs, monopolistic industries diversify into increasingly sub-optimal products (sub-optimal relative to the size of the domestic market for these products), but this cannot assure sustained growth because of the lack of a domestic capital goods sector, resulting in import leakages reducing the size of the domestic income multiplier. Furthermore, the very process itself creates a bias against the establishment of a capital goods industry, a point to which we return in Chapter 9.

Two possible exits from the impasse are examined by Merhav – government intervention and foreign trade – but it is concluded that neither is likely to rescue the underdeveloped private enterprise system from its predicament. It is to the possibility of industrialisation through the export of manufactured goods that we now turn.

## 8.5 Strategies of Industrial Development 2: The Export of Manufactured Goods

ISI and the export of manufactured goods are not, in principle, mutually exclusive (Robock, 1970, has referred to their separation as a 'false dichotomy'). Industries that were initially established to serve the domestic market should, once the period of 'infant' development is past, be able to break into export markets and thus at least partially alleviate the much publicised foreign exchange constraint. In this sense, ISI could be regarded as merely a prelude to entry into foreign markets.

In practice, however, these two strategies have generally been regarded as alternatives, with ISI assumed to be an 'easier' alternative to export promotion. In particular, it has been difficult to see how exports could be promoted efficiently, cheaply and acceptably in a manner analogous to the protection of domestic industries under ISI. But the apparent 'failure' of ISI as a development (or industrialisation) strategy and the apparent success of those economies vigorously promoting exports, has led to a reappraisal of the possibilities of export-led industrialisation. Indeed it would be no exaggeration to say that export-led industrialisation has become an article of faith amongst some development economists, international consultants and international organisations.

At the end of the 1960s, six countries accounted for approximately 78% of total LDC exports of manufactured goods to developed economies (the six, in order of importance were: Hong Kong, India, Taiwan, South Korea, Mexico and Pakistan). A further five countries (Philippines, Iran, Israel, Argentina and Brazil) accounted for another 14% of the total (Rahman 1973). These figures must be interpreted with caution. Exports accounted for 91.5% of Hong Kong's total manufacturing value added, but only 6.5% of India's, 31% and 20% of Taiwan's and South Korea's respectively, but only 2.5% of Mexico's and 10.6% of Pakistan's. Thus, as we stated above, LDCs such as India, Mexico and Pakistan must be regarded primarily as basing their industrial efforts on ISI even though, in absolute terms, they are among the largest exporters of manufactured goods from LDCs.

The most important products exported by LDCs are: clothing (23% of total LDC manufactured goods exports); non-cotton fabrics (mainly jute fabrics) (9.6%); plywood (7.0%); cotton fabrics (6.4%); leather (4.5%) and carpets (4.4%). These six products accounted for 54.9% of total LDC manufactured goods exports at the end of the 1960s (Rahman 1973).

Rahman argues that over 80% of total manufactured goods exports were labour-intensive commodities (defined as having a capital intensity less than the average capital intensity for the whole export basket). This would appear to support the argument that LDCs should specialise according to comparative advantage and produce and export labour-intensive commodities and import their capital-intensive requirements. Furthermore, other things being equal, labour-abundant economies could create more employment by following the 'outward-looking' development path and, indeed, some of those countries whose exports of manufactured goods grew most rapidly during the 1960s also had high rates of growth of industrial employment (Morawetz 1974).

Without going into the arguments concerning the relationship between trade and development, there are two major arguments against the 'outward-looking' development strategy. Firstly, it is highly unlikely that the majority of LDCs would be able to follow such a strategy, given the barriers to the export of manufactured goods imposed by the developed economies (escalating tariff structures, quota restrictions, administrative controls, 'voluntary' agreements, etc. discussed in Chapter 4). What is feasible for a few, small LDCs (with, it should be noted, a particular political and strategic value) is not possible for a large number of LDCs, many of which have relatively large industrial sectors and a significant export potential, even if it is conceded that such a strategy is in fact desirable.

But perhaps a more important argument is advanced by Frances Stewart (1973). She maintains that although the comparative advantage of LDCs lies in the production of labour-intensive goods, as long as the developed countries are mainly responsible for technological innovation, production techniques will continually move in a capital-intensive direction, and LDCs will have to adapt both products and processes to keep up with these developments if they are to remain competitive in export markets:

> Technological dependence on the developed countries will be maintained, since without the technological transfer from the developed countries the developing countries will not be able to compete in international trade. (Stewart 1973, p. 253)

Advocates of outward-looking development (for example, Keesing 1967) stress the beneficial learning effects that competition in overseas markets engenders, but there is little evidence to support the view that export-led growth will have more than a limited impact on the quality of human resources within LDCs. Such advocates consistently over-emphasise the net foreign exchange benefits of exports (capital equipment, components, raw materials, etc., may all have to be imported and there are large outflows of profits, royalties, etc. – see Chapter 9), and incentives given (especially to TNCs) are often so generous that the amount of revenue generated for host country governments is often insignificant. The dependency on foreign markets makes LDCs vulnerable to cyclical fluctuations in the capitalist world economy and some critics go further and make the point that free trade can encourage both the wrong pattern of production and consumption in LDCs.[12]

Too often the ultimate objectives of development are lost sight of. Particular strategies are promoted with almost messianic zeal, and ends and means become confused. Policies should be pursued for the efficiency and efficacy with which they lead towards the achievement of stated objectives, not because they are considered to be 'desirable' in their own right.

We return to the issues raised by the concepts of 'outward' and 'inward-looking' development strategies in the final section of this chapter.

## 8.6 Strategies of Industrial Development 3: The Export of Labour-Intensive Components

A third possibility for LDCs (which does not exclude either of the above strategies) is the export of labour-intensive components or processes. Helleiner (1973) has noted that, increasingly, TNCs are identifying specific unskilled labour-intensive activities or processes within their overall manufacturing operations and transferring these parts of the production process to LDCs, where cheap labour more than offsets the transport costs incurred. This has already occurred on a large scale in electronics (semiconductors, valves and tuners in Hong Kong, Singapore, Taiwan and Mexico); clothes, gloves, leather luggage and baseballs (sewn together in the West Indies, South East Asia and Mexico); automobile components (Taiwan, South Korea, Mexico, Thailand and India). Data are flown from the USA to the West Indies and South East Asia for punching upon tape by low-wage key punch operators and the tapes flown back to the USA; loose ammunition is sent to Mexico for loading into magazines by cheap local labour.[13]

The TNC in this case is thus transferring a labour-intensive technology and is exporting components, rather than finished goods, which do not face the barriers referred to above. But although these activities are looked upon favourably by many experts (see, for example, Myint 1972), it is difficult to see what the benefits are to the LDC, apart from the employment and income generated. The TNC has little, if any, capital invested and is thus footloose or mobile, unskilled labour is not given any real training, technological spin-off is likely to be minimal and dependence on the TNC for inputs, markets, decisions affecting output, etc. is complete. The process confirms the position of the LDCs as suppliers of cheap labour to the developed economies.

## 8.7 Dependent or Independent Industrialisation?

An important controversy has emerged within the structuralist/dependency/Marxist schools of thought concerning the nature of the industrialisation process. Dependency theorists (both Marxist and non-Marxist) argue that a process of dependent development is taking place within the LDCs, dominated by foreign corporations and interests through their control of capital, technology and markets. The concept of dependence presupposes that there is an equivalent concept of independence and Sutcliffe (1972) has attempted to clarify the idea of independent industrialisation.

Independent industrialisation should originate with and be maintained by social and economic forces within the industrialising country. Its four main characteristics, Sutcliffe argues, are: the domestic market should be paramount; the industrial sector should contain a wide range of industries (including capital goods industries); the industrial effort should be domestically financed (although actual control is more important than ownership); there should be independent technological development, consisting of the ability and opportunity to copy, develop and adapt, or at least to choose, technology suitable to the country's resources (historically a condition of development). The social and political counterpart to these factors is the existence of a class (an industrial bourgeoisie) which is both willing and able to invest in a productive manner the economic surplus that it appropriates. This class requires the powers of the state to defend and support it, which in turn must be independent both of domestic interests opposed to industrialisation (for example, landowners or commercial interests) and independent of foreign interests.

For a variety of reasons, some of which we highlight in our concluding section, capitalist development in LDCs has not led to independent industrialisation and Sutcliffe concludes that, in recent decades, 'rapid industrial growth seems to have taken place only, or at least mainly, in those capitalist countries most obviously satellised by the advanced countries', although 'this is not necessarily a permanent situation' (p. 192). For Sutcliffe, the basis of metropolitan dominance has always been the monopoly of technology (embodied in certain capital goods) that has prevented LDCs from establishing complete industrial structures because of their inability to establish industries possessing the most advanced and complex technology of that period of time.

Warren (1973) has vigorously challenged this analysis. His main points are that: the prospects for successful capitalist economic development for a significant number of LDCs are good and that substantial progress in capitalist industrialisation has already been achieved; any obstacles to this development originate within the LDCs themselves and that ties of dependence are being loosened and that the distribution of power within the capitalist world is becoming less uneven.

The attainment of political independence by many LDCs in the post-World War II period has permitted their industrial development, but even more importantly, industrialisation has been encouraged by rivalry between capitalist economies, between the western and eastern blocs and by the rise of new ruling groups within the LDCs themselves. Since independence, LDCs have increasingly improved their bargaining position and their ability to control resource-based TNCs, and although they have yet to achieve similar results with manufacturing TNCs, Warren argues that conflicts over foreign manfacturing investment occur within a long-term framework of eventual accommodation, mutually acceptable and mutually advantageous. Furthermore, Warren maintains that the establishment of capital goods industries in LDCs leads to 'automatic' technological progress and obstacles to technology transfer lie in the ability or inability of the LDCs themselves to assimilate technology, rather than in imperialist monopoly or domination. Western technological superiority is based on conditions that are losing their force and the technology that is actually transferred is more important than that which is 'blocked'. Independent industrialisation, based on Sutcliffe's four criteria, is in fact taking place rapidly within LDCs.

In general, private investment in LDCs is creating the conditions for the disappearance of imperialism as a system of economic inequality between nations: 'imperialism declines as capitalism grows' (Warren 1973, p. 41).[14] Furthermore, it is no longer necessary to associate industrialisation with a particular ruling class (and specifically not with the national bourgeoisie) and in most LDCs the role of the state is of particular importance as it assumes the role of a bourgeois ruling class before the full emergence of that class.

This brief analysis does less than justice to Warren's detailed and controversial arguments. We mention some of the criticisms of Warren's thesis in the final section of this chapter.

## 8.8 Conclusions

In this final section, we attempt to highlight some of the lessons that can be drawn from the contemporary industrialisation experience of the LDCs, in the process of which we will be able to assess the validity of the Warren thesis. We also attempt a reappraisal of the concepts of 'inward' and 'outward-looking' development strategies and end with some brief comments on the ways in which LDCs can attempt to overcome some of the problems facing them in the industrialisation effort.

Industrial development has not been a planned process in most LDCs, and in general it has been left in the hands of the private sector. Planning ministries have drawn up broad guidelines and set overall targets for the private sector, and government has intervened in an *ad hoc* and erratic manner (protection, licensing arrangements, etc.) in an attempt to influence private sector behaviour, but this is as far as 'planning' could be said to have gone.[15]

But despite rapid growth rates, there has been widespread disillusion with the achievements of industrialisation. Certainly, it is no longer in general regarded as being synonymous with development (although critics of Warren, for example Emmanuel 1974, allege that he commits this error) and some LDCs (for example Tanzania) have tended to downgrade industrialisation and promote rural development as an alternative development path. In spite of the variety of experience among LDCs, it can be said quite categorically that ISI in particular has not realised the expectations of its early advocates. Industrial growth has been isolated from the overall growth of the economy and has led to the neglect of, or positive discrimination against, other sectors of the economy (agriculture and exports).

As a broad generalisation, ISI has not alleviated the balance of payments constraint (that is, it has not saved foreign exchange), its dependence on an imported, capital-intensive technology has not created extensive employment opportunities and has not led to indigenous technological development, the process has been heavily dependent on foreign capital (or at least foreign ownership of capital from various sources – see Chapter 9 on TNCs), it has led to what many would regard as an undesirable redistribution of income and has in general resulted in stagnation after a brief period of growth. It could be convincingly argued that ISI has altered but has not broken the chains of dependency that bind LDCs to advanced economies. In addition it has emphasised the establishment of consumer goods industries, at the expense of the capital goods sector, without which independent, indigenous technological progress becomes impossible.

If generally accepted as valid, these conclusions support the arguments of the critics of Warren (especially McMichael *et al.* 1974), who in addition emphasise the limited nature of industrialisation in LDCs (much of which is 'assembly plant' operations) and its difference from capitalist industrialisation in advanced economies. They further point to the fact that the most 'successful' LDCs (in Warren's terms – countries such as Brazil, Zaire and Indonesia) are the least independent of foreign controls, and that foreign-induced industrialisation in these countries depends on the reduction or elimination of domestic forces opposing foreign economic and political domination.[16] But whatever the verdict on Warren's analysis, he forces us to re-examine the dependency thesis and reappraise the process of change that is taking place within LDCs.

If unplanned ISI leads to stagnation, and if growth through the export of manufactured goods is not a strong possibility for most LDCs, what strategies of industrialisation should these countries pursue? Will these economies at a lower level of development (mainly the economies of sub-Saharan Africa – excluding South Africa) learn from the experience of Latin America?[17]

Brazil is often put forward as an 'alternative model' of economic development. The general interpretation of Brazilian development is that opportunities for further ISI were 'exhausted' by the early 1960s, the economy had lost its dynamism and inflation had got out of hand.[18] A military coup occurred in 1964, the economic objectives of which were the control of inflation, the elimination of price distortions, the modernisation of capital markets, the introduction of incentives to direct resources to areas and sectors considered by the government to be of high priority, the attraction of foreign capital inflows and the use of public funds in infrastructure projects and certain government-owned heavy industries (especially steel, mining and petrochemicals) (Baer 1973). After a period of stabilisation between 1964 and 1967, the economy began to grow rapidly in 1968, with industry as the 'leading sector'. Brazilian growth was hailed as an 'economic miracle' and Brazil was expected by some to become the Japan of Latin America.

Briefly, the essential characteristics of the 'Brazilian model' are as follows: a redistribution of income in favour of the top 5% of income receivers[19] and functionally in favour of profits and rents, to create what Furtado (1973) refers to as a demand profile most attractive to TNCs – income must be redistributed towards those classes providing a demand for the output of domestic consumer goods industries (although this view tends to ignore the availability of credit and hire purchase facilities which permit lower income groups to purchase consumer durables); massive government investment in physical and social infrastructure facilities, power generation and the directly productive activities mentioned above; increased foreign capital inflow and a corresponding increase in both real and financial indebtedness (the increased importance of TNCs in certain sectors of the economy has been referred to as 'denationalisation' of Brazilian industry); the promotion of exports of manufactured goods, often through the use of subsidies (the share of manufactures in total exports increased from 7.2% in 1965-69 to 14.6% in 1971, Baer 1973).

Furtado concludes:

> The most significant feature of the Brazilian 'model' is its structural tendency to exclude the mass of the population from the benefits of accumulation and technical progress. The durability of the system relies heavily on the capacity of the ruling groups to suppress all forms of opposition which its antisocial character tends to arouse.
>
> (Furtado 1973, p. 127)

The alternative to the 'Brazilian model' is to recognise that industrial development in general, and ISI in particular, are not development strategies. Industrialisation can only be part of a wider development package which must include, wherever relevant, agrarian and land reform and an increase in agricultural productivity to create mass markets for domestically produced goods; the full exploitation of existing export opportunities and the creation of new exports; the re-examination of the potential for regional economic integration, especially with respect to the possibilities for cooperation in establishing essential capital goods industries and creating the research capacity to develop genuinely appropriate and indigenous technologies. Neither a strategy of ISI nor one of manufactured goods exports can by itself create an integrated industrial sector, containing capital goods industries essential for local technological advancement (a point recently emphasised in Stewart 1976).

From what has been said above, it should be clear that we must question the current usage of the terms 'inward-' and 'outward-looking development'. ISI is not 'inward-looking' in any meaningful sense of the term (especially if it is meant to imply a certain degree of self-reliance or self-sufficiency). ISI has been heavily dependent on foreign capital, technology and expertise, a different kind of dependence has been generated through changes in import structures, and it has accepted the consumption patterns, tastes, marketing techniques, etc. of the advanced economies. 'Outward-looking' strategies may be equally undesirable if, even though they lead to more rapid growth, they promote and reinforce international and internal inqualities.[20]

'Inward-looking' development must define economic, social and political objectives consistent with the resources, aspirations and commitment to development of the LDCs themselves. Ideally, it must aim at a life style different from that of the western developed economies, beginning with the identification of minimum basic needs (generally assumed to be food, clothing and shelter) and a production programme geared to meet those needs. This calls for what the Pakistani economist Mahbub ul Haq (1973) has described as a 'poverty curtain' to be drawn across the developing world, isolating its development and trade from established patterns. Whether or not such a 'curtain' will be drawn is one of the key political questions in development studies at the present time.

## Notes

1 Gray quotes from Mao Tse-Tung's Ten Great Relationships:

> We have not repeated the mistakes of some socialist countries which attached excessive importance to heavy industries at the expense of light industries and agriculture ... unlike the market situation in some countries immediately after the revolution, goods in our markets have been more plentiful ... (and) their prices are stable. This is not to say that no problems remain. There *are* problems – e.g. greater attention to light industries and agriculture than before, and adequate readjustment of the rates of investment ... to give a comparatively greater weight to investment in light industries and agriculture.
>
> (Gray 1971, p. 499)

2 Weeks does not deny that unemployment exists. Rather, he emphasises that it exists in certain circumstances: 'It exists as a widespread phenomenon only in those countries with serious land shortage, either due to population pressure or to the proletarianization of the rural population as a consequence of plantation agriculture – Mauritius is the classic example of the former, and the West Indies of the latter, while Ceylon is a case where both elements play an important part. In other countries, it is a particularized phenomenon restricted (as far as we know) to certain social and occupational groups' (Weeks 1971, p. 62). Ceylon is of particular interest in that there is an inverse association between education and employment. Against an overall rate of unemployment estimated at 14% in 1971, the figure for unemployment in the 20–24 age group was 63% among those who had passed O-level examinations and 69% for those who had passed A-levels. Unemployment of graduates was probably about 30% (ILO 1971).

3 It is interesting to compare this point (emphasised by, among others, Hirschman 1968) with Andre Gunder Frank's Centre–Periphery analysis: 'if it is satellite status which generates underdevelopment, then a weaker or lesser degree of metropolis–satellite relations may generate less deep structural underdevelopment and/or allow for more possibility of local development. ... It is also significant for the confirmation of our thesis that the satellites have typically managed such temporary spurts in development as they have had, during wars or depressions in the metropolis, which momentarily weakened or lessened its domination over the life of the satellites' (Frank 1967, pp. 11-12).

4 Raul Prebisch, the first Secretary General of UNCTAD and an early advocate of ISI, became an early critic of the type of development resulting from ISI, and stressed the need for changes in the social and economic structures of the LDCs, changes which were complementary to the process of industrialisation (see his Report to the first UNCTAD 1964).

5 Morley and Smith argue that the exclusion of intermediate demands, generated by import substitution itself, will underestimate the amount of ISI

that is actually taking place:

> If an import is to be replaced without induced rises in imported inputs or reductions in the supplies available for final demand in other sectors, production must be increased not only in the industry finally processing the good, but also in its supplier industries and so forth. In effect, the newly required intermediate output was previously 'supplied' by the import of the final product. An accurate assessment of the total supply of each sectors' products should therefore include such 'implicit' imports. (Morley and Smith 1970, p. 279)

Their results from Brazilian data show approximately one-third more import substitution than Chenery for manufacturing and 53% more for the economy as a whole. Thus a Chenery-type definition of import substitution will lead to underestimation, to an extent depending on the development of intermediate goods industries.

6 For a further discussion of these and other issues see Fane (1973) and Winston (1967).

7 Bruton (1970) also notes that '... the economic structure that the ISI approach to development spawns is no more flexible and adaptable than the one that is sought to be replaced ... (it) ... is so incompatible with the rest of the system that adjustments to changes in demands, in technology, in any part of the routine are accomplished painfully, if at all' (pp. 136-7). Furthermore the ISI economy becomes very vulnerable to import price increases, as the recent increases in oil prices have demonstrated.

8 Doherty (1970) also tentatively concludes that the balance of payments position may deteriorate as a result of ISI, depending on the sectoral composition of the ISI programme and various import propensities.

9 These are general neo-classical policy prescriptions whose objective is a more efficient allocation of resources. Most 'structuralist' writers would not attach much importance to these recommendations although an exception to this generalisation appears to be Sachs (1973).

10 The ECLA study characterised Brazil as 'one of the most perfect examples of dual economy to be found in all Latin America' (p. 54) and maintained that the various aspects of duality had been aggravated by development.

11 Baer and Maneschi (1971) build a short-run income determination model in which, in the absence of government counter-measures, stagnation is inevitable: '... import-substitutive industrialization, which occurs in a setting where there are no other basic structural changes, results in the establishment of an industrial productive capacity for which eventually there is no adequate demand ... the process is self-terminating since it neither generates sufficient income nor distributes it adequately enough to occupy the new capacity fully and keep it expanding.' (p. 183). Leff (1967) argues that Brazilian stagnation resulted from constraints imposed by lagging supplies of imports, but this view has not gone unchallenged.

12 '... it is inappropriate for developing countries to consume those goods that developed countries produce, and inappropriate for developing countries to produce those goods that developed countries consume.' (Stewart 1973, p. 256).

13 Adam (1975, p. 99) notes the rapid growth of machinery and transport equipment exports from LDCs (an annual average growth rate of almost

20% during the 1960s) and the 'engineering and metal products' category (which grew on average by 34%). But the share of the LDCs in developed market economy imports of these commodities was still less than 2% at the end of the period. Turner (1974, Ch. 7) also lays great emphasis on the increasing importance of so-called 'runaway industries'.

14 *Cf.* Lenin's *Imperialism, the Highest Stage of Capitalism* (1917).

15 This is not to deny the importance of the state's role in the majority of LDCs at the present time, nor its importance in the establishment of intermediate and capital goods industries (in India and Brazil, for example). Many LDC governments have also nationalised foreign manufacturing operations on a large scale.

16 McMichael, *et al.* (1974) conclude: 'Capitalist development in the Third World today means dependent growth in a small proportion of countries, for the benefit of a small proportion of the population.' (p. 104).

17 Economists and international organisations may have learnt the relevant lessons but governments may not have done. The Nigerian economist Professor O. Aboyade (1973) calls for an inward-looking strategy that goes beyond conventional ISI and emphasises rural development. The ILO Report on Kenya (1972) is very critical of ISI, but one still finds many references to ISI as the 'leading sector' in many African development plans.

18 In the period 1956-62, Brazil experienced an annual average growth rate of real GDP of 7.8%. It was 10.3% in 1961, 5.3% in 1962, 1.5% in 1963 and 2.4% in 1964. Wells (1973) dismisses the concept of the exhaustion of ISI opportunities as analytically incorrect and contradicted by the post-1968 boom, but as we have argued that after 1964 Brazil was not pursuing a pure ISI strategy, the latter point is irrelevant.

19 Between 1960 and 1970, the share of the top 5% increased from 27.4% to 36.3% of total income; the share of the bottom 40% of income receivers fell from 11.2% to 9.0% (Baer 1973).

20 For a perceptive discussion of 'inward-' and 'outward-looking' policies, see Streeten's Introduction to Streeten (1973).

## Bibliography

Aboyade O. (1973), 'Advancing tropical African development: a defence of inward-looking strategy', in Streeten P. (1973).

Ádam G. (1975), 'Multinational corporations and worldwide sourcing', in Radice H. (ed.), *International Firms and Modern Imperialism*, Penguin.

Arraes M. (1972), *Brazil: The People and the Power*, Penguin.

Baer W. (1972), 'Import substitution and industrialization in Latin America: experiences and interpretations', *Latin America Research Review*, Spring.

Baer W. (1973), 'The Brazilian boom 1968–1972: an explanation and interpretation', *World Development*, Vol. 1, No. 8, August.

Baer W. and Maneschi A. (1971), 'Import substitution, stagnation and structural change: an interpretation of the Brazilian case', *The Journal of Developing Areas*, January.

Baran P.A. (1957), *The Political Economy of Growth*, Monthly Review Press, New York.

Barratt Brown M. (1974), *The Economics of Imperialism*, Penguin.

Bhagwati J. and Wibulswasdi C. (1972), 'A statistical analysis of shifts in the import structure in LDCs', *Bulletin of the Oxford University Institute of Economics and Statistics*, May.

Bruton H.J. (1970), 'The import-substitution strategy of economic development: a survey', *Pakistan Development Review*, Vol. 10.

Chenery H.B. (1960), 'Patterns of industrial growth', *American Economic Review*, September.

Chenery H.B. (1971), 'Growth and structural change', *Finance and Development* Vol. 8, No. 3, September.

Desai P. (1969), 'Alternative measures of import substitution', *Oxford Economic Papers*, New Series, Vol. 21, No. 3, November.

Diaz-Alejandro C.F. (1965), 'On the import intensity of import substitution', *Kyklos*, Vol. 18.

Doherty N. (1970), 'Import substitution and the balance of payments', *Eastern African Economic Review*, Vol. 2, No. 2, December.

Emmanuel A. (1974), 'Myths of development versus myths of under-development', *New Left Review*, No. 85, May-June.

Fane G. (1973), 'Consistent measures of import substitution', *Oxford Economic Papers*, Vol. 25, No. 2 July.

Felix D. (1964), 'Monetarists, structuralists and import-substituting industrialization: a critical appraisal', in Baer W. and Kerstenetzky I., *Inflation and Growth in Latin America*, Irwin.

Felix D. (1968), 'The dilemma of import substitution – Argentina', in Papanek G.F. (ed.), *Development Policy – Theory and Practice*, Harvard University Press.

Frank A.G. (1967), *Capitalism and Underdevelopment in Latin America*, Monthly Review Press, New York.

Furtado C. (1973), 'The post-1964 Brazilian "model" of development', *Studies in Comparative International Development*, Summer.

Gray J. (1971), 'The Chinese model: some characteristics of Maoist policies for social change and economic growth', *L'Est*, Milan. Reprinted in Nove A. and Nuti D.M. (eds) (1972), *Socialist Economics*, Penguin.

Helleiner G.K. (1972), *International Trade and Economic Development*, Penguin.

Helleiner G.K. (1973), 'Manufactured exports from less developed countries and multinational firms', *Economic Journal*, March.

Hirschman A.O. (1968), 'The political economy of import-substituting industrialisation in Latin America', *Quarterly Journal of Economics*, February.

International Labour Office (1970), *Towards Full Employment: A Programme for Colombia*, Geneva.

International Labour Office (1971), 'Unemployment of the educated in Ceylon', in *Matching Employment Opportunities and Expectations. A Programme of Action for Ceylon*, Geneva.

International Labour Office (1972), *Employment, Incomes and Equality: A Strategy for Increasing Productive Employment in Kenya*, Geneva.

Johnson L. (1967), 'Problems of import substitution: the Chilean automobile industry', *Economic Development and Cultural Change*, January.

Keesing D.B. (1967), 'Outward-looking policies and economic development', *Economic Journal*, June.

Khan A.R. (1963), 'Import substitution, export expansion and consumption liberalisation: a preliminary report', *Pakistan Development Review*, Vol. 3.

Kilby P. (1969), *Industrialisation in an Open Economy: Nigeria 1945-1966*, Cambridge University Press.

Leff N.H. (1967), 'Import constraints and development: causes of the recent decline in Brazilian economic growth', *Review of Economics and Statistics*, November.

Leff N.H. and Netto A.D. (1966), 'Import substitution, foreign investment and international disequilibrium in Brazil', *Journal of Development Studies*, April.

Little I., Scitovsky T. and Scott M. (1970), *Industry and Trade in Some Developing Countries*, Oxford University Press.

Magdoff H. (1975), 'China: contrasts with the USSR', in *China's Economic Strategy, Monthly Review*, Vol. 27, No. 3, July-August.

Maitra P. (1967), *Import Substitution in East Africa*, Oxford University Press Nairobi.

Maizels A. (1963), *Industrial Growth and World Trade*, Cambridge University Press.

McMichael P., Petras J. and Rhodes R. (1974), 'Imperialism and the contradictions of development', *New Left Review*, No. 85, May-June.

Merhav M. (1969), *Technological Dependence, Monopoly and Growth*, Pergamon.

Morawetz D. (1974), 'Employment implications of industrialisation in developing countries: a survey', *Economic Journal*, September.

Morley S.A. and Smith G.W. (1970), 'On the measurement of import substitution', *American Economic Review*, September.

Morley S.A. and Smith G.W. (1971), 'Import substitution and foreign investment in Brazil', *Oxford Economic Papers*, Vol. 23, No. 1, March.

Myint H. (1972), *Southeast Asia's Economy: Development Policies in the 1970s*, Penguin.

Power J.H. (1963), 'Industrialisation in Pakistan: a case of frustrated take-off?' *Pakistan Development Review*, Vol. 3.

Rahman A.H.M.M. (1973), *Exports of Manufactures from Developing Countries*, Rotterdam University Press.

Raj K.N. and Sen A.K. (1961), 'Alternative patterns of growth under conditions of stagnant export earnings', *Oxford Economic Papers*, Vol. 13, No. 1, February.

Reuber G.L. (1973), *Private Foreign Investment in Development*, Clarendon Press.

Robock S.H. (1970), 'Industrialisation through import-substitution or export industries: a false dichotomy', in Markham J.W. and Papanek G.F. (eds) *Industrial Organisation and Economic Growth*, Houghton Mifflin.

Sachs I. (1973), 'Outward-looking strategies: a dangerous illusion?', in Streeten (1973).

Soligo R. and Stern J.J. (1965), 'Tariff protection, import substitution and investment efficiency', *Pakistan Development Review*, Vol. 5, Summer.

Steuer M.D. and Voivodas C. (1965), 'Import substitution and Chenery's patterns of industrial growth – a further study', *Economia Internazionale*.

Stewart F. (1973), 'Trade and technology', in Streeten (1973).

Stewart F. (1976), 'Capital goods in developing countries', in Cairncross A. and Puri M. (eds), *Employment, Income Distribution and Development Strategy: Problems of the Developing Countries*, Macmillan.

Streeten P. (ed.) (1973), *Trade Strategies for Development*, Macmillan.

Sutcliffe R.B. (1971), *Industry and Underdevelopment*, Addison-Wesley.

Sutcliffe R.B. (1972), 'Imperialism and industrialisation in the Third World', in Sutcliffe R.B. and Owen R. (eds) (1972), *Studies in the Theory of Imperialism,* Longman.

Sutcliffe R.B. (1973), Introduction to Penguin edition of Baran P.A., *The Political Economy of Growth,* Penguin.

Turner L. (1973), *Multinational Companies and the Third World,* Allen Lane.

ul Haq M. (1973), 'Industrialisation and trade policies in the 1970s: developing country alternatives', in Streeten (1973).

UNCTAD (1964), *Towards a New Trade Policy for Development* (Prebisch Report) United Nations.

UN Economic Commission for Latin America (1964), 'The growth and decline of import substitution in Brazil', *Economic Bulletin for Latin America,* Vol. 9, No. 1, March.

UN (1975), 'Industrialisation and development: progress and problems in developing countries', *Journal of Development Planning,* No. 8, United Nations.

Van Arkadie B. (1964), 'Import substitution and export promotion as aids to industrialisation in East Africa', *East African Economic Review,* Vol. 1, New Series.

Warren B. (1973), 'Imperialism and capitalist industrialisation', *New Left Review,* No. 81, September-October.

Wells J. (1973), 'Recent developments in Brazilian capitalism', *Bulletin of the Conference of Socialist Economists,* Winter.

Weeks J. (1971), 'Does employment matter?', *Manpower and Unemployment Research in Africa,* Vol. 4, No. 1, Montreal. Reprinted in Jolly R., De Kadt E., Singer H. and Wilson F. (eds) (1973), *Third World Employment,* Penguin.

Winston G.C. (1967), 'Notes on the concept of import substitution', *Pakistan Development Review,* Vol. VII, Spring.

# 9
# The transnational corporation and LDCs

## 9.1 Introduction

The transnational corporation (TNC)[1] has excited a great deal of interest in recent years in both developed and less developed economies as attention has increasingly been focused on the institutional framework within which goods and factors move between countries. On one side, there are those who see the TNC as making possible the use of total world resources with the maximum of efficiency and the minimum of waste and whose presence is vital for the rapid growth and development of all economies, especially the LDCs; on the other side, there are those who see the TNC as the most important aspect of the imperialist penetration of the LDCs, heightening their dependency and deepening the process of dependent development. Another group, somewhere between these two extremes but closer to the first viewpoint, would argue that within a modified framework and working within an agreed set of guidelines and rules, the TNC, through its ownership of and control over technology, capital and marketing skills, can make a unique contribution to the development effort.

At the political level, it is predicted by many (including the world managers themselves – the term used by Barnet and Müller (1974, Chapter 1) to describe the senior executives of the TNCs) that the internationalism of the TNCs, conflicting as it does with the nationalism of the nation state, will lead to the gradual demise of the latter and the development of a truly global economy. Others see the continuation of the nation state as being vital to the interests of the TNC, providing the security and stability necessary for profit maximisation and guaranteed growth.

In this chapter, we attempt to assess the impact of the operations of TNCs on the process of change and development within LDCs, paying particular attention to the claim that TNCs are a necessary and desirable vehicle for development within these economies.

## 9.2 The Characteristics of the TNC

The transnational corporation is broadly defined as a large firm which undertakes foreign direct investment in two or more countries, that is, it owns productive assets (mines, factories, etc.) in a number of countries. TNCs are responsible for the bulk of direct foreign investment, but they must be distinguished analytically from foreign investment as they also contribute other factors (skills, technology, etc.) along with the capital that they invest. TNCs defined in this way should also be distinguished from firms that are, for example, engaged solely in international trade but are not involved in international production.

Large organisations engaged in international transactions are not a new phenomenon. Hymer notes that:

> Giant corporations are nothing new in international trade. They were a characteristic form of the mercantilist period when large joint-stock companies, e.g. The Hudson's Bay Company, The Royal African Company, The East India Company, to name the major English merchant firms, organized long-distance trade with America, Africa and Asia. But neither these firms, nor the large mining and plantation enterprises in the production sector, were the forerunners of the multinational corporation.
>
> (Hymer 1972, p. 115)

The actual forerunners of today's TNCs did not begin to develop until the end of the 19th century although according to Tugendhat (1973, Ch. 1), the concept of the international company was firmly established by 1914 (especially in the production of cars, oil, chemicals and aluminium). The growth of US TNCs was fairly rapid in the 1920s, but was slower in the 1930s, although Latin America proved to be quite attractive to foreign investors in the 1930s. With respect to the majority of LDCs, large scale direct foreign investment, under the aegis of the TNC, is essentially a post-World War II phenomenon. In the late 19th and early 20th centuries, capital flows to the LDCs were mainly (but not exclusively) in the form of portfolio lending by private individuals to both private and public borrowers, to develop the production of foodstuffs and raw materials and to establish infrastructural and public utility facilities, although direct investment in mineral extraction was also of importance. The revival of the international capital market in the 1950s led to the rapid growth of private capital flows, mainly between the developed economies of North America and Western Europe, but there was also a substantial flow of direct investment to the LDCs, going increasingly into the emerging manufacturing sectors of these economies.

What distinguishes the contemporary TNC from its forerunners is not only its size and the scope of its operations but also its structure, organisation and its view of the world economy and its role in the development of that economy.

The central feature of TNCs is the predominance of large-sized firms. The four largest TNCs have annual sales greater than $10 billion[2] and more than 200 TNCs have annual sales greater than $1 billion (United Nations 1974). Vernon (1973, Ch. 1) maintains that a corporation with annual sales of less than $100 million 'rarely merits much attention' (p. 13). Nearly 200 TNCs have affiliates (an enterprise under the effective control of the parent corporation) in twenty or more countries, and growth of such companies has been very rapid. Between 1950 and 1966, for example, the number of US affiliates in all countries rose from 7,000 to 23,000. Growth was also rapid in the 1960s in the case of Japanese, French and West German TNCs.

TNCs are overwhelmingly oligopolistic in character (that is, they dominate in markets effectively controlled by a few buyers or sellers) and the essential characteristics of TNCs (technological innovation, product innovation and differentiation, heavy advertising and brand identification) are both a feature of, and reinforce, the oligopolistic market structure. Much of their behaviour, including their investment patterns in LDCs, can only be understood within the framework of oligopolistic competition. They are themselves contributors to, and products of, technological evolution in so far as developments in the fields of telecommunications, air transport, advanced computers and data processing make possible management on a global scale.

Perhaps the unique feature of the TNC is that it is able to view the world as a single economic unit and thus it plans, organises and manages on a global scale. As Barnet and Müller put it:

> The power of the global corporation derives from its unique capacity to use finance, technology and advanced marketing skills to integrate production on a worldwide scale and thus to realise the ancient capitalist dream of One Great Market.
>
> (Barnet and Müller 1974, p. 18)

Some analysts would go further and argue that the criterion for deciding whether a corporation is transnational or not is the extent to which policy is centralised and key operations integrated among affiliates.[3] Tugendhat (1973, Ch. 6) likens the head office of the TNC to the brain and nerve centre of a living organism. It is head office that evolves corporate strategy, decides on the location of new investment, allocates export markets and research programmes to various subsidiaries and determines the prices that should be charged in intra-corporate exchanges (transfer prices). Affiliates operate under the discipline and framework of a common global strategy and a common global control and, in principle at least, put the wider interests of the company as a whole before their own separate interests.

The basic objective of the TNC is to maximise global profits[4] and thus it is almost inevitable that conflicts will arise between national governments (which supposedly safeguard national interests – or at least the interests of a particular social class) and the TNC subsidiary located within its territory. Because of the latter's subservience to the parent company, its operations may give rise to a structure of inputs, outputs, costs, prices and profits that is consistent with neither the needs of the host country nor the desires of its government. As we shall see below, there are many aspects to this conflict and they are likely to assume greater importance to LDCs than in developed economies.[5]

A key to the power and influence of the TNC lies in its ownership and control of knowledge, broadly defined to include the technology of production, organisational skills and marketing skills (for both the product and the consumption 'ideology' of the home society). Often the 'soft' technology that the TNC possesses (marketing, purchasing, organisation, training, overall management, finance, etc.) may be more important than the 'hard' technology embodied in machinery and equipment. A large part of commercialised technology is in the hands of the TNCs but as the United Nations (1974) report points out, basic knowledge more often originates in government-financed research and training centres, with the research expenditure of the TNC concentrated on practical development (often aimed at product differentiation) rather than basic research. The contribution of the TNC derives from its ability to combine different types of lasting knowledge into commercially viable processes and products. Indeed, many would argue that *the* essential characteristic of the TNC is the creation, commercialisation and oligopolisation of relevant applied knowledge, *not* the ownership of fixed assets or financial resources, although not everyone would agree with this view.

From the viewpoint of the LDC, the main attraction of TNC direct investment is that technology, finance capital, managerial and marketing skills all come together in one 'package', supplying the scarce factors 'vital' to the development effort in a seemingly painless way. But the very nature of the 'package' makes it extremely difficult, if not impossible, for the LDC to discover the real costs of the various factors supplied and to evaluate the 'appropriateness' of the commodity being produced and the techniques of production utilised. There is not a great deal of empirical information available on the operations of TNCs in LDCs, especially concerning their impact on economic growth and development,[6] but even a sophisticated empiricism will not provide answers to these problems. TNCs

**Table 9.1** *Regional and sectoral distribution of stock of foreign direct investment in LDCs end 1970 ($ billion)*

| | *Latin America* | | *Europe* | | *Africa* | |
|---|---|---|---|---|---|---|
| | | % | | % | | % |
| Petroleum | 4.8 | 24.2 | 0.4 | 16.0 | 3.3 | 43.4 |
| Mining | 2.1 | 10.6 | 0.1 | 4.0 | 1.4 | 18.4 |
| Manufacturing | 7.5 | 37.9 | 1.5 | 60.0 | 1.3 | 17.1 |
| Other | 5.4 | 27.3 | 0.5 | 20.0 | 1.6 | 21.1 |
| Total | 19.8 | 100.0 | 2.5 | 100.0 | 7.6 | 100.0 |
| % | 50.8 | | 6.4 | | 19.5 | |

| | *Middle East* | | *Asia* | | *Total* | |
|---|---|---|---|---|---|---|
| | | % | | % | | % |
| Petroleum | 3.2 | 91.4 | 1.3 | 23.2 | 13.0 | 33.3 |
| Mining | — | — | 0.4 | 7.1 | 4.0 | 10.3 |
| Manufacturing | 0.2 | 5.7 | 1.8 | 32.1 | 12.3 | 31.5 |
| Other | 0.1 | 2.9 | 2.1 | 37.5 | 9.7 | 24.9 |
| Total | 3.5 | 100.0 | 5.6 | 100.0 | 39.9 | 100.0 |
| % | 9.0 | | 14.4 | | 100.0 | |

*Source:* Reuber (1973, Appendix A).

*Note:* The 'Other' category includes foreign investment in agri-business, shipping, trade, banking, tourism and consultancy.

are a (some would say *the*) key feature of the contemporary capitalist system and they can only be fully understood when they are seen as part of that wider system and analysed accordingly (Radice 1975; Baran and Sweezy 1966).[7] We are asking the wrong questions if we merely attempt to assess whether the costs of TNC activities are in some way greater than, or less than, the benefits.

## 9.3 TNCs and the Less Developed Countries

Estimates vary as to the size of the stock of foreign direct investment (f.d.i.) in LDCs. Reuber (1973, Appendix A) estimated the book value of private foreign direct investment to be approximately $40 billion at the end of 1970 (equal to roughly 25% of the world total of private foreign direct investment).[8] Of this total, direct investment in manufacturing accounts for just over 30%, 60% of which is located in Latin America (see table 9.1).

The geographical spread of direct investment and the location of TNC affiliates reflects both the spheres of interest (economic and political) and the former colonial ties of the major western powers. Seventy per cent of US affiliates are located in Central and South

America and the rest are evenly spread throughout the other LDCs. The location of the affiliates of the former major colonial powers (UK, Belgium, Netherlands, Portugal and France) reflects the extent of their past colonial empires. For example, 40% of UK TNC affiliates are in Africa and 32% in Asia (United Nations 1974, Ch. 1). Japanese TNC affiliates are concentrated in Central and South America (a very recent large-scale entry into these markets and obviously not related to previous colonial ties or spheres of influence) and Asia.

TNC investment is heavily concentrated in a few LDCs. Argentina, Brazil, India, Mexico, Nigeria, Venezuela and a group of Caribbean islands (Leeward Islands, Windward Islands, Bahamas, Barbados and Bermuda) account for 43% of the total stock of foreign direct investment in LDCs, each having a stock of over $1 billion. Another 13 LDCs account for a further 30% of the total (United Nations 1974, Ch. 1).

Historically, the extractive sector (especially petroleum) and infrastructure have been the most important areas of foreign involvement. Table 9.1 indicates that in 1970, petroleum and mining were still quantitatively the most important sectors, but as we have already noted in Chapter 8, manufacturing now accounts for 50% of the flow of current direct investment.

The control of sources of raw materials was initially a powerful force motivating direct foreign investment (Turner 1974, Ch. 2 gives some examples of raw material TNCs dominating LDCs) but recent years have seen the LDC governments becoming increasingly successful in regaining control over their non-renewable natural resources, or at least obtaining a greater share of the revenue derived from their exploitation – oil is perhaps the best example of this process. The foreign ownership and exploitation of a country's basic resources is a politically explosive issue in any economy, especially a poor one which has recently acquired political independence. The TNC has become less important as a supplier of skills, technology and capital (production technology has become standardised, patents have expired, government-owned corporations have moved into this field, and so on) for the extraction and processing of raw materials and it has thus had to develop new strategies in the light of changed economic and political conditions. The local processing of raw materials has become more important, new ownership schemes and contractual arrangements have been introduced (joint ventures, often with the TNC as a minority equity holder, management contracts, etc.) and new technologies developed, all of which demonstrate the flexibility and resourcefulness of the TNC (United Nations 1974) and/or the change in the balance of economic and political power in favour of the LDC government (Warren 1973, pp. 20-24).[9]

With respect to investment in manufacturing, TNCs are concentrated in modern, fast growing, high technology, mainly capital-intensive, brand-conscious industries. (It should also be remembered that TNCs are of increasing importance in banking, tourism, consultancy, advertising, etc.) TNCs have located affiliates in LDCs for a number of reasons – oligopolistic competition in world markets (that is, the observed tendency for TNCs to match direct investment by their rivals in particular markets), the threat of local competition, the desire to protect markets initially developed by exports and threatened by trade barriers, and the growing practice of world-wide sourcing (see Chapter 8). Also important is what Barnet and Müller (1974, Ch. 6) describe as the driving force behind global oligopolistic competition – the necessity to grow in order to maintain or increase market shares. They argue that no mature industry can afford not to expand production facilities in LDCs.

The importance of the various motivating forces, and the economic characteristics of the affiliates, will differ according to the type of activity in which the TNC is engaged. TNCs concerned with the manufacture and subsequent export of components (Chapter 8, section 8.6) are interested in labour cost differentials and the various incentives, financial and otherwise, offered by LDC governments. According to Reuber (1973, Ch. 4) (who studied 80 direct investment projects of North American, European and Japanese origin), the characteristics of these enterprises are: high degree of foreign control (100% parent company ownership is preferred), high minimum acceptable rate of return (20% per annum), short planning horizon (about seven years) and a low propensity to reinvest profits locally (transfer price mechanisms are used to export profits – see below).

In the case of what Reuber calls market development investment (that is, import substituting industrialisation (ISI) discussed in Chapter 8), the protection of the local market is the most important motivating force. The acceptable rate of return is lower (12–14%) and the planning horizon is longer (11–12 years) than is the case with the export-oriented enterprise, and there is a movement away from 100% ownership and control. Profits are more likely to be reinvested locally, but the outflow of royalty and fee payments is likely to be greater.[10]

This is not necessarily the only classification of types of direct investment that can be attempted. Streeten (1971) has argued for a classification based on the characteristics of the knowledge (whether in the field of production or marketing) that is transferred via the TNC investment. Is production knowledge specific and stable or is there a changing flow of various processes? If it is specific and stable, is it stable and simple (in which case it can be obtained through patents or licensing arrangements) or is it stable and complex (in which case technical assistance will also be required)? In the case of a changing flow of knowledge, there may be no alternative method of acquiring it other than through direct investment. The advantage of Streeten's classification is that it focuses attention on the question of alternative ways of obtaining knowledge, the value of knowledge obtained and the distribution of benefits between the supplier (the TNC) and the purchaser (the LDC) of that knowledge.

## 9.4 The TNC and Resource Utilisation and Development

It is usually assumed that TNCs are 'engines of development' in that they contribute resources not otherwise available (technology, marketing skills, etc.) or only available in insufficient quantities (capital). Alternatively, it is argued that they are able to utilise existing resources more efficiently than local entrepreneurs, thus maximising their contribution to the development effort. These arguments have been increasingly questioned in recent years, and in this section we attempt to make an assessment of the various aspects of the impact of TNCs on the economic development of LDCs.

*The Sources of Finance*

It has usually been assumed that the act of direct investment results in a direct or indirect transfer of capital to the recipient country, thus adding to the resources available for development by closing the gap that is alleged to exist between investment requirements and savings availability.

The belief that TNCs transfer large quantities of capital to LDCs is mistaken. The global investment activities of TNCs, especially in the manufacturing sector, are overwhelmingly financed from resources originating within the host economy. Estimates vary as to the extent of local financing. A UN study (Fajnzylber 1971, quoted in Cardoso 1972, p. 92, Table III) estimated that in Latin America, during the years 1957–1965, US TNCs financed 83% of their total investment from local sources, either from reinvested earnings (59%) or local borrowing (or borrowing from third countries) (24%). The equivalent figures for manufacturing only were: total 78%, internal funds 38% and local borrowing 40%. Vaitsos (1976, p. 125) quotes US Senate sources which indicate that less than 15% of the total financial needs of US-based manufacturing subsidiaries abroad originate from US sources. Furthermore, this 15% may be an overestimate in so far as various accounting practices employed by the TNCs (for example, the capitalisation of intangibles and secondhand machinery) inflate the actual contribution made. Vaitsos (1976, p. 125) further argues that the term 'foreign investment' is inaccurate in this respect – we should refer to 'foreign controlled firms' financed mainly from local sources.

The above figures show that reinvested earnings are an important source of finance for the TNC. But these reinvested earnings are, to a large extent, generated from local sources and while in one sense they are a potential addition to local savings (in so far as the TNC makes more profitable use of domestic capital than local entrepreneurs), they are under the control of the TNC and may ultimately be repatriated. Barnet and Müller (1974, pp. 153-154) quote figures which show that between 1960 and 1968, US TNCs took, on average, 79% of their net profits out of Latin America. Between 1965 and 1968, 52% of total profits of US TNCs in the manufacturing sector in Latin America were repatriated to the USA. In other words, the TNC sends out of the host country profits made on capital borrowed locally, thus reducing the rate of capital accumulation within the LDC. Nevertheless, in spite of this outflow, unrepatriated profits account for a large share of net investment in certain sectors of Latin American industry.

In many cases, TNCs buy already established local firms when they enter an LDC, rather than establish new productive facilities. This has taken place on a large scale in Latin America (in the period 1958–1967 almost 50% of all manufacturing operations established were takeovers of existing industry) and has been referred to as the 'denationalisation' of local industry. This process does not directly lead to the establishment of new productive capacity (everything depends on what the previous owners do with the proceeds of the sale – they may consume or export the proceeds, perhaps illegally, rather than reinvest them in other sectors of the economy) and, coupled with this, the 'denationalisation' of local industry has important implications for the development of a local entrepreneurial class, a point we refer to again below.

### *Financial Transfers and the Balance of Payments*

Given the paucity of existing information concerning the operations of TNCs, it is impossible to give an accurate assessment of their overall balance of payments impact. The initial act of direct investment (assuming that the capital comes from foreign rather than local sources) involves a capital inflow and thus a credit item in the balance of payments account. But the investment generates a stream of profit, interest and dividend payments, royalty payments, etc. during its life which can be repatriated and thus have a negative balance of payments effect (see, for example, table 5.2 in Chapter 5). Indirect effects on the payments position include: the extent to which the project substitutes for imports or leads to additional exports; the source of inputs (local or foreign); and the likely alternative uses of local resources utilised by the foreign investor.[11]

At a more general level, the balance of payments effect cannot be separated from the financial policies and objectives pursued by the TNC. The latter's concern with global profit maximisation will almost certainly conflict with the host countries governments' domestic objectives. In general, the LDC government will want the TNC to create as much employment as possible, to provide the maximum possible tax revenue and to save foreign exchange through ISI or earn foreign exchange through additional exports, reinvesting its profits locally, thus improving the balance of payments position. The TNC, on the other hand, may wish to maximise its transfer of funds from that particular LDC economy either to minimise its global tax payments (other things being equal, the TNC will transfer profits from a higher to a lower taxed country) or to minimise exchange risks (or any other risks – for example, the possibility of nationalisation/expropriation) that it may face. The manipulation of transfer prices (defined below) can, of course, be used to move funds into an LDC and may thus improve its balance of payments but this is likely to be the exception rather than the rule.

The minimisation of the overall amount of tax that the TNC pays on its global operations ('tax planning') is a perfectly legitimate business objective, and the TNC will use a variety of means (dividend, interest and royalty payments, capital transfers, payments for goods, services and knowledge, etc.) to achieve this objective. Tax minimisation is unlikely to be pursued at the expense of long-term global profit maximisation. For example, funds will be transferred to an economy where investment plans require them, even though higher taxes will be incurred on profits made, and thus it can be said that the TNC is maximising profits net of tax. When a number of TNCs are pursuing similar policies (that is, moving large quantities of funds in the same direction), they can weaken or destroy the national policies of even the developed economies, with respect to exchange rates, balance of payments, domestic credit availability and so on (Tugendhat 1973, Ch. 10).

The LDC may wish to attempt to control the transfer of funds between the subsidiary and any other part of the TNC and for this purpose it has a number of controls available to it (foreign exchange control regulations, tax regulations, direct controls). But a clash of interests may result and the TNC will attempt to avoid legally (or may attempt to evade illegally) the LDC regulations. The most powerful weapon that it has at its disposal in this respect is the use (or abuse) of transfer pricing.

Transfer prices (sometimes referred to as accounting prices) are the prices charged on transactions that take place within the TNC and they can deviate to a considerable extent from market prices (so-called arms-length prices). Trade within the TNC is transacted outside the sphere of the market, and in many cases a market price may not exist for the product or service being transferred (the TNC may be the sole owner or producer of the service or product). If a TNC wishes to transfer funds from a particular country, it can raise the prices that are charged for imports to the subsidiary and lower the prices that are paid for exports from the subsidiary.[12] Given the existence of international differentials in tax rates, import duties and export subsidies, the TNC alters transfer prices to maximise its global profits. Lall (1973) has listed the reasons for transfer price manipulation (apart from profit maximisation and tax minimisation). They include: the minimisation of liabilities in a weak currency; the existence of quantitative restrictions on profit remittances; the existence of multiple exchange rate systems; the possibility of political and social pressures against 'high' profits earned by TNCs and demands by local workers for higher wages; and the deprivation of local shareholders (or with the latters' agreement, the transfer of their share of profits to another country). All of these reasons can be interpreted as relating to the objective of global profit maximisation.

Tugendhat (1973, Ch. 10) argues that transfer pricing must be used with care and discretion and that the more blatant forms of transfer price manipulation are no longer possible. But LDC government agencies (customs and excise, income tax, planning and commerce ministries) in particular are unlikely to have sufficient expertise and experience to investigate all possible transfer price abuses and will not be able to match the TNC in negotiating power and ability. The pricing policy of the TNC is dictated by its head office with little or no discretion allowed to the subsidiary and this fact further weakens the ability of an LDC to control TNC activities. Vaitsos (1976, p. 122) has concluded that 'an indispensable aid to governments ... is the training of personnel who can understand the internal functioning of transnational enterprises, administer the policies and be able to negotiate with foreign factor suppliers', and one of the major functions of the newly established UN Centre on Transnational Corporations (see note 6) must be to provide technical assistance and train personnel from LDCs to bargain more effectively and efficiently with TNCs.

Even if the level of expertise available to LDCs is increased, certain types of transfer pricing abuse will still remain difficult to deal with.

It may be difficult to discover the market or arms-length price of a particular product with which to compare the transfer price and, as we have already indicated, a comparable product may not exist when TNCs are producing non-standardised products (Vaitsos 1975, p. 213, points out that 'there is no such thing as an international market for Volkswagen doors by which to estimate overpricing'). Hanson also argues that:

> finding adequate substitutes for arms-length prices is difficult in a dynamic world of changing cost functions, altered trade patterns and relocations of production for individual tradeable goods, coupled with continually changing product mixes for individual units of multinational corporations.[13]
>
> (Hanson 1975, p. 861)

It is difficult to know the extent to which transfer price manipulation occurs on a world scale. Lall (1973, table I, p. 183) estimates that in 1970, intra-firm exports of US TNCs accounted for 35% of total US manufactured exports and intra-firm imports accounted for 22% of total US manufactured imports. Overall, about one-third of total US trade in manufactured goods was intra-firm in 1970. In the case of the UK, it was estimated that in 1966, intra-firm exports accounted for 24% of total UK manufactured exports. The data quoted by Lall show that 18 US TNCs accounted for 65% of total intra-firm imports in 1965. Furthermore:

> ... if about 50 US MNEs (multinational enterprises) and a similar number of non-US MNEs controlled between them all but a minor proportion of world intra-firm trade, these 100 or so firms would be the ones controlling not only an immense quantity of resources but also the means to move its rewards around practically at will.
>
> (Lall 1973, p. 184)

These figures illustrate the *potential* for transfer price manipulation that exists and even small changes in transfer prices could have a massive effect. It is, of course, true that only a small proportion of intra-firm trade will involve subsidiaries operating in LDCs, but the absolute magnitude of intra-firm trade and the implications of transfer price manipulation will be far more important for these economies – they are less able to absorb the loss of scarce foreign exchange (which could have been as much as US $20 million for the Colombian pharmaceutical industry alone in 1968 – Vaitsos 1974, p. 48) and potential investable resources than more developed economies.

As we shall see in Chapter 10 on the choice of technique, most subsidiaries import their intermediate and capital goods requirements from the parent company or other affiliates (this is often a contractual requirement, a so-called 'tie-in' clause) and opportunities for over-pricing are thus substantial.[14] Vaitsos (1974, Ch. 4; 1975) presents figures showing that in the Colombian pharmaceutical industry, the weighted average over-pricing of products imported by foreign-owned subsidiaries amounted to 155% (that of national firms was 19%). Put another way, reported profits accounted for 3.4% of effective returns, royalties accounted for 14.0% and over-pricing accounted for 82.6% of effective returns (Vaitsos 1973, p. 319). In the electronics industry in Colombia, the over-pricing of imports ranged between 6% and 69%. In the Ecuadorian electronics industry, 29 imported products were evaluated in relation to Colombian registered prices: 16 were imported at prices comparable to the Colombian ones, 7 were over-priced by up to 75% and 6 were over-priced by about 200% (Vaitsos 1975, p. 212).

Vaitsos' conclusion is worth quoting:

> In all sectors and countries that were evaluated, significant returns to foreign factors of production appeared to accrue through the profit margins of products tied into the importation of capital and/or technology.
>
> Foreign subsidiaries in the cases investigated apparently use transfer pricing of products as a mechanism of income remission, thus significantly understating their true profitability.
>
> (Vaitsos 1974, p. 50)[15]

We must briefly mention a number of other ways in which the activities of the TNCs have a direct impact on the host country's balance of payments. TNCs make a number of other payments from host countries for the factors and services provided by the parent corporation. Payments for patents, licences, brand names and trade marks and management and service fees are all growing rapidly (UNCTAD estimates a growth rate of 20% per annum for these payments (United Nations 1974, Ch. 3)) and their total cost to six LDCs only (Argentina, Brazil, Colombia, Mexico, Nigeria and Sri Lanka) has been put at 7% of their combined exports. (The global total of royalties is put anywhere between \$3–\$5 billion per year.) But estimates of royalties are distorted by the possibilities of transfer pricing as changes in royalty flows may merely reflect changes in the TNC's global strategy with respect to the distribution of returns among different channels of income remission.

Other payments made by TNC subsidiaries to their head offices include contributions to HQ overhead expenditure, contributions to research and development, the accounting of expenses incurred before the investment as part of the equity contribution and so on (ILO 1972, pp. 455-457). The variety of means by which a TNC can transfer funds from a host country demonstrates its flexibility of operation and makes meaningless the officially declared profits on TNC operations in LDCs. The ILO Report on Kenya concludes:

> ... foreign companies have a great deal of room to manoeuvre in transferring untaxed surpluses and surpluses taxed at half the rate of profits tax out of Kenya. We consider that the amount of surplus transferred in the form of dividends after taxation might be less than half the total surplus transferred by foreign enterprises in the manufacturing sector. The particular manner in which these additional transfers are carried out makes nonsense of the regulation that the amount remitted after tax must be proportionate to the foreign share in equity capital.
>
> (ILO 1972, pp. 456-7)

TNCs may add to the availability of foreign exchange through the promotion of exports. In the case of TNCs engaged in the extraction or production of primary commodities, or in the export of components, the positive effect on the current account of the balance of payments may well be quite significant. But Barnet and Müller (1974, p. 158) quote empirical evidence showing that US TNCs in Latin America had a worse export performance than local firms for exports outside Latin America and did no better (with certain exceptions) when it came to exporting to other Latin American countries. Moreover, because 75% of these exports were intra-firm in nature, the possibilities for transfer price manipulation existed and exports were consistently undervalued on average 40% less than prices charged by local firms.

Furthermore, when TNCs transfer technology to a locally owned firm, the contract often forbids the sale of goods produced using that technology outside the host country (or the countries to which sales may be made are specified). The work of Vaitsos (1974, Ch. 4 and 1975) and others in the Andean Pact group of countries indicates that such restrictions are widespread. For four of the countries (Bolivia, Colombia, Ecuador and Peru), 81% of the contracts analysed prohibited exports totally, and 86% had some restrictive clause on exports. In Chile, more than 72% of the contracts totally prohibited exports. It is of interest to note that these restrictions were more severe with respect to locally owned firms than with foreign wholly owned subsidiaries (Vaitsos 1974, p. 57). These restrictive business practices (to use UN terminology) are very widespread, having been noted in, among other countries, India (see Patnaik 1972), Iran, Mexico, Philippines, Kuwait and El Salvador, and are one aspect of the phenomenon of technological dependence.

Overall, it is impossible to quantify with any degree of accuracy or reliability the direct and indirect effects of the operations of TNCs on the balance of payments of host LDCs. Even if there is a large positive effect, as in the case of mineral extraction and export, other aspects of the TNC's operations may be undesirable – for example, the rate of exploitation of a non-renewable resource may be too high, tax payments to the LDC too low, insufficient employment may be created and so on (although it must be remembered that all these various aspects of the operation of TNCs are open to negotiation). Tie-in clauses increase the import sensitivity of the economy already exacerbated by the process of ISI (see Chapter 8), and export restrictions prevent the development of new overseas markets and the earning of additional foreign exchange.

The LDC government may attempt to alleviate the burden imposed on the balance of payments by profit repatriation by encouraging TNCs to reinvest a greater proportion of their profits locally. But if the rate of return on foreign capital (after tax and depreciation) is greater than the rate of growth of national income and assuming that these profits are reinvested locally, then foreign capital ownership grows at a faster rate than national income. Assuming a constant capital–output ratio, foreign capital grows at a faster rate than domestic capital and an ever-increasing proportion of the domestic capital stock will be owned by foreigners. This process is not likely to be politically acceptable and must in any case end when all capital is foreign owned. The latter is, of course, a limiting case, and is highly unlikely to be realised in practice. Nevertheless, it illustrates the serious dynamic tendencies at work. Streeten summarises the dilemma faced by LDCs:

> ... either they permit or even encourage this growth of foreign capital, in which case they are faced with growing foreign ownership of their capital stock. Or else they limit this process of alienation, in which case a part of their export earnings will be mortgaged to remitting profits and repatriating capital. It is small wonder that this ineluctable dilemma has led to ambivalence and hostility towards foreign investment.
>
> (Streeten 1972, p. 213)

In general, too much attention in the past has been focused on the balance of payments effect of foreign direct investment, and the wider impact on overall resource utilisation and development has tended to be neglected. The growing literature on the TNC is beginning to rectify this situation.

## 9.5 The TNC and Taste Transfer

Barnet and Müller (1974, Chs 2 and 6) place great emphasis on the creation, by TNCs, of a 'global shopping centre' and the diffusion of the 'ideology' of the consuming society – that is, the creation of international consumption habits and standards, through the product differentiation and advertising characteristic of oligopolistic industries, throughout the developed and underdeveloped world.

An essential element of TNC power is their ability to create demands and mould tastes, and the products of the advanced capitalist economies are being increasingly consumed by the middle- and upper-income groups of the LDCs (and of course produced within these economies as ISI proceeds). An 'international elite' has come into being which, although geographically widespread, exhibits a basically uniform pattern of consumption – the same foodstuffs, soft drinks, cigarettes, automobiles, pharmaceutical products, electrical consumer goods, etc. are consumed in all countries where they are permitted access. This process has also spread to those in the lower income groups who will often consume the brand-differentiated, heavily advertised products of the TNCs, rather than the cheaper but less 'sophisticated' products of local firms.[16]

Langdon's (1975) study of the Kenyan soap industry, which contains both foreign and local firms, clearly illustrates the economic ramifications of TNC penetration. The comparison of local and foreign firms is organised around five separate but inter-linked themes, and the shortcomings of TNCs in relation to their local counterparts are strikingly exposed:

1. TNC subsidiaries are more capital-intensive (and hence generate less employment), at least partly because of the nature of the product produced. Sophisticated, brand-differentiated, secret formula toilet soaps and detergents require capital-intensive production methods ensuring standardisation and quality control; TNC marketing techniques demand smart-looking packaging which usually requires mechanisation.[17]

2. TNCs have developed fewer linkages with the Kenyan economy. Both mechanisation and the nature of the TNC products are more likely to demand imported raw materials, working against backward linkages, and the capital equipment is likely to be supplied by the parent company. The linkage possibilities that do exist (for example, packaging and printing requirements) are more likely to be exploited by other TNCs, rather than by local firms.

3. TNCs are likely to have a significant negative balance of payments effect (higher import content of output, export restrictions, surplus repatriation) as compared to local firms.

4. TNCs are likely to lead to a greater wastage of resources because of (i) lower capacity utilisation (arising from brand differentiation) and (ii) heavy advertising expenditure which is wasteful, given the scarcity of resources in LDCs.

5. TNCs are likely to exacerbate to a greater extent than local firms existing regional and social inequalities. TNCs locate with respect to, and help create, the more sophisticated urban market (in this case, Nairobi) and, as we have already argued above, the very

nature of TNC products demands an elite market (partly created through income redistribution arising from the capital-intensity of the production process). Furthermore, TNCs undercut the growth and profitability of local firms and force them to become more like TNCs in order to survive (increased mechanisation, higher advertising outlays, etc.).

What emerges from the penetration of the Kenyan economy by TNCs is a 'distorted' pattern of industrialisation. Alternative industrialisation strategies may in principle exist (based on local rather than foreign capital, for example) but in practice changes in the real world are not easy to make. Langdon concludes that:

> The MNC (multinational corporation) sector in Kenya is clearly helping to shape a class structure that depends on and supports the MNC's own role in the country ... restricting and reducing the MNC role in the Kenyan political economy, in order to promote *broadly-based* industrial development, will require a fundamental shift in power in Kenyan society.
>
> (Langdon 1975, p. 32, emphasis in original)

Langdon's second major conclusion is that the TNC, as a vehicle for the transfer of technology to LDCs, suffers from serious shortcomings, a point we return to in Chapter 10.

## 9.6 The TNC and Dependent Development

Two key aspects of the concept of the economic dependence of LDCs will be considered briefly in this section — the allegation that the activities of TNCs prevent the emergence (or destroy the existence) of an entrepreneurial class dedicated to national development (the so-called national bourgeoisie) and secondly, that TNCs prevent or retard the emergence of a domestic capital goods industry.

In those economies (mainly, but not exclusively, in Latin America) where TNCs have achieved a dominant position in the large and medium-scale industrial sector (as well as in banking, tourism, etc.), it is argued that a significant part of the domestic entrepreneurial class is transformed into what Sunkel (1973a, p. 22) refers to as 'private transnational technocracies and bureaucracies' — that is a class whose interests are tied to, and dependent on, the TNC.[18] It is not the lack of an entrepreneurial class that retards development (as has been popularly alleged in much writing on development over the past 25 years) but rather it is the penetration of the domestic economy by foreign interests that prevents the emergence of a social group which places priority on national ownership and control to achieve national developmental objectives.

Sunkel sees this penetration as being present at all levels and affecting all social classes and groups (of equal importance to the penetration of the productive structure are the economic and social consequences of technological transfer and the impact on cultural and ideological attitudes and values). This process incorporates into the new institutions and structures those individuals and groups most suited to fit into them, but expels others that have no place nor the ability to adapt. This is called the process of marginalisation (conditioned largely by the lack of, or difficulty of access to, a reasonable and stable income) and it affects all social classes within the LDC.

At a broader level, Sunkel in another article (1973b) has referred to the process as 'transnational integration' and 'national disintegration'. Certain groups and classes are incorporated into the new international industrial system being built largely by TNCs (referred to by Sunkel as TRANCOS – transnational conglomerates) whilst, as within the domestic economy, others are excluded. The classification of the domestic economy into integrated and segregated groups overlaps with the more traditional classification along class lines, and again we find integrated and non-integrated groups (referring in this case to integration into the new international industrial system) in all classes – entrepreneurs, the middle class and the working class.

This brief summary cannot do full justice to the complexity of Sunkel's arguments, but it does permit us to raise a further point concerning the transfer of technology. It has usually been assumed that any technology transferred to an LDC would 'trickle down' and permeate the whole economy (the 'spread' effects), that is technological transfer would be part of the general process of 'modernisation' (a term synonymous with 'development'). More recently, Warren (1973, pp. 30–33) has argued the case for technological spread, quoting evidence from the Middle East where the policies of the oil companies in the 1950s were alleged to have broadened the regions's technological base (local employees of the oil companies resigned and established businesses of their own, for example).

Sunkel (and others) argue that because of the centralisation of research and decision-making within the home country of the TNC, 'spread' effects may be more than offset by 'backwash' effects (defined as forces leading to greater concentration at the centre), leading to an even greater technological gap between developed economies and LDCs.[19] In this case, we should not expect the TNC to operate as a vehicle for technological diffusion and modernisation.

A crucial element in this debate is the willingness or ability of TNCs to establish capital goods industries in LDCs. A number of reasons have been put forward to support the view that the industrialisation process in the majority of LDCs has built in a bias against the establishment of domestic capital goods industries:

1. The limited domestic market for capital goods (arising from the fragmentation of domestic production and over-diversification, in turn leading to an absence of standardisation of equipment and materials) provides little incentive for domestic manufacture (Merhav 1969, p. 133).
2. Producers of final goods will strongly resist import substitution for their inputs in general and capital goods in particular because they know from their own experience that this may raise costs, lower quality and reduce reliability.
3. The risks attached to the heavy investment required for the establishment of capital goods industries may be too great given the uncertainties (both economic and political) endemic in LDCs.
4. The oligopolistic structure of the advanced capitalist economies means that a manufacturer, when deciding to invest in a new area, must take into consideration, *inter alia,* the effect of his decision on (a) his own export interests, (b) competitors' export interests, (c) customers' export interests, if any (assuming that the new plant will not compete in the national market from which the investment originated) (Arrighi 1970, p. 227). Arrighi concludes that '... the oligopolistic structure of the industrial centers strengthens the other factors ... in producing ... a sectoral pattern of foreign investment biased against the capital-goods industry'.
5. Capital-intensive techniques and the bias against the capital goods sector reinforce one another. Capital-intensive techniques favour the use of specialised machinery and this restrains the growth of demand for capital goods that could be produced in LDCs; the lack of investment in the capital goods sector in turn prevents the development of capital goods embodying modern labour-intensive technology.

We have already noted in Chapter 8 that the larger, more 'developed' LDCs (Brazil, India) have established capital goods industries and Warren (1973) makes much of the technology that has already been transferred to LDCs and the capital goods industries already established. Undoubtedly, to an increasing extent in the future, under the pressure of events and as a result of the search for profitable investment opportunities, TNCs will invest in capital goods industries, especially as the technologies required become standardised and more widely available. But unless there are both very radical changes in the geographical pattern of R and D expenditures and the objectives towards the realisation of which the expenditures are made, the most up-to-date technologies are still likely to be developed and initially utilised in the developed economies. There are no obvious reasons why TNCs should willingly surrender the monopoly they enjoy over both products and processes, although the extent to which they will be forced to compromise on this issue depends in part at least on the future course of their relationship with LDC governments.

## 9.7 Conclusions

Rather than merely summarising the arguments of this chapter, we shall attempt in this concluding section to pinpoint some of the wider economic and political implications of the foregoing analysis. In particular, it is necessary to say something about the probable future of the TNC in its relations with LDCs and their governments.

It is now a commonplace to assert that the day of the rapid and unhampered expansion of TNCs is over. The increased intensity of economic nationalism in LDCs, the nationalisation/expropriation of the assets of TNCs (especially in extractive industries), the success of OPEC and the increase in awareness of the activities of TNCs are all factors used by Turner (1973, Ch. 1), for example, to predict a shift in the balance of power in favour of LDC governments. He maintains that 'Third World governments are on the offensive against companies that for decades have had things their own way' (p. 3). Barnet and Müller (1974) although stressing the power and resourcefulness of TNCs, nonetheless feel that elites in LDCs, in order to ensure their own survival, will have to extract more from TNCs, and that they have the power to change 'the rules of the game'.

The usual framework for the discussion of these issues is illustrated by Streeten's three questions (1971, p. 242):

1. Even if the will and the political power exist, do LDC governments have the ability to control TNCs to the extent that they consider desirable?
2. Even if they have the political power, do they have the will?
3. Even if they have the will and ability, do they have the political power?

It may certainly be the case that, even though LDC governments cannot actually 'control' TNCs, they are increasingly able to obtain a larger share of the proceeds arising from TNC operations. The increase in the technical information about the behaviour of TNCs, the pooling of information between LDCs, the standardisation and greater effectiveness of laws governing the operations of TNCs, the rationalisation of investment incentive schemes, the diversification by LDCs of their trading partners, sources of technology and of capital and the opportunities for playing off one developed economy against another as competition for materials and markets intensifies, are all factors which indicate some shift in the balance of power in favour of LDCs. In Colombia, for example, the Comité de Regaliás (Committee on Royalties, a government body responsible for vetting and evaluation of technology commercialisation contracts) between 1967 and 1971 evaluated 395 contracts, of which 334 were negotiated, modified and finally approved and 61 were rejected. 'In the process of negotiations, payments of royalties were reduced by about 40% or about $ US 8 million annually' (Vaitsos 1975, p. 200).

The way Streeten's questions are framed implies a conflict between the TNC and the LDC nation state. Streeten recognises that the nation state is not monolithic and that different interests will align themselves in various ways with the TNC, and in this sense it is misleading to speak of the 'national interest' vis-à-vis TNCs. But Streeten does not pursue this issue. To do so involves a closer examination of the relationship between the TNC and the LDC government and the recognition that there need be no real conflict as such between the two. We have argued that it is unlikely that the TNC, given its objectives and *modus operandi,* will bring net benefits to the majority of the population, but neither will the policies pursued by the majority of the LDC governments. There is more likely to exist an 'unholy alliance' between the two with increasingly tough bargaining (often hostile) taking place over the distribution of rewards. But both sides will have an interest in maintaining the status quo and only radical political changes within the LDCs themselves are likely to terminate this 'partnership'.

The characteristic of the TNC that deserves emphasis is its flexibility. Although the TNC normally prefers 100% ownership of its subsidiary (especially when global control is highly centralised and when new technologies and/or products are being exploited) new forms of ownership arrangements are constantly appearing. Joint ventures (with either the LDC government or private capital), minority participation, turnkey contracts, management contracts, fade-out arrangements and so on are all becoming increasingly common.[20] TNCs will even welcome nationalisation under certain circumstances (Nixson 1971). Different institutional arrangements require that the TNC obtain its return in alternative ways (royalties instead of profits, for example).

The TNC will pursue different policies in different places at different times. For example, while ITT was attempting to bring down the Allende government in Chile, it was at the same time negotiating with the Soviet Union for the establishment of joint ventures (Sampson 1973, Chs 11–12). TNCs will live with established 'socialist' states and do business with them in an attempt to incorporate them more fully into the capitalist world economy. But they will attempt to prevent the expansion of 'socialism' and will aim at the destruction or destabilisation of political institutions or structures inimical to their continued profitable operation (Barnet and Müller 1974, Ch. 3).

Finally, we must remember the geographical mobility of those TNCs utilising the unskilled/semi-skilled labour of LDCs for the assembly or manufacture of components. These are genuinely footloose industries that can quickly move from country to country as political and/or economic conditions dictate and there is very little that LDCs, individually, can do about this.

TNCs cannot be directly blamed for the lack of development (or the direction that development is taking) within LDCs. Their prime objective is global profit maximisation and their actions are aimed at achieving that objective, not developing the host LDC. If the technology and the products that they introduce are 'inappropriate', if their actions exacerbate regional and social inequalities, if they weaken the balance of payments position, in the last resort it is up to the LDC government to pursue policies which will eliminate the causes of these problems. This is, of course, a complex political problem in itself, but the relationship between the development policies/strategies pursued and the class structure of the LDC (and the alliance of certain classes within the LDC with foreign interests) should be the central focus of the study of the political economy of development.

The final issue to be considered is the contribution that TNCs can, in principle, make to the development effort. It is currently fashionable to argue that the main contributions that the TNC can make are the access that it provides to technology, foreign markets and managerial and technical skills. Given the low organisational and technical level of many LDCs, these may indeed be indispensable elements in their development process and may only be obtainable through some form of arrangement with the TNC. In many cases, only TNCs have the financial resources and technical expertise to develop new and better products which may be essential for agricultural development (for example, pesticides), exploit mineral resources and undertake large-scale construction projects. No one would deny the importance of the TNCs *potential* contribution to the development effort, although it must still be emphasised that the generation of these new technologies further increases the dependence of LDCs on TNCs and frustrates any attempts at independent industrialisation.

But it is the structure of the arrangement with the TNC that is important, the way in which the vital factors are acquired *and the price that is paid for them.* The LDC must first put its own house in order (that is, define its development objectives and establish the structures and institutions for achieving those objectives) before it can hope to approach the TNC and strike a just bargain. This is partly a matter of training and education but it is essentially a matter of political change within the LDC itself. Without this political change, new institutional forms (joint ventures) or more effective bargaining procedures will not fundamentally affect the economic position of the majority of the population of LDCs nor eradicate the condition of underdevelopment.

## Notes

1 The United Nations has adopted the term 'transnational corporation' and we use it for the sake of convenience. It emphasises the transnationality of operations (across frontiers) without implying that ownership or management is in any sense 'multinational'. In fact, equity is largely held by the citizens and institutions of the home country and likewise senior executives come mainly from the TNCs' home countries. Appendix B of United Nations (1974a) testifies to the confusion that exists over terminology.

2 The value added by each of the top 10 TNCs in 1971 was greater than $3 billion, which was greater than the GNP of over 80 countries. The value added of all TNCs was estimated at $500 billion in 1971, which was approximately 20% of world GNP (excluding the centrally planned economies). (United Nations, 1974a, Ch. 1).

3 Jack Behrman, a former US Assistant Secretary of Commerce, quoted in Barnet and Müller (1974, p. 40). Parry (1973) argues that there is a stereotype form of international operations towards which firms with international operations are moving (and which many, of course, have already achieved). The stereotype is defined as 'that corporate structure *where operations are in two or more countries on such a scale that growth and success depend on more than one nation, and where major decisions are made on the basis of global alternatives*' (p. 1202, emphasis in original).

4 Baran and Sweezy (1968, Ch. 2) argue that the primary objectives of corporate policy are strength, rate of growth and size. These are all reducible to profitability and the search for 'maximum' profits is the search for the greatest increase in profits which is possible in any given situation. Even if profits are not the ultimate goal, they are the means by which ultimate goals can be achieved.

5 It is the case, of course, that all private investment, domestic and foreign, is motivated by considerations of profit rather than social benefit and thus a divergence exists between what is privately profitable and socially desirable. The TNC cannot logically be blamed for not 'promoting development' if it is not in its interests to do so (that is, will not increase its profits).

6 One of the functions of the UN Centre on Transnational Corporations (established in late 1975) is to establish a comprehensive information system, covering such 'priority areas where information gaps are most pressing' as transfer pricing and taxation, restrictive business practices, market concentration, sources of finance, alternative forms of management control, political activities of TNCs and many other areas. Reported in *Financial Times,* 31 October 1975. The Centre will also operate advisory services for LDC governments.

7 'Analysis of international firms and development of the theory of imperialism go hand in hand' (Radice 1975, Introduction, p. 18).

8 The United Nations (1974a, Ch. 1) estimates the total stock of direct foreign investment to be $165 billion, of which approximately $52 billion is located in the LDCs. But relative to the size of the economy, the significance of direct foreign investment is far greater in LDCs than in DCs.

9 It is interesting to speculate whether the increasing dependence of the developed economies on LDC sources of supply will lead to new attempts by the former and TNCs to regain ownership or control (perhaps even by force) of strategic raw material supplies. For an illustration of the USA's increasing dependence on imported strategic raw materials, see Barnet and Müller (1974, Table I, p. 126) and Magdoff (1969, Ch. 2).

10 A third type of direct investment is the so-called government initiated investment, largely ISI in character but not necessarily so. It is often difficult to distinguish from market development investment (Reuber 1973).

11 Streeten (1972, pp. 210-211) argues that we must distinguish between the economics of investment and the economics of private overseas investment and that 'The analysis which runs in terms of capital inflow (including retained profits) and profit outflow, crude though it is, has ... stronger logical validity and operational use than the analysis based on "indirect" effects ...' But this criticism is only valid if it is assumed that the foreign investor behaves in an exactly similar way to the domestic investor, and there are reasons for believing this will not necessarily be the case. The foreign investor will have a higher propensity to repatriate profits, *ceteris paribus,* is more likely to use an 'inappropriate' technology and will make decisions on a global, rather than a national, basis. He is also less susceptible to control than the purely national firm.

12 This process used to be referred to as over- and under-invoicing respectively, but these expressions are now used to indicate the occurrence of the practice between unrelated companies.

13 Reuber (1973, Ch. 5) argues that there are at least five reasons for doubting that profit transfers via transfer prices are as important as is sometimes suggested:

(i) tax and customs authorities, although not perfect, do provide checks on abuses by TNCs, in both home and host countries;

(ii) tax rates may often favour profit retention in host countries;

(iii) managers in host country subsidiaries have an incentive not to engage in transfer pricing because it calls into question their efficiency if their subsidiary's profits are low or zero;

(iv) the management of the parent firm may avoid transfer price manipulation to maintain greater efficiency and clearer performance criteria with which to assess the efficiency of the various subsidiaries;

(v) host country partners have a strong incentive to ensure that local profits are not repatriated through transfer pricing.

These are not totally convincing reasons but even if some of them have limited validity (e.g. point (iv)) it seems unlikely that they would override the more important objectives of global profit maximisation, tax minimisation, etc.

14 Overpricing is defined as $100(P_m - P_w)/P_w$, where $P_m$ = FOB price of imports paid by the purchasing national (in this case the Andean Pact Countries of Colombia, Peru, Chile, Bolivia and Ecuador), $P_w$ = FOB price in different world markets (Vaitsos 1974, p. 46).

15 Not only LDCs are at the mercy of TNC transfer price manipulations. There is evidence (referred to in Hanson 1975, p. 861) that Canada, Australia and the UK have all suffered adverse consequences. Presumably such countries are better equipped to deal with this problem.

16 In the case of baby foods, the creation of a 'need' by the TNCs can lead to malnutrition and even death; see Muller (1974).

17 Other factors influencing the TNCs choice of technology are discussed in Chapter 10.

18 Sunkel (1973, p. 22) quotes Celso Furtado: 'The process of formation of the local entrepreneurial class has been interrupted. The best talents that emerged from local industries are being absorbed into the new managerial class ... National independent entrepreneurship is ... restricted to secondary activities or to pioneering ventures which in the long run simply open up new fields for the future expansion of the multinational corporations ... The elimination of the national entrepreneurial class necessarily excludes the possibility of self-sustained national development, according to the pattern of classical capitalist development'. (Furtado C., 'La concentración del poder económico en los EE.UU. y sus proyecciones en América Latina., *Estudios Internacionales,* Año 1, No. 3/4, Santiago 1968).

19 Harry Johnson has argued that 'The Corporation ... has no commercial interest in diffusing its knowledge to potential native competitors ... Its purpose is not to transform the economy by exploiting its potentialities (especially its human potentialities) for development ... the main contribution of direct foreign investment will be highly specific and very uneven in its incidence' (Johnson 1971, pp. 244–246).

20 Parry (1973, p. 1216) warns that 'joint ventures need to be assessed more carefully than seems to have been done by those nations encouraging this alternative to wholly owned subsidiaries of the multinational enterprise'. Joint ventures may be charged higher than arms-length prices for parent goods and services, may have restricted access to technology and know-how and be subject to stricter export restrictions than a wholly owned subsidiary.

## Bibliography


Arrighi G. (1970), 'International corporations, labor aristocracies, and economic development in tropical Africa', in Rhodes R. (ed.), *Imperialism and Underdevelopment: A Reader,* Monthly Review Press, New York.

Baran P. (1957), *The Political Economy of Growth,* Monthly Review Press, New York.

Baran P. and Sweezy P. (1966), 'Notes on the theory of imperialism', *Monthly Review,* March 1966. Reprinted in Boulding K. and Mukerjee T. (eds) (1972), *Economic Imperialism,* University of Michigan Press.

Baran P. and Sweezy P. (1968), *Monopoly Capital,* Penguin.

Barnett R.J. and Müller R.E. (1974), *Global Reach: The Power of the Multinational Corporations,* Simon and Schuster.

Cardoso F.H. (1972), 'Dependent capitalist development in Latin America', *New Left Review,* No. 74, July–August.

Clark N. (1975), 'The multinational corporation: the transfer of technology and dependence', *Development and Change,* January.

Dunning J.H. (ed.) (1971), *The Multinational Enterprise,* Allen and Unwin.

Dunning J.H. (ed.) (1972), *International Investment,* Penguin.

Dunning J.H. (1974), 'The future of the multinational enterprise', *Lloyds Bank Review,* No. 113, July.

Dunning J.H. (ed.) (1974), *Economic Analysis and the Multinational Enterprise,* Allen and Unwin.

Fajnzylber F. (1971), *Estrategia Industrial y Empresas Internacionales,* United Nations, ECLA, Rio, November.

Hanson J.S. (1975), 'Transfer pricing in the multinational corporations: a critical appraisal', *World Development,* Vol. 3, Nos. 11–12.

Helleiner G.K. (ed.) (1976), *A World Divided: The Less Developed Countries in the International Economy,* Cambridge University Press.

Helleiner G.K. (1975), 'Transnational enterprises in the manufacturing sector of the less developed countries', *World Development,* Vol. 3, No. 9, September.

Hymer S. (1972), 'The multinational corporation and the law of uneven development', in Bhagwati J. (ed.) (1972), *Economics and World Order,* Free Press, New York. Reprinted in Radice (1975).

International Labour Office (1972), *Employment, Incomes and Equality; a Strategy for Increasing Productive Employment in Kenya,* Geneva.

Johnson H.G. (1971), 'The multinational corporation as an agency of economic development: some exploratory observations', in Ward B., d'Anjou L. and Runnals J.D. (eds) (1971), *The Widening Gap; Development in the 1970s,* Columbia University Press.

Jolly R., De Kadt E., Singer H. and Wilson F. (eds) (1973), *Third World Employment: Problems and Strategy,* Penguin.

Kindleberger C.P. (ed.) (1970), *The International Corporation,* MIT Press.

Lall S. (1973), 'Transfer-pricing by multinational manufacturing firms', *Oxford Bulletin of Economics and Statistics,* August.

Lall S. (1974), 'The international pharmaceutical industry and less-developed countries, with special reference to India', *Oxford Bulletin of Economics and Statistics,* August.

Lall S. (1975), 'Multinationals and development: a new look', National Westminster Bank, *Quarterly Review,* February.

Langdon S. (1975), 'Multinational corporations, taste transfer and underdevelopment: a case study from Kenya', *Review of African Political Economy,* No. 2, January–April.

Magdoff H. (1969), *The Age of Imperialism*, Monthly Review Press, New York.
Merhav M. (1969), *Technological Dependence, Monopoly and Growth*, Pergamon.
Muller M. (1974), *The Baby Killer*, War on Want, London.
Müller R. (1973), 'The multinational corporation and the underdevelopment of the Third World', in Wilber C.K. (ed.) (1973), *The Political Economy of Development and Underdevelopment*, Random House.
Nixson F.I. (1971), 'Nationalisation as an aid to development: the case of Uganda', *The Uganda Economic Journal*, Vol. 1, No. 1, December.
O'Connor J. (1970), 'The meaning of economic imperialism', in Rhodes (1970).
Parry T.G. (1973), 'The international firm and national economic policy', *Economic Journal*, December.
Patnaik P. (1972), 'Imperialism and the growth of Indian capitalism', in Owen R. and Sutcliffe R.B. (eds) (1972), *Studies in the Theory of Imperialism*, Longman.
Radice H. (ed.) (1975), *International Firms and Modern Imperialism*, Penguin.
Reuber G.L. (1973), *Private Foreign Investment in Development*, Clarendon Press.
Rhodes R.I. (ed.) (1970), *Imperialism and Underdevelopment: A Reader*, Monthly Review Press, New York.
Sampson A. (1973), *The Sovereign State: The Secret History of ITT*, Hodder and Stoughton.
Streeten P. (1971), 'Costs and benefits of multinational enterprises in less-developed countries', in Dunning (1971). Reprinted in Streeten (1972b).
Streeten P. (1972a), 'New approaches to direct private overseas investment in less developed countries', in Streeten (1972b).
Streeten P. (1972b), *The Frontiers of Development Studies*, Macmillan.
Streeten P. (1975), 'Policies towards multinationals', *World Development*, Vol. 3, No. 6, June.
Sunkel O. (1973a), 'The pattern of Latin American dependence', in Urquidi V. and Thorp R. (eds), *Latin America in the International Economy*, Macmillan.
Sunkel O. (1973b), 'Transnational capitalism and national disintegration in Latin America', *Social and Economic Studies*, Vol. 22, No. 1, March.
Sutcliffe R.B. (1971), *Industry and Underdevelopment*, Addison-Wesley.
Tugendhat C. (1973), *The Multinationals*, Penguin.
Turner L. (1973), *Multinational Companies and the Thirld World*, Allen Lane.
United Nations Department of Economic and Social Affairs (1974a), *Multinational Corporations in World Development*, Praeger.
United Nations Department of Economic and Social Affairs (1974b), *The Impact of Multinational Corporations on Development and on International Relations*, ST/ESA/6, New York.
Vaitsos C. (1972), 'Patents revisited: their function in developing countries', *Journal of Development Studies*, October.
Vaitsos C. (1973), 'Bargaining and the distribution of returns in the purchase of technology by developing countries', in Bernstein H. (ed.) (1973), *Underdevelopment and Development*, Penguin.
Vaitsos C. (1974), *Intercountry Income Distribution and Transnational Enterprises*, Clarendon Press.
Vaitsos C. (1975), 'The process of commercialization of technology in the Andean pact', in Radice (1975).
Vaitsos C. (1976), 'Power, knowledge and development policy: relations between transnational enterprises and developing countries', in Helleiner (1976).

Vernon R. (1973), *Sovereignty at Bay*, Penguin.

Warren B. (1973), 'Imperialism and capitalist industrialization', *New Left Review*, No. 81, September–October.

Wilber C.K. (1973), *The Political Economy of Development and Under-Development*, Random House.

Wionczek M. (1976), 'Notes on technology transfer through multinational enterprises in Latin America', *Development and Change*, April.

# 10
# The transnational corporation and the transfer of technology to LDCs

The TNC is the main vehicle for technology transfer to LDCs. Given the importance of this function, both to the TNC itself and to the recipient countries, it is not surprising that controversy should have arisen as to the way in which the task is being carried out. The technology supplied by the TNC comes in a number of different forms. For example, it forms part of the direct investment package, as we have already noted in Chapter 9. In other cases, it is transferred under licence or through management contracts to the LDC, through permission to use brand names, and so on. In yet other cases, TNC technology may be transferred as part of official aid programmes of both bilateral and multilateral aid agencies.

Controversy arises over the 'appropriateness' of the technology that is transferred (the term 'technology' is used in a broad sense to include the nature and specification of what is produced as well as the actual techniques of production). On the one hand, the supporters of the TNC argue that it is only through direct investment or licensing agreements that LDCs can acquire the technology and know-how essential for rapid development. On the other hand, critics of TNCs maintain that they transfer an 'inappropriate' technology, inconsistent with the factor endowments of LDCs.

The problem of which techniques of production LDCs should select has generated a huge volume of literature over the years. In so far as development theory has concerned itself with this issue, it has mainly concentrated on the question of labour- versus capital-intensive methods of production and has tended to ignore other aspects of the problem. In addition, it is only within the last few years that the problem of choice of technique has been examined within an institutional framework and questions raised as to how techniques are actually chosen in practice. This chapter is mainly concerned with these institutional and other factors, but for the sake of completeness, we commence with a brief discussion of the theory.

## 10.1 The Theory of the Choice of Techniques[1]

The theory of the choice of techniques for LDCs arose in connection with the initiation of development planning in those countries and had the aim of suggesting criteria for the investment choices which governments would find themselves making as planning proceeded. Drawing on orthodox static economic theory, the earliest contributions in this field proposed that the LDCs should select investment projects which utilised to the full their plentiful factors (for example, labour) and economised on scarce factors (for example, capital). Thus the 'factor intensity' criterion proposed that labour-intensive techniques should be adopted, on the assumption that labour was the abundant factor.

This can be readily illustrated using simple production theory. If labour is plentiful and capital scarce, the price of labour should be low relative to that of capital, and a small amount of capital would cost the same as a large quantity of labour, as indicated by the relative price line *AB* in figure 10.1. This line, which is determined by the ratio of the price of labour to the price of capital ($P_l/P_k$) is also known as an isocost or equal input cost line, since all combinations of capital and labour along it have the same total cost.

Given a production function for a particular product expressing output as a function of labour and capital, it is also possible to draw isoquants, such as *YY*, which indicate all combinations of the two inputs which can be used to produce any given level of output. The

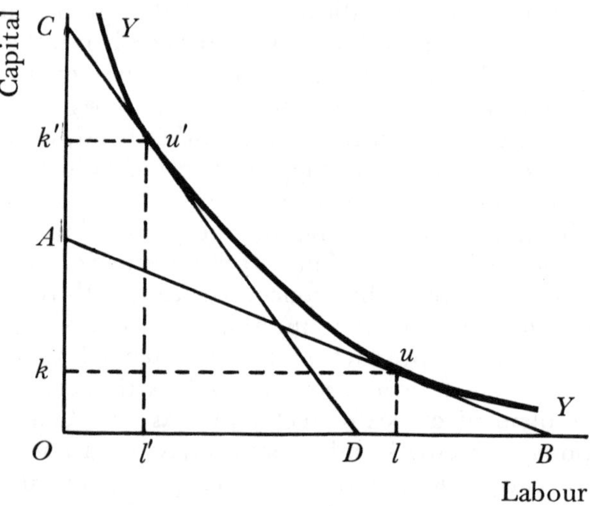


**Figure 10.1**

theory shows that the technique which maximises the profit from producing any desired level of output is given by the point of tangency between an isocost line and the isoquant for that level of output. For example, in figure 10.1, given the isocost line *AB*, the profit maximising technique for producing *Y* units of the product is shown by the point of tangency *u* which involves combining *Ol* units of labour with *Ok* units of capital.

According to the orthodox theory, unemployment will exist if wages relative to interest rates are too 'high', resulting from 'inappropriate' minimum wage legislation and over-powerful trades unions, and/or capital is too 'cheap', resulting from over-valued exchange rates and institutionally determined interest rates that are too low. Government intervention is usually blamed for creating a divergence between the market price and the social cost (the opportunity cost) of the factor of production, thus resulting in the 'distortions' that lead to the selection of 'inappropriate' capital-intensive techniques and less-than-full employment. In figure 10.1, the isocost line *CD*, representing a higher relative wage, results in the selection of a more capital-intensive production technique and a lower level of employment ($Ol'$).

An early contribution to the literature on choice of technique was the 'output–capital' criterion. This led largely to the same result as the 'factor intensity' criterion since the expectation was that if a given amount of capital was used with a greater amount of labour there would be an increase in output. Hence if the maximum output

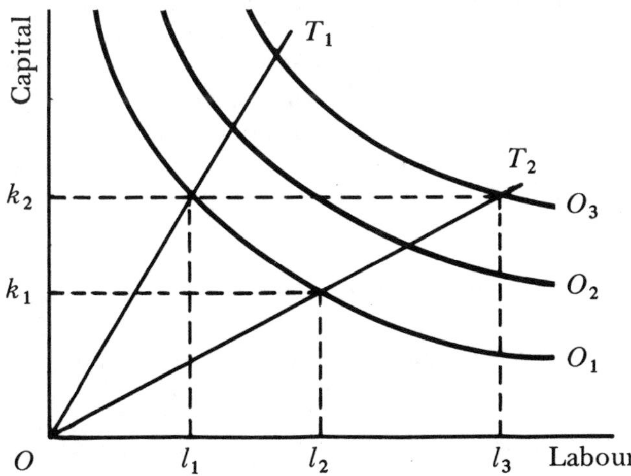


**Figure 10.2**

per unit of capital was the adopted criterion, then two urgent needs of LDCs, the creation of employment and the increase in output, would both be met. Figure 10.2 illustrates this proposition.

If the available capital $Ok_2$ is used on a project involving a capital-intensive technology $T_1$, output $O_1$ is produced and employment $Ol_1$ is created. But if the labour-intensive technology $T_2$ is used, the same output can be produced using less capital ($Ok_1$) and providing more employment ($Ol_2$). The surplus capital could then be used to expand output by additional investment using technique $T_2$. Hence output $O_3$ and employment $Ol_3$ are obtained, whilst still only using the original amount of capital.

A refinement of this criterion would accept that some projects have a long gestation period and do not produce their full output very quickly. Thus the criterion could be reformulated to have as its objective the maximisation of the discounted time stream of output per unit of capital invested, taking the time stream over the lifetime of the project. It will be noted that if a high discount rate was chosen, the criterion would result in the selection of quick yielding projects, and if a low discount rate was chosen, longer lived and later yielding projects would score highly and thus be selected.

The criterion, as originally formulated, was not explicitly concerned with the social returns or benefits resulting from any given pattern of resource allocation. It was thus generalised and extended by the formulation of the social marginal product criterion (SMP) (Kahn 1953; Chenery 1953). The SMP criterion stated that the total available capital should be so deployed that the marginal unit of capital in each industry or sector should yield the same contribution to the national product. In these circumstances, the total additional output would be maximised. Chenery's (1953) version of the SMP also proposed to include with the output contribution of each project an allowance for its contribution to the balance of payments and indeed to any other objective (for example, regional equality) that the planners felt important. Chenery also proposed to deduct from the valuation of the project the cost of inputs (labour, etc.).

Several points concerning this analysis need to be made at this stage. Firstly, there are products which it might be deemed necessary (or desirable) to produce and for which only one method (technique) exists. In this case, the issue of the choice of technique does not arise. If, however, the item is not absolutely crucial to the output pattern, then a different overall capital–labour ratio can be achieved by not producing it and producing something else instead (the question of the choice of product is discussed below). In the case of other products, a range of techniques may exist, but some techniques may be old-fashioned and inefficient in the sense that they use both more labour and more capital than the others to produce the same output.[2] These techniques would presumably not be chosen for new investment purposes, unless it was felt that for social or political reasons, an old-fashioned, inefficient, labour-intensive technique which generated immediate employment was desirable, even at the cost of there being less output than would otherwise be produced.

In general, the curve relating output to inputs of capital and labour (*YY* in figure 10.1) will not be smooth and regular as drawn in the diagram. Figure 10.1 is drawn on the assumption of an infinite number of available techniques, so that infinitely fine trade-offs between capital and labour are possible. In reality, there would only be a small number of dots on the curve and the shape of a line drawn from one to another would not have the smooth shape of the isoquant *YY*. In general, however, we would expect the line to confirm that, in producing a given level of output, a technique that required less capital than another would require more labour, that is, the line would in general slope downwards from left to right.

It should also be noted that the selection of projects according to these social optimisation criteria may run counter to the selection which would be implied by private profit maximisation. For example, techniques which are labour-intensive will only willingly be chosen by employers if labour is cheap and capital expensive. As already noted above, it is often argued that in practice labour costs in LDCs are above the level that would be dictated by the interaction of supply and demand and that capital is artifically cheap. In selecting projects, government planners could either ignore profitability altogether in favour of the social desirability implied by the above criteria, or they could adopt a system of 'accounting prices', under which the project is evaluated not by using actual wage levels and capital costs but the levels which would be a 'true' representation of the situation so far as supply and demand for the factors is concerned. Thus labour would be accorded an accounting wage which was either very low or even zero, implying that employment of additional labour has no social cost in a labour surplus economy. Also, if additional objectives are to be considered as in Chenery's SMP criterion (balance of payments contribution, etc.), then a weight has to be applied to them in line with the planners' view of their importance, alongside the main question of the output that they generate.

However, whilst these devices may assist the planners in deciding which projects are socially desirable, they do not ensure that public development agencies or private capitalists will willingly undertake them. Various policy instruments can thus be suggested to force or induce businessmen to undertake what would otherwise be socially desirable but unprofitable projects. For example, there might be a tax on capital use and a subsidy on labour costs to bring actual costs into line with the true social opportunity costs (the accounting prices). But such policies are likely to give rise to difficult political and administrative problems (for example, politically powerful interest groups may be adversely affected by higher prices for capital and will thus resist such measures) and the literature on choice of techniques has remained much more a matter of theory than of practical application. In any case, the concept of equilibrium prices leading to optimal resource allocation depends on the assumption that income distribution is acceptable, and it may well be an objective of government policy to alter income distribution (for a discussion of this issue, see Chapter 3).

A totally different criterion from those so far discussed was proposed by Galenson and Leibenstein (1955). Instead of the aim of maximising immediate output and employment, they suggested that the aim should be growth. The creation of less employment and output now may lead to more employment and output at a future date than would otherwise have been the case. To increase current employment may actually mean sacrificing the rate of growth of both employment and output, and thus the possibility exists of a conflict between maximising current output and employment and maximising the growth rates of output and employment.

In order to ensure growth, Galenson and Leibenstein suggested that the objective should be to maximise the reinvestable surplus generated per unit of output (their suggested criterion is called the 'marginal per capita reinvestment quotient'). Labour-intensive techniques might generate immediate output but very little surplus since the wage bill would be large. Capital-intensive techniques should therefore be chosen because, by minimising the wage bill, they will increase the reinvestable surplus. Put another way, capital-intensive techniques generate a high output per worker and therefore, for a given wage rate, a high surplus.

Galenson and Leibenstein present figures showing the large increases in output and employment which are possible after a few years if all the surplus is reinvested, although it must be remembered that reinvestment over time may be in a technology of a different capital-intensity from the initial investment and thus the rate of growth of employment may not be the same as the rate of growth of output. It is assumed that profits are the source of investment funds and that no savings take place out of wages. In other words, since all wages are consumed, from the point of view of growth they are a cost. It should be noted that it is the actual wage that is relevant, not an accounting wage. It must also be assumed that wage rates do not depend on the technique chosen and that the government is

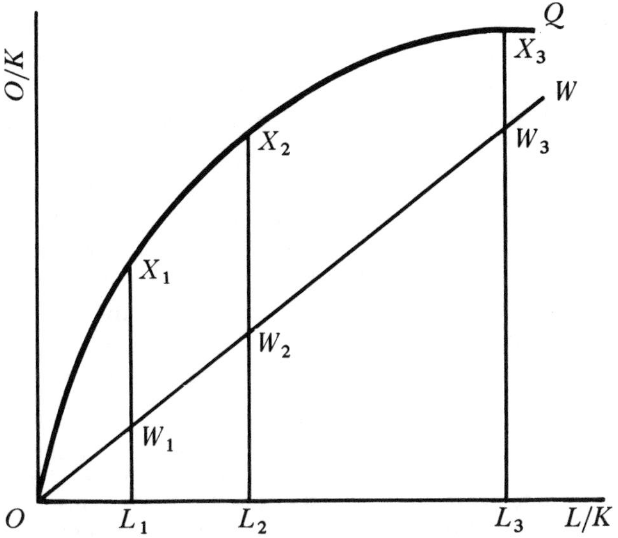


**Figure 10.3**

unable, or unwilling, to secure the savings ratio that it desires by the use of fiscal measures or forced savings. A final point to note is that this criterion accords much more closely with the entrepreneur's pursuit of profit maximisation than do the earlier criteria discussed.

Dobb (1956–57) and Sen (1957; 1968), both of whom also propounded the surplus maximisation criterion (in Dobb's case with an explicitly socialist regime in mind), nevertheless drew out the qualification that it is not necessarily the *most* capital-intensive technique which will maximise the surplus (as was implied by Galenson and Leibenstein). The surplus maximising technique depends on the slope of the function relating output to inputs and on the wage rate. A high wage rate will dictate a capital-intensive technique but a low wage rate, such as may be operative in some LDCs, will mean that a relatively labour-intensive technique will maximise the surplus.

This point is illustrated by Sen thus. In figure 10.3, the curve $OQ$ represents total output and the wage rate is shown as the slope of the line $OW$ (the height of $OW$ equals the wage bill). The surplus maximising technique is $X_2$ where the gap between output per unit of capital and the wage bill per unit of capital ($W_2L_2$) is at its maximum. The best technique from the point of view of maximising output per unit of capital and employment per unit of capital is $X_3$. The lower the wage rate (and hence the lower the slope of $OW$), the nearer does the surplus maximising technique move to becoming one and the same as the output maximising technique (in the limiting case, when the wage rate is zero, the technique maximising output and employment also maximises the reinvestable surplus). A higher wage rate will shift the point of surplus maximisation to the left (that is, towards $X_1$), thus increasing capital intensity.

Thus we see the conflict between the maximisation of current output and employment and the maximisation of the growth of output and employment. Labour-intensive techniques maximise output and employment in the short run but more capital-intensive techniques provide a greater surplus for reinvestment for more rapid growth (and hence higher employment) in the future. Stated thus, the choice becomes one between present and future welfare, and to quote Sutcliffe:

> . . . the problem of the choice of techniques cannot in theory be solved without a clear recognition that in the first place there will be a multiplicity of goals . . . some of which may conflict; nor can it be solved aside from the social rate of time preference in terms of which future alternative streams of output, consumption and employment must be ranked.
>
> (Sutcliffe 1971, pp. 168–69)

Basically this is a political question concerning the goals a society sets itself and the time horizon over which those goals are to be achieved. Can the government inflict a sacrifice on the population for the sake of benefits in the future when there is such an immediate need for output and employment now? Once again, these questions remain largely in the realms of theory. In practice, it may well be the case that one group has the sacrifice inflicted upon it and another group collects the eventual benefit.

However, methods have been suggested whereby the government's view of the desirable balance between present and future benefits can be taken into account in planners' calculations. Some allowance will probably have to be made for an increase in present consumption, given that it is likely to be more highly valued by society than future consumption. What is needed is an investment criterion which reflects both increases in current welfare and increases in future welfare brought about by the reinvestment of future surpluses arising from current investment. Eckstein (1957) advanced the marginal growth contribution (MGC) to meet this need. The MGC consists of (i) the present value of the project's direct contribution to consumption, and (ii) the present value of the consumption stream resulting from reinvestments associated with the project.

The choice of a discount rate is crucial here. A low discount rate which picks out projects whose benefits extend a long way into the future, that is have a high growth potential, implies that the government is prepared to sacrifice immediate benefits and is thinking

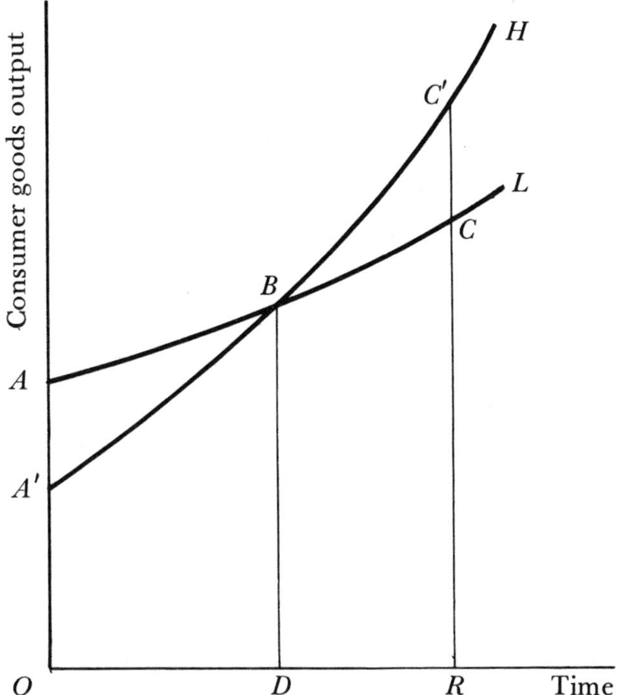


**Figure 10.4**

a long way ahead. A high discount rate would imply that the government felt the need to generate quick results. Sen (1968, Ch. 2) has also proposed a method of discriminating between quick-yielding and growth-promoting projects. He proposes the use of a time horizon, rather than a discount rate. The criterion can best be illustrated by reproducing Sen's diagram in figure 10.4.

The curves *H* and *L* show the flow of real consumption over time, each representing a different technique. Technique *H* gives a lower immediate output but a higher rate of growth than technique *L*. Until *D* is reached, technique *L* produces a higher level of output than *H* and the gap that *H* has to make up is *A′AB*. At point *R*, the area *CC′B* equals *A′AB*, that is the gap in output between technique *H* and *L* is made up and Sen calls the period *OR* the 'period of recovery' ('the period of time over which the levels of aggregate consumption are the same', Sen 1968, p. 23). In selecting a technique, a comparison is made between the 'period of recovery' and the time horizon selected by the planners. If the line *C′CR* is to the right of the time horizon, then the more labour-intensive, quick-yielding technique $L$ will be chosen. If the line $C'CR$ is to the left of the time horizon, the capital-intensive technique $H$ will be selected.

Before turning to a discussion of the factors that determine the choice of technique in practice, we must take a close, critical look at some assumptions made in the above analyses:

1. It is assumed that savings depend upon the distribution of income, that is only profits are saved while wages are consumed. But it may not be the case that wage earners do not save part of their income. They can be persuaded to save and/or the government can use direct or indirect taxes to generate a reinvestable surplus. Profit receivers may consume part of their profits, although this does not affect the selection of the surplus maximising technique if we make the, admittedly unrealistic, assumption that profit receivers consume a constant proportion of profits, irrespective of the technique used. Of far greater significance is the repatriation of profits by TNCs. In this case, capital-intensive techniques generate a reinvestable surplus which leaves the country, and this consideration seriously undermines the arguments for increasing the share of profits in national income. (Profits arising from the use of labour-intensive techniques may also be consumed or repatriated of course; all that is being argued here is that we cannot assume that the higher reinvestable surplus associated with capital-intensive techniques will be automatically reinvested.) Critics of Galenson and Leibenstein have argued that it is best to employ fiscal and monetary measures to produce an income distribution that yields sufficient savings, rather than use the choice of techniques for this purpose. Indeed, if there are no constraints (political or economic) on the amount of income that is saved, admittedly an unlikely state of affairs, it can be argued that:

   > . . . the total amount of income to be saved can be determined by the planner in any way he likes, and that he can then see that this decision is executed through the machinery at his disposal . . . If this is true then the link snaps between the choice of techniques and the proportion of income saved. Then technical choice may be made with the main purpose of maximising the amount of output, and the proportion of the output to be invested can be decided at a separate stage.
   >
   > (Sen 1969, reprinted in Meier 1976, p. 438)[3]

2. It is unrealistic to assume that the real wage rate is constant whatever technique of production is chosen. In particular, TNCs employing capital-intensive production methods are likely to pay higher wages, thus reducing the reinvestable surplus and promoting the rapid growth of consumption on the part of employed workers, rather than the rapid growth of employment (Arrighi 1970, p. 246).

3. The existence or non-existence of external economies is an

important consideration. We cannot say *a priori* whether labour- or capital-intensive techniques are more likely to generate external economies (for a discussion of this point, see Sutcliffe 1971, pp. 171–72) but they must not be neglected in either choice of project or technique.

4. The availability of other factors is important – raw materials, skilled labour (discussed in greater detail below) and foreign exchange (to import capital goods required by the investment programme if the domestic capital good sector – assuming that one exists – is unable to supply them) are all vital.[4]

5. A number of other points deserve a brief mention. As already indicated above, there may be economic and political reasons why it is considered desirable to select less efficient labour-intensive technologies which, although they involve the sacrifice of *both* current output *and* the growth of future output and employment, generate immediate employment opportunities. For example employment creation may be used as a redistributive mechanism, unemployment is regarded as demoralising, and political dangers arise from widespread unemployment (Stewart and Streeten 1969). The creation of labour-intensive urban-based activities may well, through the need to establish physical and social infrastructure facilities (houses, schools, communal services, etc.) involve a larger outlay of capital per unit of output than capital-intensive alternatives (Baran 1957, p. 286), although this will not be the case if they are located in rural areas. Labour-intensive methods may require greater amounts of working capital and this will adversely affect both their absolute and relative rates of surplus (Sen 1968, Appendix C).[5]

We discuss a number of other factors that influence the choice of technique in the section below dealing with the TNC and technological choice. To conclude this section we may quote Dobb:

> The choice between more or less capital-intensive forms of investment has nothing to do with existing factor proportions. . . It depends, not on the existing ratio of available labour to capital (treated as a stock), but on precisely the same considerations as those which determine the choice between a high and a low rate of investment . . . namely the importance to be attached to raising consumption in the immediate future compared with the potential increase of consumption in the more distant future which a particular rate of investment or form of investment will make possible. In other words, the same grounds which would justify a high rate of investment . . . would justify also a high degree of capital intensity in the choice of investment forms; and vice versa.
>
> (Dobb 1955, p. 149)

## 10.2 The Relationship between Theory and Practice

It is implicit in much of the theoretical discussion summarised above that governments are both willing and able to act according to some notion of maximising social welfare and that they can, in fact, determine the technologies chosen. Other contributors to the debate (for example, Dobb) explicitly analyse the issue within the framework of a planned (socialist) economy. But it must be emphasised that it is only in the latter case that there can be any guarantee that the surplus arising from the use of capital-intensive methods of production will actually be reinvested, thus resulting in a higher rate of growth of output and employment (although even centrally planned economies can waste the reinvestable surplus).

The importance of the distinction that must be made between free enterprise or 'mixed' economies and centrally planned economies is not always recognised. If the crucial assumptions upon which the arguments for capital-intensity are built are not realised in practice (as is the case in the majority of LDCs), the argument for capital-intensity must be treated with caution. The issues raised by Dobb above were of real importance in the Soviet Union during its industrialisation drive in the 1920s and in China at the present time. But in the majority of LDCs, other factors dominate and although these issues are still of crucial importance to contemporary LDCs, the practical context severely limits the significance of the theoretical propositions.

Before turning to a consideration of technological choice in these countries, it is instructive to note Chinese policy in the field of science and technology for purposes of comparison. While recognising that Chinese policy in this field cannot be divorced from the overall economic and political context of Chinese development, China's scientific and technological capabilities have been developed so as to improve the living standards of the mass of the population, increase agricultural and industrial production and modernise Chinese society (Rifkin 1975, p. 26). To this end, the Chinese have developed a dual sector economy using both modern and intermediate (traditional) technologies in the heavy industrial and agrarian sectors, developing small and medium sized industries throughout the economy and encouraging technological innovation in both the modern and traditional industries. Great stress is placed on self-reliance in technological progress (at both the local and national level) and the policy of 'walking on two legs' is aimed at avoiding the sectoral, geographical and social class divisions and inequalities characteristic of the majority of LDCs. The Chinese experience in this sphere, as in others, cannot be transplanted in other LDCs *in toto*. But a study of that experience illustrates the importance of clearly defined development objectives and the need for centralised control and direction, a state of affairs not found in the majority of LDCs. To what extent the comprehensive modernisation of agriculture, industry, national defence and science and technology by the end of the 20th century (enunciated as a long-term goal by the late Premier Chou En-Lai) will require an increasing dependence on imported technology is at present an open question.

## 10.3 Is There a Choice of Technique in Practice?

We saw above that the orthodox approach assumes that capital and labour are substitutable for one another and that a large number of alternative techniques is available. Indeed, the very existence of the controversy over the selection of appropriate techniques presupposes that alternative technologies both exist and are readily available for use by the LDC. In this section, we examine the plausibility of this assumption, although it should be emphasised at the outset that data on available technologies are scarce and ambiguous.

Sutcliffe (1971, Ch. 5, p. 147) has surveyed US data and tentatively concludes that in some sectors of manufacturing a choice of technology can be said to exist – tobacco, lumber and wood products, leather and leather goods, rubber products and chemicals. The sectors with the least choice are electrical and other machinery, fabricated metal products, coal and petroleum products, non-metallic mineral products, primary metals, furniture and fixtures and printing and publishing. Another group of industries (textiles, apparel, pulp and paper products and transport equipment) occupy an intermediate position. Impressionistic data from other countries suggest that foodstuffs, textile weaving, cotton spinning, clothing, woodworking, steel and wood furniture, leather goods, rubber products and bricks and roofing tiles are all technologically flexible – that is, there exists a range of alternative techniques of production embodying different factor intensities (Sutcliffe 1971, p. 148).[6]

At the risk of over-generalisation, it is probably the case that technological choice is greatest in established, basic industries (clothing, foodstuffs, household utensils, construction activities and allied industries) with low income elasticities of demand, catering for the needs of the great mass of the population. In the case of the majority of technologically advanced, sophisticated durable consumer goods (consumed by the middle/upper income groups in LDCs) and many intermediate goods industries (although there are obvious exceptions – for example, iron and steel), technological choice is likely to be limited or non-existent. There is some tentative evidence which suggests that capital goods industries (producers of machinery) are among the more labour-intensive industrial branches (Pack and Todaro 1969).

Continuous technological change is likely to reduce the range of profitable alternative techniques available. When a new technology uses less capital and labour than the existing technology (to produce the same level of output), the latter becomes unambiguously 'inferior' (see note 2) and in time will cease to exist, although variations in wages and profit margins will tend to prolong its existence. Stewart (1972, p. 106) argues that the 'stylised facts' of history suggest that new techniques use no more capital per unit of output and use less labour, thus making older techniques inferior. The most labour-intensive method available is likely to be the method used when the product was first introduced, although this method may have become inferior over time. The most labour-intensive efficient method is thus the earliest method which has not become inefficient (Stewart 1972, p. 107). In addition, the scale of output must be taken into account. The newer machine is likely to be designed for a larger scale output and thus earlier machines may remain efficient at lower output levels, but be inefficient at larger ones.

A final point to be noted is that goods are usually produced by a series of processes and each separate process may require different skills, machines, etc. requiring different relative amounts of capital and labour. (We have already seen in Chapter 8, section 8.6 that the TNC is increasingly identifying relatively labour-intensive processes within its overall operation and transferring these processes to LDCs). Scope for substitution between labour and capital usually exists in transport, packing, handling and storage operations and relative prices are likely to be a significant (but not the only) determinant of the technique chosen. We may find a situation where the main machine process is capital-intensive whereas overall, the production process may be relatively labour-intensive because of the greater labour intensity of auxiliary operations. The opposite is possible although perhaps less likely. The introduction of separate processes into the discussion thus further complicates the question of choice of technique, but widens the scope for factor substitution within manufacturing.

## 10.4 Choice of Product

The realisation that some commodities can be regarded as intrinsically more labour- (or capital-) intensive in production than others has led to attention being focused on the choice of product rather than the choice of technique. Once the choice of product is made, the question of technique will become irrelevant if there is only one way of producing a particular product. Variations in the product-mix can thus cause variations in the overall capital–labour ratio.

Dealing first with inter-industry choices (that is, the choice between different products), the demand for different products is determined, *inter alia,* by the distribution of income (and to refer back to our discussion of the TNC, by product differentiation, advertising, etc.). We have already seen in Chapter 3 that in the majority of LDCs income distribution is highly unequal and we have argued in Chapter 8 that ISI, *ceteris paribus,* increases that inequality.

ISI increasingly produces technologically advanced goods, catering for the upper income groups, for which only a limited technological choice may exist. In this case, choice of product, as influenced by the distribution of income, determines choice of technique – there may only be one 'best' way of producing a given product. If it is in fact the case that lower income groups tend to purchase goods generally produced by labour-intensive techniques and upper income groups consume goods utilising more capital-intensive techniques, it follows that a redistribution of income towards greater equality (increasing the incomes of the poor) will, through the change in the pattern of demand, lead to a change in the overall capital–labour ratio. Commodities produced by more labour-intensive methods of production (foodstuffs, clothing, basic household goods, construction materials, etc.) will be in greater demand and, other things being equal, employment opportunities in both manufacturing and agriculture will increase.

Unfortunately, the real world is not as straightforward as this. The rich consume both capital-intensive goods and labour-intensive services (domestic servants, gardeners, etc.) and high-quality, hand-made products, while the poor often spend their meagre incomes on heavily advertised 'non-essentials' (for example, Coca Cola) produced by relatively capital-intensive techniques (compared, for example, to similar goods produced by local producers). Morawetz (1974) surveys existing empirical studies of the effects of income redistribution on employment and finds that even a substantial redistribution of income would have only a marginal effect on growth and employment.

However, the empirical studies suffer from a number of defects (unreliable, highly aggregated data, unrealistic assumptions, and over-simplified models) which throw doubt on their conclusions. In any case, the generation of extensive employment opportunities is likely to be possible only within a radically altered socio-political structure. The potential arising from redistribution within existing structures (even if such were politically feasible) is extremely limited. (Refer to the discussion in Chapter 3.)

In some respects, the introduction of the problem of product choice limits still further the choice of techniques available to LDCs. If the latter wish to produce a particular good, there may be only one basic technology available (even though there may be scope for factor substitution in subsidiary operations). But once we take into account the intra-industry product mix, that is the possibility that 'more appropriate' goods are produced within each industry, the range of techniques available is increased. In the example given in the section on taste transfer in Chapter 9, the comparison was between locally based, labour-intensive laundry soaps and TNC subsidiary, capital-intensive detergents, both of which fulfilled the same functions but had different economic characteristics. The need for furniture can be satisfied by expensive products made of stainless steel, glass and leather or by simple wooden articles. Foodstuffs can be locally processed and unpackaged or be highly processed and over-packaged.

It is usual to classify products according to their physical attributes, but once products are so defined, and taking into account quality, the choice of technique is very limited – 'to produce identical physical products only one method may be possible' (Stewart 1972, p. 111). But products can be classified according to their characteristics, that is according to the needs that they fulfil. For example, a Rolls Royce is both a means of transport and a status symbol; thus a single product can fulfil a variety of needs. Similarly, a single need may be met by a variety of products – the need for shelter can be provided by a mud hut or a palace. Once needs are specified, alternative ways of meeting those needs can be examined and 'excess' or 'redundant' characteristics removed from existing products and/or new products more 'appropriate' to LDCs can be developed.[7]

Obviously, the specification of needs is not straightforward. It gives rise to technical problems (the question of what constitutes a need – see note 5 in Chapter 3) and raises key political questions concerning the degree of social control possible over consumption and hence, to a certain extent, over production. Although in principle there might exist a wide range of ways of meeting needs (once defined), in practice, within any given socio-economic environment, the choice may be severely limited.

The reasons why TNCs are unlikely to develop 'appropriate' products, at least on a large scale, are discussed in the following section.

For the present, Stewart's conclusion is worth quoting:

> The conventional distinction between choice of product and choice of technique (or choice of process) is ... an arbitrary one. If product requirements

> are sufficiently finely specified, only one process may be possible. If developing countries wish to change the factor proportions employed they must first examine the product characteristics required. The development of appropriate techniques is closely tied up with the development of appropriate products.
>
> (Stewart 1972, p. 114)

## 10.5 Choice of Technique in Practice: the role of the TNC

There is general agreement that the TNCs transfer capital-intensive technologies to LDCs, and that their efforts in the field of technological development are in the direction of even greater capital-intensity. The exception to this generalisation, already discussed in Chapter 8, section 8.6, is the transfer of unskilled labour-intensive processes to LDCs to produce components, etc. for export back to the parent company. However, such processes may still be capital-intensive relative to indigenous industries (for example, handicrafts). Technology is part of the direct investment 'package' and as we have already noted, many would argue that ownership and control of knowledge is the real key to TNC power.

We consider two main issues in this section: the reasons why 'inappropriate', capital-intensive technologies are transferred to LDCs, and the nature of the market within which this technology commercialisation takes place and the real costs to the purchasers (the LDCs) of technology.

It should not surprise us that TNCs transfer to LDCs technologies that they have developed and perfected themselves in the labour-scarce, capital-abundant economies of the developed capitalist world, and with which their managers and technicians are familiar. Indeed, TNC management may not be able to operate other technologies. It may be the case, for example, that alternative technologies simply do not exist. The limited domestic markets characteristic of LDCs and their varying stages of development and heterogeneous nature do not offer sufficient incentives for TNCs to develop separate technologies for every market within which they operate.

In addition, research and development (R and D) expenditures are overwhelmingly concentrated in the developed home economies (the United Nations (1974, Ch. 3) estimated that in the 1960s only 6% of US R and D expenditure was spent outside the USA) and the new products and processes that result are likely to be increasingly inappropriate.

Given TNC dominance of technological development, the little scientific and technological research that does take place within LDCs is more likely to be directed towards the needs and interests of TNCs (or the international scientific community) than towards the needs of the indigenous productive sectors. In Cooper's words:

> ... the scientific institutions are alienated from production activities or 'marginalised' because there is no demand for locally developed technologies from the productive sectors. Consequently science in underdeveloped countries is largely a *consumption* item, whereas in industrialised countries it is an investment item.
>
> (Cooper 1972, p. 5)

From the viewpoint of the TNC, it is global factor availability rather than the factor availability in any one LDC market that determines choice of technique. The TNC has access to capital from various parts of its organisation and from international capital markets and it is thus rational for it to use capital-intensive techniques even in labour-abundant LDCs. This 'labour abundance' is itself deceptive in so far as wages may be 'high' in relation to the productivity of the labour force and this problem is further aggravated by the 'distorted' factor prices in the LDCs (referred to earlier) which mean that there is even less incentive for the development of labour-intensive technologies. Such distortions may even lead to the substitution of capital for labour in certain technologically flexible processes (handling, packing, transport within the factory, etc.) although in the case of packaging an additional consideration is that a higher quality may be obtained through capital-intensive techniques, an important consideration if the product is exported. In these circumstances, the TNC cannot reasonably be accused of introducing an 'inappropriate' technology as it is responding rationally to local conditions.

Once we drop the assumption of homogeneity of factors of production, the qualitative aspects of the labour force in LDCs may be an important influence on choice of technique. Streeten (in Dunning 1971, p. 252) has argued that the interests of the TNC lie '... in minimising industrial relations with a foreign labour force, which may be unskilled, underfed, unhealthy, unreliable, undisciplined and perhaps hostile, and dealings with which may give rise to political difficulties'.

But the composition of the labour force available is also significant. Arrighi (1970) suggests that capital-intensive techniques are characterised by a pattern of employment in which semi-skilled labour and high-level manpower predominate, whereas labour-intensive techniques make greater use of skilled and unskilled labour. Referring specifically to tropical Africa, Arrighi argues that it is easier for the TNC to remedy the shortage of semi-skilled labour and high-level manpower (available from the parent company) than it is to remedy the shortage of skilled labour, which takes longer to train than unskilled labour and is less mobile internationally than high-level manpower. Skilled labour is thus seen as the real constraint and dictates the choice of capital-intensive techniques.

The ILO Report on Kenya (1972, Technical Paper 16) has taken the opposite view to Arrighi, maintaining that in those manufacturing sectors where both foreign and local capital compete, the foreign firm is more likely to use a more labour-intensive technology:

> '... although they are short of supervisors, they can recruit them more easily than locally owned firms (and possibly use their supervisors more productively, through better management)' (p. 451).

But the Report goes on to state that:

> '... foreign firms account for the whole of production in some inherently capital-intensive sectors. There are also signs that capital-intensive technical change is affecting the manufacturing sector, and particularly that some large foreign enterprises with brand name advantages have been able to capture and create enough of a market to make use of very capital-intensive, large-scale methods. We should expect a trend in this direction.'
>
> (International Labour Office 1972, p. 452)

In other words, it is usually the case that the presence of TNCs can be expected to lead to an overall increase in the capital–labour ratio in the manufacturing sector.

Helleiner (1975) suggests a number of other reasons why TNCs will select capital-intensive technologies: labour-intensive technologies, where they exist, are associated with small scales of production; the TNC typically produces on a large scale and it is that scale which determines the efficient factor intensity (that is, scale economies dominate factor price considerations); material inputs may be expensive and difficult to acquire in LDCs and the possibilities for capital–material substitution (mechanised handling which reduces breakages, storage facilities which reduce spoilage, etc.) are greater than for labour–material substitution; governments in the LDCs themselves may insist on the latest, more capital-intensive techniques being used and the TNCs, in the interests of 'good citizenship', bow to these pressures (Helleiner 1975, p. 169).

The available empirical evidence on whether or not TNCs use more capital-intensive techniques than local firms in producing similar products is somewhat ambiguous. Barnet and Müller (1974, Ch. 7) quote evidence from a number of surveys which indicates the relatively greater capital-intensity of TNCs.[8] Agarwal (1976) concluded that foreign firms are more capital-intensive than domestic firms in the large-scale manufacturing sector in India (capital was relatively cheaper for the TNC and labour relatively cheaper for the domestic firm).

Helleiner, on the other hand, argues that:

> In particular industrial sectors, the multinational firm has often proven more responsive and adaptable in its factor and input use, especially in the ancillary activities associated with the basic production process, than local firms; and so it perhaps should with its wide range of experience upon which to draw.
>
> (Helleiner 1975, p. 169)

Overall, the TNC will transfer a capital-intensive technology, but given its technical knowledge, experience and flexibility we should expect to observe some variations in its behaviour with respect to technology transfer and adaptation between both industries and countries. In some cases profit maximisation (or risk minimisation) will best be achieved through greater capital-intensity; in other cases, relative factor prices and technological flexibility will lead to greater labour-intensity, especially in ancillary operations. It would be surprising if the TNC did not demonstrate its ability to adapt to different and specific situations, although this point must not be overemphasised.

Having said this, the major reason for the TNC transferring a capital-intensive technology is that it is precisely through its ownership or control of this technology or knowledge that the TNC can earn monopoly profits in the host country. The marginal cost of using an already developed technology is zero for the owner of that technology (there may be costs associated with the adaptation of that technology, but these are not likely to be substantial), whereas from the buyers' point of view, the costs of independently developing that technology may be immense. Given the overall objectives of the TNC, it is perfectly rational for it to exploit its advantages in this area.

It is the TNC's monopolisation of production and consumption technology (that is, the types of products, their characteristics and the way they are produced in LDCs) that has led Vaitsos (1973, pp. 317–18) to describe the process of technology commercialisation as a bargaining process, in which the buyer (the LDC) is in a position of structural weakness in the formulation of its demand for information. The item that the buyer needs to purchase (technology) is at the same time the information that is needed in order to make a rational decision to buy it.[9]

Because of the characteristics of technology[10] the patent system is in part used to create, artificially, a scarcity which results in a price system – a price is put on inventions to make them scarce, not because they are, of necessity, scarce.[11] Vaitsos (1973, p. 322) concludes that the market price mechanism cannot defend the interests of the LDCs and that through the mechanisms already discussed (royalties, management fees, etc.) LDCs are paying too much for the technology that is actually transferred to them by TNCs.

## 10.6 Conclusions

What conclusions can be drawn from the discussion of the theoretical and real-world aspects of the choice of technique debate? Enough has been said to indicate that a straightforward answer to the question as to which techniques a LDC *should* choose cannot be expected. It is too simplistic to state merely that labour-abundant LDCs should of necessity choose labour-intensive techniques (a view uncritically advocated by too many proponents of 'intermediate technology'). The question raises fundamental political issues as to the development path to be pursued by the LDC, the nature of its goals and their realisation over time (present versus future consumption and employment, for example), and to ignore these aspects and treat the question as one of straightforward technical choice is to misunderstand the development process. Similarly, the role of the TNC and other international institutions (for example, bilateral and multilateral aid agencies) in the transfer of technology cannot be ignored. The assumption that a choice in fact exists may be incorrect in many cases, especially once we take into account the question of choice of product.

But this does not mean that the 'appropriate' techniques are not urgently needed in LDCs. Morawetz (1974, pp. 517–18) has defined appropriate technology as 'the set of techniques which makes optimum use of available resources in a given environment' and 'should be regarded as one which is suitable for particular workers producing particular products'. 'Appropriate' technologies would in general make greater use of unskilled labour, but in some cases capital-intensive methods would be more appropriate if skilled labour, rather than capital, was the main constraint.[12] In a broader sense, technologies must be 'appropriate' with respect to the wider economic and political objectives of the society in question (the value that society places on future, as compared to present, employment and consumption, for example) and also 'appropriate' with respect to scale of output, simplicity of operation, maintenance and repair and use of local inputs. The search for 'appropriate' technologies must avoid the shortfalls of the static investment criteria discussed above.

There are three possibilities of finding and implementing such technologies – they can be transferred from other countries, generated locally, or inappropriate technologies from elsewhere can be adapted to suit local needs. Morawetz sees the latter course of action as holding out the greatest hope for the future. But both it and the second alternative are conditional on the establishment of domestic capital goods industries (a point stressed by, among others, Pack and Todaro 1969, Stewart 1976 and Sutcliffe 1971), and the prior existence of a fair degree of technological competence in the adapting country.

Helleiner takes an optimistic view of the role of the TNC and argues that:

> Given sufficient incentives, there are good reasons for believing that multinational firms will become significant suppliers of more appropriate production technologies and products.
>
> (Helleiner 1975, p. 179)

Turner (1973, Ch. 6) gives some examples of TNCs moving in this direction (the development of tractors suited to conditions in LDCs) and given that it is made sufficiently profitable for the TNC to behave thus, some progress will undoubtedly be made. But it is unlikely to be on a large scale and the ultimate costs to the LDC may still be unacceptably high – what is 'sufficiently profitable' for the TNC may be ruinously expensive for the LDC.

An alternative policy is for a LDC to be more selective and purchase the components of the direct investment 'package' separately. Technology can be obtained in ways other than through direct investment by the TNC, for example, through licensing, which was used extensively by Japan, through 'turnkey' projects (the plant is built by a foreign company and then handed over to the LDC), through management contracts and fade-out or divestment agreements (the TNC agrees to run the project for a specified number of years and then sell to the government or private citizens of the LDC). Complete technological independence is neither possible (nor necessarily desirable) for the majority of LDCs. The complaint that the 'wrong' type of technologies are transferred by TNCs should not be read as a blanket condemnation of all modern imported technology. Once the LDC is in a position to determine for itself its development priorities, and better able to judge the value of what it is buying, the judicious use of imported technologies (in manufacturing, health, education, communications, etc.) will be of undoubted value to the development effort, and the importance of the TNC in developing and supplying these technologies must not be underestimated.

## Notes

1 We are using the term 'choice of technique' narrowly to mean 'technique of production' within the manufacturing sector. But the wider implications of technological choice should not be forgotten. LDCs must choose between different 'technologies' in virtually all fields – most obviously

agriculture (see Chapter 6), construction, road building, etc., but also in such fields as health and education (highly trained doctors versus medical auxiliaries; expensive urban-based schools and colleges versus mass rural education, and so on).

2 Stewart (1972, p. 99) defines efficient techniques as 'those which are not inferior to any other technique among those available', inferiority in this sense meaning that it takes more of one factor, and not less of the other factor, to produce the same output as the efficient technique.

3 Thirlwall (1971, p. 174) makes the point that if saving depends upon the total level of income as well as upon its distribution 'a compromise must be reached between maximising output per head of the employed population using capital-intensive techniques and maximising output per head of the total population using less capital-intensive techniques'.

4 In principle, these objectives can be overcome by the use of social cost-benefit analysis which attempts to assess the social profitability of a project. This involves (i) a statement of objectives (the 'objective function'); (ii) the estimation of social measures of the unit values of project inputs and outputs (shadow prices); (iii) the selection of a decision criterion to reduce the stream of social cost and benefit flows to an index, which can be used to accept, reject or rank the project relative to others. For a brief discussion see Dasgupta (1974, Ch. 9).

5 Sen (1968, Appendix C), in his classic discussion of the choice of technique in the cotton weaving industry in India, illustrates the complexity of the issues involved and concludes that 'The much discussed "technical superiority" of one technique over another seems to hold little water in this case, as the choice seems to be a genuine socio-economic one. It will depend ultimately on social factors (like the wage rate or the propensity to consume), political possibilities (like those of taxation), organisational considerations (like those influencing the marketing lag) and ethical factors (like the choice involving time)' (p. 105).

6 The editor of a recently published survey of technological choice in a number of different industries (can-making, textiles, sugar processing, cement blocks, engineering, metal working, copper and aluminium) in various LDCs concluded that 'Whether one considers the production processes themselves, e.g. in metal-working and cotton textiles, or ancillary operations such as materials handling, transport and packaging, the empirical evidence supports the existence of possibilities of substitution between capital, labour and materials' (Bhalla 1975, p. 309). Helleiner (1975) rejects the view that the non-existence of alternative technologies and technological fixities are generally acceptable explanations of the choice of capital-intensive techniques. But even though empirical work suggests that the elasticity of factor substitution is not zero (that is, labour is substitutable for capital), the theoretical and empirical problems of estimation are such that too much reliance cannot be placed on the results obtained (Morawetz 1974, pp. 515–16).

7 It is not necessarily the case that 'appropriate' products will be produced by 'appropriate' (i.e. labour-intensive) production methods, although it is generally presumed that that would be the case. Helleiner (1975, p. 175) points out that 'Technological "appropriateness" can have other dimensions than labour intensity' (e.g. foreign exchange earnings or saving objectives, inter-industry linkages).

8 One study of 1494 subsidiaries of US TNCs found no significant difference in technologies used in developed economies or LDCs in 5 out of 11 industries investigated. In the other 6 industries, there was no systematic bias for more or less labour-using technology in LDCs. (W.H. Courtney and D.M. Leipziger, 'MNCs in LDCs: the choice of technology', preliminary draft, Bureau of Economic and Business Affairs, 12 October 1973, quoted in Barnet and Müller 1974.)

9 Clark (1975) expresses the position thus: '. . . technology, or knowledge, is *inappropriable* in the sense that the more you know about what you are buying the less will be your demand price for it.'

10 Vaitsos (1973) argues that it is non-exhaustible – its use by one person does not reduce its present or future availability: it cannot be 'owned' in the traditional sense of that term; it is heterogeneous, consisting of a number of different elements (engineering blueprints, marketing knowledge, etc.) and it is not always certain what is meant exactly by technology importation.

11 Lack of space does not permit a discussion of the impact of the patent system on LDCs. It is increasingly accepted that patents have a negative effect, hindering the flow of technology to LDCs and preserving the monopoly privileges of TNCs. See Vaitsos (1972 and 1974).

12 Sutcliffe (1971, p. 186) maintains that arguments for capital-intensity are really arguments for *modern* techniques (which possess the characteristics that capital-intensive techniques are believed to have) – 'techniques which are first of all mechanised and possess the advantages of the influence of machine-paced operations on the productivity of labour, techniques giving a high and consistent quality of output and using easily available spare parts'.

## Bibliography

Agarwal J.P. (1976), 'Factor proportions in foreign and domestic firms in Indian manufacturing', *Economic Journal*, September.

Agarwala A.N. and Singh S.P. (eds) (1969), *Accelerating Investment in Developing Countries*, Oxford University Press.

Arrighi G. (1970), 'International corporations, labor aristocracies, and economic development in tropical Africa', in Rhodes R. (ed.), *Imperialism and Underdevelopment: A Reader*, Monthly Review Press, New York.

Baran P. (1957), *The Political Economy of Growth*, Monthly Review Press, New York.

Baranson J. (1969), *Industrial Technologies for Developing Countries*, Praeger.

Barnet R.J. and Müller R.E. (1974), *Global Reach: The Power of the Multinational Corporations*, Simon and Schuster.

Bhalla A.S. (1964), 'Investment allocation and technological choice: a case of cotton spinning techniques', *Economic Journal*, September.

Bhalla A.S. (ed.) (1975), *Technology and Employment in Industry*, International Labour Office, Geneva.

Chenery H.B. (1953), 'The application of investment criteria', *Quarterly Journal of Economics*, February.

Chenery H.B. (1961), 'Comparative advantage and development policy', *American Economic Review*, March.

Clark N. (1975), 'The multi-national corporation: the transfer of technology and dependence', *Development and Change*, January.

Cooper C. (1972), 'Science, technology and production in the underdeveloped countries: an introduction', *Journal of Development Studies*, October. Reprinted in Cooper C. (ed.) (1972), *Science, Technology and Development*, Frank Cass.

Dasgupta A.K. (1974), *Economic Theory and the Developing Countries*, Macmillan.

Dobb M. (1955), *On Economic Theory and Socialism: Collected Papers*, Routledge and Kegan Paul.

Dobb M. (1956–57), 'Second thoughts on capital intensity of investment', *Review of Economic Studies*. Reprinted in Agarwala and Singh (1969).

Dosser D. (1962), 'General investment criteria for less-developed countries: a post-mortem', *Scottish Journal of Political Economy*, June.

Dunning J.H. (ed.) (1971), *The Multinational Enterprise*, Allen and Unwin.

Eckstein O. (1957), 'Investment criteria for economic development and the theory of inter-temporal welfare economics', *Quarterly Journal of Economics*, February.

Galenson W. and Leibenstein H. (1955), 'Investment criteria, productivity and economic development', *Quarterly Journal of Economics*, August.

Helleiner G.K. (1975), 'The role of multinational corporations in the less developed countries' trade in technology', *World Development*, Vol. 3, No. 4, April.

International Labour Office (1972), *Employment, Incomes and Equality: A Strategy for Increasing Productive Employment in Kenya*, Geneva.

Kahn A.E. (1953), 'The application of investment criteria', *Quarterly Journal of Economics*, February.

Meier G.M. (ed.) (1976), *Leading Issues in Economic Development* (3rd edn), Oxford University Press.

Morawetz D. (1974), 'Employment implications of industrialisation in developing countries: a survey', *Economic Journal*, September.

Pack H. and Todaro M. (1969), 'Technological transfer, labour absorption and economic development', *Oxford Economic Papers*, November.

Rifkin S.B. (1975), 'The Chinese model for science and technology: its relevance for other developing countries', *Development and Change*, January.

Sen A.K. (1957), 'Some notes on the choice of capital intensity in development planning', *Quarterly Journal of Economics*, November. Reprinted in Agarwala and Singh (1969).

Sen A.K. (1968), *Choice of Techniques* (3rd edn), Blackwell.

Sen A.K. (1969), 'Choice of technology: a critical survey of a class of debates' in UNIDO, *Planning for Advanced Skills and Technologies*, New York. Reprinted in Meier (1976).

Stewart F. (1972), 'Choice of technique in developing countries', *Journal of Development Studies*, October.

Stewart F. (1976), 'Capital goods in developing countries', in Cairncross A. and Puri M. (eds) (1976), *Employment, Income Distribution and Development Strategy*, Macmillan.

Stewart F. and Streeten P. (1969), 'Conflicts between output and employment objectives in developing countries,' *Oxford Economic Papers*, July. Reprinted in Streeten (1972).

Streeten P. (1971), 'Costs and benefits of multinational enterprises in less developed countries', in Dunning (1971). Reprinted in Streeten (1972).

Streeten P. (1972), *The Frontiers of Development Studies*, Macmillan.

Sutcliffe R.B. (1971). *Industry and Underdevelopment*, Addison-Wesley.

Thirlwall A.P. (1971), *Growth and Development*, Macmillan.

Turner L. (1973), *Multinational Companies and the Third World*, Allen Lane.

United Nations Department of Economic and Social Affairs (1974), *Multinational Corporations in World Development*, Praeger.

Vaitsos C. (1972), 'Patents revisited: their function in developing countries', *Journal of Development Studies*, October.

Vaitsos C. (1973), 'Bargaining and the distribution of returns in the purchase of technology by developing countries', in Bernstein H. (ed.) (1973), *Underdevelopment and Development* , Penguin.

Vaitsos C. (1974), *Intercountry Income Distribution and Transnational Enterprises*, Clarendon Press.

Vaitsos C. (1975), 'The process of commercialisation of technology in the Andean Pact' in Radice (ed.) (1975), *International Firms and Modern Imperialism*, Penguin.

Wionczek M. (1976), 'Notes on technology transfer through multinational enterprises in Latin America', *Development and Change*, April.

# 11
# Two aspects of structuralism: inflation and migration in LDCs

This chapter discusses two of the most pressing problems faced by contemporary LDCs – continuously rising price levels and the large-scale movement of labour from the rural areas to the rapidly expanding urban areas.

The inclusion of these two separate, yet related problems in one chapter is not meant to imply that there is a direct causal relationship between them. Obviously they are indirectly related to one another in so far as they both have their roots in the structure of the LDC economy and can both be broadly regarded as manifestations of the development strategies being pursued by these countries, although inflation has, in the 1970s, become a world-wide phenomenon affecting both the developed capitalist economies and the LDCs. It can no longer therefore be viewed as a purely domestic phenomenon as far as the latter are concerned.

We have characterised the LDC economy as a distorted, disintegrated structure, subject to a number of economic, technological, sociological and political constraints, in which, in the absence of basic structural reforms, growth and development cannot be expected to proceed smoothly. Development strategies have in general been based on consumer goods import substituting industrialisation, involving a heavy dependence on foreign capital and technology (usually capital-intensive). They have also been characterised by the neglect of the rural sector in general and the supply of foodstuffs for the domestic market in particular, and an unequal distribution of income, often inherited from the colonial period but made more unequal by the economic policies pursued in the post-independence era.

Inadequate supplies of foodstuffs for the domestic market have forced prices up and governments have often responded by imposing price controls on foodstuffs, thus weakening any incentive that might exist to expand supplies. Urban workers, especially government employees, have often been able to force increases in their money wages to counteract such price rises, thus maintaining or worsening the rural–urban income differential. Low incomes in the rural areas and the lack of job opportunities have led to an increased movement of labour into the over-expanded urban areas.

To give some idea of the rate of growth of urban areas in LDCs, it is estimated that by 1985 147 cities in LDCs will have over one million inhabitants (as compared to 101 cities at the present time). Ten of these cities will have populations of over 10 million inhabitants, with Mexico City, for example, having an estimated population of approximately 18 million (Ward 1976, Prologue).

Unfortunately, there has been a marked tendency for economists interested in these questions to ignore the economic and political structure within which inflation and rural–urban migration have manifested themselves, and to reduce these complex issues to 'straightforward' technical problems. Inflation is seen in terms of an excess supply of money, rural–urban migration is seen as the attempt by a rational individual to maximise expected income, taking into account the probability of getting a job in the formal urban sector. This chapter is an attempt to redress the balance and discuss these problems within a broader economic framework. A conclusion that clearly emerges from the discussion is that economics must be supplemented by the other social sciences before we can begin to obtain a clearer, more complete understanding of these issues. The political scientist and the economist must cooperate in the study of inflation, and the work of sociologists and social anthropologists must complement that of the economist in the study of rural–urban migration. Although they were not chosen for this purpose, the two issues discussed in this chapter clearly illustrate the need for an interdisciplinary approach to development problems.

## (A) INFLATION IN LDCs[1]

### 11.1 Introduction

LDCs in the 1970s are becoming subject to increasingly severe inflationary pressures. Such pressures are both internal to LDC economies (resulting largely from the development policies being pursued) and external to them (inflationary pressures within the world economy, largely manifesting themselves through rapidly rising import prices). In the 1950s and 1960s, it could have been argued that inflation was not a general phenomenon and, with the exception of a few countries in Latin America (for example Brazil, Argentina and Chile), price levels showed a high degree of stability. Indeed, it was often argued that LDCs should be prepared to tolerate

**Table 11.1** *Percentage increases in developed and less developed countries 1965–1970.*(a)

| | *Annual average 1965–70*(b) | *Changes from preceding year* | | | | |
|---|---|---|---|---|---|---|
| | | *1971* | *1972* | *1973* | *1974* | *1975* |
| Non-oil exporting LDCs | 11 | 10 | 14 | 22 | 32 | 30(c) |
| in Africa | 5 | 4 | 5 | 9 | 19 | 19 |
| in Asia | 8 | 5 | 8 | 17 | 30 | 10 |
| in Middle East | 4 | 6 | 6 | 12 | 20 | 19 |
| in Western Hemisphere | 17 | 16 | 22 | 31 | 38 | 53(c) |
| Major oil exporting countries | 10 | 6 | 5 | 11 | 17 | 18 |
| Industrial countries (d) | 4.2 | 5.4 | 4.8 | 7.3 | 11.8 | 10.8 |
| Other industrial countries (e) | 4.5 | 7.2 | 7.3 | 7.7 | 9.8 | 10.7 |
| More developed primary producing economies (f) | 5.4 | 9.8 | 8.1 | 11.9 | 18.0 | 17.5 |

*Source:* IMF, *Annual Report 1976*, Washington DC., calculated from IMF Data Fund and Fund Staff estimates.

**Notes:**

(a) For LDCs, percentage change in consumer prices, calculated from weighted geometric means of country indices expressed in terms of local currency. Weights are proportional to GDP (in US $) in 1970. For developed economies, percentage change in GDP deflators.
(b) Compound annual rates of change.
(c) Excluding Argentina and Chile, the figures for non-oil LDCs in the last three colums are 15%, 26% and 18% respectively. With a similar exclusion, the Western Hemisphere figures in the last three colums would be 14%, 25% and 24% respectively.
(d) Canada, USA, Japan, France, Germany, Federal Republic, UK.
(e) Smaller European economies.
(f) Australia, New Zealand, South Africa, Spain, Finland, Greece, Iceland, Ireland, Malta, Portugal, Turkey and Yugoslavia.

or encourage higher rates of inflation in order to promote capital accumulation and growth.[2]

The data given in table 11.1 show that events have tended to overtake the views of academic economists and that inflation is now an endemic problem. The countries of Central and South America still experience the highest rates of price increase but there has been a significant increase in Africa and the Middle East. In general, the average rate of inflation in LDCs throughout the period covered

(1965–1975) has been significantly higher than the average rate for the major industrialised and other developed economies.

The data on price increases in LDCs should be treated with caution. Data are limited, and those that are available often have severe limitations. The majority of LDCs do not compile GNP deflators so that cost of living indices and/or indices of wholesale prices are frequently the only price series available. Both of these measures have serious defects. The wholesale price index is frequently heavily weighted with the price of imports and exports, which tend to be domestic equivalents of international prices rather than measures of domestic prices, while the cost of living index is usually based upon a limited sample of goods and services purchased in the major urban areas and is thus unrepresentative of the consumption patterns of the majority of the population located in smaller urban centres and rural areas. In practice, cost of living indices are usually employed as they are often the only measure available or are the least unsatisfactory of the measures of domestic price increases available. Nevertheless, these provisos do not in any way lessen the significance of inflation in LDCs.

## 11.2 Inflation and Growth

As we have already noted above, it has often been argued that inflation could be used as a growth promotion mechanism. Specifically it was argued that inflation, through the redistribution of income towards profits (largely because of the time lag between price rises and rises in wages and other costs) would increase savings, as it was assumed that profit receivers had a higher marginal propensity to save than wage earners. Inflation would draw more resources into the growth process through the stimulating effect that it was likely to have on the level of economic activity and, indirectly, would create the conditions for greater flexibility as it would permit necessary relative price changes in conditions of downward price rigidity (Thorp 1971, p. 196). Finally, if it was argued that government investment was necessary for the elimination of bottlenecks constraining growth, and if the only way to carry out that investment was by government deficit spending, the creation of conditions conducive to growth would also lead to inflation. Linked to this idea was the concept of self-liquidating inflation. Inflations which created capital were self-destructive in so far as the new capital produced a stream of consumer goods which eventually dampened or eliminated the inflationary pressures, although much depended on how quickly the new capital became productive and on how productive it was

(Lewis 1966, pp. 130–38). Inflation in this sense was a form of taxation, transferring resources to the government.[3]

Empirical evidence concerning the relationship between inflation and growth is inconclusive, although there is some suggestion that high rates of inflation (10% or above per annum) have a detrimental impact on rates of growth. In the contemporary world, it would be unusual to find LDC governments explicitly using inflation as a growth promoting mechanism (although it may be used for other purposes) and even though, as we discuss below, many writers in the structuralist tradition prefer inflation to stagnation, once the structural constraints regarding growth have been eliminated or at least substantially alleviated, financial stability provides the most suitable environment in which to promote growth and development.

In this context, it is of interest to note that one poor country that has not suffered from inflation in the past 25 years is China. The Chinese themselves (see for example, Peng Kuang-hsi 1976) place emphasis on the need for a balanced budget within the socialist planned economy (that is, a restructured economy where the crucial bottlenecks have been eliminated) and Donnithorne (1974) too stresses the maintenance of strict budgetary discipline.[4] It is also of relevance to note that China has had a low dependence on foreign trade (at least until recently) and is thus immune to inflationary pressures within the world economy.

## 11.3 The Relevance of 'Orthodox' Analysis of Inflation

The work of many economists on the causes of inflation in LDCs has started from an explicit rejection of concepts and theories formulated within the developed, industrialised economies of the West. The Latin American 'structuralist' school of thought (discussed in the following section) which emerged in the 1950s was concerned with the inapplicability of the concepts of 'cost-push' and 'demand-pull' and their critique, together with the work of others, is still of relevance.

Before discussing these ideas, however, we must briefly summarise some of the main aspects of contemporary inflation theory. Contemporary 'orthodox' analysis is based on the relationship between aggregate demand and supply. Inflation originates in conditions of excess demand, arising either from increases in the money supply not matched by increases in output or from increases in costs, especially increases in wages (and controversy exists as to which of these factors is of greatest importance). The Phillips curve, which incorporates both demand-pull and cost-push factors, expresses

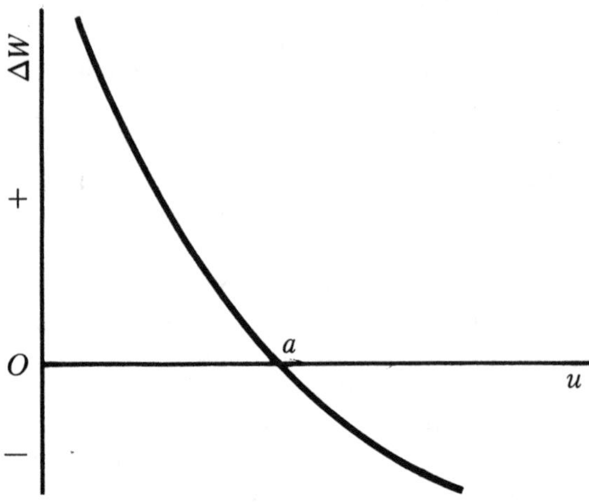


**Figure 11.1** The Phillips curve

graphically the relationship between the rate of change of money wages ($\Delta W$) and the percentage of the labour force unemployed. The existence of frictional unemployment means that even when the rate of change of wages is zero, unemployment is positive (point *a* in figure 11.1).

The Phillips curve has more recently been modified to take into account expectations and it is postulated that the rate of change of wages will equal the expected rate of price change plus an adjustment related to the excess demand for labour (as measured by the level of unemployment). The reformulated Phillips hypothesis predicts that if a closed economy is operated with permanent excess demand (that is, unemployment is permanently below its 'natural' level), inflation will persistently accelerate.

Complementary to the development of the Phillips curve has been the emergence of the monetary theory of the balance of payments, which represents a revival and extension of the price – specie – flow mechanism, originally advanced by David Hume in the 18th century. Assuming a stable demand for money function, the monetary theory of the balance of payments predicts that prices within a country respond to changes in the domestic money supply. In turn, the balance of payments responds to changes in the relative prices of goods between countries, and consequently this affects both the domestic money supply and the domestic price level. In other words, in an open economy, the supply of money is given by the sum of domestic credit and international reserves. Changes in the balance of payments affect the latter and thus the overall supply of money within the economy. In a world of fixed exchange rates where each economy is operating at the full employment level of output, the rate of inflation in the world price level is determined by the rate of expansion of the international money supply and, in equilibrium, each country takes this world inflation rate as its own rate of inflation.

We noted in Chapter 2 the reservations expressed by many economists concerning the transfer of theories and concepts from one socio-economic system to another (the 'limitations of the special case'). The idea of 'misplaced aggregation' (that is, the analysis of dissimilar items in terms of a single category) is particularly useful for our critique of the relevance of 'orthodox' theories of inflation to LDCs. The latter focus attention on the 'natural' rate of unemployment but, given the disintegrated and fragmented nature of LDC economies, concepts such as full employment or the 'natural' rate of unemployment have no meaning.[5] In addition, the use of the concepts of aggregate demand and supply, and the postulation of a ceiling to aggregate demand in real terms, which is set by aggregate supply, is open to criticism in the context of an LDC. The latter's economy is characterised by factor immobility, market imperfections and rigidities and disequilibrium between demand and supply in different sectors of the economy. Under-utilisation of resources in some sectors (for example, manufacturing) coexists with shortages in other sectors of the economy, and market imperfections and technological constraints prevent the movement of resources in response to market signals.

In these conditions, it is questionable whether the 'orthodox' interpretation of inflation, in terms of aggregate demand and supply, can be applied. It can be argued that there is no overall (or global) limitation on aggregate supply. Rather, limitations are diverse and specific, and thus inflation must be analysed taking into account the structural composition of the economy. Myrdal (1968, p. 1962) has rejected the idea of a single ceiling and along with the Latin American 'structuralists' has argued for an interpretation of inflation which stresses '. . . the fragmentation, the disequilibria, and the lack of balance between supplies and demands in different sectors of the economy and between different groups in the community'. In other words, inflation is seen as resulting from the existence of a number of specific bottlenecks or constraints in the economy.

## 11.4 Structuralist and Monetarist Explanations of Inflation

The debate over the causes and consequences of inflation in Latin

America has largely been between two groups loosely labelled structuralists and monetarists. Each group broadly represents a certain type of approach to the problem of inflation in particular, and to economic development in general. In addition, the two groups are usually distinguished by differences in political ideology, structuralists usually being 'of the left' and monetarists 'of the right' (Felix 1961). Thus, although the terms 'structuralist' and 'monetarist' are merely convenient labels and do not necessarily indicate a coherent school of thought, there are important differences between them as to the cause of inflation and possible cures, especially with regard to the need for, and efficacy of, orthodox stabilisation programmes.

*The Structuralist View*

The structuralists argue that inflation is inevitable in an economy that is attempting to grow rapidly in the presence of structural bottlenecks or constraints, defined by Thorp (1971, p. 185) as 'certain fundamental facets of the economic, institutional and socio-political structure of the country which in one way or another inhibit expansion'. Inflation usually accompanies the transition of the LDC from an 'outward-orientated' export-based economy to an 'inward-orientated', domestic-market based economy (in which, as we have already seen in Chapter 8, ISI plays a key role). The fundamental changes in the socio-economic structure that are required by such economic development cannot be brought about by the price mechanism operating within very imperfect market structures characterised by limited resource mobility, and thus shortages and disequilibria appear.

The structuralist analysis is concerned with the identification and analysis of these alleged bottlenecks (the basic or structural inflationary pressures, to use Sunkel's (1960) terminology).[6] The key bottlenecks are generally taken to be (i) the inelastic supply of foodstuffs, (ii) the foreign exchange constraint and (iii) the budget constraint.

With respect to the agricultural sector bottleneck, it is argued that urbanisation and rising incomes have led to a rapidly increasing demand for foodstuffs which cannot be met by the agricultural sector. The supply response is poor because of the structural constraints within the sector – the domination either by large non-capitalistic latifundia which are not profit maximisers, or by minifundia operating almost at a subsistence level and hardly integrated into the market economy.[7] The inelastic supply constitutes a structural inflationary factor. As Sunkel notes with respect to Chile:

> ... the stagnation of global agricultural production cannot be attributed to market, demand and/or price conditions, but must be due to factors inherent in the institutional and economic structure of the main part of the agricultural sector itself.
>
> (Sunkel 1960, p. 115)

The second major bottleneck, the foreign exchange constraint, arises because the rate of growth of foreign exchange receipts is not sufficient to meet rapidly rising import demands generated by accelerated development efforts, rapid population growth and the industrialisation effort which takes place in an environment of technological limitations, structural imbalances and imperfect factor mobility. Import shortages and rising import prices trigger off cumulative price rises; balance of payments difficulties eventually force countries to devalue their currencies and this in turn adds to domestic inflationary pressures, especially when the elasticity of demand for imports is very low.[8]

The third bottleneck, identified by some structuralist writers but not others, is the lack of internal financial resources (the budget deficit). Development efforts increase the scope of necessary government involvement in the economy (especially in the provision of social and physical infrastructure facilities), but government revenue rarely expands sufficiently rapidly to meet the growth of expenditure. Tax structures are regressive and tax collecting bureaucracies are sometimes ‘antiquated, inefficient and ... corrupt’ (Baer 1967, p. 10). The insufficiency of revenue is usually overcome by recourse to deficit financing which has inflationary consequences.

In addition to the basic inflationary pressures, Sunkel (1960) identifies exogenous inflationary pressures. These include upward movements in the prices of imported goods and services (the increases in the prices of oil, fertilisers and foodstuffs are good examples) and major increases in public expenditure arising out of natural disasters or political pressures. Finally, we have cumulative inflationary pressures which are induced by inflation itself. These pressures are an increasing function of the rate and extent of inflation and they include the orientation of investment (preference for safe, non-productive investments), expectations, the negative impact of inflation on productivity (including distortions introduced into the price system by price controls) and the lack of export incentives.

For the various structural constraints to give rise to price increases, which in turn lead to a rapid and continuous increase in the price level, there must exist an effective transmission or propagation mechanism which permits the manifestation of the various inflationary pressures. If various classes or groups in society did not attempt to maintain their relative positions in the face of price increases, the chances of an inflationary spiral being generated would be reduced and the increase in prices would lead to a redistribution of income. In Chile, Sunkel (1960) argued that the propagation mechanism resulted from the inability of the political system to resolve two major struggles of economic interests, namely, the distribution of income between different social classes and the distribution of productive resources between the public and the private sectors of the economy. The propagation mechanism is thus seen as:

> ... the ability of the different economic sectors and social groups continually to readjust their real income or expenditure: the wage-earning group through readjustment of salaries, wages and other benefits; private enterprise through price increases, and the public sector through an increase in nominal fiscal expenditure.
>
> (Sunkel 1960, p. 111)

One of the major components of the propagation mechanism is the budget deficit which leads to an increase in the supply of money. Public expenditure is not easily reduced and revenue not easily increased. The public sector deficit thus represents '... the existence of a number of structural problems which preclude the realisation of a balanced-budget policy' (Sunkel 1960, p. 122). To the structuralist, the increase in the supply of money is a permissive factor which allows the inflationary spiral to manifest itself and become cumulative – it is a symptom of the structural rigidities which give rise to the inflationary pressures, rather than the cause of inflation itself. An increase in the supply of money is a necessary condition for the rise in the overall level of prices but it is not a sufficient condition.

*The Monetarist View*

The Latin American monetarists argue that inflation originates in and is maintained by expansionist monetary and fiscal policies, comprising government deficit spending, expansionist credit policies and expansionary exchange operations of central banks. The rate of inflation will be reduced (and the concomitant distortions in the economy eliminated) via the curbing of excess demand through monetary and fiscal policies, the control of wage increases and the elimination of over-valued exchange rates.

Monetarists do not deny the existence of constraints but they argue that they are not structural or autonomous in nature. They result from the price and exchange rate distortions which are generated by the inflation itself and government attempts to reduce the rate of price increase. For example, they argue that the alleged structural inelasticity of food supplies in fact results from the all-too-frequent administrative control of food prices, the result of attempts by governments to protect urban consumers and avoid growing pressures for wage increases. This interference in the operation of market forces has a disincentive effect on food producers, but it is a distortion induced by administrative controls and is not inherent in the structure of land ownership. High prices for some items, for example food, are necessary to induce an adequate supply, but within the context of the overall control of the money supply and the re-allocation of resources through the market mechanism, high prices for such items are offset by low prices for others, and hence inflationary pressures are not generated. Monetarists further argue that the slow growth of exports is policy-induced rather than structurally induced. Exchange rates are typically over-valued and development efforts 'inward-looking'.

Monetarists thus admit the existence of constraints but reverse the causal relationship. The bottlenecks in the economy that retard growth will be eliminated when inflation is brought under control. The majority of monetarists recognise the 'social priority of development' but argue that stable and sustained growth can only be achieved in an environment of monetary stability (Campos 1967). Structuralists, on the other hand, are often accused of favouring inflation as a means of accelerating growth but in general this is not the case. They are concerned with the problem of making stability compatible with development but argue that price stability can only be achieved through economic growth, which is a long-run process. Short-run stabilisation policies, although effective in reducing the rate of inflation, impose heavy social and economic costs and retard the processes of structural change necessary for longer-term growth and development. In effect, structuralists prefer inflation to stagnation, it being regarded as the lesser of two evils.

The basic differences between the two schools of thought can best be seen in their conflicting attitudes to stabilisation policies. The monetarist solution – the removal of budget deficits, the restraint of credit and the elimination of 'distortions' in the market mechanism (especially the establishment of an 'equilibrium' rate of exchange) – form the basis of IMF-sponsored stabilisation programmes. Structuralists do not deny that monetary variables are partial determinants of inflation, in so far as inflation could not continue for long without monetary expansion, but argue that, even if total demand were reduced, the underlying structural inflationary pressures would still persist, ready to manifest themselves at a later stage. Thorp (1971, pp. 204–207) has characterised the numerous Latin American stabilisation policies as 'costly failures' and, even within a monetarist perspective, they have been criticised for underestimating the political problems associated with stabilisation programmes and failing to identify bottleneck sectors where investment would have to be maintained or accelerated (Campos 1967, pp. 117–120).

## 11.5 Empirical Evidence

An important investigation of one aspect of the structuralist analysis has been carried out by Edel (1969) in his study of the alleged food supply bottlenecks in eight Latin American countries. He tests the propositions that (i) food supply has lagged behind the required rate of growth, and (ii) that this agricultural lag has been associated with inflation, balance of payments difficulties and stagnation. The adequacy of food supply is defined as that rate of autonomous growth of production (resulting from the adoption of new techniques, increases in the labour force and area of production, etc.) sufficient to satisfy demand without any change in relative prices.

Edel found that in Mexico, Brazil and Venezuela, supply outpaced or at least approximately equalled food requirements. Taking into account price changes, five countries with inadequate growth rates (Chile, Colombia, Peru, Uruguay and Argentina) had increasing relative prices and thus inadequate growth could not have been a function of price deterioration. He did not find a perfect relationship between food supply and inflation but the evidence justified the conclusion that

> ... the direction of the relationship is the one indicated by the structuralist theory that less adequate food production means more inflation, as well as relative rises in the food prices, more food imports, and slower growth in other sectors of the economy.
>
> (Edel 1969, pp. 135–36)

Furthermore, the degree of price control on foodstuffs did not appear to be related systematically to agricultural performance for the countries studied, whereas there was evidence that land tenure and low productivity were related to one another.[9]

In his study of Brazil, Kahil (1973) analysed four alleged structural constraints. These were the agricultural sector bottleneck, the inadequate mobility of capital, the external sector bottleneck and the effects of rapid urbanisation (increased private and public demand for goods and services and increased costs of supplying food to the urban areas). He argued that structural weaknesses did not play a significant role in the evolution of the price level over the period studied (1946–1964). The aggravation of these structural weaknesses was more an effect than a cause of inflation. Price rises were caused by large and growing public deficits, a too rapid expansion of bank credit in the early period and unnecessarily large and increasingly frequent increases in legal minimum wages at a later stage. These factors interacted in such a way that it was impossible to distinguish cause from effect, and thus the basic causes of inflation appeared to have become mere parts of the structuralist propagation mechanism.

Kahil qualifies his monetarist conclusion by arguing that the factors ultimately responsible for inflation were political rather than economic. The two major policy aims of the 1950s were rapid industrialisation and the winning of the allegiance of the urban masses, at the same time serving the interests of other politically important groups (big industrialists, bankers, etc.). Inflation was thus the outcome of the attempt by the state to promote growth and development and grant privileges (albeit temporary and illusory) to mutually antagonistic groups or classes. We discuss the implications of these conclusions below.

Harberger's (1963) influential study of Chile covers the period 1939 to 1958, during which inflation was almost continuous and the cost of living index rose over eightfold. Within the monetarist framework, Harberger regresses the annual rate of price change in the cost of living index upon the percentage change in the money supply during the same year and the preceding one and the percentage change in real income in that year. Wage changes are used as an additional independent variable in the regression equation.

The results of the analysis support the monetarist interpretation, with each of the monetary variables statistically significant and the inclusion of the wages variable failing to increase the overall explanatory power of the monetary variables. The importance of wage changes lies in their importance as 'transmitters' of inflation from one period to the next, responding to the monetary expansion of the past period and including monetary expansion in the subsequent period.

Vogel (1974) has extended the Hargerger model to sixteen Latin American countries for the period 1950–1969. The dependent variable is the consumer price index and the independent variables are money supply (currency plus demand deposits), real income and past changes in the rate of inflation (as a proxy for the expected cost of holding real balances). On the basis of his results, Vogel concludes that:

> the most important result of the present study ... is that a purely monetarist model, with no structuralist variables, reveals little heterogeneity among Latin American countries, in spite of their extreme diversity. The substantial differences in rates of inflation among these countries cannot under the present model be attributed to structural differences, but must rather be attributed primarily to differences in the behaviour of the money supply.
>
> (Vogel 1974, p. 113)

In reviewing other work on inflation in Latin America, Vogel notes that very different conclusions about the monetarist-structuralist controversy have been reached from essentially similar findings. He suggests that further work is needed on the determination of the money supply and that structural variables could be added to the model. Even if a purely monetarist model can adequately explain the causes of inflation, stabilisation policies may have to be more than purely monetarist in character, given that rates of inflation take up to two years to adjust to changes in the money supply and that this may be a longer period of austerity than can be tolerated politically by the majority of Latin American regimes.[10]

Argy (1970) has attempted to assess the contribution of structural elements to inflation using data for 22 countries for the period 1958–1965. He constructs a variety of indices to test four structural hypotheses – the demand-shift hypothesis (shifts in the composition of demand, as distinct from generalised excess demand, cause upward shifts of the price level), the export instability hypothesis (fluctuations in export earnings will tend to create a long-term upward movement in the price level), the agricultural bottleneck hypothesis and the foreign exchange bottleneck (both discussed above). Two additional variables are included in some of the regressions – the government deficit rate and the rates of change in the money supply.

Argy concludes that the results for the structuralist variables are poor (except for the fact that there is a slight tendency for countries where food prices have risen most relative to the cost of living to have higher rates of inflation) but that the monetary variables perform well – 'In every case the addition of a monetary variable to structuralist variables improved substantially the results' (Argy 1970, p. 83).

Argy's study clearly shows (as the author himself admits) the difficulties involved in testing the structuralist position. It is very difficult to specify correctly and construct indicators which adequately encompass the essence of the alleged structuralist constraints. For example, to test the foreign exchange bottleneck, Argy uses (i) the average annual percentage change in the terms of trade and (ii) the average import ratio (imports over gross domestic production). But neither of these measures indicate the *capacity* to import and are thus not a satisfactory test of the (*ex ante*) balance of payments constraint. There is also likely to be significant multicollinearity between the independent variables used in the regression analysis.

The conclusion that monetary variables have a high correlation with the rate of inflation should be treated with caution and monetarists can be criticised on these grounds. Evidence of correlation fails to provide an understanding of the underlying causal relationships that exist between structural constraints, monetary expansion and inflation. Structuralist writers can be criticised on the grounds that they have often devoted insufficient attention to the nature of the propagation mechanism in general and the expansion of the money supply in particular (which is necessary, other things being equal, for the manifestation of spiralling price rises). Structuralist assertions that increases in the money supply are merely permissive may tend to obscure the wider socio-economic framework within which this policy option is chosen by, or forced upon, the government. Both structuralists and monetarists can accept the proposition that changes in the money supply occur in response to political factors, but the basic question remains as to whether these changes permit or are the actual cause of the inflationary process.

## 11.6 Towards a General Theory of Inflation for LDCs

Inflation has been, or is becoming, a problem endemic in most LDCs. Up until now, most attention has been concentrated on Latin America and the structuralist analysis has been very influential. But to what extent is the structuralist analysis applicable to LDCs outside Latin America?

It could be argued that the emphasis placed by structuralist writers on two or three specific bottlenecks and their presentation of a somewhat rigid and mechanical analysis of the operation of those bottlenecks leads to over-generalisation, which is often easy to refute with specific examples, and to the downgrading in importance of the actual (as opposed to the hypothetical) policy options that a government has open to it. In principle, all structural constraints can be alleviated, or eliminated, by the pursuit of the 'correct' policies – land and agrarian reform can break the agricultural sector bottleneck, the balance of payments position can be eased by restrictions on the import of non-essentials, and so on. In this restricted sense, monetarists are right in claiming that constraints are policy induced, although it does not necessarily follow that monetarists would themselves advocate such policies.

But within a given socio-political environment, a government is 'forced' to pursue certain policies (inflation is an 'easier' political alternative than land reform or a reduction in the consumption of upper-income groups) and although the result is a policy-induced constraint, it is no less the outcome of a particular economic, political and institutional structure. The concept of a structural constraint cannot be divorced from the specific socio-political and historical framework within which it is operative.[11]

What therefore needs to be developed is a broadly based structural analysis of inflation, specific to each country, and encompassing a wide range of potential bottlenecks. Myrdal (1968, pp. 1928–29), for example, argues that bottlenecks in such sectors as electricity generation, fuel, imported raw materials, transport, repair facilities and credit facilities are all important in generating inflationary pressures. Attention must be focused on the broader socio-economic, institutional framework which LDC governments both influence and are a part of, and within which development objectives are specified and policies implemented. Within this framework, the propagation mechanism is of considerable importance. If specific social groups or classes are unable to regain their previous position relative to other groups after an inflationary increase in prices has led to a fall in their real living standards, relative price changes will not lead to an inflationary spiral. They will lead to a redistribution of income, and the relationship between inflation and income distribution is of crucial importance. In particular, the distribution of economic, and hence political, power determines the range of policy options any particular government is likely to pursue and the process of inflation itself alters the economic and political power structure of the inflating economy.

It is evident therefore that the analysis of inflation cannot be separated from the problems of underdevelopment and development. Any study which omits social, political and institutional factors will obscure the real issues involved and will quite illegitimately reduce a complex economic and socio-political problem to a straightforward technical one.

## (B) RURAL–URBAN MIGRATION IN LDCs

### 11.7 Introduction

A major feature of the economic development of the now developed western industrialised countries was the large-scale movement of labour from the land and its increasing concentration in expanding urban areas. In general, the creation of urban employment opportunities in these countries matched the growth of the urban labour force. In contrast to this historical experience, contemporary LDCs are faced with problems of rapid urban population growth, largely resulting from rural–urban migration. It is estimated that between 1950 and 1970 migration accounted for 45–55% of urban population growth and 55–65% of the growth in the number of urban workers (Bairoch 1975, p. 151). LDCs are also facing increasingly severe urban unemployment problems, the result of the inability of urban-based economic activities (especially manufacturing in the 'modern' sector) to expand employment opportunities sufficiently rapidly to absorb productively the growing labour force (discussed in Chapter 8).

A high degree of labour mobility is both necessary and desirable in an expanding economy, but contemporary rural–urban migration (one aspect of labour mobility) is more likely to have a negative impact on economic development. The rapidly expanding urban areas can be characterised as 'parasitic' development in so far as they absorb a large volume of resources, financial, physical and human, but make only a limited contribution to the development effort.[12] The rural areas are adversely affected in that, contrary to the popular misconception of teeming, overcrowded areas, they often suffer from a general labour shortage (Godfrey (1969) cites West Africa as an area with a labour deficiency in agriculture) and migration is often selective with respect to age and educational levels. The stagnation of the rural areas and rapid expansion of shanty towns surrounding the urban centres, plus the growth of employment in the so-called 'informal sector',[13] all attest to the detrimental impact of rural–urban migration in contemporary LDCs.

Amin (1974, p. 66) has noted that modern migrations are of labour rather than peoples and the migrant comes into a receiving society that is already organised and structured and which often accords the migrant an inferior status. We are concentrating in this section on net rural–urban migration, but it should be remembered that migration can also be rural–rural or urban–urban (and, less likely, urban–rural). In the more developed, urbanised LDCs, urban–urban migration (from smaller urban centres to the metropolitan area) may be significant (as for example in Chile (Herrick 1965)), although inter-urban migration is often merely a relay point in the rural–urban chain (that is, the migrant moves to a smaller urban centre before moving to a larger one). In West Africa, Amin (1974, p. 69) notes the importance of rural–rural migration, the migrant leaving one rural area and moving to another because of greater possibilities of producing for the export market. Although we have dismissed (net) urban–rural migration as insignificant, sociologists have noted that the pattern of migration (especially in Africa) is circulatory, that is, migrants return to the rural areas at the end of their working life (Garbett and Kapferer 1970). Finally, for the sake of completeness, we may note the phenomenon of international migration, the most important aspect of which is, from the viewpoint of the LDCs, the loss of educated and skilled manpower to the developed, western economies (the so-called 'brain drain').

## 11.8 The Theoretical Framework

Traditionally, migration studies emphasised the importance of 'push-pull' factors. Poverty and the lack of economic opportunities would 'push' labour from the rural areas while the attractions of the urban areas (job opportunities and opportunities for education, marriage, the attraction of the 'bright lights', etc.) 'pulled' labour to the towns. Obviously, migration in the real world must be the result of some combination of these two sets of forces and thus it can be hypothesised that net rural–urban migration is some function of rural–urban income differentials, taking into account the probability of getting a job in the urban area. This approach implies that the predominant cause of rural–urban migration is economic, a conclusion non-economists appear to accept (Gugler 1969, p. 137), although social and psychological factors must also be taken into account.

The best known model of economic development (Lewis 1954; extended and refined by Ranis and Fei 1961; see Chapter 2) is based on the assumption that the existing real wage differential between the rural and urban areas is the sole determinant of rural–urban migration and migration will continue as long as this differential exists. The possibility of large scale open employment in urban areas is not explicitly considered by the model. The reinvestment of the surplus by capitalists leads to the expansion of the capitalist sector and the creation of more jobs, until surplus labour is absorbed and the labour supply schedule ceases to be perfectly elastic.

Reality has not matched this interpretation of the development process. As we have already noted, large-scale net rural–urban migration has continued in the face of growing urban unemployment. Todaro (1969) has argued that the large pool of unemployed and under-employed in the urban sector must affect the potential migrant's 'probability' of finding a job in that sector. Consequently, when analysing the determinants of urban labour supplies, he argues that we must examine not only prevailing real income differentials but also the rural–urban *'expected'* income differential, that is, the income differential adjusted for the probability of finding an urban job (Todaro 1969, p. 138).

Migration is seen as a two-stage process. The unskilled worker migrates to the urban area and initially spends some time in the 'informal' urban sector from which he moves, in the second stage, to a more permanent modern sector job. An important aspect of this model is thus the length of time spent looking for a formal sector job, and it follows that the urban wage premium must be high enough to offset the potential income loss involved in being unemployed for a considerable length of time. The migrant must thus balance the probabilities and risks of being unemployed in the city (or employed in the informal sector at a much reduced income) for a certain period of time against the favourable urban wage differential (Todaro 1969, p. 140) and must perceive the urban wage as being sufficiently high to compensate for the loss.[14]

Before taking a critical look at the Todaro model, we must briefly consider the policy implications that flow from it. Migration and urban unemployment are positively related in so far as any attempt to increase urban employment opportunities without reducing the rural–urban income differential will eventually lead to even greater unemployment.[15] Rising labour productivity in the urban sector will, if it is permitted to increase the rural–urban income differential, lead to increased migration and even greater unemployment. Likewise, the introduction of labour-intensive technologies in the urban sector, while leaving the differential unchanged, may lead to both higher employment and unemployment in that sector.

All these points lead to the conclusion that rural life must be made more attractive. Agricultural productivity and incomes must be raised, thus reducing the differential; rural employment opportunities expanded, both farm and non-farm; and physical and social infrastructural facilities (roads, schools, health facilities, etc.) introduced or improved. The regeneration of the rural areas and the narrowing of rural–urban inequalities are the necessary preconditions for preventing further over-urbanisation, reducing the level of urban employment and stemming the emigration from the land.

The Todaro model of rural–urban migration has been extremely influential, in part because the migrant can be conceived of as acting in a rational, income maximising manner, rather than responding irrationally to the lure of the bright lights of the city. In principle, Todaro's urban real income variable, $Y_u(t)$, includes all the elements that constitute urban real income–money wages, urban amenities and the other attractions of urban life. Likewise, rural real income, $Y_r(t)$, includes, in principle, all factors which affect the migrant's rural income and must incorporate such variables as the system of land tenure, inheritance laws, social structures, and so on. In principle, the Todaro model encompasses all these elements. The landless labourer and the small farmer, the displaced share cropper and the educated youth all migrate in response to economic incentives in a perfectly rational, consistent manner. In a sense, therefore, the model is able (or at least should be able) to incorporate and 'explain' all observed patterns of migratory behaviour, but a closer inspection reveals that it does not provide a necessary understanding of the real factors and forces involved in any given situation. Thus what appears to be the major strength of the model (its generality) is in fact its major weakness.

Todaro's theory of migration falls within the general framework that treats migration as a form of investment in human capital. The migration decision is viewed in a costs and returns framework, such that the decision to migrate will not be taken unless expectations are that the costs of migration (money and non-money) are equal to or less than the difference in the present discounted values of the streams of benefits in the rural and urban areas. The decision to migrate is taken by an autonomous individual, unconstrained by considerations of sex, class, age or race, abstracting from the economic and social structures of which in reality the migrant is a part. But individual actions and decisions are not made independently of society and we need to examine the economic and social structure and analyse the behaviour of individuals within that structure.[16] The rural–urban real income differential is one aspect of a particular socio-economic system and one manifestation of the development path being pursued at that particular time and place. The differential arises as a result of the policies being pursued (with respect, for example, to urban development, industrialisation, rural development, etc.) and migration must thus be viewed within this broader analytical framework.[17]

The logical corollary of this argument is that Todaro-type models of migration are tautological (if it is assumed that the migrant is an income maximising individual, he will obviously move to that area where the chances of success seem greatest). Such models only have an explanatory value if the real income differential, adjusted to take into account the probability of getting a job in the modern sector, was the *basic* cause of migration (Amin 1974, p. 90). Furthermore, there is evidence that migrants do not come indifferently from all poor regions and are not recruited from all individuals who constitute their populations. In Tanzania, for example, the 'poor' Masai do not migrate whereas a large number of farmers from the richer region of Kilimanjaro do, a phenomenon only 'explained' by the Todaro model if the expected income differential is greater for the latter than for the former.

As we have already noted above, although economic factors are the prime determinants of the decision to migrate, non-economic factors are of importance. It has been argued by some sociologists (for example, Garbett and Kapferer 1970) that migration must be viewed as a process, rather than as a static, once-only phenomenon,[18] taking account of the total context within which migration occurs and the factors related to this overall context which influence the decisions of the migrants at various points in their migratory careers. The choice is made with reference to both economic and sociological alternatives in that the individual may attempt to maximise gains in terms of a number of alternatives, for example, maximisation of the migrant's income, the educational opportunities for his/her children, the migrant's political position and influence, and so on. Various factors act as constraints on one another and in the process of making a choice, individuals generate constraints which affect the pattern of future choices. Specific choices are open to an individual at a certain time in life or at a certain point in his/her career, but not at others; for example, marriage and children alter the range of options open. Various social attributes (skill, education, etc.) affect the range of alternatives open to the migrant, thus affecting the pattern of migration, and access to information is also an important consideration.

We must also examine the choices faced by individual migrants as they are affected by the structure of social relationships. Relatives and friends play a crucial role in the migratory process, providing information on job opportunities, accommodation and food while the migrant is looking for a job, and so on.[19] Migration must thus be understood in terms of the total array of economic and social relationships, including both urban and rural relationships. Within this field, the individual has his/her decisions constrained by his/her position in a particular structure of social relationships, and the individual's choices are contingent on, and constrained by, the choices of others. Todaro-type models present, to say the least, an incomplete picture in so far as they over-emphasise monetary rewards and in practice exclude social relationships.[20]

Two further points must be briefly discussed before we consider some empirical studies. The first concerns the role of the informal sector. The Todaro model ignores this sector (apart from acknowledging the fact that the migrant may spend some time there before finding modern sector employment) but we have already noted in Chapter 8 that it is incorrect to assume that a person is unemployed merely because he/she is unable to find a wage job in the modern sector of the urban economy. The migrant may even actively seek to earn his/her living in the informal sector and it is thus both inaccurate and derogatory to assume that all those outside the formal sector are unemployed. A three-sector model at the very least is required to analyse the migratory decision (rural sector, modern urban sector, 'traditional' or informal urban sector) and we also need to analyse the historical evolution of urbanisation in each particular LDC.

The second point concerns the rural–urban income gap. There has been a marked tendency to exaggerate the size of this gap (the term 'labour aristocracy' is often loosely and inaccurately used to refer to certain parts of the 'modern sector' urban labour force). Amin (1974, p. 108) has argued that a loose comparison between urban wages and rural incomes is dangerous, given (i) the differences in types of consumption in urban and rural areas (high rents and food prices in urban areas, expenditure on transport, entertainment, etc., and what Lewis (1954) refers to as the difference in 'conventional standards', with workers in the capitalist sector acquiring tastes and a social prestige which conventionally are recognised by higher real wages) and (ii) the often considerable differences in the amount of work needed to earn a reasonable income (the urban worker is likely to have to work harder). The distribution of income is also likely to be more unequal in the urban area. Amin concludes:

> . . . we express serious doubt concerning the thesis of a widening difference between the income of the farmer and those of unskilled urban workers . . . on the whole, the most significant difference is not the divergence between the income of the peasant and the wage of the unskilled urban worker, but the gap which separates both the peasantry and the lowest class of urban workers from the new social classes which developed during the last decades of colonisation and after independence (notably administrative bureaucracies) . . . The migrants are an impoverished proletariat. On the urban labour market as well as on the plantations they occupy the lowest positions and are the worst paid . . . In a very general way migration serves to provide cheap labour to the host areas.
>
> (Amin 1974, p. 109)

## 11.9 Empirical Evidence

Rather than attempting to give a detailed summary of the various empirical analyses of rural–urban migration, we will first summarise some of the major conclusions to emerge and then look at one study in greater detail.

1. It is generally found that there is an inverse relationship between the propensity to migrate and the distance from the nearest large urban centre (although distance is closely related to cultural and social differences between regions and to the flow of information) (Beals *et al.* 1967; Caldwell 1967, 1968, 1969; Sahota 1968).
2. Migrants move in response to income differentials; the study of Beals *et al.* (1967), although it is concerned with inter-regional rather than rural–urban migration, clearly showed that migrants moved to regions with high wage levels.
3. There is a positive relationship between the size of the rural centre and rural–urban migration (Caldwell 1967, 1968, 1969); greater urbanisation or population density in either the origin or destination region increases migration (Beals *et al.* 1967).
4. Caldwell found that a disproportionate fraction of the wealthier households of a village were 'migrant households', that is they were linked by absentees or returnees to the town; the explanation given was that 'many migrants send remittances back home and many returnees bring back money and possessions, while,

at the same time, better off households are more likely to send their children to school and so intentionally or unintentionally equip them for town jobs' (Caldwell 1968, p. 367).

5 There is a strong association between the presence of friends or relatives in the urban area and migration; they provide temporary accommodation and information and thus 'chain migration' is an important phenomenon (the term is used by Caldwell but the phenomenon is also noted by Sahota 1968).

6 There is some dispute over the relationship between education and migration. Beals *et al.* (1967) conclude that the direct effect of education is to reduce migration, arguing that this disproves the hypothesis that educated people migrate because they are dissatisfied with rural life. But Knight (1972) maintains that the effect of education is to raise the expected rural–urban income differential and increase the probability of getting a job in the modern sector. Caldwell finds a strong positive association between education and rural–urban migration – 'schooling itself turns people towards town life' (Caldwell 1969, p. 60) – arguing that the content of school courses is an important influence alienating children from rural life (but Godfrey (1973) regards this as an over-simplification).[21] A more recent study (Barnum and Sabot 1976, p. 77) concludes that the more formal education a rural resident has, the greater is his propensity to migrate. Both the rural–urban income differential and the net return to migration increase with education.

Godfrey's (1973) study which we will look at in greater detail, incorporates and develops much of the material of the earlier empirical works already referred to. He attempts to test the Todaro hypothesis although he argues that it is difficult to translate into testable terms as, strictly speaking, it deals with the migrant's subjective expectations and is thus not refutable. Reformulating the hypothesis, net rural–urban migration is predicted to vary directly with the differential between the urban wage-rate and average rural income, and inversely with the degree of difficulty of getting a job in the modern sector (approximated by the total supply of labour to urban areas minus the number employed in the modern sector, expressed as a proportion of total supply of labour to urban areas).

The country studied is Ghana over the period 1955–1965. The period 1960–1965 was marked by a tough wages policy, and as the urban–rural income differential fell, and the difficulty of getting a modern sector job increased, the Todaro model would predict a lower rate of rural–urban migration for this period. But even taking into account data deficiencies, the evidence suggests a higher rate of migration in 1960–65 than in 1955–60. Data inaccuracies are unlikely to be responsible for this seemingly perverse result and thus Godfrey firstly attempts to respecify the model. He argues that the informal sector must be incorporated into the model and that other variables should also be included in the migration function – the gap in social and infrastructural assets (health facilities, water supplies, etc.), the number of kinsmen already resident in urban areas (the influence of chain migration), changes in attitudes explainable solely in sociological and/or political terms and an educational variable.

With respect to the latter, Godfrey rejects the so-called 'white-collar hypothesis' (educated people migrate because they have been taught to despise the rural environment and to aspire to urban, white-collar employment) and argues that:

> ... having acquired a certain level of education, a school-leaver may feel it necessary to leave the village, irrespective of the state of the urban labour market because the acquisition of that level of education differentiates him from his age-group to the extent that he feels himself to be in the 'migrant' category. As enrolment ratios rise, so, of course, does the level of education that performs this function.
>
> (Godfrey 1973, p. 71)

Education is in principle incorporated into the Todaro model because it can be argued that the expected urban income and the probability of getting a modern sector job are positively related to the migrant's educational level. Godfrey argues that education also has an effect on migration quite separate from the effect on expected income. The Ghanaian data show a continuous increase in the number of people leaving schools in rural areas with a certain minimum primary education and a first-level rural enrolment ratio that only began to rise significantly after 1961. His argument is that the higher the enrolment ratio, the less is the school-leaver differentiated from the rest of his age group and this to a certain extent offsets the increase in the number of school-leavers on the migrant flow. In other words, when education is felt to confer a distinction between the educated and the rest, migration is stimulated, but as more children receive education up to any given level, the less the distinction is felt and operates only at a higher educational level. Thus Godfrey is saying that education and migration are positively related to one another, both in terms of increasing the economic incentive to migrate (à la Todaro) and in altering the school-leaver's perception of himself/herself. But as the proportion of children entering school rises, the level of education required to fulfil the latter function also rises.

However, even with the educational variable included, Godfrey still feels that additional explanatory variables need to be included in the migration function, in particular the number of kinsmen already in the urban area. If this was in fact an important variable, it would give a built-in dynamic to the migration process and would make the control or diminution of rural–urban migration more difficult. Godfrey concludes that in order to better understand the migratory process

> The most promising alternative to an aggregative, probabilistic approach may be that of micro-studies of particular villages or particular groups within villages over time, with the aim not so much of statistically 'explaining' as of understanding what is going on.
>
> (Godfrey 1973, pp. 74–75)

The empirical studies clearly show the dominance of economic motives in the migratory decision, but even taking into account the concessions that some economists have made towards the inclusion of sociological variables, the methodological framework used is still that of the autonomous, income-maximising individual. Necessary policy measures, on the other hand, on which there is general agreement, stress the need for radical changes of a structuralist nature in government policies – integrated rural development programmes, the development of labour-intensive techniques in the rural sector to create extensive employment opportunities, the redirection of the educational system towards the needs of rural development and the creation of an appropriate balance between urban and rural areas. It could be argued that only countries that have already undergone significant political and social change would be in a position to implement such far-reaching measures. For countries that have not undergone such changes, large-scale rural–urban migration is likely to remain a significant problem.

## Notes:

1 This section draws heavily on Kirkpatrick and Nixson (1976).

2 Thirlwall (1974) argued that when studying LDCs outside Latin America, 'the impression remains that capital accumulation and employment growth may have been sacrificed for the sake of financial stability' (p. xii).

3 We should beware of assuming a straightforward relationship between deficit finance and inflation. Myrdal (1968) maintains that the size of the deficit does not provide a yardstick measuring the effects of the budget on inflation, because:

'(i) Expenditures, taxes and loans vary and have varying effects on the timing, direction, and size of demand and supply in different domestic markets and also on all of these factors in relation to foreign transactions; simple aggregation is therefore misplaced.

(ii) The effects of the budget cannot be separated from the effects of a number of other policies that do not appear in the budget; this would imply illegitimate isolation.
(iii) The budget covers only a small part of the whole economy, and therefore many important areas are left in the dark.' (Myrdal 1968, p. 2025)

4 Donnithorne (1974) argues that excess demand has been chronic (as illustrated by the need for rationing, price controls and high black market prices) but has not been allowed to get out of control. The political framework (of which she obviously disapproves) is of importance in this respect.

5 Concepts such as 'employment' and 'unemployment' imply a homogeneous, mobile, adequately trained, wage-earning labour force willing and able to work and responding to incentives. But Streeten (1972, Ch. 5, p. 55) argues that 'In a society of isolated communities, some of them apathetic or with religious prejudices against certain kinds of work, illiterate and unused to cooperation, the notion "Labour Force" does not make sense'.

6 The price increase stemming from the bottleneck is not a once-and-for-all change in relative prices, leading to a reallocation of resources and no change in the overall price level. Rather it may trigger off an inflationary spiral: 'Price increases that, in a different institutional setting, would be confined to a few items and carry their cure with them, will in an underdeveloped country tend to spread to other items and be self-defeating' (Myrdal 1968, p. 1929).

7 Balogh (1961, p. 57) argues that it is not accurate to state that the owners of the latifundia and minifundia act irrationally. Large-scale landowners are interested in the maximisation of their incomes over time, constrained by the minimisation of effort and risk (both economic and political); the small farmers and sharecroppers have little interest in improvement: 'Their lack of capital and access to credit at reasonable terms makes risks connected with improvement unbearably high. Should anything go wrong, even their wretched existence would be jeopardized'.

8 It is useful to contrast the foreign exchange gap hypothesis with the monetary theory of the balance of payments outlined earlier in the text. According to the foreign exchange gap analysis, the balance of payments deficit is a source of inflationary pressures, whereas according to the monetary theory of the balance of payments, a deficit reduces the domestic money supply and thus reduces pressure on prices. In the former case, the elimination of the deficit encourages economic development and alleviates inflationary pressures; in the latter, the move from a deficit to a surplus on the balance of payments is accompanied by rising prices.

9 Myrdal (1968, pp. 1257–58) comments: 'Prices of agricultural products and government price policies play, of course, a vital role in determining the course of agricultural output in the West, and naturally Western economists who happen to touch on the problems of underdeveloped countries often naively assume that these countries could stimulate agricultural production by raising farm prices. Western experts who have studied the South Asian agricultural situation are more careful. Like their South Asian colleagues, they do not count much on price support as a means of raising agricultural production'.

10 This argument perhaps understates the case. Output is likely to remain depressed and unemployment high for an even longer period, thus increasing the economic and social costs of orthodox stabilisation policies. It is not certain that Vogel's regression results justify the conclusion he reaches. One critic argues that monetarists would not defend the use of the same monetarist model to every Latin American country, that there are significant differences in the inflationary process in Latin America and that what is needed is a detailed comparative analysis of different groups of countries over some given time period. See Betancourt (1976).

11 Sunkel (1960) emphasises this point: '... inflation does not occur *in vacuo* but as part of a country's historical, social, political and institutional evolution' (p. 108).

12 Wilsher and Righter (1975, p. 22) argue that many would go a step further and describe LDC cities as 'cancers not catalysts'. Their book gives a graphic description of conditions in the rapidly expanding urban areas of contemporary LDCs.

13 The term 'informal sector' is used to describe the low-income, small-scale, self-employed, unorganised sector of the urban economy. It includes a wide range of labour-intensive activities, both legal and illegal, usually without access to modern sector facilities (credit, government assistance) and often positively discouraged and harassed by legislation and the police.

14 Todaro's model of rural–urban migration is set out as follows. It is assumed that the percentage change in the urban labour force as a result of migration during any period is governed by the difference between the discounted streams of expected urban and rural real income, expressed as a percentage of the discounted stream of expected rural real income:

$$\left(\frac{\dot{S}}{S}\right)_t = F\left[\frac{V_u(t) - V_r(t)}{V_r(t)}\right]$$

where:

$\dot{S}$ = net rural–urban migration

$S$ = existing urban labour force

$V_u(t)$ = discounted present value for expected urban real income stream over unskilled workers planning horizon

$V_r(t)$ = discounted present value of expected rural real income stream over same planning horizon

It is further assumed that the planning horizon is identical for each worker (assumed to be 60 months), the fixed costs of migration are identical for all workers and that the discount factor is constant over the planning horizon and identical for all potential migrants.

Permanent rural income (that is, the present value of the expected income stream over $n$ periods) is expressed thus:

$$V_r(0) = \int_{t=0}^{n} Y_r(t)e^{-rt}dt$$

where:

$Y_r(t)$ = net expected rural real income in period $t$ based on average real income in $x$ previous periods

$r$ = discount factor reflecting the degree of consumption time preference of the typical unskilled rural worker.

Permanent urban income is represented thus:

$$V_u(0) = \int_{t=0}^{n} p(t) Y_u(t) e^{-rt} dt \; - \; C(0)$$

where:

$Y_u(t)$ = net urban real income in period $t$

$C(0)$ = initial fixed costs of migration and relocation in the urban sector

$p(t)$ = probability of finding a modern sector job in time period $t$.

The inclusion of $p(t)$ means that even if $Y_u(t) - Y_r(t)$ was positive, the 'expected' differential, $p(t)Y_u(t) - Y_r(t)$ could be negative. $p(t)$ depends on the probability of being selected from the pool of urban 'traditional sector' workers in the current or previous time periods. The length of time spent in the urban 'traditional sector' is thus of importance. The probability of being selected is equal to the ratio of new modern sector employment openings in period $t$ relative to the number of accumulated job seekers in the urban 'traditional sector' at that time.

15 A factual example can be given. In 1964 and 1970, the Government of Kenya concluded two 'Tripartite Agreements', between itself, the employers federation and the trades unions. The major provisions of the 1970 agreement were:

(i) the government and employers agreed to expand employment by 10% of their regular establishment;
(ii) employees agreed to a 12 month wage standstill;
(iii) there were to be no strikes or lockouts during the period of the agreement.

The registration of those seeking employment under the agreement totalled 290,911. Only 46,680 jobs were created by the scheme, 30,203 in the private sector and 15,477 in the public sector (an increase of 7.3% for the two sectors combined, although this was not necessarily a net addition to employment). The ILO Report (1972) concluded that 'Both agreements succeeded in generating a certain amount of additional employment in the short-run. Yet they probably contributed more to raising expectations than to realizing them. ... The additional employment generated almost certainly has had no lasting effect. ... Those who had been forced to provide more employment than they needed were waiting for natural wastage and expansion to absorb it' (p. 542). Harbison (1967, p. 183 footnote) characterised the 1964 agreement as a 'colossal failure' and concluded that 'the volume of unemployment, as a consequence of the expansion of the modern labour force in response to the prospect of more jobs, was probably increased rather than decreased'.

16 Developing this point, Godfrey (1973, p. 73) argues that we should perhaps discard the Todaro approach with its 'implicit definition of the decision-maker as an economic man who will act consistently at different points in time. It may make more sense to distinguish between at least two decisions made at different points in time – the initial decision whether or not to migrate and the later decision, faced after a period of unemployment, whether or not to return to traditional farming ... these two decisions, although made by one individual, are made by two different people'. Apathy, frustration and fatalism may become the dominant personality traits of a migrant unemployed for a long period of time – the experience makes the migrant a 'different' person.

17 Amin (1974, pp. 88–9) makes a similar point when he argues that the distribution of the factors of production is not given *a priori* and distributed geographically unequally but rather is the result of the development strategy being followed: 'Economic (so-called 'rational') choice and notably the decision of the migrant to leave his region of origin, is then completely predetermined by the overall strategy determining the allocation of factors'.

18 In Central and Southern Africa, for example, the pattern of migration is circulatory in that many migrants return to the rural areas at the end of their working life.

19 Mayer's (1961) study of Red Xhosa and School Xhosa in East London (South Africa) illustrates how individuals are constrained in their actions by a particular structure of social relationships. The School Xhosa adapt well to urban life and stay for long periods, the loose-knit social network permitting a cleaner break to be made with the village and greater independence in the town. The Red Xhosa, on the other hand, are badly adapted to urban life, staying for short periods only. They have a close-knit social network, maintain close ties with their homelands and rely on contacts in the town to help them.

20 Two points deserve brief mention although lack of space prevents fuller discussion: (1) economic, cultural and social factors are not independent of one another. The economic structure of society both influences and is influenced by values, attitudes and institutions. The distinction between 'economic', and 'non-economic' or 'personal' factors must thus be used with care; (2) the concept of rationality is used in a normative or ideological manner. The migrant is 'rational' if his/her objective is the maximisation of income, but other forms of behaviour may be perfectly rational, given a different system of economic organisation, social structure, cultural values and so on. What is considered rational in one society would be considered highly irrational in another. Economic rationality is neither timeless nor universal.

21 There is much in Caldwell's work which is of interest and value, but lack of space prevents discussion here. Chapter 4 (Caldwell 1969) in particular presents fascinating information on migrants' attitudes to rural push and urban pull factors.

## Bibliography

### Inflation

Argy V. (1970), 'Structural inflation in developing countries', *Oxford Economic Papers,* March.

Baer W. (1967), 'The inflation controversy in Latin America: a survey', *Latin American Research Review,* Spring.

Balogh T. (1961), 'Economic policy and the price system', *UN Economic Bulletin for Latin America,* March. Reprinted in Balogh T. (1974), *The Economics of Poverty* (2nd edn), Weidenfeld and Nicolson.

Betancourt R.R. (1976), 'The dynamics of inflation in Latin America: comment', *American Economic Review,* Vol. 66, No. 4 September.

Campos R. de O. (1967), *Reflections on Latin American Development,* University of Texas Press.

Donnithorne A. (1974), 'China's anti-inflationary policy', *Three Banks Review,* No. 103, September.

Edel M. (1969), *Food Supply and Inflation in Latin America,* Praeger.

Felix D. (1961), 'An alternative view of the "monetarist" – "structuralist" controversy', in Hirschman A.O. (ed.) (1961), *Latin American Issues: Essays and Comments,* The Twentieth Century Fund, New York.

Harberger A.C. (1963), 'The dynamics of inflation in Chile', in Christ C. *et al.*, *Measurement in Economics: Studies in Mathematical Economics and Econometrics in Memory of Yehudi Grunfeld,* Standford University Press.

Kahil R. (1973), *Inflation and Economic Development in Brazil, 1946 – 1963,* Clarendon Press.

Kirkpatrick C.H. and Nixson F.I. (1976), 'The origins of inflation in less developed countries: a selective review', in Zis G. and Parkin M. (eds) (1976), *Inflation in Open Economies,* Manchester University Press.

Lewis W.A. (1966), *Development Planning,* Allen and Unwin.

Myrdal G. (1968), *Asian Drama,* Penguin.

Peng Kuang-hsi (1976), *Why China has No Inflation,* Foreign Languages Press, Peking.

Sunkel O. (1960), Inflation in Chile: an unorthodox approach', *International Economic Papers,* No. 10.

Thirlwall A.P. (1974), *Inflation, Saving and Growth in Developing Economies,* Macmillan.

Thorp R. (1971), 'Inflation and the financing of economic development', in Griffen K. (ed.) (1971), *Financing Development in Latin America,* Macmillan.

Vogel R.C. (1974), 'The dynamics of inflation in Latin America 1950–1969', *American Economic Review,* Vol. 64, March.

### Rural–Urban Migration

Amin S. (1974), 'Modern migrations in Western Africa', in Amin S. (ed.) (1974), *Modern Migration in West Africa,* Oxford University Press.

Bairoch P. (1975), *The Economic Development of the Third World since 1900,* Methuen.

Barnum H.N. and Sabot R.H. (1976), *Migration, Education and Urban Surplus Labour: The Case of Tanzania,* Development Centre, OECD, Paris.

Beals R.E. Levy M.B. and Moses L.N. (1967), 'Rationality and migration in Ghana', *Review of Economics and Statistics,* November.

Caldwell J.C. (1967), 'Migration and urbanisation', in Birmingham W., Neustadt I. and Omaboe E.N. (eds), *A Study of Contemporary Ghana*, Vol. II, *Some Aspects of Social Structure*, Allen and Unwin.
Caldwell J.C. (1968), 'Determinants of rural–urban migration in Ghana', *Population Studies*, Vol. XXII, No. 3.
Caldwell J.C. (1969), *African Rural–Urban Migration*, Hurst.
Garbett G.K. and Kapferer B. (1970), 'Theoretical orientations in the study of labour migration', *The New Atlantis*, Vol. 2, No. 1.
Godfrey E.M. (1969), 'Labour-surplus models and labour-deficit economies: the West African case', *Economic Development and Cultural Change*, Vol. 17, No. 3, April.
Godfrey E.M. (1973), 'Economic variables and rural–urban migration: some thoughts on the Todaro hypothesis', *Journal of Development Studies*, Vol. X, No. 1, October.
Gugler J. (1969), 'On the theory of rural–urban migration', in Jackson J.A. (ed.) (1969), *Sociological Studies 2*, Cambridge University Press.
Harbison F.H. (1967), 'The generation of employment in newly developing countries', in Sheffield J.R. (ed.) (1967), *Education, Employment and Rural Development*, East African Publishing House, Nairobi.
Herrick B.H. (1965), *Urban Migration and Economic Development in Chile*, MIT Press.
International Labour Office (1972), *Employment, Incomes and Equality: a strategy for increasing productive employment in Kenya*, Geneva.
Jolly R. (1970), 'Rural–urban migration: dimensions, causes, issues and policies', paper for *Cambridge Overseas Studies Committee Conference.*
Knight J.B. (1972), 'Rural–urban income comparisons and migration in Ghana', *Bulletin of Oxford University Institute of Economics and Statistics*, May.
Lewis W.A. (1954), 'Economic development with unlimited supplies of labour', *Manchester School*, May.
Mayer P. (1961), *Townsmen or Tribesmen: Conservatism and the Process of Urbanisation in a South African City*, Oxford University Press, Cape Town.
Ranis G. and Fei J.C.H. (1961), 'A theory of economic development', *American Economic Review*, September.
Sahota G.S. (1968), 'An economic analysis of internal migration in Brazil', *Journal of Political Economy*, March/April.
Streeten P. (1972), *The Frontiers of Development Studies*, Macmillan.
Todaro M. (1968), 'The urban employment problem in less developed countries: an analysis of demand and supply', *Yale Economic Essays*, Fall, Vol. 8.
Todaro M. (1969), 'A model of labour migration and urban unemployment in less developed countries', *American Economic Review*, March.
Ward B. (1976), *The Home of Man*, Penguin.
Wilsher P. and Righter R. (1975), *The Exploding Cities*, Deutsch.

# Author Index

# Subject Index